Using Learning Standards and Assessment

Enhancing Children's Social Development

Supporting Children's Communication Skills

Curriculum Development

Supporting Children's Creativity

Supporting Children's Cognitive Development

Becoming a Professional

NINTH EDITION

The Whole Child

Developmental Education for the Early Years

JOANNE HENDRICK
UNIVERSITY OF OKLAHOMA, EMERITA

PATRICIA WEISSMAN

Merrill
Upper Saddle River, New Jersey
Columbus, Ohio

Library of Congress Cataloging-in-Publication Data
Hendrick, Joanne
    The whole child : developmental education for the early years / Joanne Hendrick, Patricia Weissman.—9th ed.
        p. cm.
    Includes bibliographical references and index.
    ISBN-13: 978-0-13-715305-3
    ISBN-10: 0-13-715305-8
    1. Education, Preschool—United States. 2. Early childhood education—United States. 3. Preschool teachers—
Training of—United States. I. Weissman, Patricia. II. Title.
    LB1140.23.H46 2010
    372.210973—dc22

                                                                                        2008039966

Vice President and Editor in Chief: Jeffery W. Johnston
Acquisitions Editor: Julie Peters
Editorial Assistant: Tiffany Bitzel
Development Editor: Bryce Bell
Senior Managing Editor: Pamela D. Bennett
Senior Project Manager: Linda Hillis Bayma
Project Coordination: Heather Willison, S4Carlisle Publishing Services
Senior Art Director: Diane C. Lorenzo
Cover Image: SuperStock
Cover Design: Candace Rowley
Photo Coordinator: Lori Whitley
Media Producer: Autumn Benson
Media Project Manager: Rebecca Norsic
Senior Operations Supervisor: Matthew Ottenweller
Operations Specialist: Susan Hannahs
Vice President, Director of Sales & Marketing: Quinn Perkson
Marketing Manager: Erica DeLuca
Marketing Coordinator: Brian Mounts

This book was set in Goudy by S4Carlisle Publishing Services. It was printed and bound by Edwards Brothers. The cover was
printed by Lehigh Phoenix.

Chapter Opener Photo Credits: Pam Oken-Wright, **pp. 2, 54, 340;** Joanne Hendrick, **p. 30;** Benjamin La Framboise,
pp. 80, 160, 180, 200; Barbara Schwartz/Merrill, **p. 108;** Leslie Gleim, **p. 138;** Lori Pickert, **pp. 222, 294;** Rebecca
Weissman, **p. 244;** Leisa Maloney, **p. 268;** Sojin Yi, **p. 316;** Camille Tokerud/Image Bank/Getty Images, **p. 356.**

Pearson® is a registered trademark of Pearson plc
Merrill® is a registered trademark of Pearson Education, Inc.

Pearson Education Ltd., London
Pearson Education Singapore, Pte. Ltd.
Pearson Education Canada, Inc.
Pearson Education–Japan
Pearson Education Australia PTY, Limited

Pearson Education North Asia, Ltd., Hong Kong
Pearson Educación de Mexico, S.A. de C.V.
Pearson Education Malaysia, Pte. Ltd.
Pearson Education Upper Saddle River, New Jersey

Merrill
is an ... is an imprint of

www.pearsonhighered.com

10 9 8 7 6 5 4 3 2 1
ISBN-13: 978-0-13-715305-3
ISBN-10:   0-13-715305-8

REVISING THIS BOOK ABOUT
EARLY CHILDHOOD EDUCATION IS
ALWAYS STIMULATING. IT HAS BEEN
AN INTERESTING TASK FOR ME TO
SET DOWN WHAT I KNOW ABOUT
THIS AREA AND THEN TO WITNESS
THE CHANGING NEEDS THE PAST
FEW YEARS HAVE BROUGHT TO THE
FORE. IF IT IS ALSO HELPFUL TO
BEGINNING TEACHERS AND TO THE
CHILDREN THEY SERVE, I WILL BE
PLEASED INDEED.

JOANNE HENDRICK

Overview

The Whole Child is a practical methods book for foundational or introductory courses in early childhood education. It explains how to teach young children from infancy through grade 3 in ways that foster healthy development. It helps pre-service teachers understand what children need from the learning environment in order to thrive. For that reason, it focuses on the child and pictures him or her as composed of a number of selves: the physical self, the emotional self, the social self, the cognitive self, and the creative self.

A Focus on the Domains—The Five Selves

The discussion of the physical self includes not only large- and fine-muscle development but also how to best handle routines because such things as eating, resting, and toileting contribute much to physical comfort and well-being. For the emotional self, the book considers ways to increase and sustain mental health, to cope with crises, to use guidance to foster self-control, to cope with aggression, and to foster self-esteem. Included for the social self are ways to build social concern and kindness and learning to value the cultures of other people. The cognitive, or intellectual, self is considered in terms of language and literacy development, the development of reasoning and thinking skills via the *emergent* approach, and the development of specific reasoning abilities. Finally, the creative self covers the areas of self-expression through the use of art materials and creativity as expressed in play and applied in thought.

    The Whole Child is based on the premise that physical and emotional health are fundamental to the well-being of children, that education must be developmentally appropriate if that well-being is to prosper, and that children need time to be children—time to be themselves, to do nothing, to stand and watch, and to repeat again what they did before. In short, they need time to live in their childhood rather than through it. If we offer the young children we teach rich and appropriate learning opportunities combined with enough time for them to enjoy and experience those opportunities to the fullest, we will enhance childhood, not violate it.

Inviting Features of This Textbook

New! myeducationlab A Web-based resource site, *MyEducationLab*, includes video, classroom artifacts, strategies, case studies, and more. Referenced in the pages of this text, these resources give real-life classroom examples to illustrate early childhood concepts and appropriate practices in action. Assignable questions are available in "Activities and Applications," while "Building Teaching

Go to MyEducationLab and select the topic "Guidance." Under Activities and Applications, watch the video *Promoting Socially Appropriate Behavior in Kindergarten.* How do these teachers create a classroom climate that fosters positive interactions for the children?

Skills and Dispositions" offers more elaborate exercises. Other resources include a lesson plan builder, portfolio builder, guidance about your first year of teaching, and more.

To start using MyEducationLab, activate the access code packaged with your book. If your instructor did not make MyEducationLab a required part of your course or if you are purchasing a used book without an access code, go to www.myeducationlab.com to purchase access to this wonderful resource!

This edition also includes:

- New information on **standards and assessment** and the implications for early childhood education
- Expanded age range from **infants and toddlers through third grade**
- The importance of **advocacy** for children, families, and the profession
- New discussion about considerations for the new teacher in **clarifying values and priorities**
- Additional new material as diverse as discussions of the **No Child Left Behind Act** to **integrated curriculum** to **multiple intelligences** to **intentional teaching**
- **Revised charts** on children's development, the development of block play, and Reggio-inspired examples of emergent curriculum
- Explanations of the basic tenets of **Vygotsky's, Piaget's, Gardner's, and Bronfenbrenner's theories** as well as their **implications** for early childhood education
- An emphasis on the development of reasoning and thinking skills via the **emergent approach**
- Practical examples of how teachers adapt the **Reggio Emilia** approach in American classrooms, including discussion and examples of documentation
- **"Related Organizations and Online Resources"** identify especially interesting and relevant resources available at low or no cost to students

The Whole Child is coordinated with the popular television series based on *The Whole Child*, funded by the Annenberg CPB Project. This series, available in Spanish and English, was produced under the guidance of an advisory committee that included Lilian Katz, Joan Costley, Irving Siegel, Carol Phillips, Ruby Burgess, Eli and Rosaline Saltz, Barbara Ferguson-Kamara, Frederich Goodman, and Jane Squires.

Continuing Features

- Material is presented in a warm, practical approach based on more than 30 years of experience teaching adult students and young children.
- Emphasis is on teaching methods that focus on children and their developmental needs rather than on science or art per se.
- The authors, who have visited and studied the Reggio schools for over a decade, include explanations of the Reggio Emilia approach and suggestions for integrating aspects of that philosophy.
- Entire chapters are included on multicultural, nonsexist education (chapter 4) and welcoming children who have special educational requirements into the life of the school (chapter 5).

Instructor and Student Resources

The following resources are available for download by adopting instructors from www.pearsonhighered.com. Click on Educators, then register and download any of the following ancillaries:

- **New!** A Web-based resource site, *MyEducationLab,* includes video, classroom artifacts, strategies, case studies, and more. Referenced in the text, these resources give real-life classroom examples to illustrate appropriate early childhood practices in action.
- An expanded *Online Instructor's Manual* includes "predicaments" for class discussion and suggested assignments.
- An updated *Online Test Bank,* also available in **BlackBoard** or **WebCT** course management formats, offers multiple choice, true/false, and essay questions for every chapter.
- Complete instructor's slides for every chapter are available in **PowerPoint** format for enhanced classroom presentation.

Acknowledgments

I owe so much to so many people that it is an impossible task to mention them all.

Some of these people are old, familiar friends and influences from my past. They include the students and parents and staff who contributed to my knowledge of early childhood. In addition, I am forever in debt to my mother, Alma Berg Green, who not only began some of the first parent education classes in Los Angeles but also taught me a great deal about young children and their families.

I am also indebted to Sarah Foot and her wonderful Starr King Parent/Child Workshop, which convinced me that my future lay in early childhood education, and to my own children who bore with me with such goodwill while I was learning the real truth about bringing up young people.

As far as the book itself is concerned, I would like to thank Murray Thomas for teaching me, among other things, how to write and John Wilson for convincing me that some things remained to be said and changed in early education. To Chester and Peggy Harris, I am forever indebted for a certain realistic attitude toward research, particularly in the area of cognitive development.

Of course, time does not stand still, so now I want to add to my list of early childhood friends and associates. As the new edition of *The Whole Child* goes to press, the people at Pearson/Merrill have been of great assistance. In particular I want to thank Kevin Davis, Publisher, and Julie Peters, Editor.

Finally, it gives me considerable pleasure that Patty Weissman is the co-author for the ninth edition. While continuing the philosophy and practical approach that has characterized previous editions of *The Whole Child*, Patty Weissman contributes a fresh background of institutional and family child care. In addition, she is thoroughly acquainted with the Reggio Emilia Approach because she was an early editor of *Innovations in Early Education: The International Reggio Exchange.* I know as you enjoy the latest edition of *The Whole Child* you will come to respect Patty as much as I have and that you will agree I am leaving my precious book in good hands.

—Joanne Hendrick

I wish to thank Joanne Hendrick for her contribution to early childhood education—and to my own education—through her creation of *The Whole Child*. I first encountered the text as a student some 30 years ago and I felt as if I had found a friend. I believed Joanne Hendrick to be someone who understood my experiences as a novice teacher, someone who appreciated my hard work and confusion as well as the deep sense of satisfaction I was beginning to feel from teaching. Through her delightful humor and down-to-earth wisdom, I came to trust the author and allowed her to pull me, reluctantly, into the world of educational theory (a world I now love). Joanne Hendrick was the first person who led me to think that the ideas of Erikson, Piaget, and Vygotsky are not only far from boring, they are awesome and true and very useful.

My learning from Joanne Hendrick continues as we now collaborate on the revision of *The Whole Child*. I am extremely grateful for this experience. I hope that my efforts result in at least one hardworking and perhaps confused novice teacher feeling as if she has found a friend.

I also wish to thank my other notable mentors: Rosalyn Saltz, founder of the Child Development Center at the University of Michigan–Dearborn and Eli Saltz, former director of the Merrill-Palmer Institute. Separately and together, they are a powerhouse of good ideas, good practices, good teaching, and most importantly, good hearts.

I am grateful to have worked or studied with so many wonderful and inspiring educators. Whether our encounters were brief or extended, they had an impact on my professional development and understanding of teaching. These include Sue Bredekamp, Carol Brunson Day, Louise Cadwell, Carolyn Edwards, Joan Firestone, George Forman, Brenda Fyfe, Amelia Gambetti, Lella Gandini, Karen Haigh, Pam Houk, Judith Kaminsky, Felicitas Kartiwan, Lilian Katz, Loris Malaguzzi, Rebecca New, Baji Rankin, Carlina Rinaldi, Libby Sheldon-Harsch, Eva Tarini, Sharon Tsuruta, Charlie Vincent, and Lynn White.

My colleagues at Pearson/Merrill have been an invaluable help. In particular, I appreciate the assistance (and patience) of Julie Peters and Linda Bayma.

Leslie Gleim, Benjamin La Framboise, Lori Pickert, and Pam Oken-Wright deserve mention for their beautiful photographs. The photos that accompany this text were made possible by the cooperation of families and staff at the Child Development Center, University of Michigan–Dearborn; Drayton Avenue Cooperative Nursery School, Ferndale, MI; Early Childhood Center, Wayne State University College of Education, Detroit, MI; Merrill-Palmer Child Development Laboratory, Wayne State University, Detroit, MI; Mid-Pacific Institute, Honolulu, HI; St. Catherine's School, Richmond, VA; and White Oak School, Monticello, IL. The high caliber of these programs is evident in the photographs, and students will learn from them for years to come.

The ninth edition has moved with the times and includes much new material. For their many suggestions in this regard, I would like to thank the following reviewers: Junie Albers-Biddle, University of Central Florida; Mary Beth Miller, Fresno City College; Regina Miller, University of Hartford; Dawn S. Munson, Elgin Community College; and Barbie Norvell, Coastal Carolina University.

Finally, I am forever grateful for all the children who have instructed me in life—from my first "batch of babies" at the Infant Development Center of San Francisco, to the Gorilla Group at Step One Nursery School in Berkeley, to my own dear offspring, Rose and Tony.

—Patricia Weissman

BRIEF CONTENTS

CONTENTS

chapter 9

Strengthening the Development of the Emotional Self   200

chapter 10

The Social Self: Encouraging Social Competence in Young Children   222

chapter 11

The Social Self: Fostering Self-Discipline and Conflict Resolution Skills   244

Note: Every effort has been made to provide accurate and current Internet information in this book. However, the Internet and information posted on it are constantly changing, and it is inevitable that some of the Internet addresses listed in this textbook will change.

There was a child went forth every day,
And the first object he look'd upon, that object
he became,
And that object became part of him for the day or
a certain part of the day,
Or for many years or stretching cycles of years.

The early lilacs became part of this child,
And grass and white and red morning-glories, and
white and red clover, and the song of the
phoebe-bird,
And the Third-month lambs and the sow's pink-
faint litter, and the mare's foal and the cow's calf,
And the noisy brood of the barnyard or by the
mire of the pond-side,
And the fish suspending themselves so curiously
below there, and the beautiful curious liquid,
And the water-plants with their graceful flat
heads, all became part of him.

The field-sprouts of Fourth-month and Fifth-
month became part of him,
Water-grain sprouts and those of the light-yellow
corn, and the esculent roots of the garden,
And the apple-trees cover'd with blossoms and the
fruit afterward, and wood-berries, and the
commonest weeds by the road,
And the old drunkard staggering home from the
outhouse of the tavern whence he had
lately risen,
And the schoolmistress that pass'd on her way to
the school,
And the friendly boys that pass'd, and the
quarrelsome boys,
And the tidy and fresh-cheek'd girls, and the
barefoot negro boy and girl,
And all the changes of city and country wherever
he went.

His own parents, he that had father'd him and she
that had conceiv'd him in her womb and
birth'd him,
They gave this child more of themselves than that,
They gave him afterward every day, they became
part of him.

The mother at home quietly placing the dishes on
the supper-table,
The mother with mild words, clean her cap and
gown, a wholesome odor falling off her person
and clothes as she walks by,
The father, strong, self-sufficient, manly, mean,
anger'd, unjust,
The blow, the quick loud word, the tight bargain,
the crafty lure,
The family usages, the language, the company, the
furniture, the yearning and swelling heart,
Affection that will not be gainsay'd, the sense of
what is real, the thought if after all it should
prove unreal,
The doubts of day-time and the doubts of nighttime,
the curious whether and how,
Whether that which appears so is so, or is all
flashes and specks?
Men and women crowding fast in the streets, if
they are not flashes and specks what are they?
The streets themselves and the facades of houses,
and goods in the windows,
Vehicles, teams, the heavy-plank'd wharves, the
huge crossing at the ferries,
The village on the highland seen from afar at
sunset, the river between,
Shadows, aureola and mist, the light falling on
roofs and gables of white or brown two miles off,
The schooner near by sleepily dropping down the
tide, the little boat slack-tow'd astern,
The hurrying tumbling waves, quick-broken crests,
slapping,
The strata of color'd clouds, the long bar of
maroon-tint away solitary by itself, the spread of
purity it lies motionless in,
The horizon's edge, the flying sea-crow, the
fragrance of salt marsh and shore mud,
These became part of that child who went forth
every day, and who now goes, and will always go
forth every day.

Walt Whitman
There Was a Child Went Forth (1871)

The Whole Child

Developmental Education for the Early Years

CHAPTER one

What Is Good Education
for Young Children?

What to reply when a friend says your job is really just babysitting?

Whether early education really makes any difference?

What constitutes a good program for infants and young children?

Why people are so excited about something called Reggio Emilia?

. . . IF YOU HAVE, THE MATERIAL IN THE FOLLOWING PAGES WILL HELP YOU.

Educating the mind without educating the heart is no education at all.

Aristotle (384–322 BCE)

Child care is only easy when you don't know what you're doing.

Jim Greenman (1998, p. 6)

Children have the right to fulfill and also expand all of their potential, a process that can be accomplished by recognizing and valuing children's capacity to socialize, by giving them affection and trust, by satisfying their needs and desires to learn.

Loris Malaguzzi (1993, p. 9)

Teaching young children can be one of the best, most deeply satisfying experiences in the world. Children from infancy to age 8 years go through fascinating, swiftly accomplished stages of development. They are possessed of vigorous personalities, rich enthusiasms, an astonishing amount of physical energy, and strong wills. There is no other time in human life when so much is learned in so brief a period (MacDonald, 2007; National Research Council and Institute of Medicine, 2000; Schiller, 2001; Shore, 1997).

This phenomenal vigor and burgeoning growth present a challenge to the beginning teacher that is at once exhilarating and frightening. The task is a large one: The teacher must attempt to build an educational climate that enhances the children's development and whets their appetites for further learning. The milieu must also nourish and sustain emotional health, encourage physical growth and muscular prowess, foster satisfying social interactions, enhance creativity, develop language skills, and promote the development of mental ability. Moreover, this must all be garbed in an aura of happiness and affection to establish that basic feeling of well-being that is essential to successful learning.

With such a large task at hand, it is not surprising that the beginning teacher may wonder somewhat desperately where to begin and what to do—and that is what this chapter is all about.

REALIZE YOU ARE PART OF A NOBLE PROFESSION

Early childhood education in the United States can trace its beginnings to the philosophy of Friedrich Froebel, who founded the first German kindergarten in 1840. Froebel's kindergartens were based on allowing children free-choice activities, creativity, social participation, and motor expression in a welcoming and stimulating environment prepared by the teacher.

In the late 19th century, American children often began working at the age of 10 after completing 3 years of school. Susan Blow, an educator in St. Louis, devoted her life to the education of young children and opened the first public kindergarten in 1873 based in Froebel's theories in order to improve children's lives. Many of the best practices in early education today have roots in these early kindergartens. Play was viewed as a primary means for children's learning, children were seen as progressing through developmental stages, and the teacher set the environment and stimulating activities to enhance learning.

Interest in the study of children and awareness of the value of educating their parents in wholesome child-rearing practices began to grow around the beginning of the 20th century. Along with the burgeoning interest in child development came a companion interest in preschool education and child care. This began abroad, where such leaders as Maria Montessori and the McMillan sisters pioneered child care as a means of improving the well-being of children of the poor.

In 1907 Maria Montessori, an ardent young reformer-physician, began her *Casa dei Bambini* (Children's House). That child care center was originally founded as part of an experiment in refurbishing slum housing in an economically distressed quarter of Rome (Loeffler, 1992). Supporters of that cooperative housing venture found that young children left unattended during the day while their parents were away at work were getting into trouble and destroying the property that people had worked so hard to restore. They therefore wanted to work out some way for the children to be cared for. Under Montessori's guidance, Children's House emphasized health, cleanliness, sensory training, individual learning, and the actual manipulation of materials (Hainstock, 1997; Montessori, 1912). Since Montessori believed that individual experience with self-correcting materials must come before other learning could take place, language experience, the use of imagination, and dramatic play were not recognized as being of much importance (Beatty, 1995).

In England, too, the pathetic condition of young slum children was being recognized. In 1911 two English sisters, Margaret and Rachel McMillan, founded their open-air nursery school. The McMillans had been interested in socialism and the women's movement. Through these concerns they came to know the condition of the London poor. They were horrified to discover that many children were running around shoeless in the London slums, suffering from lice, malnutrition, and scabies. Like Children's House, their school stressed good health, nourishing food, and adequate medical care. Unlike Children's House, it emphasized the value of outdoor play, sunshine, sandboxes, and regular baths. The McMillans advocated teaching children together in small groups. They stressed building independence and self-esteem. They also believed that young girls had natural gifts for working with children, so they gave them paid, on-the-job training as they worked with the children (Bradburn, 1989; McMillan, 1929).

In the United States, childhood education witnessed a flowering of interest in the early 1900s as well. *Progressive education,* one of the most influential movements in the early childhood field still today, was developed at the University of Chicago Laboratory school under the direction of John Dewey at the beginning of the 20th century. Progressive education prevailed in elementary schools, yet many of the practices currently used in preprimary programs grew out of Dewey's then-radical philosophy of "child-centered education." Dewey believed that education should stem from the child's interests and real experiences in the world, help the child think critically, and meet all the child's needs—physical, social, emotional, and intellectual—to develop into a moral citizen and member of a democratic community (Mooney, 2000).

"Nursery" education began to blossom in this country in the early 1920s. A group of women at the University of Chicago began the first parent cooperative nursery school in 1916. In 1919 Harriet Johnson opened the City and County School, which later metamorphosed into Bank Street. Abigail Eliot began the Ruggles Street Nursery School in Boston in 1921—the same year that Patty Smith Hill founded a laboratory nursery school at Columbia Teachers College.

As interest in nursery-level education grew, the academic community began to offer training in the field, and professional associations were formed. For example, at the Merrill Palmer School of Motherhood and Home Training (which later became the prestigious Merrill Palmer Institute), a nursery school was provided where students participated in an 8-hour laboratory experience each week. They studied child care management, health, nutrition, and social problems—not very different from what students do, at least in part, today.

In 1925 Patty Smith Hill (1942/1992) called a meeting of early leaders in the field to discuss issues of concern in the care of young children. In 1929 the National Association of Nursery Education was founded. That association has continued and is now known as the National Association for the Education of Young Children (NAEYC). It has grown to more than 100,000 members and provides an annual conference attended by 24,000 people (NAEYC, 2007). For over 20 years, NAEYC has developed an accreditation system designed to ensure high-quality standards in early childhood programs. Over 10,000 preprimary centers were NAEYC accredited in 2007 (NAEYC, 2007). Information about NAEYC is included in the Related Organizations and Online Resources section at the end of this chapter.

The field of early childhood education has a noble history that has resulted in a proliferation of programs designed with the very best intentions for young children. People who enter the field usually do so out of a genuine sense of caring about children—certainly not for a love of money! (The issue of compensation will be discussed later in this chapter.) Most of us in early childhood education—like John Dewey or Maria Montessori or Patty Smith Hill—want to make a difference in children's lives and by doing so, help to create a better society. This begs the question that has probably crossed every early childhood teacher's mind: Is all our hard work effective? Can we really make a difference?

CAN EARLY EDUCATION MAKE A DIFFERENCE?

For several decades, research on early childhood education has sought to investigate the effects of various kinds of programs on the development of young children. The results of these investigations have been at times discouraging and at times heartening. In addition, since the 1990s, scientists investigating brain development have discovered a number of findings that support the significance of good early childhood education (MacDonald, 2007; Rushton & Larkin, 2001; Rutledge, 2000; Stephens, 2006b; Schweinhart, 2008; Shore, 1997; Washington, 2002).

It is important to know about the results of such studies because most members of the general public, including parents and legislators, are still uninformed about the potential value of early education and persist in seeing it as "just babysitting." If we are tired of this misguided point of view, we need to have the results of these studies on the tips of our tongues so that we can explain the value of our work with young children to those who need to be better informed about it.

Brain Development Research

For centuries, the study of the human brain was limited to the realm of theory since researchers were unable to investigate a normal living brain without surgery. The development of noninvasive brain scanning technologies in the 1990s, as well as new means for studying brain waves and chemistry, now allow neuroscientists to see how the brain functions without causing distress to the person being examined. Recent studies have looked at the brains of young children, infants, and even fetuses. A wealth of neuroscientific data has accumulated that shows how the child's brain develops.

The new brain research provides early childhood educators with a deeper understanding about teaching and learning. Several findings are relevant for those who work with infants and young children:

- The brain development of infants and toddlers proceeds at a staggering pace, and the human brain is most active during the first 3 years of life.

- Early experiences have an impact on the actual structure of the brain.

- Early experiences have a decisive impact on how a person functions as an adult.

- There are prime times, particularly in the early years, for acquiring different kinds of knowledge and skills.

- Positive experiences in the first years of life enhance brain development, whereas negative experiences, such as abuse or maternal depression, can interfere with development.

- Warm, responsive care during infancy is critical to healthy development (MacDonald, 2007; Shore, 1997; Stephens, 2006b). Figure 1.1 describes the ways in which teachers can put these findings into practice.

Recent research on early brain development and school readiness suggests the following broad guidelines for the care of young children:

- Ensure health, safety, and good nutrition.

- Develop a warm, caring relationship with children. Show them that you care deeply about them. Express joy in who they are. Help them feel safe and secure.

- Respond to children's cues and clues. Notice their rhythms and moods. . . . Respond to children when they are upset as well as when they are happy. Try to understand what children are feeling, what they are telling you (in words or actions), and what they are trying to do. Hold and touch them; play with them in a way that lets you follow their lead. Move in when children want to play; and pull back when they seem to have had enough stimulation.

- Recognize that each child is unique. Keep in mind that from birth, children have different temperaments, that they grow at their own pace, and that this pace varies from child to child. At the same time, have positive expectations about what children can do and hold onto the belief that every child can succeed.

- Talk, read, and sing to children. Surround them with language. Maintain an ongoing conversation with them about what you and they are doing. Sing to them, play music, tell stories, and read books. Ask toddlers and preschoolers what will come next in a story. Play word games. Ask toddlers and preschoolers questions that require more than a yes or no answer, like "What do you think . . .?" Ask children to picture things that have happened in the past or might happen in the future. Provide reading and writing materials, including crayons and paper, books, magazines, and toys. These are key prereading experiences.

- Encourage safe exploration and play. Give children opportunities to move around, explore, and play (be prepared to step in if they are at risk of hurting themselves or others). Allow them to explore relationships as well. Arrange for children to spend time with children of their own age and other ages. Help them learn to solve conflicts that inevitably arise.

- Use discipline to teach. Talk to children about what they seem to be feeling and teach them words to describe those feelings. Make it clear that while you might not like the way they are behaving, you love them. Explain the rules and consequences of behavior so children can learn the "whys" behind what you are asking them to do. Tell them what you want them to do, not just what you don't want them to do. Point out how their behavior affects others.

- Establish routines. Create routines and rituals for special times during the day like mealtime, naptime, and bedtime. Try to be predictable so the children know they can count on you.

Figure 1.1
Tips for teachers on the day-to-day care of young children's brains

Source: Adapted from Rethinking the Brain: New Insights into Early Development *(pp. 26–27), by R. Shore, 1997, New York, NY: Families and Work Institute. Reprinted with permission.*

Effects of Early Childhood Education

The research on children in the Perry Preschool Project is probably the most important long-term study of the effects of early education on children's development. Begun in 1962, that research is still continuing, and the data have been consistent over more than four decades of investigation. Researchers found substantial differences between the experimental group who had experienced the benefits of a good preschool program (the Perry Preschool) and a similar group who had not had those experiences as they reached adulthood. Fewer of the Perry Preschool children had been in trouble with the law, more of them had graduated from high school, and more of them had jobs after graduation (Schweinhart, Montie, Yiang, Barnett, & Belfield, 2005; Weikart, 1990). The most recent data indicate that this trend toward self-sufficiency was continuing as the group reached age 40. They continued to have fewer arrests and significantly higher incomes, and many more of them owned homes than did those in the control group. When these results are translated into taxpayer dollars saved, the money amounts to about $195,621 (in 2000 dollars) per participant—a return of $12.90 for every dollar originally invested in the preschool program (Schweinhart et al., 2005).

The Perry Preschool studies are presented because they are the most widely publicized pieces of research on this subject, but you should realize that they are among many studies that now support the value of well-planned early education on children's development and success in later life (Barnett, Jung, Wong, Cook, & Lamy, 2007; Isaacs, 2008; National Early Childhood Accountability Task Force, 2007).

Benjamin La Framboise

What the research tells us: Develop warm, caring relationships with each child.

Research Implications for Teaching

The Perry Preschool studies and the research on brain development lead us to an important conclusion: Good early education has long-lasting positive effects on children and on society. Teachers of young children wield a considerable power. With that power comes the responsibility to provide the best possible care and education for the infants and young children under our watch. The first step for the beginning teacher is to understand the theoretical foundations that underlie early childhood education. As teachers, we make theoretical choices throughout the day—whether we are aware of them or not. This includes everything from how we structure the day to the types of questions we ask to the experiences and materials we provide. The more informed we are in our choices, the more positive our impact on the children will be.

THEORETICAL FOUNDATIONS OF EARLY CHILDHOOD EDUCATION

All teachers (and parents) have their own ideas about what is right for children. Everyone has beliefs about how children should behave, what course their development should follow, and what the appropriate experiences are for their age. Many times this understanding of childhood comes from one's own upbringing and is not reflected upon in a conscious way. As a beginning teacher, you would be wise to think about your own childhood and the expectations you have for children before entering the classroom. Theories of development and teaching methods that have been tried and tested for decades—sometimes centuries—should inform teaching practices. By studying theories and the "best practices" that have grown out of theory, teachers can provide the type of early education that is most beneficial to children.

Developmental Approaches

Many theories regarding early childhood education are based on the premise that child development is a continually unfolding process. Children pass through stages, and their interests and learning are directly related to this growth or developmental process. The developmental approach is used in the majority of early childhood programs in the United States today.

This book takes a developmental approach and views the child as being "whole" but composed of a number of developing selves: the physical self, the emotional self, the social self, the cognitive self, and the creative self. It is important for teachers to understand how each aspect or *domain* of development occurs and how each area influences and is influenced by the others.

There has been considerable research examining the typical development of children and describing the normal course of children's growth in charts of developmental norms (see Appendix A). This knowledge base has led to a movement within the field of early childhood education known as *developmentally appropriate practice* (DAP). *Developmentally appropriate* means the learning activities planned for children are placed at the correct level for their age and are suited to individual children's tastes, abilities, and cultures. By following the DAP guidelines developed by NAEYC, teachers do not use developmental charts to try to speed up development, but to better understand and plan for each child (Copple & Bredekamp, 2009). This is especially important for children with special needs who benefit from a supportive environment that enables them to capitalize on their strengths, rather than one that focuses on their delays in comparison to the norm (Larkin, 2001).

Psychoanalytic Theory

Contributions of Sigmund Freud

One of the most influential theories on the field of child development is Freud's theory of personality development. In the late 1800s Sigmund Freud began investigating the human mind. Although trained as a physician, Freud became interested in how early childhood experiences led to mental problems in adulthood. He developed a treatment for patients that consisted of having them talk at length about their past experiences, a technique known as *psychoanalysis*. In Freudian theory, early child-rearing practices are viewed as a crucial, defining aspect of development (Freud, 1922/1959).

Freud also proposed a series of developmental stages that all humans pass through. Each *psychosexual* stage relates to the chief source of bodily pleasure. For example, the infant seeks oral gratification, whereas toddlers' sexual energy is focused around the anus and the process of elimination (keep in mind this is the time that toilet training usually takes place). Early childhood educators also work with children who are in the *phallic* stage or *early genital* stage (3 to 6 years), when there is often intense interest in their (and others') genitals (Freud, 1922/1959).

Although Freudian theory has been criticized as being outdated or sexist, his contribution to our understanding of childhood impulses and behavior is enormous. A knowledge of Freudian theory can help teachers understand the developmental appropriateness of a 2-year-old who grabs toys (an example of what Freud termed the "id" or the child's basic drive for self-gratification) or a 4-year-old who seems fascinated with his or her genitals. In addition, many other theories relevant to early childhood grew from a base of Freudian theory.

Contributions of Erik Erikson

One important theory in early childhood was developed by a Freudian-trained psychoanalyst, Erik Erikson. Many early childhood programs today are based in part on Erikson's *theory of psychosocial development*. Like Freud, Erikson believed children pass through stages of development; however, he saw these stages as more socially motivated rather than sexually motivated. Erikson's *eight stages of psychosocial development* trace personality development through the life span.

Of particular interest to early educators are Erikson's first four stages. In the stage of *trust versus mistrust* (from birth to approximately 12–18 months), the baby learns whether the world can be trusted. During this stage it is essential that a deep, intimate bond or *attachment* is formed between the infant and the caregiver for healthy development to proceed. During the stage of *autonomy versus shame and doubt* (12–18

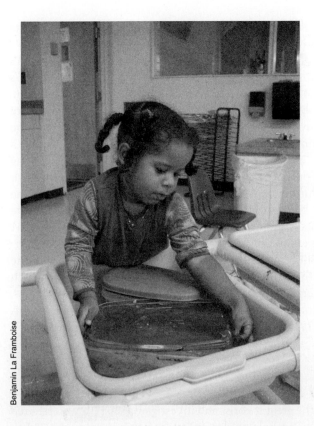

Benjamin La Framboise

A sense of purpose develops as the child uses initiative to try out new things.

months to approximately 3 years), the child develops a sense of self. If independence is repressed, the child begins to have self-doubts and feel ashamed. Much of the behavior attributed to the so-called terrible twos can be explained by Erikson's theory. The 2-year-old who refuses to put on a jacket or who answers almost every question with an emphatic "No!" is expressing a healthy need for autonomy. In the stage of *initiative versus guilt* (3 to 6 years), a sense of purpose develops as children use their initiative to try out new things and experience success with their ideas. If the child is met with disapproval and failure, a lasting sense of guilt can develop. The fourth stage of *latency* generally takes place in elementary and middle school (6 to 12 years). During this period, children develop a sense of either industry or inferiority. They learn through their own persevering efforts that pleasure can be derived from a job well done. It is important for the child to discover pleasure in being productive and to develop feelings of success. The child's relationships with peers become increasingly important (Erikson, 1963).

Family-Ecological Theory

Contributions of Urie Bronfenbrenner

The ecological theory of Bronfenbrenner does not look at child development itself but at the environments in which children develop. He called his theory ecological because ecology is the science of the relationships between beings and their environments (Bronfenbrenner, 1979).

Bronfenbrenner proposed four levels of environment which affect the child's development. The first level, or *microsystem,* refers to the setting for the child's behavior such as the activities, participants, and their roles in the child's life. The child's family structure, neighborhood, playmates, and child care arrangements are examples of the child's microsystem. The second level, or *mesosystem,* refers to the links among the various settings in which the child spends time. For example, a school-age child's mesosytem in the United States might include the links among home, school, church, neighborhood, and extracurricular activities such as sports or after-school programs. The third level is the *exosystem,* which includes settings the child does not actually enter but that affect the child indirectly. For example, the child is affected by the parents' workplace although he or she may never go there. Other examples of the child's exosystem are the local community structure and services, the school board, and all forms of the mass media such as television and the Internet. The fourth level of the child's ecological system is the *macrosystem,* which refers to the culture and overall society in which the child lives. Social values, beliefs, customs, and institutions all have an important impact on the child's development (Bronfenbrenner, 1979).

Active Learning, Constructivist Theories

Contributions of Jean Piaget

You will find that the work of the great theorist and investigator Jean Piaget is referred to again and again throughout this volume. His more than half-century of research into the developmental stages and characteristics of children's cognitive processes is invaluable, as are both his emphasis on the importance of dynamic interaction between children and the environment as children *construct* what they know for themselves, and his emphasis on the significance of play as a medium for learning (DeVries & Kohlberg, 1990; Frost, Wortham, & Reifel, 2008).

However, many scholars and teachers are not satisfied with restricting themselves solely to Piagetian *constructivist theory* because they believe that Piaget did not say enough about social relationships, creativity, or emotional health. This is because Piaget's primary interest was the investigation of children's thought processes.

A point of view closely related to Piagetian constructivism but more comprehensive is the *developmental-interactionist* approach of the Bank Street and High/Scope programs (Bank Street, 1998; A. Epstein, 2003). This approach sees children as developing human beings in whom knowing about things (the intellectual self) combines with feeling about them (the emotional self). In this point of view the impetus for growth lies in part within the maturing individual, but it also occurs in part as a result of the interaction between the child and the environment and people to whom the child relates.

This interaction is important because children are regarded as being active participants in their own growth. Children learn by constructing and reconstructing what they know as they encounter a variety of experiences and people who widen and enrich their knowledge. The teacher's role is one of guiding, questioning, and enabling—not just stuffing children with an assortment of facts and rewards for good behavior.

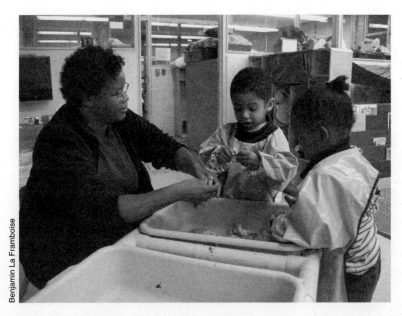

The teacher's role is one of guiding, questioning, and enabling—not just stuffing the child with an assortment of facts and rewards for good behavior.

Contributions of Lev Vygotsky

In recent years Lev Vygotsky (1978) has become known as yet another educational theorist who has contributed helpful insights about the way young children learn and develop. Vygotsky reminds us how important the influence of culture and social interchange is to mental growth. Adults and more knowledgeable peers who transmit these social values and information assist the child's growth. They do this by interacting and encouraging children to operate at the growing edge of their mental abilities—the area of "assisted performance" termed by Vygotsky as *the zone of proximal development* (often abbreviated as the ZPD).

Vygotsky identified social play as the premier or "leading" activity that enables young children to operate in that zone since play requires the use of imagination, symbolic language, and observation of social rules requiring self-regulation. In addition to play, Vygotsky devoted considerable time to defining the role of the teacher. He advocated that teachers should sense which skills are about to emerge in each child and seek to develop them. Development should be accomplished by delicately assisting children—first by finding out what they already know and then by using dialogue and various experiences to assist them to advance to a further point in their growth. This technique of "scaffolding" a child's learning, that is, supporting and assisting the child before new learning and skills emerge, has been shown to be very effective for both children with special needs and children with typical development (Barnes & Whinnery, 2002; Larkin, 2001).

The Reggio Emilia Approach

The teachers in Reggio Emilia, Italy, are confident about the preschool child's abilities (Gandini, 2008; Malaguzzi, 1998; Rinaldi, 1993). They see the child as strong, competent, capable of constructing thoughts, and having great potential to offer to the world. In this approach, the teacher becomes a compass that may point the child in a particular direction, and education is seen as an ever-developing process that cannot be predetermined because it emerges bit by bit.

The 32 children's centers in the town of Reggio Emilia are places where children and teachers interact—listening and talking with each other—to explore subjects thoroughly by exchanging ideas and trying out those ideas. Teachers select an aspect of the children's interests to develop further, an aspect that presents problems for them to consider and solve (or, as Reggian teachers put it, "provokes" the children into thought). A particular interest may be pursued in depth over several months, depending on how intrigued the children become with the topic.

The results of these joint investigations are then transformed by the children into visible products that communicate what they have found to other people. Since the children are too young to write, the staff encourages them to express what they know by using all sorts of other languages, or what educators in Reggio have termed "the hundred languages of children." It might be the language of paint, or clay, or cardboard structures, or concoctions of bent wire bedecked with tissue paper, or shadow plays.

American early childhood education already espouses many ideas basic to the Reggian philosophy. In fact, there are many similarities between the Reggio approach and progressive education as developed by Dewey: parent involvement; fostering creativity; learning by doing; and inquiry-based, child-centered, hands-on, cooperative learning (D. L. Black, 2000; Mooney, 2000). But we are also tantalized by evidence of the exceptional abilities demonstrated by these young Italian children, particularly because observers report that it is the children themselves who are doing the work and accomplishing it without strain—and in a delightful, joyful setting. It is hoped that inclusion of information about the Reggio approach in *The Whole Child* will encourage the exploration of many of its principles in our own work with children in this country. There will be further discussion of the Reggio approach, as well as the theories of Piaget and Vygotsky, in chapters 14 and 16.

PEARSON
myeducationlab

Go to MyEducationLab, at www.myeducationlab.com, and select the topic "Curriculum/ Program Models." Under Activities and Applications, watch the video *Discovery in a Study of Birds.* How does this curriculum support active learning? Which educational theory is this type of curriculum based upon?

Behaviorist or Learning Theory

Although developmental theories form the theoretical basis of this text, there is one other theory that warrants our attention. The term *behavior modification* tends to bring scowls to the faces of many teachers who object to the potential for manipulation inherent in that approach. However, it is important to understand its positive value as well. Learning theorists who practice behavior modification have accumulated a great deal of carefully documented research that substantiates their claims that this approach, which rewards desirable behavior and discourages undesirable actions, can be a powerful avenue for teaching (Carpenter & Nangle, 2001; R. Thomas, 1999). It has proved its usefulness particularly in work with children with a variety of disabilities (McLean, Wolery, & Bailey, 2004).

Behavior modification theorists maintain that children learn as a result of rewards (for example, teacher attention or praise) or punishments (such as scolding or the way some teachers use, or misuse, the dreaded "time-out chair"—similar to putting a dunce cap on the child's head!). It is true that a program based solely on the deliberate manipulation of children's behavior is repugnant, but it is also true that *all teachers use this technique constantly and extensively whether they realize it or not*. Every smile, every frown, every positive or negative bit of attention a child receives either encourages or discourages future behavior. Therefore, rather than blindly condemning such theory, why not become aware of how often we employ such strategies on an informal basis and acknowledge their power?

FROM THEORY TO PRACTICE

Thus far we have seen that the history of early childhood education is rich and quite wondrous in all that it has accomplished since the first U.S. public kindergarten opened in 1873. We have also noted that early education has a strong, positive impact not only on children's development but on society as well. Finally, we've discussed the different theories that we can apply in our teaching so that we provide the best education and care for young children. The rest of this chapter will equip you with practical information about the types of programs in which you can expect to find work and how to go about integrating theoretical ideas into practice as you begin your teaching career.

Go to MyEducationLab and select the topic "Curriculum/Program Models." Under Activities and Applications, observe constructivist theory put into practice in one of the following videos: *Head Start, Montessori, High/Scope,* or *Reggio Emilia.*

TYPES OF EARLY CHILDHOOD EDUCATION

Over 13 million preschool-age children are in child care arrangements today (Children's Defense Fund [CDF], 2005). It is now more common for a child under the age of 5 to be in child care than to be at home with a parent (CDF, 2005; U.S. Census Bureau, 2005). Certainly the current demand for early care is due to the number of mothers with young children who are in the paid labor force: Today approximately 63% of mothers with children under age 6 work outside the home (CDF, 2005). In the year 2005, over 75% of mothers with school-age children worked in the paid labor force, creating a need for before- and after-school programs in elementary schools (Cahony & Sok, 2007) in addition to preschool programs.

It is unlikely that the demand for children's early education programs will lessen in the near future. Mothers will continue to find employment outside the home for a number of reasons, including economic necessity and self-fulfillment. Those entering the field of early childhood education will find a wide range of student teaching possibilities and work available to them in just about every community throughout the country.

All Programs Include Children with Special Needs

Individuals with Disabilities Education Act (IDEA), Parts B and C

IDEA is our nation's special education law, the federal education program that assists states in implementing services for individuals with disabilities, birth through 21 years of age. Part B provides services to children ages 3 to 21 years. Part C provides services to infants and toddlers. IDEA ensures that all children with disabilities have available to them a "free appropriate public education." IDEA mandates that public programs, such as Head Start or the public schools, include children with special needs. During the 2000–2001 school year, close to 600,000 children with disabilities ages 3 to 5 years received services under IDEA Part B. This number represented approximately 5% of the total population of preschool-age children in the year 2000 (U.S. Department of Education, 2001). Novice teachers should become familiar with IDEA and the many ways in which children with a variety of special needs are included in preprimary and primary programs (see chapter 5 for more in-depth discussion of *inclusion*).

Center-Based Care

The most prevalent form of preprimary care and education is provided in a nonresidential child care center, usually serving 13 or more children. The majority of preschoolers with a mother in the labor force are in child care centers (U.S. Census Bureau, 2005). Center-based programs are licensed by the state, and regulations vary widely from state to state. Quality in centers varies enormously as well, as there is no national "quality control." Centers that have gone through a voluntary process of NAEYC accreditation, however, tend to have higher quality programs (Whitebook, Sakai, Gerber, & Howes, 2001).

Teaching situations range from half- to full-day care of infants up through prekindergarten children. The center could be funded by parents, the state, a parent's employer, a church, a private charity, and/or the federal government. It could be part of a chain or operate as an independent center. It might be located in a new facility or in make-do circumstances, on a college campus, or in a church, a public school, or its own building. It could be a public preschool program for 4-year-olds or a Head Start Center, part of the military child care system operated by the U.S. Department of Defense, or restricted to serving families of low income. It may be staffed by teachers with a Child Development Associate (CDA) or college degree in early childhood education (AA, AAS, and BA degrees), by people working on those degrees, by those possessing a master's or even PhD, or by people who meet only the criteria of being 16 years old and having a high school degree and no criminal record. The variations for children and teachers are truly mind-boggling. Today, *universal pre-k* or preprimary programs that are sponsored by states are the main source for preschool education. Each state has its own system of delivery as well as its own standards and forms of assessment, all of which is discussed further in chapter 6.

Compensatory Programs

Head Start is the best known of the compensatory programs since it exists on a nation-wide basis. Some states also fund additional preschool programs designed to educate children from families with low incomes. Although termed *compensatory* because they were originally intended to compensate for deficiencies in the child's home environment, current investigations have found greater strengths in the homes than had previously been noted. Now the programs seek to honor these strengths, as well as to compensate for lags in verbal and mental development that are associated with poverty (Head Start Bureau, 2004).

Head Start was created in 1965 by the federal government to provide comprehensive education, health, nutrition, and parent involvement services to children and their families who are living in poverty. More than 21 million preschool-age children have benefited from Head Start. In 2003 there were over 900,000 children enrolled in Head Start programs, the majority of them (87%) 3- and 4-year-olds (Head Start Bureau, 2004). With the reauthorization of the Head Start program in 1994, Congress established a new program for low-income families with infants and toddlers and pregnant women, which is called Early Head Start.

Montessori Schools

Placement of student teachers in schools that base their curriculum on the teachings of Maria Montessori is usually quite difficult to arrange unless the students are participating in an academic program philosophically based in the same tradition. This is because Montessori schools require their teachers to undergo training specifically related to Montessori's precepts. Occasionally students who do not meet this criterion can find employment as an aide or during the summer in such schools, thereby gaining at least some exposure to the methods and philosophy of that distinguished educator (Hainstock, 1997).

Demonstration or Laboratory Schools

Demonstration or laboratory schools are typically connected with teacher training institutions or with research programs. They can be wonderful places for students to begin their teaching because they are the most likely of all the kinds of schools to be child and student centered. Ideally, students should have teaching opportunities in both laboratory and real-life schools so that they receive a balance of ideal and realistic teaching experiences.

Family Child Care

Family child care, where care is provided for a small group of children in the provider's own home, is another facet of the early childhood profession. Frequently used for infants and toddlers, family child care has the virtues of providing children with a smaller, more intimate environment, more flexible hours, and a more homelike atmosphere. Providers often prefer this setting because it offers opportunities for increased income while keeping their own youngsters as part of the group, and it offers personal independence in curriculum planning and scheduling. Some family child care homes are licensed by a state agency although most are unlicensed (Galinsky, Howes, Kontos, & Shinn, 1994). Licensing regulations vary from state to state, with the total number of children allowed ranging from 6 to 12. As is true for center-based care, fees, and hence a provider's income, vary widely, as does the quality of care.

Public School Programs

Elementary Grades K–3

Early childhood teachers in public elementary schools should be aware of the No Child Left Behind (NCLB) Act of 2001. This federal legislation requires states to ensure that qualified teachers are in every public school classroom and that schools use research-based learning standards. Schools are required to assess children's performance in reading, language arts, science, and math tests annually in grades 3 to 8, and schools, school districts, and states are held accountable for children's performance results (Yell & Drasgow, 2005). The NCLB Act has greatly affected the curricula used in elementary schools, and those who teach in public primary schools should be knowledgeable about their state's standards and assessments. Chapter 6 contains more detailed discussion of the NCLB Act.

A Final Thought About Programs

Wherever you end up in your student placement or teaching career, you will bring with you your own set of values, approaches, and teaching methods—what you might think of as your "tool kit." It is wise to start assembling this early on, learning from others what has worked for them and discovering what works for you. When you observe exceptionally good teachers, take note of the things that they do, what makes them effective, and which approaches are being used. What's in that experienced teacher's tool kit that you might borrow?

The following explains the approaches that form the basis of *The Whole Child*, culled from many years of research and work with young children, as well as from observing some exceptionally good teachers. For more information about getting started in your teaching placement, see Appendix B.

BASIC PREMISES OF THIS BOOK

Besides advocating that a curriculum be provided for every self, this book is based on additional basic premises. The first premise is that the purpose of education is to increase competence and mastery in all aspects of the developing self. It is much more important to teach children to cope by equipping them with skills than to stuff them full of facts. This is so because confidence in their coping ability is what underlies children's sense of self-worth. Skills empower children.

The second premise is that physical and emotional health are absolutely fundamental to the well-being of children. Any program that ignores that fact is building its curriculum on a foundation of sand.

The third premise is that children learn most easily by means of actual, involving experiences with people and activities. This is best accomplished in an open, carefully planned yet flexible environment where children must take responsibility and make decisions for themselves and where they have ample opportunity to learn through play.

The fourth premise is that children pass through various stages as they develop. Piaget has, of course, thoroughly demonstrated this in regard to intellectual development, but it has been heavily documented for the other selves as well (Gesell, Halverson, Thompson, & Ilg, 1940; MacDonald, 2007; Shore, 1997).

The fifth premise is that children do not exist in isolation as they develop. As Bronfenbrenner (1979) and Vygotsky (1978) remind us, we are all surrounded by ever-widening influences of family, community, and the world beyond—all of which affect the direction and degree of our growth.

Children need time to be children.

The final premise is that children need time to be children. The purpose of early education should not be to pressure and urge youngsters on to the next step in a hurried way. Recent research provides evidence that placing academic pressure on young children is a precursor to negative attitudes toward school and decreased academic accomplishments in later grades (Hirsh-Pasek & Golinkoff, 2003; Schweinhart & Weikart, 1997; Wien, 2004).

Children need time and personal space in which to grow. They need time to be themselves—to do nothing, to stand and watch, to repeat again what they did before; in short, they need time to live *in* their childhood, rather than *through* it. If we are sensitive to their concerns and offer the young children we teach rich and appropriate learning opportunities combined with enough time for them to enjoy and experience those opportunities to the fullest, we will be enhancing that era of childhood, not violating it.

PUTTING PREMISES INTO PRACTICE: PLANNING A GOOD DAY FOR CHILDREN

No matter what setting you work in as a teacher, the following ingredients are all essential for creating quality education for young children.

Good Human Relationships Are a Fundamental Ingredient of a Good Day

For warmth and personal contact to flourish, the day must be planned and paced so that opportunities for person-to-person, one-to-one encounters are numerous.

In practical terms, this means groups must be kept small and the ratio of adults to children must be as high as possible, especially with regard to infants. To provide optimal care, it is recommended that the maximum group size for infants is six, with each adult caring for no more than three babies (Copple & Bredekamp, 2009; Lally et al., 2003).

Many occasions must also be provided for the children to move freely about, making personal choices and generating individual contacts. Such arrangements permit numerous interludes in which informal learning experiences can be enjoyed and human caring can be expressed. The moments may be as fleeting as a quick hug when the teacher ties a pair of trailing shoelaces or as extended as a serious discussion of where babies come from. It is the *quality* of individualized, personal caring and the chance to talk together that are significant.

Families Must Be Included as Part of the Life of the School

Mounting research confirms that inclusion of families in the educational process, whether in home tutoring programs or the school itself, results in longer lasting educational gains for the child (Mendoza, Katz, Robertson, & Rothenberg, 2003; National Research Council and Institute of Medicine, 2000). Family inclusion is also a fundamental cornerstone of the Reggio approach, in which parents participate in day-to-day interactions, discussions of relevant issues, excursions, and celebrations (Gandini, 2008; Spaggiari, 1998).

High-Quality Education Must Be Developmentally Appropriate

If the material is at the right developmental level, the children will be drawn to it and want to learn about it (Copple & Bredekamp, 2009; Rushton & Larkin, 2001; Wien, 2004). In contrast, when children are pushed too far ahead of their current levels and the curriculum is unsuited to their abilities, it's like pushing them into deep water before they can swim: They're likely to dread the water and avoid it when they can. At this early stage of schooling, it is crucial for children to decide that learning is something to be pursued with verve, not that it is difficult and anxiety provoking. For this reason it is vital that teachers have a good grasp of the developmental characteristics of children at various ages, understand how they are likely to progress as they grow, and plan the curriculum to stimulate that growth without making it so difficult that children give up in despair.

High-Quality Education Is Individualized

Teachers must see every youngster not only in terms of what they know in general about child development, but also in terms of what each particular child is like developmentally and culturally. This is the real art of teaching. Fortunately, in preprimary programs, the small group size and intimacy make it possible for teachers to know each youngster well and to plan with particular individuals in mind, particularly those with special needs. Excellent elementary teachers also find ways to connect with and respond to each child in the classroom.

Joanne Hendrick

A good program needs to be developmentally appropriate. This is just about challenging enough to intrigue but not discourage these young threes.

High-Quality Education Honors Diversity in Its Many Forms

Ever since its original publication in 1973, *The Whole Child* has included an entire chapter advocating cross-cultural education and another on inclusion of children who have special needs into the group. Everyone's experience is enriched when children from a variety of backgrounds are included in the school.

High-Quality Education Uses Reasonable and Authentic Methods of Assessment to Find Out More About the Children

Assessing young children is a risky and problematic business (Shonkoff & Meisels, 2000; Epstein, Schweinhart, DeBruin-Parecki, & Robin, 2006), particularly in this time of mandatory testing for Head Start and elementary school children. At best, assessments can identify skills, needs, and promising potentials of such young children; at worst, they can use totally inappropriate methods of evaluation (McAfee, Leong, & Bodrova, 2004).

Perhaps the most desirable way to think of assessment for the majority of young children is as an opportunity to record growth and deepen teachers' and parents' insights about particular children. There are a variety of ways that teachers can generate such records. These include information contributed by families, simple checklists based on developmental charts, snapshots or even videotapes of children's special accomplishments such as block structures or other creations, an occasional painting, and weekly anecdotal records citing events or interactions related to the child that the teacher thinks are significant (McAfee et al., 2004). Many infant caregivers find it useful to keep notes throughout the day. In addition to recording information about feeding, diapering, and such, it is a good way to note new developments, such as a new tooth or an attempt at crawling, to communicate to parents. Records are most helpful when they are begun early in the year so that progress can be noted as it occurs.

It is important to keep in mind that many early childhood teachers today must adhere to state and federally mandated standards and assessments. This is true for Head Start teachers, many who work in state-sponsored preschool programs, and public elementary school teachers. Teachers need to be aware of which educational standards and assessments are required in their school.

When more comprehensive assessments are needed, it is best to refer the family to someone who specializes in that area. See chapter 5 for a discussion about how to make effective referrals.

High-Quality Education Has a Balance Between Self-Selection and Teacher Direction; Both Approaches Are Valuable

The idea that young children can be trusted to choose beneficial educational experiences for themselves goes back in educational theory about a hundred years to Dewey—and even earlier than that! Currently this concept is being used in Reggio Emilia, as well as continuing its tenure in the majority of American child care centers. By allowing children to pursue their own interests in depth, rather than restricting them to the 20 minutes allotted for "creative expression," respect for children's abilities and natural intelligence is demonstrated. When children are respected in this way, their self-expression *and* self-esteem flourish.

Self-selection needs to be balanced with opportunities for group experiences, too. Some of those experiences are small, casual, and informal, as when a group of interested children gathers around the teacher to discuss where the snow went and how to make it return. Some, such as large-group times and mealtimes, require more management by the teacher. These more formal situations are essential ingredients in the early childhood program because they provide opportunities to make certain that all the children are included in thinking and reasoning activities every day.

Felicitas Kartiwan

The joy of creative expression!

High-Quality Education Should Be Comprehensive

One aspect of planning that deserves special consideration is that the curriculum should be comprehensive in coverage. As mentioned earlier, a valuable way to think about this is to picture the child as being composed of a number of selves: the physical self, the emotional self, the social self, the cognitive self, and the creative self. This book is based on this division of the child into selves, since experience has shown that various aspects of the curriculum fall rather neatly under these headings and that the five selves succeed in covering the personality of the child.

The physical self includes not only large- and fine-muscle development but also the handling of routines because such things as eating, resting, and toileting contribute much to physical comfort and well-being. For the emotional self we consider ways to increase and sustain mental health, to use discipline to foster self-control, to cope with aggression, and to foster self-esteem. Included for the social self are ways to build social concern and kindliness, learning to enjoy work, and learning to value the cultures and abilities of other people. Finally, the cognitive, or intellectual, self is considered in terms of the development of language and generalized and specific reasoning abilities. The creative self covers the areas of self-expression through the use of art materials and creativity as expressed in play and applied in thought.

High-Quality Education Has Stability and Regularity Combined with Flexibility

Young children need to know what is likely to happen next during the day. This means that the order of events should be generally predictable. Predictability enables children to prepare mentally for the next event; it makes compliance with routines more likely and helps them feel secure.

However, time schedules and routines should not be allowed to dominate the school. Sometimes overconformance to time schedules happens because teachers are creatures of habit and simply do not realize that juice and raisins do not have to be served at exactly 9:15. Rather than sticking to clock time, it is better to maintain an orderly but elastic schedule wherein play periods and investigative activities can be extended at those times when the majority of the children are involved in activities that interest them intensely.

High-Quality Education Has Variety

Children Need Many Different Kinds of Experiences, as Well as Changes in Basic Experiences

Variety should certainly be incorporated into a program for young children. Many teachers think of variety of experience in terms of field trips or covering different topics such as families or baby animals. But another kind of variety that should also be considered is variety in everyday basic learning experiences. What a difference there is between the school that has the same pet rat and bowl of goldfish all year and the school that first raises a rabbit, then borrows a brood hen, and next has two snakes as visitors. Lack of variety is also apparent in schools that offer the omnipresent easel as their major "art" experience or others that set out all the blocks at the beginning of the year and leave it at that.

Children Need Changes of Pace During the Day to Avoid Monotony and Fatigue and to Maintain a Balance of Kinds of Experiences

The most obvious way to incorporate variation of pace is to plan for it in the overall schedule. For example, a quiet snack can be followed by a dance period.

Additional opportunities to meet individual temperamental requirements of children must be allowed for. Quieter, less gregarious children need to have places available where they can retreat from the herd, and more active youngsters need the escape hatch of moving about when they have sat beyond their limit of endurance.

Some kinds of programs appear to have special problems associated with pacing. For example, some compensatory programs attempt to cram so much into such a short time (playtime, story time, snack, lunch, special activity time, not to mention visits from the psychologist, field trips, and special visitors) that the day goes by in a headlong rush of children being hurried from one thing to the next without the opportunity to savor any experience richly and fully. At the other extreme, some child care programs offer a variety of activities and changes of pace during the morning but turn the children loose in the play yard for 3 interminable hours in the afternoon.

Learning Must Be Based on Actual Experience and Participation

Children learn best when they are allowed to use all their senses as avenues of learning. Research has shown that young children with disabilities learn best when they are actively engaged in activities (Barnes & Whinnery, 2002; Larkin, 2001; S. A. Raver, 1999). Participatory experience is an essential ingredient in early childhood education. This means the curriculum must be based on real experiences with real things, rather than limited to the verbal discussions and pictures commonly (though not necessarily ideally) used when teaching older children.

Because educators ranging from Dewey to Piaget to the teachers of Reggio Emilia have emphasized the value of real experience as being fundamental to successful education since the beginning of the 20th century, one might think this principle need not be reiterated. The persistent influx of word-oriented rather than action-oriented teaching materials on display in the commercial exhibits of most conferences on early childhood, however, and the fact that these materials continue to sell make it evident that this point must be stated very clearly: Young children learn best when they can manipulate material, experiment, try things out, and talk about what is happening as it takes place. Talking without doing is largely meaningless for a child of tender years.

Play Is an Indispensable Avenue for Learning

Another long-held value in early childhood education is an appreciation of play as a facilitator of learning. Teachers who have watched young children at play know the intense, purposeful seriousness they bring to this activity. Play is the medium used by children to translate experience into something internally meaningful to them. Play clarifies concepts, provides emotional relief, facilitates social development, and creates periods of clearly satisfying delight. Sometimes teachers see its value only as a teacher-controlled, structured experience used to achieve a specific educational end (e.g., role playing after visiting the fire station), but it is crucial that there be ample time in the curriculum for children's self-initiated play. There is no surer way to tap into the children's real concerns and interests.

The Program Should Be Reflected on Daily

Once a curriculum is planned and put into action, it is also necessary to evaluate the results, and these reflections need to go beyond such statements as "What a terrible day!" or "Things went well!"

Instead teachers should ask themselves the following questions:

- What special interests emerged that I can respond to when planning curriculum pathways?
- How did the day go? Did any hitches and glitches occur?
- If so, how can I rearrange plans and activities so that they move more smoothly for the children next time?
- What did the children learn today?
- How are the children with special problems getting along?

And finally the most valuable question of all:

- How can I help each child experience success tomorrow?

Thoughtful answers to questions like these will go a long way toward helping build a more effective curriculum for the children as the year moves on.

High-Quality Education Promotes Ethical Standards for Teachers

"Our paramount responsibility is to provide safe, nurturing, and responsive settings for children." So states *The Code of Ethical Conduct and Statement of Commitment,* a position statement developed by NAEYC (2005). This position statement reflects the core values of the early childhood profession's largest organization and was developed after months of dialogue among the NAEYC membership, made up of teachers, directors, professors, and leaders in the field of early childhood education. The Code of Ethical Conduct sets the stage for all that we do with children and families, affirming how important and lasting our work can be. We have a great responsibility ahead of us, and the Code of Ethical Conduct helps us navigate the often-confusing issues regarding children, families, colleagues, and community and society. The code inspires us to make a genuine commitment to early childhood education and to take seriously the vital role we play in children's lives (see Related Organizations and Online Resources at the end of this chapter to access the NAEYC Code of Ethical Conduct).

High-Quality Education Should Encourage Advocacy

Part of our ethical responsibility extends beyond being a good, developmentally appropriate teacher whom the children and families adore. If we are truly committed to providing the best for young children, then we must advocate for massive changes in our early care system. It is an unfortunate fact that many in this world do not place much value on children or on children's teachers. This is reflected in the low wages and high turnover rates in the early education profession.

Studies have shown that when teachers are well compensated and given the proper educational support, they provide higher quality care (Honig & Hirallal, 1998; Whitebook et al., 2001). When the opposite is true, it is the children who suffer: Teachers may have unrealistic expectations for children's behavior, punish them inappropriately, and create a climate of failure and fear in the classroom. Additionally, children suffer the results of teachers feeling so frustrated and unappreciated that they quit their jobs, leaving the children to make new connections with new teachers over and over again throughout their most formative years.

We all have a responsibility to advocate on behalf of children, families, and families of children with special needs so that early childhood education, of which most children now partake, does not inflict harm on our developing citizens. You are encouraged to become informed about the important issues regarding children and families, and to connect with others who are working to create a better situation. Figure 1.2 offers suggestions for how to get started advocating for children, families, and families of children with special needs.

Let's keep in mind that early childhood education is built on a foundation of struggle and the intense efforts of those dedicated to providing children with a better world. Early education programs grew from taking children off the streets to give them the basics of food, shelter, and comfort. Look how far we have come since those times. Although teachers sometimes feel frustrated or "burned out," we should remember how our efforts can succeed. As historian Henry Adams put it in 1907, "A teacher affects eternity; he can never tell where his influence stops" (p. 20).

- Become informed about the educational, social, and political issues that affect children and families. Appendix C lists some of the most important journals that will keep you abreast of current trends and issues. In addition, a simple way to stay informed is to sign up for the Connect for Kids free, nonpartisan e-mail newsletter at http://www.connectforkids.com or visit the Web site to view their national and state-by-state listing of children's advocacy groups.

- Join with others to make your voice heard. At the end of each chapter is a list of some of the most vital, relevant organizations. By joining an organization such as the National Association for the Education of Young Children or the Children's Defense Fund, you support their work and benefit from their many educational and teacher support services. There is no better antidote to burnout than to attend a meeting of impassioned and committed early childhood educators!

- Communicate with families. Once you are aware of the issues that affect children, start discussing them with the children's families in your program. You can provide them with information that will help their family directly (such as recommending an organization that helps find services for children with disabilities after a diagnosis has been made), and you can also encourage the family's advocacy as well.

Figure 1.2
Suggestions for advocating on behalf of children, families, and families of children with special needs

Patricia Weissman

Pleasure, enjoyment, humor, and laughter should be very much a part of the children's day.

The Day Should Be Pleasurable

One way we can affect children for the long run is by helping them form a positive attitude toward school and learning. Probably the most significant value a teacher can convey to children is the conviction that school is satisfying and that they want to return the next day. This point has been deliberately left until last to give it special emphasis in case you have begun to feel bogged down with the sober-sided responsibilities of providing a good program for young children.

The experience not only should be pleasurable for the children but also should be a joy for the adults. Young children have their trying moments, but they are also delightful. They see the world in a clear-sighted way that can lend fresh perspective to the eyes of their teacher, and their tendency to live for the present moment is a lesson to us all. Pleasure, enjoyment, humor, and laughter should be very much a part of each day in early childhood education.

SUMMARY

Early childhood education has a noble history that can teach us important lessons for current best practices. Beginning teachers should make use of educational theories that have been tried for many years in order to be most effective.

After more than four decades of research on the effects of early education, and with the addition of recent brain research, the evidence indicates that high-quality education for young children and their families has a lasting, positive impact.

Certain elements are emerging that appear to be common to the majority of effective early childhood programs and schools. These include good human relationships, family inclusion, and a curriculum that is developmentally, individually, and culturally appropriate. High-quality early education uses reasonable and authentic methods of assessment, incorporates a balance of self-selection and teacher direction, and educates all the child's five selves.

High-quality education for young children is basically orderly but also flexible; it provides for variety in experience, levels of difficulty, and pacing; and it is based on the principles that learning should be the result of actual experience, that play is a significant mode of learning, and above all that the center should be a place of joy for both children and staff. High-quality teachers adhere to ethical standards and work as early childhood advocates.

Questions and Activities

1. Select a basic activity, such as using tricycles or easel painting, that tends to stay the same throughout the year in many schools, and suggest some variations that would add interest and learning to the activity.
2. Describe some situations in your own educational background in which the learning was primarily accomplished by means of direct instruction, and other situations in which the emphasis was on learning by means of experience and participation. Which method did you prefer? What were the advantages and disadvantages of each of these approaches?
3. As a beginning teacher, how do you feel about the prospect of having parents at school? If a father is helping at school on the day his youngster has a temper tantrum and refuses to come in to lunch, would it be easier to handle this situation if the father were not there? Do you agree completely that parents should be welcomed at school? Why or why not?

Diversity Question

1. How can a teacher best use developmental norms when working with children who have special needs?

Predicament

1. Suppose a parent said to you after touring the school, "Your fees are so high! My babysitter charges less than you do, *and* comes to the house and does the cleaning, too. I don't see why it costs so much to take care of some little kids!" What should you reply?

Self-Check Questions for Review

Content-Related Questions

1. What research findings can you cite to support the thesis that early childhood education is beneficial?
2. What are some of the theoretical foundations of early childhood education, and why should teachers be familiar with them?
3. List several ways in which teachers might generate records that will help them and the parents assess how much the children have learned and what they are like.
4. List and discuss the ingredients that should go into a good day for young children.
5. Name the five selves discussed in this chapter, and tell what aspects of the child each self includes.

Integrative Questions

1. Give an example of a situation with a 3-year-old and with a 7-year-old in which it would be appropriate to use a behavior modification technique.

2. Compare the developmental-interactionist philosophy of teaching to a behavior modification approach. What do they have in common, and in what ways do they differ?

3. This chapter describes several concepts common to both American and Reggian teaching philosophies: These include learning by doing, inquiry-based learning, and child-centered learning. Explain what you think each of these terms means, and provide a specific example that illustrates how you might implement each of these practices in your classroom of 4-year-olds.

Reference for Further Reading

Copple, C., & Bredekamp, S. (Eds.) (2009). *Developmentally appropriate practice in early childhood programs serving children birth through age 8*. (3rd. ed.). Washington, DC: National Association for the Education of Young Children. This indispensable resource spells out good teaching practices that are appropriate at the preschool level. It remains the most influential publication on this subject in the field.

Related Organizations and Online Resources

Center for the Child Care Workforce, a project of the American Federation of Teachers Educational Foundation (CCW/AFTEF). The center's mission is to ensure that the early care and education workforce is well educated, receives better compensation, and has a voice in their workplace. Find out about the Worthy Wage Campaign, a grassroots effort to improve compensation and work environments, at http://www.ccw.org.

Head Start and Early Head Start. Head Start is the most successful and longest running national school readiness program for families with low incomes in the United States. Early Head Start, in cooperation with Zero to Three, is a program to provide services for infants through age 3 years. Reach Early Head Start at http://www.ehsnrc.org and Head Start at http://www.nhsa.org.

National Association for the Education of Young Children (NAEYC). This is the largest membership organization for early childhood educators. Many excellent resources are available, as well as its journal, *Young Children*. NAEYC is an invaluable resource organization for everyone in the early childhood profession. The DAP guidelines and Code of Ethical Conduct can be downloaded from the Resource section at http://www.naeyc.org.

National Dissemination Center for Children with Disabilities (NICHCY). Funded by the U.S. Department of Education, NICHCY is a central clearinghouse for information about disabilities in children and IDEA, the law authorizing special education, among other topics. Information is available at http://www.nichcy.org.

Zero to Three. This is a nonprofit organization that provides excellent resources about the first 3 years, including a monthly journal, and the coordination of the Early Head Start program. Information is available at http://www.zerotothree.com.

CHAPTER two

Working
with Families

Why certain families seem supportive of your program while others seem critical?

How to open a discussion with parents about a problem their child is having?

How to increase families' interest and participation in their children's learning?

. . . IF YOU HAVE, THE MATERIAL IN THE FOLLOWING PAGES WILL HELP YOU.

Young children—in the United States and around the world—are growing up in a greater variety of families than ever before. Babies enter families through birth, adoption, or fostering; they are conceived through intercourse or assisted reproductive technology; they live in families formed by marriage and remarriage, in cohabiting heterosexual families, in lesbian- and gay-headed families, and in single parent families.

Emily Fenichel (2003, p. 2)

We cannot know and understand each child unless we know and understand each child's family.... We need to be willing to hear what it is parents really want, to figure out a way of engaging them in conversations that are respectful of where they are as we seek to understand how they feel about their children.

Maurice Sykes (2001, p. 57)

No   matter how dedicated and meticulous we are about establishing a good life for the child at school, teachers must never forget that the most significant part of the young child's environment lies outside the school. Quite rightly, there is a much more profound influence in the child's life: the home and the members of the child's family. Thus it makes good sense, if we hope to establish the best total environment for the child, to include the family as an important part of the early educational experience (Berkowitz & Bier, 2005; Guralnick, 2001; Mendoza et al., 2003; Powell, 1998). For children with special needs, family involvement is especially crucial. As the 26th Report to Congress on the Implementation of Individuals with Disabilities Act (IDEA) emphasized, family involvement improves educational results for children with disabilities (U.S. Department of Education, 2004). Family involvement is such a strong predictor of success that it is a required component for both IDEA and Head Start programs (see chapters 1 and 5 for more discussion about these programs). In the elementary grades, family involvement is equally as important: The single best predictor of student success in school is the level of parental involvement in a child's education (Berkowitz & Bier, 2005).

There are a number of formal and informal ways to build links between home and school. Such involvement can be as varied as making home visits, inviting family members to volunteer in the classroom, or asking them to serve on the advisory board. All these avenues encourage interchange and communication between families and teachers if they are well done. Infant caregivers and home care providers find that close bonds with the child's family come with the territory.

Although our work is primarily with young children, some of our most lasting and important work is with adults. To be the best teachers for young children, we must also develop our skills in communicating with adults. One communication skill lies at the heart of them all: the ability to talk with others in a sincere, nonthreatening way.

OPENING THE DOOR TO GOOD COMMUNICATION

The first step to good communication with families begins with our attitude. Too often teachers view parents and family members in a negative way, with trepidation or judgment. Some teachers dread conferences and rush through them as quickly as possible, and others refuse to let parents in their classroom. Research has shown that parent involvement not only enhances children's academic achievement and behavior at school but also improves overall program quality and staff morale (Berkowitz & Bier, 2005; Mendoza et al., 2003; Michigan Department of Education, 2002; Powell, 1998). For the benefit of the children, teachers must avoid an "us versus them" mentality and instead welcome families into their children's programs as partners.

UNDERSTANDING FAMILIES

Family Diversity

Just as each child is unique, so too is each family with its own dynamics, psychology, and ways of being (R. M. Barrera, 2001; Mendoza et al., 2003). Our job is to understand

Ricardo Changeux

Ricardo Changeux

Michal Heron/PH College

Teri Stratford/PH College

Eugene Gordon/PH College

Celebrate the diversity of families.

33

the child's family culture and to support it as best we can. When we meet with families for the first time, it is important to ask questions as well as offer information. By asking for input, we convey to families that their experiences are valued and an essential part of their child's education. In this way, teachers and families can work together as a team to provide the best possible environment for the child.

Teachers must find out what each child's family situation is from the start. Gone are the days when the typical family consisted of a breadwinning father who was married to a stay-at-home, child-rearing mother: Only 13% of all families in the United States fit that model, and three out of five preschoolers have their mother in the labor force (Children's Defense Fund [CDF], 2005; Cohany & Sok, 2007; U.S. Census Bureau, 2005). Families in the United States reflect the same diversity that is seen throughout our society. It behooves early childhood professionals to approach children's families with an open mind and an open heart, with no preconceived notions about what a proper family should be.

As Figure 2.1 shows, teachers should be prepared to work with children who live in all sorts of family situations. Children today often come from nontraditional families

- 1 in 2 will live in a single parent family at some point in childhood.
- 1 in 3 is born to unmarried parents.
- 1 in 3 will be poor at some point in their childhood.
- 1 in 4 lives with only one parent.
- 1 in 5 was born poor.
- 1 in 5 is born to a mother who did not graduate from high school.
- 1 in 5 has a foreign-born mother.
- 3 in 5 preschoolers have their mother in the labor force.
- 1 in 6 is poor now.
- 1 in 6 is born to a mother who did not receive prenatal care in the first three months of pregnancy.
- 1 in 8 has no health insurance.
- 1 in 8 has a worker in the family but is still poor.
- 1 in 8 is born to a teenage mother.
- 1 in 12 has a disability.
- 1 in 13 was born with low birthweight.
- 1 in 13 will be arrested at least once before age 17.
- 1 in 14 lives at less than half the poverty level.
- 1 in 24 lives with neither parent.
- 1 in 28 is born to a mother who received late or no prenatal care.
- 1 in 60 sees their parents divorce in any year.
- 1 in 83 will be in state or federal prison before age 20.
- 1 in 146 will die before their first birthday.
- 1 in 1,339 will be killed by guns before age 20.

Figure 2.1
Key facts about American children

Source: From The State of America's Children Yearbook 2004, Children's Defense Fund. *Reprinted with permission.*

Support the involvement of men in children's lives.

that can be headed by a single parent, a grandparent, or a teenager. To be effective with all the children in our care, we must welcome each family with openness and respect, even if their family structure is different from our own.

Many children today are being raised by single men or fathers who are highly involved caregivers. It is important for teachers to acknowledge and support the involvement of men in children's lives. Teachers can make men feel welcome and valued in child care programs by encouraging their participation, directing questions at them as well as at mothers, and making sure all family communication is made in a nonsexist way. Further discussion about the involvement of men in early childhood can be found in chapter 4.

Challenges to Working with Families

In these times when more than 65% of all mothers with preschool-age children work outside the home (CDF, 2005), the additional burdens of fatigue and guilt may take an additional toll on parent energies. The results can be that although the parents remain as loving and concerned as ever, the time for contact between school and home is diminished.

When families *do* have contact, they, like the teacher, feel vulnerable to criticism. After all, their child, who is an extension of themselves, is on view. First-time parents particularly can be quite frightened of the teacher's opinion, and all families yearn to know that the teacher likes their child and that the child is doing well.

Parents of infants face additional challenges, often feeling conflicted, if not outright guilty, when they leave their baby in the care of others. It is now more common for infants and toddlers to be in a child care program than to be cared for at home by a parent (CDF, 2005; U.S. Census Bureau, 2005). When parents leave their baby in child care, they are taking a big leap of faith: They are trusting the caregiver to love and take good care of their child—and they can't help worrying about the many things that could go wrong. Good infant caregivers know that parents who have their baby in child care often experience stressful amounts of worry, anxiety, and guilt.

Suggestions for Establishing a Good Relationship Between Family and Teacher

Probably the most essential ingredient in a satisfactory relationship between teacher and family is that the teacher has the child's welfare truly at heart and is genuinely concerned about the child. Our experience has been that when families believe this to be true—which means, of course, that it has to *be* true and not just something the teacher *wishes* were true—when families really sense the teacher's goodwill, they will forgive the teacher any inadvertent transgressions, and the relationship will warm up as trust develops.

Genuine concern and caring can be expressed in a variety of ways. Faithful caretaking is one way. For example, the preschool teacher takes pains to see that everything the children have made is valued by being put in their cubbies for them to take home, their belongings are kept track of, noses are wiped when they need to be, and although the children may not be the pristinely clean youngsters at the end of the day that they were upon arrival, they are tidied up and have had their faces washed before their family members pick them up. Teachers also show they care by carefully enforcing the health and safety regulations and by planning a curriculum that is interesting, varied, and suited to the needs of individual children. It is especially important to convey this to the families of children with special needs. Assure these families that you are paying attention to their children and making every effort to adapt the program to meet their needs.

Families of infants need to know their baby is in good hands. Many infant caregivers find it useful to keep notes throughout the day that record such things as feeding times and what was eaten, diaper changes, and bottles and medicine given. In addition, we need information from the family on a daily basis: How did the child sleep last night? Is he or she getting a new tooth or ready to try a new food? This sort of communication should be built into infant and toddler programs so that it occurs naturally every day. Brief written notes about something the child did that day, telephone calls, casual conversation, and scheduled meetings all contribute to effective communication with families (Gonzalez-Mena & Eyer, 2006; Honig, 2002; Lally et al., 2003).

Another way for the teacher to show concern is by expressing genuine interest in each child to the family. For example, it is always sound practice to comment on something the child has enjoyed that day. It may be the statement, "I think Nathan is making friends with our new boy, Manuel; they spent a lot of time with the trains in the block corner today," or it might be, "Maggie really loves our new bunny; she fed him and watched him half the morning." These comments assure the parent that the child has had attention and that the teacher is aware of the child as an individual, rather than as just one of the troop. Teachers in the elementary grades can pass on important developmental information gleaned through assessments and child evaluations, and have particular responsibility for discussing these issues with parents: alerting them to when assessments take place and how they will be used.

Teachers can also demonstrate they truly care about the children and their families by learning about different points of view concerning child rearing that families from cultures other than the teacher's own may have (R. M. Barrera, 2001; Gonzalez-Mena, 2007; Mendoza et al., 2003). As Gonzalez-Mena (2007) points out, not only may points of view differ in a general way from group to group, but also attitudes toward the value of their own backgrounds vary within members of that group. These attitudes range from the desire of the parents to have their children blend completely with the dominant culture to an equally strong desire to have their youngsters respect and retain the parents' personal values related to their own culture. As Figure 2.2 illustrates, there are many steps teachers can take every day to ensure that family diversity is respected in the classroom.

Still another kind of caring can be indicated on a subtler level by letting the family know that the teacher is on the child's side *but not on the child's side as opposed to the family's.* Occasionally teachers fall into the fantasy of thinking, "If only I could take

- Treat grandparents/guardians/lesbian and gay nonbiological parents as parents.
- Display pictures and posters on the walls depicting all types of families.
- Use forms that say parent/guardian not mother/father.
- Include family of origin and sexual orientation in your nondiscrimination statement.
- Learn what children call family.
- Use books depicting family diversity, diversity in general.
- Get rid of out-of-date books and wicked stepmothers.
- Use natural classroom situations to talk about different families and all differences.
- Integrate various families into your language and everyday play (two moms, two dads, adoption, stepdad . . .).
- Teach children about feelings, empathy, and accepting differences.
- Use a variety of bulletin board ideas: Our Families, Who Cooks Dinner at My House, What I Like to Do with My Family.
- Make "All About Me," "All About My Family" books.
- Play the "How are we different, how are we the same?" game.
- Have a variety of play people for your dollhouse to represent a variety of families.
- Be sensitive during holidays; ask parents what would be appropriate.
- Encourage parents to visit, read, do an activity, come on a field trip.
- Find out what you can do to help their child.
- Emphasize to the children that *family* is the people who love them and take care of them.

Figure 2.2
Suggestions for embracing all families and teaching the value of family diversity

Source: Adapted from Working with Nontraditional Families *by L. Eisenbud, 2002, Child Care Information Exchange, 144, pp. 16–20. Reprinted with permission.*

that child home with me for a week and provide a steady, loving environment." Or sometimes a child will say in a rush of affection, "Oh, I wish you were my daddy (or mommy)!" To avoid an emotionally confusing and difficult situation for the child, it is important to clarify the teacher's role. The teacher can handle this by gently replying, "We are having fun, and I like you, too; but, of course, you already have a daddy (or mommy). I'm your teacher. I take care of you at school, and your parents take care of you at home." This avoids rivalry and makes a friendly alliance between parents and teacher more likely.

It is difficult to be on the family's side if the teacher blames them for all the child's problems. Such disapproval, even if unspoken, cannot help being sensed by families (Baker & Manfredi/Petitt, 2004; Murphy, 1997). In any situation in which you feel critical, you might find it helpful to ask yourself, if you were this child's parent, with that particular set of problems and circumstances, could you do much better?

As the teacher, you can put parents at ease by letting them know that you are concerned about the child, that you are on both the child's and the family's sides, and that you do not think everything the child does is the family's fault. After all, families, like teachers, also want what is best for their children. A sense of common, shared concern is worth working for because once family members feel its existence, they are freer to work with the teacher on the child's behalf.

Of course, sometimes, despite our best intentions, a relationship with a child's teacher may not be so harmonious. When this is the case, it can be helpful to know how to handle such encounters.

WHAT IF THE RELATIONSHIP IS NOT GOOD?

It is inevitable that, from time to time, a parent or guardian will make teachers so angry it is almost impossible to resist the temptation to lose one's temper in return—a response that usually makes things worse. Fortunately there are alternative ways of coping with angry feelings that can help teachers (and other people) retain control of themselves and the situation.

The Preamble: What to Do Before the Situation Arises

A good way to begin is to know one's own points of vulnerability. You might picture these points as being a series of red buttons people can push—red buttons that, when pushed, make you see red, too! Different things make different people angry. For some teachers it's the person who is bossy and domineering, whereas for others it's the parent who is always late or who sends the child to school with a deep cough and runny nose. Whatever the buttons are, it is helpful to identify them in advance; once they are identified, it is possible to summon the extra reserves of self-control that are needed when someone begins to push one.

Coping with the Initial Encounter: What to Do When That Button Is Pushed

Surviving an encounter with an angry adult is really a three-part process. It includes the immediate first encounter, what happens afterward, and the final resolution of the situation.

When confronted with an angry complaint, rather than jumping right in with a defensive reply, the more effective approach is to wait a minute before responding and actually *listen* to what the person is saying (Baker & Manfredi/Petitt, 2004). These precious seconds provide valuable lead time that allows an opportunity to recognize the anger inside oneself and to consider the reply before saying something you'll regret later.

Next, instead of defending or explaining, take time to rephrase what the complainer is saying, adding a description of the person's feelings. *There is no more effective way of dealing with strong feelings than using this response.* For example, you might say, "You don't want me to . . . ," or, "You're upset because I. . . ."

After the person has calmed down, it may be appropriate to explain your side of the situation, or it may not. Many times, when a matter of policy is in question ("You mean you lost her mittens again?" or, "If you let that kid bite Kim once more, I'm calling licensing"), the wisest thing to do is refer it to the director or at least say you'll need to discuss it with the person in charge. This tactic is called "referring it to a committee," and it serves the invaluable purposes of spreading around the responsibility for the decision, as well as providing a cooling-off period.

For the bravest and securest teachers, there is another way to cope with the initial encounter. After listening and rephrasing an attack, some people are comfortable enough to put their own honest feelings into words. "I'm feeling pretty upset (angry, frightened, worried) right now about what you've said. I don't know what to say. Let me think it over, and I'll get back to you." This kind of self-disclosure is too risky for some people to attempt, but it is an effective way of dealing with feelings for those who feel able to try it.

What to Do After the Complainer Departs

The problem with controlling anger as we have suggested is that it does not always melt away after the attacker has left. It is important that teachers respect families' privacy rights and refrain from talking about the encounter with every teacher on the playground! However, the opportunity to ventilate feelings in a safe place is a wonderful luxury that eventually can lead to forming constructive solutions to whatever problem exists. Discussing the situation with your director, principal, or another trusted professional—*in private, away from the children and other parents*—can offer much-needed support as well as help solve the problem.

It is also useful to think through the best- and worst-case scenarios during that discussion. Facing up to the worst that could happen when you speak with the family again and the best that might happen will reduce anxiety a great deal and increase confidence when the meeting actually takes place.

The Return Engagement

One benefit of waiting and then returning to discuss an emotion-laden problem is that the other person has had time to calm down, too. He or she may even be a little ashamed about what happened, so it may be necessary to help the person save face.

It can also be helpful to include a third person in the discussion, particularly if the problem has been "referred to a committee." Many times this person is the director, principal, or someone else who can support both teacher and parent.

This is the point at which various alternatives for solving the problem can be proposed, so it is a good idea to have several such possibilities in mind that are acceptable to the school and that allow the parent the opportunity to participate in the final solution, too.

Whatever that solution turns out to be, if you have listened, rephrased, dealt with your own anger in safe surroundings, and offered explanations or solutions, it is probable that the parent will see you as a reasonable person. You will have the comfort of knowing you have done nothing that you need be ashamed of at a later date.

MAINTAINING GOOD RELATIONSHIPS: KEEPING THE LINES OF COMMUNICATION OPEN

Fortunately most relationships with families do not involve such difficult encounters. For these families, too, it is important to keep communication lines open. Thus it is necessary for teachers to be accessible in two senses of the word. First, they must be approachable because they care about the children; second, they must be physically available when the parents are around the school.

In preprimary programs it is possible and even desirable to arrange the schedule so that one teacher is free to greet families during the first and last 15 minutes of the day or during peak arrival and departure times. If the teacher is free from other responsibilities at that time, it is possible to see each parent for countless casual meetings and to build relationships of friendliness and trust more easily. The sheer informality of this encounter robs it of a good deal of threat. Chatting right by the door, the parents know they can hasten away if the conversation takes too threatening a turn. In addition they

Informal contacts as families come and go build comfortable relations between teachers and parents.

are likely to see the teacher in a variety of moods and predicaments, which increases the teacher's humanity.

This repeated, consistent contact is far superior to relying solely on the more formal and frightening "conference" that may occur once or twice a semester. After a comfortable, everyday relationship is well established, an occasional conference with a longer uninterrupted opportunity to talk can be used to better advantage.

A helpful way to broaden teacher-parent communication skills is to think over past encounters with a parent to determine who is doing most of the talking. If this analysis reveals that the teacher is talking most of the time, it probably means that either the chats are too hurried or the teacher needs to make certain he or she is truly listening to what the parent has to say.

COUNSELING WITH FAMILIES

Once lines of communication are open, the question remains, "What do we do then?" When people talk together, many levels of relating can exist between them. During the year all these levels can be used by the teacher, depending on the situation.

The simplest level is a verbal or written message in which the teacher may say to the family, "This is what we did in school today," or, "Tanya learned to ride the scooter today." On this level at least the family knows that the teacher wants them to know what is happening at school. Most new relationships have to start about here.

On another level the teacher acts as the supportive information provider and general comforter. In this guise the teacher interprets the child's behavior to the family on the basis of extensive experience with other children. For example, the simple information that many 4-year-olds relish "disgraceful" language can be a great relief to a family secretly tormented by the worry that they suddenly have a pervert on their hands.

At yet another level the parent-teacher relationship has more of a counseling flavor to it. This is guidance, but not guidance in the sense that the teacher tells the parents what to do. Guidance means the teacher works with the family in terms of conscious motivation and behavior to help them discover what may be causing various behavior problems in the child and to help them figure out how to cope with them. Even novice teachers can do considerable good by offering themselves in a guidance role to parents in need of help, especially if they concentrate on listening rather than prescribing (Baker & Manfredi/Petitt, 2004).

Excluding the occasional special situation in which more professional help is required, what families need in order to work out a difficulty is the chance to talk out how they feel and evaluate whether a tentative solution is right for them and their unique child. Tremendous comfort comes to a distressed family when they are given the opportunity to air a problem with someone who can listen attentively and who is not too shaken by the confession that the children have been sitting behind the back fence doing you know what! Allowing them to express their feelings of shame, or occasionally even anguish, over their child's behavior is a positive benefit to offer families in a counseling situation.

It is also true that teachers, who have known literally hundreds of children, do have a broader background of experience than most parents. It seems only right to pool this knowledge with the family's as long as the teacher's alternatives are offered in such a way that the family feels free to accept or reject them. Families will be able to use this range of knowledge most easily if teachers point out that no matter how much they know in general about children, they will never know as much about the individual child as the family does.

Instead of providing instant answers to all problems posed by families, the teacher will find it more useful to ask such questions as "Why don't you tell me what you've tried already?" or "What are your thoughts about what to do next?" By asking the family questions, the teacher encourages the participation that will lead to more successful solutions.

Another cornerstone of good counseling is patience. It seems to be human nature that we want instant results, but change often takes a long time. One of the authors of this text used to despair when she made a suggestion that was ignored. She was most concerned on the occasions when she referred a family to a specialist and they declined to act on the referral. Her implicit assumption was that if the family did not do it then, they never would. Happily she found this to be a false assumption. To be sure, parents may not be ready this year to face the problem of Ari's temper tantrums and hyperactivity, but they have at least heard that the possibility of a problem exists, and the next professional person who approaches them may have greater success because the ground has been prepared.

PRACTICAL POINTERS ABOUT CONDUCTING A CONFERENCE

Getting ready for the conference is as important as the conference itself since neither teachers nor families want to waste time just chatting. Preparation may involve accumulating a series of quick observations or developmental checklists if these are used by the school. Some teachers also take photographs of significant events or activities the youngster has participated in and find that sharing these at the beginning of the conference starts conversation off on a friendly note. When these as well as other materials are assembled in a portfolio, it provides a useful, consistent record of how and what the child is doing during the time at school.

In addition to these tangible documents, it helps focus the conference to think through the points to be covered before beginning, but at the same time it is important to remember that a conference is just that: It is an opportunity to *confer and collaborate*. So, while making plans on what to cover, it is also essential to allow plenty of time and opportunity for parents to talk and to raise concerns of their own. Always bear in mind that even more important than exchanging information is building and maintaining the bond of warmth and trust between teacher and family (Koch & McDonough, 1999).

It is helpful to *set a clear time limit at the beginning* so that you and the family can pace yourselves. This avoids a sense of rejection when the teacher must end the conference.

 ### Avoid Interruptions

Of course, avoiding interruptions is easier said than done sometimes, but most parents resent the teacher's or director's taking a telephone call during a conference. Doing so not only interrupts the flow of talk but also infringes on the parents' rightful time, and parents of young children are often paying a caregiver for the privilege of attending (the child, of course, should not be present).

Beginning the Conference

Perhaps the best way to begin a conference is to encourage families to express their concerns first. "Have you special things in mind you want to talk over about Sarah?" Even though their initial response may be, "Well, no, not really," this kind of early opening question often enables families to bring something up later in the conference they were too shy to mention at first. More frequently, however, the parent will leap at this chance and start right in with a genuine concern, often phrased as a return question: "Well, I was wondering, how is she . . .?" It is gratifying how often this concern is related to that of the teacher.

Some additional nonthreatening ways to get the ball rolling include sharing with the parents the most positive traits you see in their children, what you like about them, who they play with and what they enjoy doing at school, and all the new things their children are interested in or learning. If you do have problems or concerns with a child, it is important to leave those until after you have already expressed your appreciation for the child. By starting out with a sharing of positive information, the family can see that you truly have the child's best interest at heart when you have to bring up a more difficult topic.

During the Conference, Stay as Relaxed as Possible

Take time to really listen to what the parent says. (A good way to monitor yourself is to check whether during conversations you are usually busy formulating a reply in your own mind. If you find yourself doing this habitually, it is probably an indication that you should focus your attention more completely on the speaker and be less concerned about your response.) If you think of the conference as being a time for the family to do most of the talking, it will help you at least to share the time more equally.

Drawing the Conference to a Close

As the time to close draws near, you can signal this in several ways. (Remember that the wise teacher has mentioned the potential limit in the beginning in some tactful fashion.) These ending signals are as varied as shifting a little in your chair and (in desperate circumstances in which past experience has indicated that a parent is insensitive to time limits) having someone primed to interrupt in a casual way.

It is always worthwhile to sum up what has been said as part of the closing process: "I am really glad we had a chance to talk. Even though Rosie is getting along so well, it never hurts to touch base, does it? I'll remember what you said about the allergy tests. We'll make sure she gets water instead of milk and that the other children understand and don't tease her about it," or, "I'm sorry to hear your family's going through that. We're here if there's something we can do to help. Give me a ring any time, and meanwhile we'll do those special things with Kelly we worked out today and let you know how they turn out."

What to Do After the Conference

It is vital to follow up on any promises or plans you and the family have made together. For the busy teacher who has spoken with 15 or 20 families, it can be all too easy to forget something or to defer doing it. But for the families who have only that one particular

The conference is an opportunity to collaborate and confer.

conference to recall, it is much easier to remember! If you wish to maintain a condition of trust between you and the families you serve, it is necessary that *you* remember, too. This is one reason why it is valuable to make notes immediately following the conference. They can serve as a reminder of promises and plans that should be carried out.

Notes also provide useful take-off points for the next conference. One of the authors has even known them to be valuable in court, when the teacher was asked to document that a parent had demonstrated a faithful interest in the well-being of her child by attending a series of conferences during the year.

Finally, Remember That Information Shared by Parents During a Conference Is Confidential

It is unethical, as well as unwise, to repeat what was said in private to anyone else unless that person (the director or principal, perhaps, or another teacher who works with the child) has a genuine need to know that information (certainly if you are concerned about the child's welfare, you must contact the appropriate agency right away). Indeed, if you foresee the need to share such material with another person, it is a good idea to ask the family first (except, of course, in cases of abuse or neglect). That way you do not risk violating their trust. The National Association for the Education of Young Children (NAEYC) has developed a code of ethical conduct that reinforces the importance of confidentiality for early childhood educators and can assist teachers in behaving ethically (NAEYC, 2005).

Limits to Guidance Work

When planning and carrying out conferences, we must also recognize that some behavior and development problems are beyond the teacher's ability, training, and time to handle. It is vital to be clear about where to draw the line and how far to go in guidance work. One rule of thumb is "When in doubt, refer." If the situation looks serious or does not respond to matter-of-fact remedies, it is time to suggest a specialist. In general it is too risky and takes more advanced training than a typical teacher possesses to draw implications and offer interpretations to parents about deep, complex reasons for behavior. Fortunately we can rely on highly trained, skilled specialists to solve serious problems, so let's leave Oedipus and his troublesome kin to our psychiatric cohorts. However, keep in mind that when making an outside referral, you must do so with the utmost sensitivity to reassure the family and let them know they can rely on you for support.

BEYOND THE CONFERENCE: FURTHER STRATEGIES FOR INVOLVING FAMILIES

Joyce Epstein of Johns Hopkins University encourages family involvement in their children's education at six different levels. These levels of family involvement should be supported by teachers throughout the program and throughout the year—not only at conference time. "The main reason to create such partnerships is to help all youngsters succeed in school and in later life" (Michigan Department of Education, 2002, p. 3). Epstein's framework for the six types of involvement include:

Go to MyEducationLab and select the topic "Curriculum/Program Models." Under Activities and Applications, watch the video *Head Start* and consider how family involvement helps children succeed.

1. *Parenting.*   Teachers can help families establish a home environment that supports their children's learning. Teachers can also support parents in their own growth and education through parent education workshops and other suggestions for parent learning (courses to support family literacy, college, or GED classes). Finally, teachers should assist families in finding local support programs for health, nutrition, and other social services.

2. *Communicating.*   In addition to parent conferences, teachers should establish effective forms of school-to-home and home-to-school communication. This includes phone calls, newsletters, information about standards and assessments, as well as making use of language translators to assist families as needed.

3. *Volunteering.*   Teachers actively recruit and organize family support in the classroom and school. A parent room and resource center is a good way to welcome family involvement.

4. *Learning at home.*   Teachers provide families with information about how they can help their children at home through reading and homework help. Elementary teachers should provide families with information on the skills their children need in all subjects at each grade.

5. *Decision making.*   Teachers include parents in school decisions and develop parent leaders and representatives in the school structure. Teachers encourage participation in the PTA/PTO or other family organizations, school councils, and parent committees. In addition, families are encouraged to join advocacy groups to lobby for school reform and improvements.

6. *Collaborating with community.*   Teachers identify community resources and services to strengthen school programs, children's development, and family practices. Teachers provide families with information about community health, cultural, recreational, social support, and other programs and services. They help to link children's learning skills and talents with extracurricular programs.

FAMILIES IN CRISIS

Young children are as subject to stress and strain when a crisis strikes their families as adults are, but this may be difficult for the family to recognize. They often hope that if nothing is said, the children will be unaware of the problem. Or they may be so overwhelmed by the crisis that they have little emotional reserve available to help the children through their troubles at the same time. But children are keen sensors of emotional climates, and they are aware of telephone conversations, comments by neighbors, media news reports, and so forth. Indeed, the secrecy and avoidance often practiced by families when crises occur may serve only to deepen the child's anxiety. It is far better, then, to reduce this misery when we can by facing facts squarely and by providing as much stability as possible than to worsen the problem by failing to deal with it (Alat, 2002; Close, 2002; "Helping Young Children," 2001; K. Miller, 2003).

It is important to realize that adverse circumstances do not always weaken children. Children are remarkably resilient. Even in the most dire of situations children are often able to rise above in a way that is a marvel and inspiration to adults (Edelman, 2001; Kersey & Malley, 2005; Levin, 2003; Wolkoff, 2002).

WHAT CONSTITUTES A CRISIS?

We usually think of a crisis as being something sudden, and surely death or illness or a trip to the emergency room falls in this category. Other crises are of longer duration: the mental illness or substance abuse of a parent, a divorce, a new baby, physical abuse, moving to a new neighborhood, and even adjusting to child care outside the home.

Some crises are unhappy events—loss of a job, for example—and some are happier occasions—a marriage, perhaps, or the adoption of a child. The one thing all crises have in common, whether sudden or chronic, unhappy or joyful, is that they all involve change. These changes occur far more commonly than one would wish. For example, it is projected that nearly half of all babies born today will spend some time in a one-parent family usually as a result of separation or divorce (CDF, 2005), 1 in 3 children will be poor at some point in their childhood (CDF, 2005), and 1 in 20 children will lose one or both parents by age 15 (Dougy Center for Grieving Children, 1999).

SOME GENERAL PRINCIPLES FOR HELPING FAMILIES DEAL WITH CRISES

There is no other time in life when the family is more important to the child than during a time of crisis (Pawl, 2002). Teachers, psychologists, social workers, and sometimes police officers may also offer meaningful aid, but the family is the most significant influence; for this reason the fundamental goal of the teacher should be to support the family as well as possible. There are a number of ways to accomplish this.

Make Certain the Families Understand That It Is Better to Include Children in the Situation than to Exclude Them

Particularly in matters of death, serious family illness, or job loss, adults may attempt to shield children from what is happening, but as mentioned before, children always know when something is wrong. Families may not realize how frightened this can make youngsters when they are left to fantasize about the nature of the trouble or the reason for it. It is the primeval fear of the unknown. To remedy this, the teacher should encourage the family to explain in simple terms *but not gory detail* the nature of the emergency (K. Miller, 2003; Hogan & Graham, 2001).

The same recommendation applies to expressing feelings: Children should be allowed to participate in feelings of concern or grief, rather than be excluded (Hogan & Graham, 2001; Levin, 2003; Willis, 2002). This principle should be followed within reason. The point to get across to the family is that it is all right for children to understand that grown-ups sometimes feel sad or frightened or upset—as long as this is mingled with steady assurances from family members that the child will be taken care of and that life will continue (NAEYC, 2001; Pawl, 2002; Willis, 2002).

Try Not to Overreact, No Matter What the Family Tells You

Teachers can be of little help if they allow themselves to become as upset as the families are over a crisis, although no one can deny that crises such as suicide or the rape of a 4-year-old are deeply shocking to everyone. However, if teachers can present a model of relative calm as well as concern, they can influence families to behave in the same manner. By providing information on what will help the child, they can encourage the institution of rational steps in dealing with the situation.

Benjamin La Framboise

Teachers can present a model of relative calm as well as concern and they can provide information that will help the child.

Teachers should also guard themselves against being overcome with pity for a youngster or the parents since pity is not beneficial for the family, either. One little boy, returning to school after his mother died, was greeted by a teacher who threw her arms around him and burst into tears, saying, "Oh, you poor baby! What are you and your father going to do now?" This unfortunate response overwhelmed the boy and froze him into an inexpressive state from which it was very difficult to retrieve him. One would think that an adult would have more sense, but crises do strange things to people.

Do Not Violate the Privacy of the Family

Particularly when something sensational has happened, be it a car accident or a home burning to the ground, it can be tempting to participate in the tragedy by gossiping about it with others. It is impossible to avoid discussion of such events entirely when they are common knowledge in the community, but care should be taken to keep private details private. For one thing, any families who hear the teacher repeat such personal details are bound to conclude that the teacher will gossip about their personal affairs, too. For another thing, behaving in this way is a breach of professional ethics (NAEYC, 2005).

Offer Yourself as a Resource

Being a good listener is one way to offer yourself as a resource as long as parents do not come to feel that you are mainly interested in the sensational aspects of the crisis or that you cannot wait for them to stop talking so that you can offer advice. Remember also that sometimes families do not want any help; this desire must be respected, too.

Sometimes, after the emergency aspect has subsided, parents find it helpful when the teacher lends them a good reference book. If the resource center has a reserve of at least a few such basic books on hand, they can be instantly available when needed.

Finally, the teacher can also be a resource for referral to other supporting agencies. It is necessary to be careful of offering referral resources too hastily lest the family interpret this as your wanting to get rid of them and their uncomfortable problem. Sometimes, however, it is better not to wait. Crises that result from a sudden deep shock or trauma, such as being in a severe automobile accident, experiencing rape, or witnessing a murder or suicide, require immediate psychological attention (Hogan & Graham, 2001).

Child Abuse, Neglect, Sexual Molestation, and Emotional Maltreatment

Recognizing Child Abuse

Teachers have the ethical and often a legal responsibility to report any suspected child abuse (NAEYC, 1997, 2005). This is referred to as *mandated reporting*. Teachers should understand that when we make a report to the proper agency, we do not have to prove—or even feel certain—that abuse has occurred. It is not the teacher's role to determine culpability, but to protect the child from harm *if there is any suspicion at all*. We must all be knowledgeable about what to look for and what to do when there is the possibility of abuse. Figure 2.3 details the common signs of abuse and neglect.

The following signs may signal the presence of child abuse or neglect.

The Child:

- Shows sudden changes in behavior or school performance.
- Has not received help for physical or medical problems brought to the parents' attention.
- Has learning problems (or difficulty concentrating) that cannot be attributed to specific physical or psychological causes.
- Is always watchful, as though preparing for something bad to happen.
- Lacks adult supervision.
- Is overly compliant, passive, or withdrawn.
- Comes to school or other activities early, stays late, and does not want to go home.

The Parent:

- Shows little concern for the child.
- Denies the existence of—or blames the child for—the child's problems in school or at home.
- Asks teachers or other caretakers to use harsh physical discipline if the child misbehaves.
- Sees the child as entirely bad, worthless, or burdensome.
- Demands a level of physical or academic performance the child cannot achieve.
- Looks primarily to the child for care, attention, and satisfaction of emotional needs.

The Parent and Child:

- Rarely touch or look at each other.
- Consider their relationship entirely negative.
- State that they do not like each other.

Signs of Physical Abuse

Consider the possibility of physical abuse when the child:

- Has unexplained burns, bites, bruises, broken bones, or black eyes.
- Has fading bruises or other marks noticeable after an absence from school.
- Seems frightened of the parents and protests or cries when it is time to go home.
- Shrinks at the approach of adults.
- Reports injury by a parent or another adult caregiver.

Consider the possibility of physical abuse when the parent or other adult caregiver:

- Offers conflicting, unconvincing, or no explanation for the child's injury.
- Describes the child as "evil" or in some other very negative way.
- Uses harsh physical discipline with the child.
- Has a history of abuse as a child.

Signs of Neglect

Consider the possibility of neglect when the child:

- Is frequently absent from school.

Figure 2.3

Common signs of child abuse and neglect

This fact sheet was adapted with permission from Recognizing Child Abuse: What Parents Should Know. *Prevent Child Abuse America. © 2003. Published by the National Clearinghouse on Child Abuse and Neglect Information.*

- Begs or steals food or money.
- Lacks needed medical or dental care, immunizations, or glasses.
- Is consistently dirty and has severe body odor.
- Lacks sufficient clothing for the weather.
- Abuses alcohol or other drugs.
- States that there is no one at home to provide care.

Consider the possibility of neglect when the parent or other adult caregiver:
- Appears to be indifferent to the child.
- Seems apathetic or depressed.
- Behaves irrationally or in a bizarre manner.
- Is abusing alcohol or other drugs.

Signs of Sexual Abuse

Consider the possibility of sexual abuse when the child:
- Has difficulty walking or sitting.
- Suddenly refuses to have clothing changed.
- Reports nightmares or bedwetting.
- Experiences a sudden change in appetite.
- Demonstrates bizarre, sophisticated, or unusual sexual knowledge or behavior.
- Runs away.
- Reports sexual abuse by a parent or another adult caregiver.

Consider the possibility of sexual abuse when the parent or other adult caregiver:
- Is unduly protective of the child or severely limits the child's contact with other children, especially of the opposite sex.
- Is secretive and isolated.
- Is jealous or controlling with family members.

Signs of Emotional Maltreatment

Consider the possibility of emotional maltreatment when the child:
- Shows extremes in behavior, such as overly compliant or demanding behavior, extreme passivity, or aggression.
- Is either inappropriately adult (parenting other children, for example) or inappropriately infantile (frequently rocking or head banging, for example).
- Is delayed in physical or emotional development.
- Has attempted suicide.
- Reports a lack of attachment to the parent.

Consider the possibility of emotional maltreatment when the parent or other adult caregiver:
- Constantly blames, belittles, or berates the child.
- Is unconcerned about the child and refuses to consider offers of help for the child's problems.
- Overtly rejects the child.

Figure 2.3
Common signs of child abuse and neglect—*Continued*

What to Do When Abuse Is Suspected

Teachers who discover evidence of abuse are very upset about it. They may find it difficult to believe that such a "nice" family could do a thing like that and thus they deny it, or they may be so frightened for the child's safety that they do not think clearly and therefore act impulsively. For this reason, before going any further with this discussion, *it is important to emphasize that handling such cases requires skill and delicacy* (NAEYC, 1998b, 2005). The consequences of unsuccessful management may be so serious that we cannot risk jeopardizing such chances by acting in an ill-considered way. *Therefore, teachers must not suddenly plunge into the problem by accusing the parents or even reveal suspicions by questioning them or the child too closely.* Instead, if they suspect a case of abuse, they should contact whatever agency or individual in their community has the responsibility for handling such cases and report it. *They should ask these people for advice and do what they tell them, to the best of their ability.*

How to Find Help

The agency the teacher should seek out is whatever agency in the community is responsible for children's protective services. These agencies go by different names in different parts of the country: Department of Social Services, Social Rehabilitation Service, Bureau of Children and Family Services, and so forth. Still another way to locate protective services is to ask the public health nurse whom to call. If no such agency exists, as is sometimes the case in small or rural communities, the police department, a mental health clinic, a child psychologist or psychiatrist, or a knowledgeable pediatrician should be asked for help. The organization Child Help USA can also be of assistance in filing a report; they can be reached at the National Child Abuse Hotline (1-800-4-A-CHILD).

Action Should Be Prompt

Since abusers often repeat their behavior, prompt action is advisable; yet teachers sometimes hesitate to get involved. The teacher should realize that all states now have mandatory reporting laws and that many of these specifically identify teachers as being among those people *required* to report cases in which abuse is suspected (NAEYC, 1998b, 2005). Understand that this means in many states a teacher can be prosecuted for *not* reporting suspected child abuse. Even when teachers are not specifically mentioned, the law is generally on the side of anyone reporting such a case "in good faith." Besides the necessity of conforming to the law, *reporting such cases is an ethical and moral responsibility the teacher must not overlook* (NAEYC, 1998b, 2005).

Helping the Child's Family After the Referral Has Been Made

Even when teachers have taken the expert's advice and have handled the referral successfully, and even if the family is receiving help, teachers must still deal with their feelings about the child and the family. The relief to families that such a respite provides, as well as the protection and education of the child it affords, means that continuing at school is important. Here we are confronted with a paradox. Teachers are more than likely experiencing feelings of revulsion and outrage over what the parents have done, and their impulse may be to judge and punish them. Yet experts tell us that what the parents need, among many other things, is understanding and acceptance— which they may have been woefully short on in their own childhoods.

Helping the Child While the Family Is in Treatment

Most material having to do with the treatment of child abuse deals with the treatment of the adults or amelioration of the family's environment, but the child needs help, too—help that must go beyond the simple level of physical rescue. In particular, it is important with such youngsters to emphasize the building of trust and warmth between them and their teachers; steadiness and consistency are invaluable elements of such trust building. The enhancement of self-esteem is also important to stress. *Referral for psychological counseling for the child is recommended.*

Above all, every effort should be made to retain the child in school; to maintain consistent, regular contact with the other people working with the family; and to be as patient and caring with both the child and the family as possible.

SUMMARY

Sensible caution and referral to an expert are advisable under some circumstances, but teachers can offer a lot of help and work with families in many ways to bring about a happier life for their children. To do this, it is first necessary to overcome various problems that make communication between families and teachers difficult. One of the most effective things teachers can do is make it clear to the family that they have the welfare of the child at heart and that they want to join with the family to help the child. Teachers can also take care to be available when the parent wants to talk, and they can provide the opportunity for many easygoing, casual contacts.

Once the lines of communication are open, teachers can offer help by serving as friendly listeners who assist the family in assessing the nature of the difficulty and in proposing alternatives until they find the one best suited for family and child. Teachers who assume this guidance function offer families what they need the most: an accepting attitude, an open ear, and a warm heart.

Questions and Activities

1. In what ways can teachers make the child care center or school "family-friendly"? List some specific actions you would take to encourage family involvement and communication.
2. Have the class divide into pairs. One person in each pair should select a problem or difficulty to discuss while the other person listens. Before making any other reply, the listener must first restate in his or her own words what the speaker is saying; that is, the listener's primary task is to be open to the feelings and import of the communication. Then shift roles and have the speaker practice this sort of listening and responding.

Diversity Questions

1. What types of families can early childhood teachers expect to work with? Think of a family structure that is different from your own, and list three ways in which you can convey to the family and child that they are welcome in your program.
2. Select children in your group who appear to require special diagnostic help of some kind. List the reasons for your conclusion that they need help. With another student, practice how you might broach the subject of referral with the family. It is helpful to practice this with one "parent" who is resistant, one who is overly agreeable, and one who is obviously upset about your suggestion.

Predicament

1. You are now head teacher in a class of 3-year-olds. One afternoon a mother is half an hour late picking up her child. When you ask why she is late, she snarls, "None of your damn business," and yanks her child out the door. How would you handle this situation?

Self-Check Questions for Review

Content-Related Questions

1. Give some practical examples of ways that teachers can show families that they really care about their children.
2. List and describe the three-part process involved in dealing with an angry complaint.
3. What do families really need in a conference?
4. List some practical pointers for conducting a successful conference.
5. Why is it important to get families involved in their child's program?
6. How might the needs of families who have their infant in child care be different from the needs of families of older children?

Integrative Questions

1. Britney, a 6-year-old girl in your group, has taken to pinching children, grabbing toys, and displaying other destructive behaviors. You are quite concerned and ask her parents whether they could come to a conference with you. Give three examples of what you would say to these parents during the conference that would blame them for their child's behavior. Be sure to use actual quotations.
2. Now that Britney's parents are really mad at you, suggest an angry sentence or two they might say

in reply. Then, for each of the sentences, phrase a response that would describe their feelings back to them.
3. Now suggest some approaches you could use instead that would *not* blame Britney's parents for her behavior.

Reference for Further Reading

Baker, A. C., & Manfredi/Petitt, L. A. (2004). *Relationships, the heart of quality care: Creating community among adults in early care settings.* Washington, DC: National Association for the Education of Young Children. This is a very comprehensive guide to working with adults.

Related Organizations and Online Resources

Child Help USA, National Child Abuse Hotline, 1-800-4-A-CHILD. Information and resources are available online at http://www.childhelpusa.org.

Children's Defense Fund (CDF). Since 1973, CDF has worked toward reducing the numbers of neglected, sick, uneducated, and poor children in the United States. Many resources to support families can be found at http://www.childrensdefense.org.

Clearinghouse on Early Education and Parenting (CEEP). Publications and information to the worldwide early childhood and parenting communities can be found at http://ceep.crc.uiuc.edu.

National Black Child Development Institute (NBCDI). For over 3 decades, the NBCDI has worked to build family support services. Information is available at http://www.nbcdi.org/.

National Center on Fathers and Families (NCOFF). The center is dedicated to research and practice that expand the knowledge base on father involvement and family developments. Information can be found at http://www.ncoff.gse.upenn.edu.

CHAPTER three

Fostering Creativity in Play

Whether play is as important as some people claim it is?

How to encourage play without dominating it?

Why some teachers think blocks are so important?

. . . IF YOU HAVE, THE MATERIAL IN THE FOLLOWING PAGES WILL HELP YOU.

Play is the purest, the most spiritual, product of man at this stage and is at once the prefiguration and imitation of the total human life—of the inner, secret, natural life in man and in all things. It produces, therefore, joy, freedom, satisfaction, repose within and without, and peace with the world. The springs of all good rest within it and go out from it.

Friedrich Froebel (1889, p. 25)

Through our years of research, we have come to the conclusion that play is to early childhood what gas is to a car. It is the very fuel of every intellectual activity that our children engage in.

Kathy Hirsh-Pasek & Roberta Golinkoff (2003, p. 214)

I believe that play is as fundamental a human disposition as loving and working.

David Elkind (2004a, p. 36)

When the first edition of *The Whole Child* went to press, only a few citations were available concerned with research and the value of play. Thirty years later it is a happy fact that citations dealing with theory, research, and practice related to children's play abound (Jones & Cooper, 2006; Elkind, 2007; Frost, Wortham, & Reifel, 2008; Hirsh-Pasek & Golinkoff, 2003; Koralek, 2004; Saracho & Spodek, 2003; Zigler, Singer, & Bishop-Josef, 2004).

And yet, despite increasing evidence that play is the serious business of young children and that the opportunity to play freely is vital to their healthy development, early childhood teachers find that many administrators and parents continue to misunderstand and underestimate the importance of play in the lives of children.

Teachers of young children must be prepared to explain and defend the value of basing large parts of their curriculum on play. For this reason, the following pages include an extensive analysis of the many contributions play makes to the development of the whole child and how we can support play in early childhood settings and early elementary school classrooms.

PURPOSES OF PLAY

Play fulfills a wide variety of purposes in the life of the child.

Play Fosters Physical Development

On a very simple level, play promotes the development of *sensorimotor skills*, or skills that require the coordination of movement with senses, such as using *eye-hand coordination* to stack blocks (Frost et al., 2008; Morrison, 2004; Tokarz, 2008). Children spend hours perfecting such abilities and increasing the level of difficulty to make the task ever more challenging. Anyone who has lived with a 1-year-old will recall the tireless persistence with which the child pursues the acquisition of basic physical skills.

Strenuous, physical play is especially important today when obesity among children and adults has reached an all-time high. An estimated 64% of all adults in the United States are seriously overweight or obese. Approximately 10% of all children age 2 to 5 years and 15% of older children are overweight (Association for Childhood Education International [ACEI], 2004). It is crucial that early childhood programs offer children the opportunity for active, gross-motor play every day, as habits and attitudes toward physical activity are formed early in life and continue into adulthood.

Outdoor Play Connects Children to Nature and Their Environment

Playing outdoors allows children to experience their natural environment with all their senses "open." They can breathe fresh air and feel the invigoration of their hearts pounding as they charge up a hill. Children learn about the variety of creatures that may live in their area, explore the life cycle when they discover a cocoon or squashed ant, and experience fully with their senses how everything seems different after the rain. Where does the sun go when it is cloudy? Where does the wind come from?

Benjamin La Framboise

Children must have the opportunity for active, gross-motor play every day.

Questions about nature arise spontaneously through outdoor play and provoke children into thought and, if properly supported by the teacher, into deep investigations of the world. It is vital that we allow all children—urban, suburban, and rural—to discover the world outside and learn to appreciate the environment around them. Children with disabilities, too, can discover the world and appreciate the environment through outdoor play. We must accommodate our programs to meet the needs of children with disabilities by encouraging their outdoor activity. After all, discovering the beauty of nature is one of the lasting delights of childhood.

Play Fosters Intellectual Development

Both Piaget and Vygotsky asserted that play is a major influence in cognitive growth (Curwood, 2007; Hirsh-Pasek & Golinkoff, 2003; Zigler et al., 2004). Piaget (1962) maintained that imaginative, pretend play is one of the purest forms of symbolic thought available to the young child. Vygotsky (1978) also extolled the value of such fantasy play, arguing that during episodes of fantasy and pretend play, when children are free to experiment, attempt, and try out possibilities, they are most able to reach a little above or beyond their usual level of abilities, referred to as their zone of proximal development.

Play also offers opportunities for the child to acquire information that lays the foundation for additional learning (Cavanaugh, 2008; Curwood, 2007; Elkind, 2007;

Benjamin La Framboise

Imaginative, pretend play is one of the purest forms of symbolic thought available to the young child.

Jones & Cooper, 2006; Montie, Xiang, & Schweinhart, 2007; Ramani & Siegler, 2007; Zigler et al., 2004). Play fosters children's math, science, and literacy understanding and skills (Cavanaugh, 2008; Elkind, 2007; Jones & Cooper, 2006; Zigler et al., 2004). For example, through manipulating blocks the child learns the concept of equivalence (two small blocks equal one larger one). Through playing with water the child acquires knowledge of volume, which leads ultimately to developing the concept of reversibility (if you reverse an action that has changed something, it will resume its original state).

Language has been found to be stimulated when children engage in play (Bergen, 2004; Cavanaugh, 2008; Isenberg & Quisenberry, 2002; Tokarz, 2008). Ramani and Siegler (2007) found that Head Start children's math abilities improved after playing numerical board games, in part due to the use of "math-related language" that occurs naturally during the games and which is an important precursor to math learning (Cavanaugh, 2008). Riojas-Cortez (2001) found that children's play in a bilingual classroom helped to extend the children's use of language experimentation in both languages.

Play Enhances Social Development

One of the strongest benefits and satisfactions stemming from play is the way it enhances social development (Elkind, 2007; Ginsburg, 2007; Jones & Cooper, 2006). Playful social interchange begins practically from the moment of birth (Bergen, 2004; Copple & Bredekamp, 2009).

As children grow into toddlerhood and beyond, an even stronger social component becomes evident as more imaginative pretend play develops. The early research of Smilansky and Shefatya (1990) demonstrated the positive effects of play on social development. Their methodological analysis has proven to be a helpful way of looking at children's play and is widely used by early educators today. They speak of dramatic and sociodramatic play, differentiating between the two partially on the basis of the number of children involved in the activity. *Dramatic play* involves imitation and may be carried out alone, but the more advanced *sociodramatic play* entails verbal communication and interaction with two or more people, as well as imitative role playing, make-believe in regard to objects and actions and situations, and persistence in the play over a period of time.

Sociodramatic play in particular also helps children learn to put themselves in another's place, thereby fostering the growth of empathy and consideration of others. It helps them define social roles: They learn by experiment what it is like to be the baby or the mother or the doctor. And it provides countless opportunities for acquiring social skills: how to enter a group and be accepted by them, how to balance power and bargain with other children, and how to work out the social give-and-take that is the key to successful group interaction (Elkind, 2007; Hirsh-Pasek & Golinkoff, 2003; Jones & Cooper, 2006; Koralek, 2004).

Piaget maintained that children in the concrete operational stage, approximately 7 to 11 years old, engage in playing games with rules. It is through this type of game playing that children learn what rules are, how to follow them, and the consequences when rules are not followed. Larger issues emerge, such as fairness and cheating, and inform the child's developing sense of social mores and personal moral behavior. In

PEARSON
myeducationlab

Go to MyEducationLab and select the topic "Child Development." Under Activities and Applications, watch the video *Building with Blocks*. Which domains of learning are supported through this type of play?

Karen Monster

One of the strongest benefits and satisfactions stemming from play is the way it enhances social development.

Piagetian theory, the importance of playing games in the early elementary years is crucial to the child's social and moral development (Curwood, 2007; Elkind, 2007).

Play Contains Rich Emotional Values

The emotional value of play has been better accepted and understood than the intellectual or social value because therapists have long employed play as a medium for the
expression and relief of feelings (Elkind, 2007; Koralek, 2004; O'Connor, 2000). Children may be observed almost anyplace in the early childhood center expressing their
feelings about doctors by administering shots with relish or their jealousy of a new baby
by walloping a doll, but play is not necessarily limited to the expression of negative
feelings. The same doll that only a moment previously was being punished may next
be crooned to sleep in the rocking chair.

Omwake cites an additional emotional value of play (Moffitt & Omwake, n.d.).
She points out that play offers "relief from the pressure to behave in unchildlike ways."
In our society so much is expected of children and the emphasis on arranged learning
can be so intense that play becomes indispensable as a balance to pressures to conform
to adult standards.

Finally, play offers children an opportunity to achieve mastery of their environment. In this way, play supports the child's psychosocial development, as discussed in
chapter 1, promoting the development of autonomy, initiative, and industry. When
children play, they are in command. They establish the conditions of the experience
by using their imagination, and they exercise their powers of choice and decision as
the play progresses.

Play Develops the Creative Aspect of the Child's Personality

Play, which arises from within, expresses the child's personal, unique response to the
environment. It is inherently a self-expressive activity that draws richly on the child's
powers of imagination (Elkind, 2007; Jones & Cooper, 2006; Isenberg & Quisenberry,
2002; Jalongo, 2003). As Nourot (1998) has said, "The joyful engagement of children
in social pretend play creates a kind of ecstasy that characterizes the creative process
throughout life" (p. 383).

Play increases the child's repertoire of responses. *Divergent thinking* is characterized
by the ability to produce more than one answer, and it is evident that play provides
opportunities to develop alternative ways of reacting to similar situations. For example,
when the children pretend that space creatures have landed in the yard, some may respond
by screaming and running, others by trying to "capture" them, and still others by engaging them in conversation and offering them a refreshing snack after their long journey.

Play Is Deeply Satisfying to Children

Probably the single most important purpose of play is that it makes children—and
adults, too—happy. In a study of 122 preschoolers in eight various child care settings,
98% of the children cited play as their favorite activity. In addition, researchers found
that the highest quality centers offered the most opportunities for free play and allowed extended time for children to play. Even in the centers that were rated "low

quality" (where teachers were observed yelling at children and punishing them frequently), the children made play the central focus of their day, liked play best, and expressed happiness because they were able to play (Wiltz & Klein, 2001). Regardless of their situation, almost all children find happiness in play.

DEVELOPMENTAL STAGES OF PLAY

As is true in so many other areas, children's play progresses through a series of stages. There are two widely accepted methods of classifying these developmental stages. The first classification system used for identifying stages of play has its roots in Piaget (1962). In this theory, play is divided into stages according to the way children use play materials. Thus play begins at the *functional level* (simple, repetitive, exploratory activity as simple as a baby playing with his toes or a 2-year-old squeezing dough through her fists). The second stage is *constructive play* (activity that has some purpose or goal, such as pouring water to fill a bucket), which develops into *dramatic play* (play involving pretend circumstances) and finally proceeds to the fourth stage, *games with rules*.

[handwritten margin note: 4 stages of play]

The two middle levels of play, constructive and dramatic (or fantasy) play, are of most interest to preschool teachers. Constructive play is most frequently seen in children ages 2 to 4 years, and it is characterized by children learning the uses of simple or manageable play materials and then employing them to satisfy their own purposes. For example, a child might learn how to string beads and then make a necklace. Dramatic play increases in frequency as children mature, and the golden age of sociodramatic role playing develops between ages 4 and 7, although we see the beginnings of this play in much younger children. At this level we see children assigning roles as varied as "daddy" or "baby" or "doggie" to themselves and others around them.

Children in the early elementary grades begin to enjoy games with rules, including board games, simple card games, computer games, and organized sports. The importance of games with rules in elementary school children's development cannot be emphasized enough. It is through games and the developing understanding of rules that the child becomes fully socialized. According to Piaget, socialization through game playing is a universal part of development. Through game playing, children learn how to cooperate, negotiate, resolve conflicts, and express themselves to others (Piaget, 1950).

The second commonly used system for identifying stages of play was developed by Parten (1932, 1933). It divides play according to the kind of social interaction that is taking place among children. In this system of classification, play develops from *solitary* through *parallel play* (playing beside but not with another child), to *associative play* (playing together), and ultimately to *cooperative play* (playing together with role assigning and planning).

[handwritten margin note: Stages of play Parten]

This division into steps is not a mutually exclusive one, however. Although solitary play happens more frequently with younger children, there are varying levels of sophistication in solitary play. Therefore the teacher should not assume that solitary play by older children is generally regressive and undesirable. It is particularly important to recognize the value of such individual playful preoccupation in child care centers and elementary classrooms, where children are almost relentlessly in contact with other people all day long. Children need the opportunities to think and develop their ideas through play by themselves, as well as while in the company of

other children, and they need opportunities for privacy, too. Of course, if solitary play continues too long or is the only kind of play indulged in by a 4-year-old, it should be cause for concern but some of this less social play is to be expected and even encouraged for most young children.

Parallel play also continues to have its uses even after group play has developed, and it is often used by 3-year-olds as an effective way to enter a group: the children first playing alongside and then with the group as they work their way into the stream of activities. Perhaps teachers could deliberately use this strategy with 3-year-olds, encouraging them to play beside the other children as a stepping stone to more direct social encounters.

Educational Implications

Although preschool teachers are likely to see functional, constructive, and dramatic play, they will rarely come across the final Piagetian stage—games with rules—because this kind of play is the prerogative of older children. The child care center teacher should realize that organized, competitive games are developmentally inappropriate as well as uncreative for young children. Activities such as relay races, dodge ball, and kick the can are loved by second and third graders but do not belong in centers for younger children (Copple & Bredekamp, 2009; National Association for Sport and Physical Education [NASPE], 2002; S. W. Sanders, 2002).

The teacher should be prepared for the somewhat chaotic quality of creative play because it is impossible to organize inspiration before it happens. But this chaos can be productive, and the teacher can maintain reasonable order by picking up unused materials and returning them to their place and by seeing that the play does not deteriorate into aimless running about.

Elementary school teachers have the difficult task of satisfying mandated standards while satisfying the child's need to play. In recent years, the trend has been to reduce the time allotted for children's play in kindergarten and the early primary grades. After the No Child Left Behind Act became federal mandate in 2001, the pressure on schools to prepare children for testing in the primary grades led to increased emphasis on academics. Many elementary classrooms have done away with block areas, dress-up centers, free-play time, and even recess. It is important that primary-grade teachers understand that academic learning such as reading, writing, and math concepts can be enhanced through play (Elkind, 2007; Ginsburg, 2007). Additionally, while achievement on academic tests is important, learning to *enjoy* learning and having a positive attitude toward school are also important lessons in the early grades (Curwood, 2007; Elkind, 2007).

FACTORS LIKELY TO FACILITATE CREATIVE PLAY

Allow Children's Ideas to Develop and Avoid Dominating the Play

Teachers should do their best to avoid dominating the play experience and seek instead to foster children's abilities to express themselves in their own unique ways. Such teachers help children base their play on their own inspirations because the teachers are convinced youngsters can be trusted to play productively without undue intervention and manipulation (Elkind, 2007; Montie et al., 2007).

This freedom for children to generate their own ideas can be difficult for some teachers to allow. Indeed some teachers are so eager to use play as a medium for teaching that they cannot resist overmanipulating it in order to provide a "good learning experience." For example, one teacher had taken the children to the fire station for a visit. The next day, overwhelmed by the temptation to use play as an avenue for teaching, she set out all the hats, hoses, ladders, and pedal trucks she could muster, and as the children walked in the door, she pounced on them, announcing, "I have the most wonderful idea! Remember when we went to the fire station yesterday? Well, why don't we play that here today? Maria, you can be the chief. Now, who wants to hold the hose?"

Children may learn a good deal about fire engines this way, and if this is the real purpose, very well. However, the spontaneous, creative quality of the play will be greatly reduced by using this approach. It is generally better to wait until the children express an interest and then to ask them how you can help and what they need.

Here is an example of a teacher who uses this approach in responding to the children's own interests. Notice how she tries to extend their play experience and learning without directing it herself. This is in the form of a question posed on the Reggio Emilia Internet discussion group*:

> I had a wonderful block building activity take place in my 4-year-old class. Recently, the children began to use the ledge of the chalkboard as the base of their construction. I found them working away, adding blocks here and there, talking to each other, and asking each other for help and assistance.
>
> I listened to the children as they worked with each other and continued to fill in the spaces. I asked as many open ended questions as possible and stood back with pride as they experimented with size and shapes and balance. The "masterpiece" was completed to their satisfaction when they realized the tallest student in the group could no longer honor their request to place blocks any higher.
>
> I documented as much as I could with my camera. The following day, we revisited the "masterpiece" as I wrote their dictation. I have been pleasantly surprised that the work is still in one piece on the ledge of the board and the children have been very respectful of "the work of others."
>
> Now I have some thoughts as to where I would like to go with this, but of course the children will have to continue to lead this activity. However, I would love to somehow project the work onto a piece of canvas to be traced and discussed. I would also love for them to add some color to the work on canvas. Ultimately the canvas could become a backdrop to a story developed by the children. We shall see if any of this comes about. I feel that this is such a treasure for the class that more could happen. I do not want to lose any moments with them. Help please with thoughts, ideas, and recommendations.
> Thanks,
>
> Martha Bateman
> _____
> Beaufort Elementary School, Beaufort, S. Carolina (2004, September 6). A little advice needed.

_____

*Message posted to REGGIO-L, http://ecap.crc.uiuc.edu/listserv/reggio-l.html Reprinted with permision.

The two examples of differing approaches to children's play clarify the distinction between *teacher direction* and *child-initiated play with teacher support*. However, there are some circumstances in which the teacher must assume a more direct, intervening role since some children come to the center with poorly developed play skills. Studies indicate such intervention has produced rich dividends for these children, such as increased receptive language (ability to understand), increased expressive language skills (greater vocabulary and command of grammar), higher intellectual competence, more innovation and imaginativeness, reduced aggression, better impulse control, and better emotional and social adjustment. Because of these benefits, sociodramatic, make-believe play should be included as a vital element in every preschool and kindergarten day. During such play, teachers should help the children gain social skills rather than focus on content or subject matter.

The problem with recommending consistent intervention in some children's play is that this can be tricky advice to give beginning teachers because many beginners have great difficulty maintaining the subtle blend of authority and playfulness required to sustain this role. Instead they either overmanage and overwhelm the children or reduce themselves to "being a pal." It is vital to remember that even when teaching children with special educational needs, *the purpose is not to dominate but to stimulate play*. The teacher should make interventions accordingly, stepping in only when necessary and withdrawing whenever possible. The following suggestions are intended to illustrate some effective ways of doing this.

SOME PRACTICAL WAYS TO STIMULATE AND EXTEND PLAY

To be most helpful to the children, it is important to pay attention to what they are playing and to think a little ahead of what is happening so that the teacher can encourage the play to continue *before* it languishes.

One way to do this is to ask the children what will happen next. For example, if they are playing "going to the market," the teacher might ask, "Now that you've got all those big bags of groceries, I wonder how you're going to get them home?"

Suggesting additional roles for bystanders to fill can also extend play. Perhaps a child on the sidelines is yearning to join the others at the airplane/rocket site. The teacher could ask a question such as, "Gee, how's that airplane going to fly without any gas?" [pause] "Perhaps Ryan could use that hose and help you."

It is also very important to provide enough time for play to develop. It takes time for children to recruit other players, conceive and assign roles, and get the play under way.

And finally, never forget the value of enriching and extending the play by the use of language: putting into words what the children are doing. Making these comments while the play is going on, recapping it in large group, and recalling yesterday's or last week's play by means of pictures or discussion at the start of the next self-select period will delight the children, as well as increase their own ability to think about what they are doing or have accomplished already (Klein, Worth, & Linas, 2003).

Make a Special Point of Including Children Who Have Disabilities in Play

It can be an unfortunate fact that children who have various disabilities are often not included in the play of other children at school. This can be attributed to a variety of reasons including inexperience (on both sides), being at a different developmental level than other children, or having limited communication skills because of restricted hearing abilities or vision problems. Then, too, sometimes these children have been overly sheltered from contact with other children or have spent an unusual amount of time in special education situations in which the emphasis has been on drill and practice, rather than in a more playful environment. Such children in particular need the relief offered by play.

Whatever the reason for the limited participation, these children, like all other children, are entitled to and benefit from endless, rich opportunities to experience the joy of playful living. However, it may require more special attention from the teacher than is typically necessary to bring this about (Doctoroff, 2001; Sandall, 2004).

A variety of specific suggestions is incorporated throughout *The Whole Child* and more thoroughly in chapter 5, but a quick summary is included here of a basic approach that will encourage play to develop. Remember to explain in matter-of-fact terms to the other children the nature of the child's disability and to suggest some appropriate ways they could include the youngster in the activity. Be careful always to include activities in the curriculum plan at which you know the child with the disability can be successful. Keep an attentive eye on what is happening in order to promote as much success as possible during the play experience, and be sure to commend the children in a low-key way for that success when it is appropriate to do so.

Cast Yourself in the Role of Assistant to the Child as You Help Play Emerge

Fostering creative play demands that teachers add another skill to their repertoire: the ability to move with the child's play and support it as it develops. This does not mean they play with the children as their peers, anymore than it means they should sit on the sidelines being thankful the children are busy and not in trouble. Rather, teachers who are skilled in generating creative play sense what will enhance the play and remain ready to offer suggestions that might sustain or extend it should this become necessary. Such teachers cast themselves in the role of supporter or facilitator of the child; they imagine themselves inside the child's skin and see the play from that point of view. This gives them an empathic understanding that enables them to serve the child's play needs well. Sometimes this insight is expressed by as simple a thing as going to the shed and getting out a variety of ropes, chains, and hooks for a construction project. Sometimes it is evident on a subtler level as the decision is quietly made to delay snack so that play may build to a satisfying climax.

Some of this empathic ability may go back to remembering what it was like to be a child oneself, and some of it may be related to opening oneself to sensing the children and taking time to "hear" them. It is a skill well worth cultivating because it makes possible the perception of the children's play in terms of what they intend. This enables the teacher to nurture the play by sensitively offering the right help at the right moment.

Benjamin La Framboise

Cast yourself as facilitator or supporter of children's play.

   Putting children in command of the play situation is valuable not only because it fosters their creative ability but also because it strengthens their feelings of mastery. When the teacher becomes the assistant and helper and defers to the children's judgment, they are free to determine what will happen next in their play. They exercise their ability to make choices and decisions. As mentioned previously, Erikson (1963) maintained that becoming autonomous and taking the initiative are fundamental tasks of early childhood. Creative play presents one of the best opportunities available for developing these strengths (Elkind, 2007; Klein et al., 2003; O'Connor, 2000).

A Rich Background of Actual Life Experience Is Fundamental to Developing Creative Play

Children build on the foundation of real experience in their play. The richer and more solid the background of experience that children accumulate, the more varied the play will become. Field trips, holidays, and experiences with many ethnic groups, as well as things brought into the school in the way of science experiments, books, and visitors, will increase the base of experience upon which they can build their play. There is no substitute for this background (Isenberg & Quisenberry, 2002). In addition, this is one way in which elementary teachers can infuse math, science, and literacy learning into playtime.

Offer Many Opportunities for Outdoor Play

Playing outdoors is essential for the healthy growth and development of children, and being outdoors stimulates children to play (Greenman, 2003; Perry, 2004; Wellhousen, 2001). In addition to promoting fitness and a connection to nature, as mentioned previously, outdoor play allows children a sense of freedom that cannot be found anywhere else, and opens their minds to so many new possibilities and adventures. Today's children stay indoors and are more sedentary than ever before, and their experiences in the natural world have been reduced (Curwood, 2007; Louv, 2008; Natural Learning Initiative, n.d.). Currently, children spend as much time indoors sitting before electronic media (television, computers, video games) as they do playing outdoors (Kaiser Family Foundation, 2006).

Teachers should allow plenty of time for children to play freely outside: running, jumping, twirling, skipping, and so on, to their hearts' content. When children are outdoors, all their senses are stimulated and so too is their creativity. Children often make up their own games and challenges, but teachers should also actively engage children in outdoor play rather than assume it's fine to just let them run about without any interaction with the teacher. Cooperative games and challenges, such as "Let's all see how fast we can get to the tree while hopping," can be introduced easily to engage all children in outdoor activity. However, we should keep in mind that games with rules, such as soccer or tag, are not developmentally appropriate for preschoolers but are most appropriate for second and third graders. Finally, it is important to seek out natural settings in which children can play and explore such as parks, cornfields, or a walk in the woods so that they experience the beauty of nature firsthand as a part of their play. Even a simple walk around the neighborhood can open up a world of fascination for the young child and a sense of connection to the natural environment.

Equipment Plays an Important Role in Facilitating Play

Buy Equipment That Encourages the Use of Imagination

The kinds of equipment the teacher provides have a considerable influence on the play that results. Children younger than age 3 benefit from the use of realistic play props when involving themselves in pretend play. Then, as the children mature and their ability to represent reality through imagination increases, it becomes more desirable to offer them less realistic items to play with. Thus a young 2 1/2-year-old may play house more freely, using actual cups and saucers, whereas a 4-year-old may simply pretend he is holding a cup in his hand with equal satisfaction.

Of course, this is not meant to suggest that 3- and 4-year-olds should never have realistic playthings to enjoy. We all know that dolls, dress-up clothes, and little rubber animals are beloved at that age and act as powerful enhancers of play. However, teachers should not go overboard on supplying every little thing. Some things are best left to the child's imagination, or as educators at the famous Pikler Institute for infants and toddlers say, "The more active the toy, the more passive the child" (Sussna Klein, 2002).

Where larger pieces of equipment are concerned, however, teachers can make their money go further and enhance the potential variety of play experiences for the children by buying equipment that can be used in a variety of ways and that is not overly realistic (Curtis & Carter, 2003; Klein et al., 2003). Boards, blocks, and ladders, for example, lend themselves to a hundred possibilities, but a plywood train tends to be used mostly as a plywood train the children just sit in. A good question to ask before investing a lot of money is, How many ways could the children use this? If you can think of three or four rather different possibilities, that's a good indication the children will use their imaginations to think of many more.

Children in the primary grades benefit from more complex play and educational materials. Since children at this age are more concerned with friends and the social world than preschoolers, the teacher should offer games and materials that lend themselves to social interaction and cooperation. Materials can also facilitate academic learning, including math, science, language, and literacy at this age (Bronson, 2004).

Select a Wide Variety of Basic Kinds of Equipment

When equipment is selected, choices should reflect a good range and balance. This means that careful attention must be paid to all areas of the curriculum, both indoors and outdoors.

Change Equipment Frequently

Rather than having everything available all the time, change accessories in the basic play areas such as the housekeeping area and the block corner. Changing attracts different children, keeps life fresh and interesting for them, and encourages them to play creatively. Adding boys' clothes or an old safety razor (minus the blade, of course), or bringing the guinea pig for a visit might break the monotony in the housekeeping corner. Using trains, rubber animals, dollhouse furniture, or the cubical counting blocks could provide variety in the block area. Moving play equipment to a new location is another fine way to vary play and foster creativity. Boys, for example, are more likely to play house if the stove and refrigerator are out on the grass or if the house is made of hollow blocks for a change. Different locations attract different customers.

Rearrange Equipment Frequently and Recombine It in Appealing and Complex Ways

Besides moving equipment to new places, it is also valuable to consider how it can be recombined. What if we moved the mattress to the base of the low wall? Would this attract (and protect) the 2-year-olds while they teeter along its edge or jump freely from it? What if the refrigerator box were moved near the climbing gym with boards, ladders, and sawhorses provided nearby? What if the pots and pans from the sandbox were included in this play?

An important concept to understand here is the one presented early on by Kritchevsky and Prescott (1977) and Shipley (1993) but still relevant today. They pointed out that *simple* play units such as swings or tricycles have low absorbing power; that is, each item soaks up only one child at a time for play. When two kinds of materials or equipment are combined, such as when digging equipment is added to the sandbox, the play unit becomes *complex*. This has stronger absorptive power for children than the simple units. Better yet are the *super play units*. These units, which combine three or more kinds of equipment and materials at once (e.g., sand, digging tools, water), do an even more effective job of drawing groups of children into cooperative play for extended periods. Evidently if we wish to draw children into interactive, creative play, we should do all we can to concoct these superunits for their delight.

Of course, teachers do not have to produce all the ideas for recombining equipment and enriching play. If the children are encouraged and their ideas supported, they will contribute many fruitful ideas for such elaborations and recombinations on their own, thus providing an additional outlet for their creative ideas.

Store Equipment in Convenient, Easy-to-Reach Places

The teacher must also arrange adequate storage for these materials. Good storage will keep equipment available and save the teacher's sanity as well. Storage can actually make or break a play situation, so it is well worth the time, effort, and money involved to solve this problem adequately. Material should be conveniently arranged so that it can be reached easily, and, of course, it should be returned to the same place after use to expedite locating it the next time it is needed. Labeled shelves, racks, hooks, and storage closets that are large enough all help. In addition, storage should be located close at hand so that the teacher may continue to provide supervision while getting out something the children have requested.

Keep Play Areas Safe and Attractive

The general appearance and presentation of the play areas will inspire (or discourage) children to play there. All areas should be set up at the beginning of the day in a fresh, appealing way. New touches should be added here and there to spark interest and avoid dull repetition.

Play is also better encouraged if materials are not allowed to degenerate into a shambles during playtime. No one wants to wade through a welter of costumes on the

Create and maintain appealing play areas.

floor or build in a chaos of blocks dumped and abandoned in that corner. Attractiveness fosters attraction, and the teacher bears the primary responsibility for creating and maintaining appealing play areas.

A Final Thought

One last reminder: Children need plenty of freedom, time, and materials if they are to become maximally involved in imaginative play. They need the freedom to move from one activity to another as their tastes dictate, they need uninterrupted time to build a play situation through to its satisfying completion, and they need enough materials to furnish a challenge and provide a feeling of sufficiency. Making these resources available is a good way to say to children in tangible terms that their needs are met, indeed their *right* to play is respected.

SPECIFIC ACTIVITIES TO ENCOURAGE CREATIVITY IN PLAY

Creative Dramatic Play—"Just Pretending"

In addition to the many virtues discussed earlier in the chapter, creative dramatic play such as dress-up, birthday party, and playing house provides unparalleled opportunities to use the imagination and play "as if" something were true. The potential for intellectual development that this implies cannot be overemphasized (Bergen, 2004; Elkind, 2007; Isenberg & Quisenberry, 2002; Jones & Cooper, 2006). Usually pretend play involves more than one child at a time and contains a lot of role assigning and role assuming ("Now, you be the father and I'll be . . . "). Three-year-olds tend to play a simple version of "house," but 4-year-olds love to embellish the premises with dogs, cartoon characters, naughty children, and interesting domestic catastrophes. All these activities develop the use of language because the children will discuss and describe among themselves what is happening ("Let's get the babies and pretend they've been in that mud again"). Teachers should encourage this use of imaginative language whenever possible.

Dress-up clothes and props can enhance the play, but having unstructured materials available that may be used in many ways is even more desirable because it helps the children be inventive and use their imaginations. Thus a scarf may become a hat, an apron, a blanket, or even a child's wished-for long hair.

Older children also need to exercise their imaginations in unbound free play during the school day. Through child-controlled play, they learn important social lessons of give-and-take, rule making and enforcement, and where they fit in the social world of peers. Pretend-play materials and costumes, puppets, and play scenes help ready the primary school child for real-life activities.

Suggested Variations

Some teachers enjoy assembling play kits for the children. This is all right as long as the teacher resists the tendency to supply every little thing or to offer such specific equipment that no room is left for developing a creative use for a familiar material. It is essential to vary dress-up clothes and housekeeping accessories regularly. Using different hats and costumes, pans, empty food packages, or a milk bottle holder and bottles can kindle new interest. Dress-up clothes for both sexes should be provided. Hats, vests, and old firefighters' jackets and boots will find favor with boys, but both sexes should be encouraged to try all kinds of garments. Ethnic costumes are a nice variation and often enhance the image of the child who lends them, but be sure these are not valuable, treasured mementos. Doctor play is always popular, partly because it represents thinly veiled concerns about sexual differences and partly because it offers invaluable chances for children to play out their fear of doctors, shots, and being hurt. The teacher should be available for interpretation and control when such play takes place. Additional variations in props that have found favor in our school include a modest amount of paraphernalia donated by a local fast-food chain, obsolete typewriters and other business equipment, a birthday party box, wedding veils and bouquets, backpacks and camping gear, and, always, cowboy/cowgirl accessories such as an old saddle and plenty of boots.

Block Play

Blocks are one of the timeless, classic play materials that have withstood the many comings and goings of ideologies and theories of early childhood education. From the beginning of the early childhood field, educators have extolled the benefits of block play for young children (Froebel, 1889; Hill, 1942/1992). No matter what theory of learning is espoused by which educator, children have continued to play with blocks with concentrated devotion (Elkind, 2007; MacDonald, 2001).

The sheer variety of kinds of blocks available for use in schoolrooms attests to their appeal. These range from large hollow ones through unit blocks to the so-called cubical counting blocks (which have so many other wonderful uses besides counting!). In addition, well-designed types of interlocking blocks are available that foster the development of fine-muscle abilities. There is no such thing as having too many blocks!

Unfortunately because of their initial expense, many schools stint on this kind of equipment, but there are ways around that problem. Initially cardboard blocks can serve as a reasonable substitute for the more expensive hollow ones, or someone with an electric saw can make an inexpensive but copious set of unit blocks from pine until the school can begin acquiring the longer lasting maple variety. Then every year additional blocks should be included without fail in the equipment budget.

Infants begin to stack objects (a primitive block-building skill) almost as soon as they are able to sit up, and children continue to use blocks with satisfaction throughout their elementary school years if they are given this opportunity. Blocks provide endless opportunities for the development of emerging perceptual-motor skills. Stacking, reaching, grasping, lifting, shoving, carrying, and balancing are only a few of the countless motor skills practiced in block play (see Figure 3.1).

Possibilities for emotional satisfactions abound as well. What teacher has not seen a shy child build a corral and seek safety within it, or a pent-up child send blocks toppling down, or two little boys construct block houses and establish families firmly within their confines?

Infants and Twos	**What they do**	**What they learn**	**What they need**
	Manipulate/feel blocks with hands Put blocks in mouth Reach for blocks Drop blocks repeatedly, especially if in a high chair Knock down a stack of blocks Older infants (approximately 8–12 months) will look for a hidden block Toddlers love to stack big foam blocks as high as they can and knock them down	Physical properties of objects Eye-hand coordination Lessons of gravity Cause and effect Object permanence 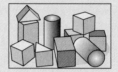	Lots of blocks in different shapes that they can grasp Soft, vinyl-covered foam blocks that won't hurt when mouthed and can be washed after use Thin plastic or empty cereal-type boxes that can be knocked down Large, soft foam blocks for toddlers Medium-sized wood blocks in a variety of shapes and colors for toddlers

Threes and Fours	**What they do**	**What they learn**	**What they need**
	Match, group, and classify blocks by size, shape, and color Build tall stacks of blocks Build structures and roads Will start building without a design in mind, then label it afterward Make patterns with blocks Begin to use blocks in pretend play scenarios	Beginning math concepts such as matching, grouping, classification Problem solving Fine-motor and gross-motor control Visual-spatial relations Balance and gravity The power of their imagination Confidence in their ability to create	Lots of different types of blocks: a good set of wood unit blocks including arches, pillars, ramps, and curves; large hollow blocks; small color cubes; interlocking blocks such as bristle blocks or snap blocks Props such as play animals, people, vehicles, trees to embellish pretend play

Fives, Sixes, Sevens, and Eights	**What they do**	**What they learn**	**What they need**
	Build elaborate structures: cities, roadways, castles, houses, etc. Think about and plan what they intend to build Use blocks to represent real-life places and things Build structures specifically for their pretend play scenarios Tell stories about their structures Build cooperatively with others Match, group, classify, and arrange blocks in patterns	Logico-mathematical concepts including classification, seriation, number, and spatial relations How to express ideas using symbols or pretend objects Communication skills Planning, follow-through, cause and effect	Many different types of blocks and materials, including miniature multicultural people, vehicles, mechanical items (pulleys, drawbridges, inclines) Wagon, buckets, platforms Large hollow blocks Lots of space and time for building 

Figure 3.1
Developmentally appropriate block play

Blocks provide unparalleled opportunities for understanding visual-spatial relationships.

Blocks lend themselves readily to achieving large effects quickly, thereby building ego-expanding structures of considerable height and large dimensions, which help the child feel strong and masterful, as well as provide opportunities to be creative.

Blocks provide unparalleled opportunities for understanding visual-spatial relationships. What does a structure look like when viewed from one side and then the other, or when seen from above or peered up at from underneath? They also provide opportunities for developing insight into mathematics and physics as the children struggle with cause-and-effect relationships when unbalanced towers topple down or roofs remain in place.

Blocks are also strong in their contribution to the child's learning the intellectual operations basic to Piagetian theory. They offer many opportunities for the child to grasp important developmental principles (Kamii, Miyakawa, & Kato, 2004; MacDonald, 2001). Blocks have also been found to be very productive elicitors of language.

Finally, blocks foster the development of creative play (MacDonald, 2001). By nature they are unstructured and may be used to build anything that suits the child's fancy. Older children enjoy planning such structures in advance, but younger ones will content themselves with the experience of stacking and balancing for its own sake and perhaps assign a useful function to the construction at a later point in the building (Kamii et al., 2004).

Suggested Variations

Accessories that may be offered to stimulate block play are legion and can add a lot of attractiveness to the area. However, teachers should not overlook the value and delight inherent in presenting block play with blocks alone. When accessories *are* used, the touches of color they can lend add beauty as well as stimulation to the play. Dollhouse furniture and rug samples, small rubber animals, and miniature people are all successful additions. Variations in blocks themselves, such as gothic arches, flat "roofing" blocks, spools, and cubical counting blocks, add embellishment. Not all the blocks should be offered all the time; it is sound to save the arches, switches, or triangular blocks and ramps and offer them as interesting variations when the more common varieties begin to pall. It is also fun to build block pens for the rats and guinea pigs, although this requires careful supervision from the teacher for the animals' protection. Trains, tracks, cars, trucks, boats, and airplanes are also delightful to use with block materials.

Outdoors the addition of boards, sawhorses, ladders, and old bedspreads and parachutes will extend large block play in a satisfactory way. Large, sturdy boxes and concrete pipes are additional accessories that make good combination units with blocks, and wagons and wheelbarrows are handy for carrying blocks about and delivering them to many locations in the yard.

Water Play

Water play is one of the freest, finest play opportunities we can offer children. Although inexperienced teachers often dread it because they fear the children may become too wild or overstimulated, the opposite of this behavior is usually the case. Water play is absorbing and soothing; children will stay with it a long time and come away refreshed and relaxed if it is well presented. It is also valuable because it offers children many opportunities to work through conflicts resulting from the demands of toilet training (there is no better present for a newly trained 2-year-old than a sprinkling can!), it provides relief from pressures and tensions, and it stimulates social play. Sometimes children will play companionably with others while using water, even though they remain isolated the rest of the day.

Activities such as pouring and measuring help develop eye-hand coordination. Children also acquire intellectual concepts having to do with estimating quantity (how much will the cup really hold?), with Piagetian conservation (but it looks like more in the tall bottle!), and with physical properties of water (what became of the water when we poured it on the hot sidewalk?).

Water play should be offered several times a week to provide maximum satisfaction for the children. In winter a large indoor bathroom with a drain in the floor is an invaluable asset. When water play is set up in such a location, spills run off quickly. Water can be offered in deep dishpans or sinks but is best offered in larger containers, such as galvanized laundry tubs, water tables, concrete-mixing tubs made of plastic, or even wading pools.

Suggested Variations

Too many schools limit this kind of play to hand-washing or dabbling in the sink. Although these activities are certainly better than not having water available at all, they stop far short of what children really require for this experience. Many variations can be employed for a change, although basic water play always remains a favorite. Running water from the hose is a fine thing to offer, although it is, of course, a warm weather activity. Water can be used in conjunction with a sandbox or mud pit with real pleasure. In addition, water can be offered to use in sinking, floating, pouring, and quantifying experiments. Unbreakable bottles and containers, as well as various sizes of sieves and funnels, can be saved for this purpose. Ice is a fascinating variation to offer, or washing activities with dolls, doll clothes, preschool furniture, cars, or tricycles can be presented. Scrubbing vegetables, watering the garden, and washing dishes should not be overlooked as additional variations, which have the added appeal of participating in meaningful work. Making a variety of pipes and joints available for assembling and using with water is fascinating to children and teaches them some valuable concepts about cause and effect. Adding sponges, bubbles, or a little color will also change the appeal of the water and create additional interest.

Mud and Sand

Mud and sand have wonderful, messy, unstructured qualities that make them among the most popular creative play materials in early childhood education. They offer rich tactile sensory experiences and provide emotional relief as well: Messing and slopping through water and sand or mud are relaxing and are thought by some psychologists to provide relief from the stringent toilet-training demands of our society. These materials also facilitate a lot of social interaction. Older children play imaginatively and cooperatively with each other while digging tunnels, constructing roads, and carrying on "bake-offs"; but sand and mud are also rewarding for younger children to use, and they often settle down to this activity in a particularly absorbed and satisfied way. In short, the chance to mix, stir, pour, measure, mold, and squish sand and mud is an indispensable component of the curriculum.

Since this experience is often restricted at home, it is particularly important to offer it consistently at the center, where it can be planned in advance and is relatively easy to clean up. It is good planning to locate the sandbox as far from the school door as possible, in the hope that some of the sand will shake off clothes on the way back inside, and it is also sound to check pants cuffs when the play has been especially vigorous, to reduce the likelihood of dumping the whole sandbox on the carpet. The sandbox should have a wide border around it so that children may sit on it and stay warm and dry when the weather is chilly. A waterproof chest beside it will make storage of commonly used equipment easier; plastic laundry baskets also make good containers because they allow the sand to fall back into the sandbox.

Mud is different from sand, and the school should provide chances for the children to play in both of these materials. A mud hole and the opportunity to dig deep pits and trudge around in mud are interesting to children, so a place in the yard should be set aside for this purpose. (If the holes are deep, it will be necessary to fence them off for safety's sake.) Children will dig astonishingly deep pits if given room, good tools, time, and opportunity, and the satisfaction of doing this work is plain to see on their faces.

Suggested Variations

It is a shame to leave the same old buckets and shovels in the sandbox day after day when so many interesting variations may be employed. All kinds of baking and cooking utensils make excellent substitutes and may be readily and cheaply acquired at rummage sales. Toy trucks and cars are nice to add, too, particularly if they are wooden or sturdy plastic, since metal ones rust and deteriorate quickly if they are used outdoors. Sturdy tools of various kinds are good to use. (Remember that when digging large holes, children need real shovels—just as they need real hammers and saws at the woodworking table.)

Gardening is another useful variation of digging and working with mud. Since digging is the best, most involved part of gardening from the children's point of view, several weeks of this experience should be offered to the children *before* seeds are planted. The other part of gardening that young children enjoy the most is watering. Although this can be done with a hose that has a sprinkling head attached, it is easier to control if sprinkling cans and a big tub of water for filling them are provided instead. This allows the children to water to their hearts' content without washing the seeds away or creating undue runoff.

Computer Play

Many teachers are offering a new type of play to today's young children: computer games and programs. Most elementary schools include computer games in the curriculum. Certain children are drawn to computer play and choose it over other

Many children are drawn to computer play, and it's always more fun with friends.

self-select activities regularly. Teachers find that many children love the thrill and excitement of computer play. It stimulates their imagination and sense of humor, and some children just can't seem to get enough! One out of four 5-year-olds uses the Internet (U.S. Department of Education, National Center for Education Statistics, 2003), and many classrooms are equipped with computers (McNair, Kirova-Petrova, & Bhargava, 2001; National Association for the Education of Young Children [NAEYC], 1996).

The use of computers can enhance children's development, or, without thoughtful attention on the part of the adult, it can have deleterious effects. For example, girls tend to use computers less frequently than boys (Heft & Swaminathan, 2002; McNair et al., 2001). Additionally, wealthier schools have more and better equipment resulting in inequitable availability of educational resources. Early childhood teachers must keep these problems in mind when using computers, and provide computer access and activities for children that are free from bias.

On the positive side, computer use can enhance children's development, offering opportunities for collaborative play, learning, and creativity. Children prefer using the computer with other children, and the ensuing play can be rich in social and language interaction (Haugland, Bailey, & Ruiz, 2002; NAEYC, 1996). Teachers must ensure that the computer experiences they offer children are not only fun but also enriching, that they are developmentally appropriate, and that they refrain from violence or violent solutions to problems—such as "blowing up" a mistake (NAEYC, 1996). A good guide for selecting developmentally appropriate software is provided by Haugland et al. (2002), and all teachers who use computers should consult the NAEYC *Position Statement on Technology and Young Children—Ages 3 Through 8* (1996). Computers can be used in the preprimary and primary classroom in a developmentally appropriate way to foster language and literacy development, as well as thinking and reasoning skills. Figure 3.2 offers suggestions for how teachers can promote positive computer experiences for young children.

- Locate the computer center within the classroom, not in a separate location.
- Make sure there are several chairs for more than one participant.
- Don't just leave the children on their own; interact with them, ask questions, and support their experiences.
- Make sure that a child isn't sitting at the computer for more than an hour without moving about, or that a child doesn't consistently select computer play at the expense of other activities—particularly physical fitness.
- Pay attention to who is using computers in your classroom, and make sure all children receive equal opportunities by inviting children to play who seem reluctant (more often girls).
- Ensure that all programs and Web sites have developmentally appropriate content that is bias-free, nonviolent, and prosocial.

Figure 3.2
Tips for promoting positive computer experiences for young children

SUMMARY

Play serves many valuable purposes in the life of the child. It provides occasions for intense practice of sensorimotor skills; the symbolic nature of imaginative play fosters development of the intellect and generates increased understanding of events; it enhances academic skills learning in the primary grades; play facilitates role playing and develops social skills; it furnishes opportunities to work through emotional problems and to experience the relief of acting like a child instead of an adult; and it provides many occasions for children to be creative by using their imaginations and abilities to think in divergent ways. Best of all, play provides endless opportunities to experience joy and delight.

Teachers who wish to foster the creative aspects of play will seek to extend it but avoid dominating it. They will purchase, plan, and arrange equipment so that creativity will be enhanced. They will allow many opportunities for play outdoors. But above all, teachers who wish to foster creativity in play will cast themselves in the role of assistant to the children, seeking to move with and support their play as it develops and to serve their play needs to the best of the teachers' ability.

Questions and Activities

1. Take time to make a brief record of the play of several children during the coming week. Can you find evidence in these observations that play is used symbolically by children to translate experience into a deeper understanding of events? Did you find evidence that children employ play to express emotions and work these through? Did you observe any instances in which the children generated new, divergent solutions to problems by trying them out in play?
2. What is the difference between overcontrolling play and acting in a supportive, fostering role that encourages it to develop in greater depth? Role-play the same play situation, demonstrating differences between these two approaches.
3. Survey the play yard of your school. List the different play units around which activity occurs. Do some appear to generate more imaginative activities than others? Identify what properties these units possess in common. How are they alike?

Diversity Question

1. How would you help to integrate a child with disabilities, such as blindness or developmental delays, into the children's play? Give specific examples of what you might say and do.

Predicament

1. Suppose a parent comes to you after touring the school and says dubiously, "It looks nice enough here, but don't they ever learn anything? Don't they ever do anything but play around here?" How would you reply?

Self-Check Questions for Review

Content-Related Questions

1. Explain how play helps each of the five selves of the child (physical, intellectual, emotional, social, and creative) develop.
2. List and describe the four Piagetian developmental stages of play and then list and describe the four stages of play identified by Parten. What is the difference between the two systems of classification?
3. What are three ways teachers can encourage creativity in play?
4. Describe how equipment may influence the play of children. Be sure to give several examples to illustrate your answer.
5. Pretend you are escorting a visitor around your center and compose an answer to this question, "Why do you have such a large block corner? Aren't they an awful lot of trouble to pick up all the time?" Be sure you explain the educational benefits of this material.

6. Now explain to that same person why you make a point of offering water, sand, and mud play to the children.

Reference for Further Reading

Koralek, D. (Ed.). (2004). *Spotlight on young children and play*. Washington, DC: National Association for the Education of Young Children. A wonderfully informative collection of articles about children's play, its development, and what teachers can do to support it.

Related Organizations and Online Resources

American Association for the Child's Right to Play. *IPA/Newsletter*. This international association publishes various materials such as the *IPA/Newsletter* and conducts meetings that champion the child's right to play. Information is available at http://www.ipausa.org/.

Association for Childhood Education International (ACEI). This international organization promotes and supports the optimal education and development of children, and influences the professional growth of educators and the efforts of others who are committed to the needs of children in a changing society. ACEI position paper, *Play: Essential for all children*, is available at http://www.acei.org.

National Association for the Education of Young Children (NAEYC). Many excellent resources about play are available, as well as in their journal, *Young Children*. The NAEYC Position Statements can be downloaded at http://www.naeyc.org.

Playing for Keeps. The purpose of this national nonprofit organization is to promote and support the role of play in our culture. Many resources for teachers and families can be found at http://www.playingforkeeps.org.

CHAPTER four

Providing Cross-Cultural, Nonsexist Education

What to do about name calling and racial insults?

What to say when a youngster says to a Muslim child, "Why does your dad wear a white thing on his head?"

How to help children value everyone, no matter what their race or color or gender?

What to tell a 4-year-old who asks where babies come from?

. . . IF YOU HAVE, THE MATERIAL IN THE FOLLOWING PAGES WILL HELP YOU.

I hear the train a comin',
A comin' round the curve.
She's using all her steam and brakes
And straining every nerve.
Get on board, little children,
Get on board, little children,
Get on board, little children,
There's room for many-a-more.
The fare is cheap and all can go,
The rich and poor are there.
No second class aboard this train,
No difference in the fare!
Get on board, little children,
Get on board, little children—
Get on board, little children!
There's room for many-a-more!

Anonymous

The wonderful lines of the old gospel tune, "No second class aboard this train, no difference in the fare!" sum up what is meant by *equity in education* because in a well-presented cross-cultural, nonsexist curriculum there are no second-class children and surely no differences in what children must do or be in order to be allowed on the train with the other children.

Perhaps you are thinking indignantly, "What do you mean! Of course there are no second-class children," but the truth is that sometimes teachers *do* treat some children as being second-class people.

TEACHERS' ATTITUDES

Many examples of the way prejudice shows through in teachers' attitudes were presented by Hoot, Szecsi, and Moosa (2003), who reviewed studies of teacher attitudes toward Islam. The majority of non-Muslim primary school teachers admitted to knowing very little about Islam and they believed the Muslim population numbered less than 20,000 in the United States (the figure is closer to 6 million). Perhaps most shocking was that only 2 out of 218 respondents in one study felt that the basic beliefs of Islam might be different from those espoused by Islamic extremists. Despite the fact that Muslims (followers of the religion of Islam) represent diverse cultures and political systems and number more than a billion worldwide, only about 5% of the elementary school teachers interviewed said they would be willing to teach children that Muslims were not all terrorists. Islam is the second largest and most rapidly growing religion in the world. Clearly, teachers in the United States must confront their own ignorance and prejudices in order to create a peaceable classroom that promotes cross-cultural understandings for all.

Children from low-income and diverse linguistic, cultural, and ethnic backgrounds have a higher risk of academic failure (Adams, 2008; Bowman, 2006a; Cuellar, 2007; Mann, Steward, Eggbeer, & Norton, 2007). Teachers often have lower expectations for African American students, who are three times more likely to be expelled than non-Black students for the same offense (Adams, 2008). Although there is increased diversity in U.S. families' cultural backgrounds, teachers are ill-prepared to effectively include them in early childhood settings and schools (Adams, 2008; Bradley & Kibera, 2006; Cuellar, 2007; Holloway, 2003; Mann et al., 2007). Additionally, even when teachers espouse an antidiscrimination viewpoint, the actual methods they use in the classroom run counter to their multicultural intentions and, in fact, often cause considerable harm to the culturally and language diverse children in their classes (Falconer & Byrnes, 2003).

Sexist prejudice shows through in the different ways some teachers treat boys and girls. A study by Chick, Heilman-Houser, and Hunter (2002) revealed differences in teacher behavior toward boys or girls. Boys received more attention (both positive and negative) even when there were fewer of them, caregivers used linguistic bias when talking to children, and the classroom toys and materials were often stereotypical. Another teacher behavior the researchers observed—and one that many of us might be guilty of—was that teachers commented more on girls' dress, hairstyles, and helping behavior, whereas boys received more comments on their size and physical skills. It is no wonder that a recent study of elementary school children found that the majority of girls felt pressure to be thin and dress right, as well as reporting a lot of pressure to "please everyone" (Girls, Inc., 2006). We should be careful about what we say to children when complimenting or greeting them and avoid this subtle form of stereotyping. Certainly we can think of better comments to say to children besides, "Oh, your hair looks so pretty today!"

Can Such Attitudes Be Changed?

Fortunately the answer to this question is yes—at least to some degree. Although we must realize that attitudes and responses to groups, or individual representatives of certain groups, stem from long-ingrained habits and prejudices, teachers can change, and children can, too (Adams, 2008; Bowman, 2006a; Bradley & Kibera, 2006; Derman-Sparks & ABC Task Force, 1989; Gonzalez-Mena, 2007; Gurian & Stevens, 2005; Mann et al., 2007; National Association for the Education of Young Children [NAEYC], 1995).

For many years attempts at changing racist and sexist attitudes in early childhood seemed to concentrate on the more superficial aspects of differentness such as celebrating ethnic holidays and putting up pictures of female physicians and firefighters. Now a growing edge of work in the area of cross-cultural and nonsexist education is striving to reach beneath these surface manifestations of goodwill and to suggest ways to build deeper, more emotionally and socially meaningful relationships between people. For example, such vintage books as the earliest edition of *The Whole Child* (Hendrick, 1975) and *The Anti-Bias Curriculum* (Derman-Sparks & ABC Task Force, 1989), and more recently *Skilled Dialogue: Strategies for Cultural Diversity in Early Childhood* (I. Barrera, Corso, & Macpherson, 2003) and *Diversity in Early Care and Education: Honoring Differences* (Gonzalez-Mena, 2007), have provided practical ways to move toward more substantive changes in attitudes.

SUGGESTIONS FOR CONTROLLING AND OVERCOMING EXPRESSIONS OF PREJUDICE

Desirable as it may be, it is not always possible for people to overcome deeply held convictions about what other people are like. Everyone has negative opinions—prejudices—about someone. Some teachers may be genuinely unconcerned about skin color but find they are critical of unmarried or same-sex couples, or overweight people, or how welfare recipients spend their money, or people who use profanity, or those who chew tobacco.

An important part of controlling the expression of that prejudice lies in honestly admitting to oneself that it exists. Once you recognize that the dislike or even hatred exists, you can begin to control expressing it. It is an interesting illustration of the principle "Feel what you wish, but (at least) control what you do about those feelings."

Go to MyEducationLab and select the topic "Diverse Learners." Under Activities and Applications, watch the video *Integrating the Home Experiences of Culturally Diverse Students in the Classroom, Part 1.* What types of cultural biases do teachers sometimes have about bilingual students? How can these biases be overcome?

At the very least it is possible to monitor oneself and practice the "bias-proofing" suggestions advocated by G. Thompson (in Hopkins, 2008, p. 32):

1. Honestly examine your own background and feelings with regard to cultural differences.
2. Show all students that you care about them equally.
3. Respect children's developmental level based on who they are as individuals, not their ethnic or racial background.
4. Beware of judging families that are different from your own. Try to understand the culture of the family.
5. Never allow racist comments or behavior in your classroom. Model and teach respect for diversity.
6. Maintain high expectations for all your students.
7. Provide students with the school experiences that are crucial for later school success and meeting academic standards. For example, teach appropriate test-taking behaviors in elementary school.
8. Acknowledge when you have a negative opinion about a child and make that child your "star student." Spend extra time observing and connecting with the child, focusing on positive attributes.

The following pages contain many suggestions for ways to show that the teacher values the specialness of each child and every family background. Some suggestions are obvious such as planning a curriculum that includes everyone. Some, where human relationships are concerned, are more subtle.

But no matter what the teacher does or says, what matters most of all—what really sets the tone and what people sense almost instantly when they walk into the room—is the true character of the teacher. The teacher who practices a combination of decency, respect, and fairness toward self and toward others establishes the climate of mutual positive regard so necessary for effective multicultural education.

The teacher's character establishes a climate of mutual positive regard so necessary for multicultural education.

Broaden Your Frame of Understanding and Acceptance; Find Out What People Are Really Like!

Of course, if acquiring information about the family viewpoints, values, and learning styles of Mexican American or Hopi children results in stereotyping (assuming that every Mexican American or Hopi child is a cookie-cutter replica of every other one), the value of such education is destroyed.

But if such information is used to further understanding of the children's and family's attitudes and behavior, that insight paves the way for liking and warmth to flourish. Indeed, such information can even help teachers overcome their own cultural deprivation. For example, the teacher who knows that owls are regarded as birds of ill omen and death by the Navajo will not include them in Halloween decorations, nor will a teacher feel embarrassed by the Japanese mother who brings a small gift each time she visits the school.

Ethnic studies programs and even some colleges of education offer a wealth of information on particular cultures, and teachers should take such courses whenever they can. Participation in ongoing discussion groups can also be extraordinarily helpful. Presentations at regional and national NAEYC conferences can also widen one's perspective. Even just reading about the characteristics of various groups can build appreciation and sensitivity to variations in cultural style. Such resources not only broaden our frames of reference but may also help us avoid offending those we never intended to hurt.

A wonderful quotation from Tolstoy that comes to mind sums it all up: "Everyone thinks of changing the world, but no one thinks of changing himself." If we could only learn to understand and accept some differences as being just that, *differences*, without condemning them, it could be the beginning of changing ourselves and accepting a wider, warmer, more understanding view of the world and the children we care for.

IS EARLY CHILDHOOD TOO SOON TO BEGIN CROSS-CULTURAL, NONSEXIST EDUCATION?

Do such young children really notice the ethnic or gender differences of other children? If not, perhaps they are too young to require instruction. Might it not be better to ignore these issues and practice "color blindness," rather than make children self-conscious about such differences when they are so young?

Although some teachers might still prefer to answer yes to this question, research on the perception of differences in skin color shows that children as young as age 3 notice the skin color of African Americans and Mexican Americans (Anti-Defamation League [ADL], 2005; Derman-Sparks & Ramsey, 2006; Hoyt, 2005; York, 2003). Typical questions and comments by preschool children such as, "Is Mexican my color?" and "I didn't know that babies came out Black," provide continuing evidence of their concern with and awareness of racial and cultural differences.

Awareness of ethnic differences precedes the development of prejudice, so we must also ask, When do positive or negative *attitudes* toward ethnic differences begin to surface? Two- and 3-year-olds are increasingly aware of physical characteristics, such as hair color, skin hue, and sex differences. Some may exhibit "preprejudice behaviors" such as being fearful of someone who looks different or has a disability. Between the ages of

PEARSON
myeducationlab

Go to MyEducationLab and select the topic "Diverse Learners." Under Activities and Applications, view the classroom artifact *Tina's Self-Portrait.* How does the child's ethnic/cultural background play a role in her self-concept?

3 and 5 years, most children have acquired a sense of their own ethnic identity and possibly negative attitudes toward those who are different (ADL, 2005; Hoyt, 2005).

Awareness of physiological differences begins as early as age 2, as any teacher of young children can attest, and children will comment freely on such differences unless they are suppressed. One has only to listen during any toilet period in a children's center to hear such remarks as, "Why don't she have a hole in her pants?" or, "Don't you use that thing to wet on me!"

These kinds of comments and questions from children, as well as the more formal research already cited, make it clear that the children are indeed revealing a dawning awareness of ethnic and gender differences and developing feelings about these differences at a very early age. If we want them to learn at this same sensitive time that such differences are to be valued rather than scorned—that is, if we wish to combat the formation of bias and prejudice at the earliest possible moment—then we must conclude that early childhood is the time to begin (ADL, 2005; Bowman, 2006a; Bradley & Kibera, 2006; Derman-Sparks & ABC Task Force, 1989; Derman-Sparks & Ramsey, 2006; Gonzalez-Mena, 2007; Gurian & Stevens, 2005; NAEYC, 1995, 1997).

WHAT DO CROSS-CULTURAL AND NONSEXIST EDUCATION HAVE IN COMMON?

Perhaps you have been startled to find cross-cultural and nonsexist topics linked together in one chapter even though it is now clear that the common problem of bias ties them together. They are linked together also because two underlying educational principles apply to both subjects. One principle is that we want children to value their *unique* identities in relation to both their ethnic background and gender role. The other principle is that we want children to learn that people of all races and both sexes have many *needs and abilities in common,* and we must recognize these held-in-common needs and abilities and encourage their satisfaction if we want to enable all children to make use of their potential.

In the following pages these principles are applied first to cross-cultural and then to nonsexist education.

PRINCIPLES OF CROSS-CULTURAL EDUCATION

Recognize and Honor Cultural and Ethnic Differences: Encourage Cultural Pluralism

When weaving the cross-cultural strand into the curriculum, it is helpful to recall its two basic threads: (a) teaching that everyone has many unique and precious differences to be shared and appreciated and (b) teaching that all people have many basic needs in common. The first thread, honoring diversity, is sometimes termed *teaching cultural pluralism.* The emphasis in the following pages is placed primarily on that thread since it appears to be the area in which teachers need the most help.

Value Individual Children for Their Special Qualities: Teach Cultural Pluralism

Sometimes we get so wrapped up in thinking about children's cultural backgrounds that we temporarily forget all the other talents and quirks that make that child unique, but we must always remember that culture and gender aren't the only things that matter. The child's cheerful grin, cleverness at block building, and ready sympathy when someone cries are part of the child, too. In real life we must be careful not to dwell so much on only one or two characteristics—in this chapter, cultural/ethnic background and gender—that we lose sight of the whole child.

Most particularly we do not want any children ever to feel "on display" because they have been singled out for attention. Instead, the basic learning about cultural pluralism should be that everyone is worthwhile and that all children bring with them special things they have learned at home that they can share for the benefit of the group.

Relate Cross-Cultural Learnings to the Here and Now

Just as other learnings are linked with reality, cross-cultural learnings should be linked with current experiences in which the children are actually involved. For example, it doesn't make much sense for teachers to retreat to quaint pictures of little Dutch girls when they begin to talk about people of different cultures if the children cannot relate to the example.

An interesting example of an effective way of helping children relate cross-cultural experiences to the here and now of their daily lives comes from some teachers at Pacific Oaks College who have been doing just that with considerable success—so much so that it is now considered a classic in the field and used widely in early education programs across the country. They have developed what is called "The Anti-Bias Curriculum" (Pacific Oaks College Faculty, 1985), and they define the purpose of that curriculum as being to "empower people to resist being oppressed or to resist oppressing others." The work includes dealing with concerns about bias against gender and disabilities, as well as about racial prejudice.

Although space does not permit a review of all their ideas here, it is hoped that providing a taste of what they suggest will inspire interested readers to pursue the matter further on their own (Derman-Sparks & ABC Task Force, 1989; Derman-Sparks & Phillips, 1997; Derman-Sparks & Ramsey, 2006). The curriculum, which emerges from day-to-day life experiences at the school, stresses the importance of fostering direct, open communication with children that helps them become aware of racially oppressive beliefs and learn that they can begin to counter these beliefs with positive action.

The teaching varies with the child's age, of course, in order to be developmentally appropriate. For example, they favor providing 2-year-olds with direct information about race, such as the fact that the brown color of skin does not wash off and is not dirty; whereas they encourage older 5-year-olds to participate in more activist possibilities. These have included helping the children recognize examples of unfair practices and take action to correct them. One instance involved the children writing to an adhesive bandage company advocating the development of bandages not geared to pinkie-white skin, and another involved painting over a wall near their school that had been covered with racist graffiti.

How much more meaningful it is to children to offer such down-to-earth experiences that are closely related to their own lives and that include activities they can do and enjoy. The satisfaction they experience while participating in such real-life activities can build a foundation of positive attitudes toward other cultures on which we can build more advanced concepts at a later date.

Beginning Steps: Include Concrete, Visible Evidence of Cultural Diversity

Whenever Possible, Build Bridges by Using the Child's Dominant Language.   Someone should be available in every schoolroom who can understand what the child has to say and who can communicate in the child's own language. Even such simple courtesies as learning to pronounce the child's name as the family does, rather than Anglicizing it, can make a difference. Teaching English as a second language and the use of Black English are discussed more fully in chapter 12. Of course children need to learn to speak English, but a bicultural or multicultural program is a farce if we deny children the right to also use their own dominant language or dialect.

Provide a Cross-Cultural Link Between Home and School.   In recent years we have witnessed the publication of more authentic stories about African American, Indian, Mexican American, and Asian children and fewer books containing stereotypes or with primarily middle-class Caucasian characters (Hall, 2008). Records and pictures are also available, but it is not necessary to depend on only commercial sources. Children often know rhymes and songs from their families, and the teacher can learn these with the parents' coaching and then help children teach them to the group. Most homes have music CDs, but this is a resource frequently ignored by teachers who may deem the music not to their liking. However, many of the children's homes are saturated with rock or country music or Latin American rhythms, and using such music in school can draw children into movement and dance who spurn less colorful songs about little duckies waddling around the fish pond.

Stories brought from home, ethnically accurate and attractive dolls, and integrated pictures are also good choices. *Such cross-cultural materials should be available consistently, rather than presented as isolated units.* Dolls, pictures, books, and music from many cultures should be deliberately, though apparently casually, woven into the fabric of every school day.

Make yourself aware of the families' cultural customs and incorporate them into the school. According to Rebecca Maria Barrera (2004), president of the National Latino Children's Institute, "Latinos tend to do things as a family. So if you set up a parents' night, don't expect Latino parents to find a babysitter. Instead, the whole family will come, and every parent will want to bring something to eat" (p. 46). Rather than keeping a strict policy of no siblings at school functions, invite the cultural exchange and show your respect for the families' ways.

Serve Familiar Food.   This is another excellent way to honor particular backgrounds and to help children feel at home. Sometimes a shy child who appears to be a poor eater is actually just overwhelmed by the strangeness of the food served. Food in some child care centers and elementary schools still seems to be planned with the best of nutritional intentions but with total disregard of local food patterns and customs. This situation can be remedied by asking families for suggestions about appropriate food, by using recipes from ethnic cookbooks, and by employing a cook who comes from a

Benjamin La Framboise

Cross-cultural materials should be available to children all the time—not just when presented as a "learning unit."

culture similar to that of the majority of the children. Children can also be encouraged to bring recipes from home that they can cook at school, or family members may have time to participate in this way. As the children feel more at ease, it can also be fun to branch out and visit local markets and delicatessens that specialize in various ethnic foods.

The Special Family Customs of the Children Should Be Considered, Too. For example, we discovered the reason why one Arab American child was not eating much lunch was that he had been taught it is good manners to refuse food the first time it is offered!

Holidays and other special occasions are also good times for children to share various customs. For example, one young boy in our group lit Hanukkah candles and explained very clearly their purpose and the custom of gift giving.

A note of caution should be inserted here about the need to increase our sensitivity to the way some people feel about certain holidays. For example, some American Indian groups have come to feel increasingly angry about the stereotyped presentation of Indians during the Thanksgiving season. All too often Indians in these circumstances are presented as wearing feathers in their hair and dancing around, war whooping as they go, and their real contribution toward helping the Pilgrims, as well as the way the White people ultimately responded, is overlooked. For this reason some Indian groups have gone so far as to observe Thanksgiving as a time of mourning for the Wampanoag Indians—the people who helped the Pilgrims so generously during those early days and who have almost completely disappeared (Derman-Sparks & ABC Task Force, 1989; Derman-Sparks & Ramsey, 2006).

Suggestions That Foster Deeper Cross-Cultural Understanding

Building Good Human Relationships: Going Beyond Foods, Books, and Holidays

The problem with listing such ideas as those above is that so many teachers seem to think this is all there is to multicultural education, whereas it is actually only the beginning. We must realize that the basic purpose of providing multicultural experience is *not* to teach the children facts about Puerto Rico or Japan or to prove to the community that the teacher is not prejudiced. *The purpose of a multicultural curriculum is to attach positive feelings to multicultural experiences so that each child will feel included and valued and will also feel friendly and respectful toward people from other ethnic and cultural groups.*

When you get right down to it, all the multiethnic pictures and recipes and books in the world will not make much difference if teachers, in their hearts, cannot appreciate the strong points of each child and family and help the other children appreciate them, too.

Isaura Barrera (2003) suggests three guiding principles for building cross-cultural bridges: Respect, reciprocity, and responsiveness should form the basis of any teacher's multicultural approach (p. 9). Figure 4.1 demonstrates how teachers can put these principles into practice.

Dealing with Racial Comments and Slurs at School

Preprimary teachers often ask how they should reply when a 3- or 4-year-old comments on the difference in skin color of a classmate.

Generally there are two kinds of comments. The first is the kind of information-seeking question cited previously by Derman-Sparks and coworkers (Pacific Oaks College Faculty, 1985): "Will it rub off?" or "How come her backs [of hands] are brown but her fronts are pink?" Such comments should be welcomed (rather than brushed aside in an embarrassed way) because they provide opportunities to clear up confusions about skin color. Our African American head teacher has taught us all never to allow such opportunities to slip past. She is quick to explain and demonstrate that skin color does not wash off and that it is not dirty. She also points out that people may be different colors on the outside but that we are all the same color on the inside.

---

1. Show respect for every child, every family, every colleague. Be sure to acknowledge there are many different viewpoints. Respect other people's right to their own perspective.

2. Show reciprocity by inviting dialogue and discussion. Make sure others feel they can voice their ideas and that they will be heard by you. Engage in back-and-forth communication where everyone's opinion counts equally. Ask for others' opinions as much as you voice your own.

3. Show responsiveness by letting people know you have listened. Actively convey that you understand and respect their views.

Figure 4.1
Suggestions for building cross-cultural bridges based on respect, reciprocity, and responsiveness

The second kind of comment is more difficult to handle. When 4-year-old Jan yells at Jamal, "You dirty nigger, get off my trike!" it is easy for teachers to feel so upset and angry they lose sight of the probable reason why such a young child resorts to such an ugly slur.

First, it is necessary to remember that 3- and 4-year-olds do not comprehend the full extent of the insult—just as they rarely comprehend the true meaning of *son-of-a-bitch*. What they *do* know about these words is that they have a strong emotional power to hurt, and the children who use these words use them because they *are* angry and they *do* intend to hurt. This means the problem has to be dealt with in two parts.

The first part has to do with pointing out to both children the real reason why Jan is angry. She is angry because she does not want Jamal taking her trike, not because he is African American. It is important for Jamal to understand this to protect his self-esteem. It is important for Jan to realize that it is not the color of the person taking her trike that matters but the fact that she does not want *anyone* taking it. *She needs to learn to attach anger to its real cause, rather than displace it by substituting inaccurate or incorrect reasons.* This not only helps prevent the formation of prejudice but also is a basic principle of mental health everyone needs to learn and practice: *Always admit to yourself why you are really angry. Don't displace anger: Face facts.* Following this clear labeling of the reason for the fight, coupled with a brief description of each child's feelings ("I can see you're mad, and I can see you don't want to wait"), the argument has to be settled just as any other fight would have to be.

The second part of the problem, which is more likely to be mishandled, must also be faced. No one likes having their feelings hurt, and name calling of any sort is intended to and does hurt feelings. Although the usual advice about such matters is that if "bad" language is ignored it will go away, experience in the real world of early education has shown that sometimes ignoring such words works but usually it does not. It is also true that some name calling hurts worse than others; when this is the case, it is essential for the teacher to be firm and clear with the children about what is acceptable and to stop what is not. Certainly racial insults must never be tolerated.

These standards of acceptability vary from school to school. As the original author of this text wrote:

> My own level of tolerance is that although I can ignore many insults and bathroom words, I will not tolerate racial or sexist insults to myself or to anyone else. So after dealing with the social contretemps just described, I would take Jan aside for a quiet, firm talk about hurt feelings, reiterating the rule: "We do not use the word *nigger* because it hurts too much. When you're mad at Jamal, hold on to the trike and tell him, 'You can't have the trike—I'm using it now. You have to wait til I'm done,' *but we do not use the word* nigger *in our school.*"
>
> As the moment presents itself, I would also point out to Jamal that Jan was mad at him because he grabbed her trike and that she wanted to get even by calling him "nigger." Next time, he had better ask for the trike instead of just taking it. I would also make a big point with him that just because somebody says you're something or calls you a name doesn't make it true. *You* know who you are, and you don't have to let yourself be hurt by unkind people who are trying to make you feel bad. Someone who calls you a bad name is doing it to hurt you, so do your best to brush it off. Don't give the person that satisfaction.

Teachers in the elementary grades must also be watchful in protecting children from racial slurs and hatred. Unfortunately, when there is increased diversity in the student population without an accompanying anti-bias program at the school, racism can arise as students segregate themselves and view other ethnic groups as threatening. Holloway

(2003) reviewed the research on racial intolerance and reported that about 13% of middle to high school students had been called a derogatory name within the previous 6 months based on their race, ethnicity, religion, disability, gender, or sexual orientation. About a third of the students had seen hate-related graffiti at school. Elementary schools can begin proactive, anti-bias education by offering:

- Multicultural assemblies and special events
- Opportunities for diverse student populations to mix
- Conflict resolution training for children and staff
- Diversity in hiring staff
- Professional development on diversity and equity issues
- Support for bilingual students

The problem of helping minority children deal with such attacks is a difficult one and could fill a book by itself. It is important for children to be able to respond with dignity and keep control of themselves. They might respond by saying, "Call me by my name!" or say, "Don't call me that again." Early educators can teach young children a range of strategies that include ignoring the taunt, walking away and then returning with a reply, getting help from someone else, combining a response with getting help, and sharing the sadness at home. Creating a school climate where children stand up for each other against attacks will help reduce racist behavior and offer much-needed support to the victim. Providing the continuing countermeasure of building pride in ethnicity, which was discussed earlier in the chapter, is probably the strongest defense of all.

Involve and Honor All Families

As recommended earlier, teachers should seek to acquaint themselves with various cultures by reading, taking courses, learning the language, and so forth, but it is important to emphasize here that the most vigorous and lively source of ethnic learning is right on the school's doorstep—namely, the families themselves. In the long run, cooperative sharing of themselves and their opinions and skills will teach the teacher and the children the most about the personal strengths of family members. As a matter of fact, it would be difficult to conduct a multiethnic classroom without drawing on these resources.

Successful Communication Is Vital.   The teacher who is unafraid of parents and who genuinely likes them will communicate this without saying anything at all; there is really no substitute for this underlying attitude of goodwill and concern for the children. All families appreciate the teacher who has the child's welfare genuinely at heart, and this mutual interest in the child is the best base on which to build a solid teacher-family relationship. Since listening is so much more important than talking, teachers should particularly cultivate that ability in themselves (R. M. Barrera, 2001; I. Barrera et al., 2003; Gonzalez-Mena, 2007).

Other facts about communication can help when speaking with English learners. A friend of one of the authors to whom English is a foreign language suggests that teachers speak more slowly (but not more loudly!) and without condescension when talking with family members who are learning English. Sometimes writing words down in English also helps because some people read English better than they understand the spoken word.

It is also worthwhile to go to the trouble of having a translator handy when necessary. This person may be another adult, but sometimes it can even be a child who is bilingual. Notices sent home stand a much better chance of being read if they are written in the language of the home. Both languages should be printed side by side to avoid the implication that the one that comes first is better.

Welcome Family Volunteers. The problem with making families feel at ease and glad to participate in the school program is that they are always a little out of their element in the beginning. Perhaps it would be fair to require the teacher to visit and help out in the families' homes on a turnabout basis. If this were possible, it would certainly help teachers gain a better insight into how it feels to step into a strange situation in which the possibility of making fools of themselves is quite likely.

Oftentimes, teachers ask family volunteers to wipe off tables or help in the kitchen, or let them simply stand around, smiling a lot but knowing in their hearts their time is being wasted. Visitors may prefer simple tasks in the beginning because these are familiar and not threatening, and because they do not want to make waves or antagonize the teacher. Keeping them at such tasks, however, is fundamentally denigrating, teaches the children that families are not important at school, and deprives the children of the unique contribution such people can make when they are properly encouraged. For example, instead of setting up the tables for lunch, a mother might share with the children a book she has kept from her own childhood or bring pictures of her family's latest trip to India, or help the children make her child's favorite recipe, or bring the baby for a visit and let the children help bathe him (this presents an especially nice opportunity to teach about the universal similarities of human beings). Last fall one father in our group who is a member of the Wichita tribe helped the children make an authentic (and tasty) squash and cornmeal dessert. The children were delighted, and his son was ecstatic!

Remember that the fundamental purpose of providing these experiences is to create emotionally positive situations for the children and the adults who are involved. For this reason the teacher should concentrate on doing everything possible to help visitors feel comfortable and successful. It takes considerable planning, but the results are worth it.

Although it is not fair to put family members on the spot and ask them to control a group of children they do not know, it can be genuine fun and very helpful to have family volunteers come along on field trips during which everyone can be together and everyone takes some responsibility.

Families can often provide ideas for excursions, too. The children at our center greatly enjoyed a visit to a communal organic garden one spring, and they also loved a trip to a pizza parlor owned by one of the families.

Make Visitors Welcome for Meals. One of the wisest policies of the Head Start program has been its welcoming, open attitude at mealtimes. People are often spontaneously invited to share meals with the children in a Head Start center, and it is true that breaking bread binds people together in basic friendliness. If possible, this is a good policy for all schools to follow. When finances cannot support this drain, visiting parents can order lunch a day in advance and pay a nominal fee to defray the cost.

Trust and Use Family Expertise on the Advisory Board. All programs receiving federal funds are required to have advisory boards that must have at least 50% parent representation to be legal. But many schools use such boards as rubber stamps and present parents with programs and plans literally for approval, rather than for consideration

Cynthia Cassidy/Merrill

Involve and honor all families in the classroom.

and modification—a policy that certainly does not make families feel welcome or respected. A much better way to make plans is to trust the families. It is unlikely they will suggest activities or policies detrimental to the children; and when differences arise, they can usually be settled by open discussion, which educates everyone.

Teachers who seek out families' suggestions because they value their practical experience with their children will find that this approach reduces the families' feelings of defensiveness when the teacher happens to be better educated or better paid. If meetings are held during times when child care is available, more board members are likely to attend. Attendance also increases when families' suggestions are actually used and when family members are thanked sincerely for coming.

Increase the Number and Variety of Children in the School Who Come from Various Ethnic and Cultural Groups

As mentioned earlier, some schools and Head Start–type groups are luckier in the assortment of children who come naturally to their doors than other schools. Such multiethnic contacts can introduce children at an early age to the values of an integrated society. They can teach the basic fact that Lucia's face is not brown because it is dirty and can couple this learning with the fact that Lucia is fun to play with because she is such a skilled block builder.

Show Respect for People of Differing Ethnic Origins by Employing Them as Teachers

Cross-cultural learning in the children's center should be based on real ongoing experiences with real people whenever possible. This means, for example, that when we talk about how to emphasize that Mexican people are effective human beings, it is just not satisfactory at such an early level to use the historical examples recommended in many Hispanic curriculum guides. Historical figures are so remote and intangible that they do not mean much to young children.

A much more effective way of teaching children that people of all ethnic backgrounds are important is to employ them in positions of power. Many schools employ minority group members as aides. But this is far from enough. Children are quick to sense the power structure of the school, and they need to see people of all ethnic backgrounds employed in the most respected positions as teachers and directors. Only 7% of public school teachers are African American, and for Black male teachers that figure goes down to 1% (Adams, 2008).

Professional associations can and should help remedy these deficiencies by encouraging their local colleges to recruit heavily among ethnic groups other than Anglo, and they can also help by offering scholarships to sustain such students through college. Even a modest book scholarship may mean the difference for some young people between going to a community college or working in a fast-food outlet. Several of the Related Organizations and Online Resources listed at the end of this chapter offer varying types of support and information.

EMPHASIZING THE SIMILARITIES AS WELL AS VALUING THE UNIQUENESS OF PEOPLE

Not only do children and families need to have their cultural uniqueness welcomed and valued, but they also need to learn that all people have many things in common and that they are alike in some fundamental ways.

Teach the Commonality of Biological and Psychological Needs

One way to teach the similarities of all people is to emphasize the commonality of biological and psychological needs. Thus, when talking about the children's favorite food or what they traditionally eat for various holidays, the teacher can remind them that no matter what we like to eat best, everyone gets hungry and everyone likes to eat something, or the teacher can point out at the right moment that it feels good to everyone to stretch and yawn or to snuggle down in something warm and cozy.

The same principle can be taught in relation to emotions: Everyone gets mad sometimes, everyone wants to belong to somebody, most people want to have friends, and most children feel a little lost when they leave home for school.

In addition, the teacher can draw the children's attention to the fact that people often use individual, unique ways to reach a goal that most people enjoy. For example, Molly's father plays the guitar, whereas Heather's mother uses the zither; but they both use these different instruments for the pleasure of making music and singing together with the children.

Help Families Look Beyond Various Differences to Focus on Common Goals

Schools of various types can provide opportunities for friendships to form and thrive. Cooperatives are famous for doing this, of course, but it can also be accomplished in other groups. Advisory boards can draw families into projects that focus on the children and benefit everyone. This activity can take the form of a potluck dinner, with a slide show of what the children have been doing; it can be a series of discussions on topics chosen by the parents; it can be a workday combined with a picnic lunch for which everyone pitches in to clean and paint and tidy up. (There is nothing like scrubbing a kitchen floor together to generate a common bond.) It makes little difference what is chosen, as long as it results in the realization of a common goal and creates opportunities for everyone to be together in a meaningful, friendly way.

Keep Working Toward the Basic Goals of Socialization That Teach Children to Consider the Rights and Needs of Everyone

Finally, the teacher should remember that working toward the goals of socialization will help children learn that everyone has the same basic rights and privileges and that everyone is respected and treated fairly at school. The social goals most important to emphasize in relation to cross-cultural education are (a) developing empathy for how other people feel, (b) learning that everyone has rights that are respected by all, and (c) gaining skill by cooperating, rather than achieving satisfaction by competing and winning over others. If these social skills are fostered, living in the group will be a good experience for all the children, and a healthy foundation will be laid for a more truly integrated society in the future.

CAN TEACHING ABOUT CULTURAL UNIQUENESS AND SIMILARITY OF NEEDS BE COMBINED?

There is at least one way to teach young children these two concepts—that people are enjoyably unique and that they have many similar needs in common at the same time. The staff at our child care center gradually evolved this approach after passing through two earlier stages.

During the first stage, in an effort to make experiences more real for the children, students and staff tended to bring in objects from other cultures for the children to pass around and look at during group time, or the items were displayed on a table, accompanied by books and pictures about the culture. This was basically a beginning attempt to honor cultural uniqueness. We now refer to this as "our museum period."

During the second stage we increased the here-and-now aspect by doing a lot of the sort of thing described in the first part of this chapter. We cooked ethnic foods together and enjoyed them, or we celebrated a holiday or made a piñata and talked about the many wonderful ways of satisfying hunger or having parties. We still continue to offer many of these stage 2 experiences during the week, and the children continue to appreciate them.

However, the staff remained unsatisfied with these approaches. It just did not seem to us that we were helping the children grasp the reality and value of other cultures and appreciate the common humanity that binds us all. With such young children we thought we needed to link things together in more explicit and literal ways—ways they could really understand and enjoy.

To accomplish *this* goal we developed a third stage. In this current stage we are offering the children comparative experiences through which they can actually try out what it is like to sleep in a Czech feather bed, a Guatemalan hammock, and our child-sized "American" bed, and we make these comparative play experiences available for a week at a time.

In another example we set up a comparison between Japanese and Western eating styles. On the Japanese side the children took their shoes off upon entering, sat on low cushions, and used bowls and chopsticks as they partook of ramen noodles and Japanese cookies. (Our Japanese children were gratifyingly proficient with chopsticks!) On the Western side they wiped their shoes on a mat, sat on low chairs, used plates and bowls, and had noodle soup and wheat crackers. In the offing is an experience comparing the different methods by which mothers carry their babies around, and one of our students has just finished a comparison of Navajo and Anglo weaving whereby the children tried out a Navajo-style loom.

Elaborate experiences like these are a lot of fun but are also a lot of work. Fortunately experiences do not have to be this fancy to get the point across. During a warm spring rain last year one student brought some banana leaves (often used in Thailand when it rains), and the children delighted in using them and comparing them with their more familiar umbrellas. Another easy comparison to offer is a simple tasting experience. For example, it is interesting to compare French bread, tortillas, matzo, and pita bread, or various cheeses, or fruits that come from different countries such as mangoes, oranges, and guavas. For a more extended experience, grow Native American seeds such as amaranth, Hopi blue corn, Navajo watermelons, and Zapotec pleated tomatoes.

Once again, remember that families can make invaluable contributions of advice and resources if you decide to attempt stage 3 activities, and it is most beneficial when these experiences are family related and based on the cultural backgrounds of children in the group.

Please understand that these more concentrated experiences do not constitute our entire approach to cross-cultural education. If they did, that would be too much like reverting to "Japanese Day" or "Cinco de Mayo." We continue to make certain that multiethnic materials such as books, pictures, puzzles, and other equipment are used throughout the school on a matter-of-fact, daily basis. The purpose of the stage 3 activities is to accentuate that a human need can be met in more than one satisfactory way and, most important of all, that many of these ways are *fun*.

The most important element remains the teachers and the example of decency and respect they model every time they relate to a child in the classroom. The first step teachers must take is to familiarize themselves with each student's cultural and family background. Lily Wong (2004), director of Children and Family Studies in Singapore, reminds us there can be enormous diversity within a larger ethnic group, ". . . you should recognize that there is more than one group of Asian children. There is a distinct difference between children from the nations of China, Japan, Korea, and Vietnam, and children from other parts of the continent. . . . Each group has different customs, and teachers should work with parents and community leaders to find out what they are" (p. 48).

ENCOURAGING EQUITY BY PROVIDING A NONSEXIST EDUCATION AND HELPING CHILDREN VALUE THEIR OWN SEXUALITY

Today, when educational emphasis tends to be placed on the value of nonsexist education, it may be necessary to mention that it is also important to teach children about reproduction and sexual differences and to help them value their femaleness or maleness.

Even though many of us want to enable children of both sexes to step beyond the narrowly restricted ideas of sex roles and stereotypes that currently exist, we must be careful to help them value their basic sexuality as well since that is an important and deeply elemental part of every individual's personality. If children grow up with the idea that sexuality is unimportant or not valued or, worse yet, that reproduction and sex are smutty topics to be snickered about and investigated in secret, we may have unwittingly undone much of what we hoped to accomplish by adding a nonsexist emphasis to teaching.

Teaching Simple Physiological Facts

The more open and matter-of-fact teachers and families can be about differences in the anatomy of girls and boys, the more likely it is that children will not need to resort to "doctor" play or hiding in corners to investigate such differences "on the q.t." Open toileting has long been the rule in most preschool settings because when children use the same toilets, secrecy about sexual differences and toilet practices is avoided. This policy also generates opportunities for the teacher to supply answers to things young children wonder about such as why boys urinate standing up whereas girls urinate sitting down. The teacher makes simple statements about these matters: "Yes, boys and girls are made differently. Boys have penises, and so they stand up to urinate. Girls have vulvas, so they sit down to urinate." If little girls still want to know why they cannot urinate while standing up, the teacher can invite them to try it. There is no substitute for learning by experience! Casualness and answering the questions actually asked, rather than ones the teacher is nervously afraid the children will ask, should be the order of the day. With older children, too, it is important to use accurate words such as *vagina* or *penis* when referring to boys' and girls' genitalia. We adults need to remember to discuss the anatomy of little girls as well as that of little boys even though that part of the anatomy is not as apparent.

Sometimes it helps clarify matters if the adult replies to questions by asking what the child thinks the answer is; this can provide a clue to how complicated the adult explanation should be. Sometimes, though, such a return question embarrasses older 4-year-olds who are sophisticated enough to suspect they should not be asking about such things anyway, and questioning in return can cause them to stop asking. So it takes a delicate perception of each child to know whether to respond with a question or just to answer as simply and clearly as possible. Of course, if you want to keep the line open for more questions, it is deadly to betray amusement at some of the naive answers you will receive.

Since every child's self-concept is intimately tied to his or her sense of sexual worth, we must be careful to teach that each sex has an important role to play in reproduction. When grown, girls have the opportunity to carry and bear children, and boys, when grown, help start the baby growing. Then mothers and fathers work together to care for the baby following its birth.

Bear in mind when discussing the dual roles of parenting that it is necessary to think about the child's home situation. So many children now come from single-parent homes that this has to be gently taken into account in such discussions so that children do not feel "different" or peculiar if they have only one parent. And yet, it is these very children who may be least experienced with mother-father roles and who need the most help in understanding the ideal mutuality of the parenting relationship. It takes a combination of sensitivity and matter-of-factness without sentimentality or pity to deal with this problem successfully.

Once past the matter of simple anatomical differences, many adults still dread questions about reproduction and because of their discomfort either evade them (just as they avoid discussing race) or give such confused or elaborate replies that the children are bewildered. Therefore, it can be reassuring to learn that the kind of question most young children are likely to ask is, "Where did the baby come from?" or "How will it get out?" This level of questioning, common to 3- to 5-year-olds, can be answered with simple language that a baby is growing inside the mother's uterus or that it will be born through a special hole women have between their legs, near where their urine comes out but not exactly the same place.

For the slightly older child who wants to know how the baby gets inside to start with, it is far better to tell the truth rather than to talk about animals or seeds. This is because when children see animals mating, it really looks like fighting to them. The problem with the "planting seeds" idea is that it encourages them to think too literally about this concept in terms of what they already know about gardening. One little girl asked after such a discussion, "Well, what I want to know is, when you picked out that seed, did it have my picture on it?"

To avoid such misconceptions, the original author of this text suggests the teacher or family member explain that the mother and father start the baby growing in the mother by being very loving and close with each other and that when they are feeling this way, the father fits his penis inside the mother's vagina and a fluid passes into her that joins with the mother's egg and helps the baby start growing. This explanation is preferred because it is truthful and accurate and also because it mentions the role of warmth, caring, and mutual responsibility as being important parts of the experience.

Masturbation

Another aspect of helping children value their own sexuality deals with self-pleasuring masturbatory behavior so that children are not shamed by the teacher's reprimand and do not come to feel their sexual impulses are unclean or "bad."

The pioneering research into sexual behaviors by Masters and Johnson has long shown that masturbation is commonplace in adult males and females (Masters, Johnson, & Kilodny, 1994) and it is in children, too (Shelov & Hannemann, 2004). The question that confronts teachers once they admit the frequency and normality of the behavior is what to do about it, since it is still true that masturbating is not acceptable public behavior. It seems wisest to take the child aside and explain that you realize such behavior feels good but that it is something people do only in private.

Meeting the Special Needs of Boys in School

Still another aspect of helping children value their own sexuality has to do with recognizing the boys' needs for high-physical-energy activities and meeting their needs for role models in the school. Although it is difficult to talk about this without having it misinterpreted as advocating sexist practices, experience has shown it is necessary to remind female teachers how important it is to provide young boys many experiences that fit their needs and that do not feminize them because the temptation is to approve of "female type" activities and reward those with positive attention (Gartrell, 2006; Gurian & Stevens, 2004, 2005; Mercurio, 2003).

Boys' physical activity needs appear to differ from those of girls (Desouza & Czerniak, 2002; Gartrell, 2006; Gurian & Stevens, 2004, 2005; Mercurio, 2003). Research shows boys tend to engage in more rough-and-tumble play than girls and that they are more physically aggressive than girls are after age 2 (Desouza & Czerniak, 2002; Gartrell, 2006; Gurian & Stevens, 2004, 2005). But female teachers tend to suppress this vigor and energy since it is contrary to the teachers' own behavior patterns and also makes running a classroom more difficult (Gartrell, 2006; Gurian & Stevens, 2004, 2005; Mercurio, 2003). Although all children need opportunities for vigorous physical activity, boys do seem to need it especially, and we must provide for meeting that need. Their play requires large, sturdy equipment, plenty of space, and a teacher who genuinely welcomes such activity, rather than regards it as a threat to the ability to control the children.

Boys not only must be supplied with enough room to move and to let off steam but also must have the chance to form relationships with men who can serve as models for them (Gartrell, 2006; Gurian & Stevens, 2004, 2005; Mercurio, 2003). In an age when the divorce rate remains high and many unmarried women are electing to raise their children rather than surrender them for adoption, many children come from single-parent, mother-centered homes. The effect on boys' developing sense of masculinity in these mother-centered, father-absent homes varies. In view of the fact that over 90% of early childhood and elementary school teachers are female, every effort must be made to provide boys with adult male role models (S. P. Johnson, 2008; Menteach, 2006).

Common sense, however, cannot help encouraging one to believe that the presence of a father facilitates sex role development at every age (although evidence also suggests that boys can develop normally without it). Girls also benefit from such experience because it probably helps them develop concepts of masculinity and femininity. For these reasons centers and schools should do all they can to provide boys and girls consistent contacts with men who care about children.

Incidentally one of the continuing and unfortunate examples of sexism in our society is the fact that few men are employed as early childhood teachers. In 2006 the U.S. Department of Labor reported that 97.7% of people employed as preschool and kindergarten teachers were women. This disparity is attributable to several factors: gender stereotyping (the perception that such work requires the nurturing qualities commonly attributed to females rather than to males), the feeling for men of being an outsider in the female culture of child care, the low pay and low status of the profession, and the rising concerns about the potential for accusations of child abuse (Menteach, 2006).

These difficulties mean that we need to think of ingenious ways to include men as participants in the school day. High school and college men can often be employed as aides, and occasionally warmhearted fathers, grandfathers, uncles, and the mother's boyfriend will volunteer to show up regularly and spend time with the children. All the contacts, though admittedly not as satisfactory as a father's continuing presence in the home, will help both boys and girls formulate their concepts of what it means to be a man or woman in our society and ideally will help boys and girls grow up to be sturdy, capable men and women themselves.

Benjamin La Framboise

Encourage and support men in their role as teachers of young children.

Suggestions for Providing a Nonsexist Curriculum

"Are boys really better than girls at analyzing problems?" "Are girls really better than boys at nurturing and comforting others?" The answers to these questions remain unclear and certainly controversial. Early research in the 1990s indicated that there were no significant behavioral differences between boys and girls (Jacklin & Baker, 1993; Kindlon & Thompson, 1999). However, teachers have consistently noticed differences in school behaviors, attitudes, and achievement. One such difference in schools across the nation is that boys account for two thirds of all learning disability diagnoses and 90% of discipline referrals (Gartrell, 2006; Gurian & Stevens, 2004, 2005).

Michael Gurian, who has developed a "nature-based approach" to education, uses recent brain research to support his thesis that girls' and boys' brains are "wired" differently. According to Gurian & Stevens (2004), "The hippocampus . . . is larger in girls than in boys, increasing girls' learning advantage, especially in the language arts" (p. 22). Differences in brain functioning account for girls outperforming boys in reading, writing, and overall school achievement, and boys' inclination for abstract-spatial learning. Gurian does not suggest that girls and boys be segregated from different learning domains, but rather that teachers use this knowledge to encourage boys' and girls' learning in all areas equally.

One way that ideas about sex roles can be changed to be more equitable without undermining the child's pride in gender is by presenting an open curriculum that provides opportunities for both sexes to participate in all learning activities, rather than restricting children to obsolete sex role expectations. Teachers should work to develop wider competence and equal privileges for both sexes. Providing boys *and girls* opportunities to practice with "boy-preferred" toys such as blocks, dominoes, and building toys improves the children's visual-spatial ability—a skill on which boys typically score higher.

This skill is fundamental to later achievements in such fields as architecture, mathematics, and engineering and so is one well worth fostering in children of both sexes. Surely activities such as woodworking and blocks should be freely available to girls, just as opportunities to enjoy dressing up or sewing should be available to boys. The chance to experience a full range of roles enriches the knowledge of each sex, does not produce sexual perverts, and, ideally, deepens understanding and empathy for the opposite sex.

It is, of course, important not only to offer wider opportunities to girls but also to offer them to boys. For example, opportunities for additional male roles should be included in homemaking such as scaled-to-comfortable-size men's clothing for workers of various kinds. These garments should be freely available for use by both sexes, and boys should be encouraged to join in formerly female-dominated activities such as cooking and caring for children. Teachers may encounter a bit more resistance from boys when such cross-gender activities are first proposed than they will from girls. This is because girls are less criticized by their peers when they engage in "masculine preferred" activities than boys are. Even when teachers encourage boys to cook or to engage in self-expressive art activity, other boys do criticize them for such behavior, so it is well to be on the lookout for such remarks by their peers and discourage them when possible.

Research has shown that most of the early childhood curriculum stresses skills girls already possess but that boys often lack—leading to more behaviors that teachers view as difficult and respond to in a negative way (Gartrell, 2006; Gurian & Stevens, 2004, 2005; Mercurio, 2003). These include emphasis on verbal activities (e.g., large-group time), small-muscle activities (e.g., cutting, painting), and assistance in gaining impulse control. Participation in these activities, which is determined primarily by female teachers, is virtually obligatory.

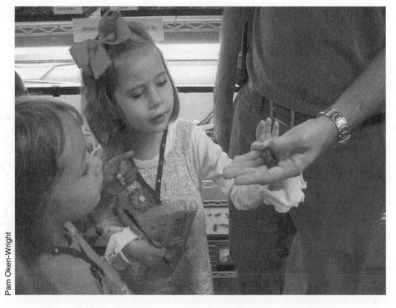

Encourage girls to investigate subjects usually reserved for boys—such as science (and encourage boys to explore areas usually reserved for girls). These girls are becoming familiar with a Madagascar hissing cockroach.

However, much of the curriculum that might remediate deficiencies in little girls' education is left to "choice and chance." Participation in such activities as block play and large-muscle activities that might also aid in developing spatial awareness are part of self-select time (as is selection of various science activities).

Based on brain research and the work by Gurian and Stevens (2004, 2005), Figure 4.2 offers suggestions for providing an education that supports girls' and boys' natures and patterns of development.

The Research Study in this chapter shows how preschool children's learning styles and preferences reflect gender differences, in this case, with regard to science and the study of insects. The authors make several recommendations based on these results to ensure more equitable learning opportunities for boys and girls. As the research by Desouza and Czerniak so clearly indicates, it is essential to provide equal opportunities for girls and boys, for example, science experiences and encouragement for girls. Since boys in school are in an environment managed mostly by female teachers, it is also essential to provide boys with opportunities that enhance their development as healthy males.

Importance of Evaluating Educational Materials

All teachers should take a closer look at the materials they offer for educational activities. More nonsexist, multiracial materials in the form of puzzles, lotto games, and dolls are becoming available, but these materials are rarely sufficient for the needs of the school. Teachers should also expect to make many of their own items.

Although it remains necessary to search out adequate activity materials, the good news is that multicultural and nonsexist books are increasing in number (Hall, 2008) and are quite readily available. *Across Cultures: A Guide to Multicultural Literature for Children* (East & Thomas, 2007) is an annotated bibliography of multicultural books for preschoolers through the elementary grades. Appendix E offers some helpful guidelines to follow when the supply of these materials ebbs and flows as the market dictates. Publishers print what the public will buy. If we want to have a continuing supply of good-quality books that represent the cultures of all the children we teach, we have to write to publishers and make our desires known.

Importance of Attitude and Modeling

More basic than all the nonsexist curriculum in the world is the need to sensitize women and men to the negative consequences of unconsciously biased sexist teaching. What happens to the self-esteem of young boys who are criticized by female teachers for their high-energy, aggressive response to life? What effect does the constant use of such words as mailman, fireman, and policeman have on young girls and their anticipation of future occupations?

Or on a positive note, what do children conclude when they see their female teacher confidently using the electric drill to install a new chalkboard or their male teacher matter-of-factly sewing a button on a child's shirt?

We do indeed have a long way to go in raising our awareness and control of the long-ingrained patterns of behavior and speech that perpetuate sexist and racist teaching, but we have come a long way, too. The danger to guard against is that complacency may permit us to become careless or to stop trying. Doing that opens the way to recapitulating the racist/sexist problem.

Ways to encourage boys' full and healthy development

1. Provide boys with role models and a variety of situations to help encourage a range of emotional responses. Caregivers should provide an environment that promotes communication and acceptance of emotionality. Give boys encouragement and the words they need to express what they are feeling.

2. Communicate with boys in a way that appreciates their dignity and self-worth. Understand that boys may have more difficulty expressing their feelings; therefore, it is important to ask specific questions.

3. Acknowledge and understand that boys have a high activity level. It is important to provide plenty of time and a variety of places and physical activities for the release of this energy.

4. Free boys from feeling ashamed when they are afraid or vulnerable. Let them know they don't always have to win, be the strongest, or never cry. Help them understand that kindness and empathy stem from inner strength.

5. Use the guidance approach discussed in chapter 9 to help boys develop flexible, effective self-regulation skills. Punishment and anger from the teacher result in more anger or defiance from boys rather than the development of self-discipline.

6. Provide positive male role models in the classroom. Make sure boys see men around them in a variety of roles. Allow opportunities for boys to get close to adult men whether they are teachers or family volunteers.

7. Use beadwork and other manipulatives to promote development of fine-motor skills.

8. Make learning experiential and kinesthetic.

Ways to encourage girls' full and healthy development

1. Organize activities that require spatial exploration.

2. Offer activities for practice in large-muscle coordination and development of large-motor skills (increase structured gym activities).

3. Provide equipment that enhances investigatory activity, for example water and sand tables to explore science concepts.

4. Plan activities that permit learning from following directions.

5. Organize tasks that require cooperative groups of three or more children in which girls take a leadership role and learn negotiation skills.

6. Plan tasks that encourage distance from adults.

7. Provide opportunities for experimenting with a wide range of future career options.

8. Post photos around the room of girls' successes particularly in nontraditional roles.

Figure 4.2
Ways to encourage full and healthy development of children

RESEARCH STUDY

Gender Differences in Preschoolers' Science Learning and Social Behavior

Research Question: Desouza and Czerniak wanted to know if boys and girls exhibited the same behaviors in both free play and during teacher-directed activities. They also wanted to know, more specifically, which social behaviors boys and girls exhibited during science activities and how each gender approached scientific subjects.

Research Method: Researchers looked at 4- and 5-year-olds over 2 years at a university early childhood center. The observed activities took place in a large, center-based classroom. The researchers took turns observing free play and group time activities. Science topics were introduced during group time, including the study of mammals, reptiles, birds, insects, amphibians, and plant life.

Research Results: Desouza and Czerniak found that girls played more in the housekeeping area and with puzzles, while boys played more with cars and blocks. Boys played more with boys, and girls played more with girls. The researchers found that boys were more active, aggressive, and more often violent than girls. Girls displayed more caring behavior in general, and more specifically toward animals.

The researchers also found that boys had more general knowledge of animals and insects and displayed more curiosity and spontaneity toward science activities. Also, girls tended to seek attention and help from teachers, while boys tended to resist offers of help. Finally, girls showed more fear and negative reactions toward insects.

Implications for Teaching: This study had a small sample size of 49 children, and the researchers caution against generalizing their findings to other children. However, significant gender differences were found, and when teachers understand these differences, they can work to provide better educational experiences in which both girls and boys benefit.

The researchers suggest teachers do the following to encourage equitable learning opportunities for boys and girls:

- Help to channel aggressive tendencies into positive learning experiences; for example, boys and girls can work together to build a stable block structure. This type of experience provides a chance to teach science concepts and for both boys and girls to develop spatial abilities.
- Set up cooperative learning situations, so that girls' learning isn't inhibited as it is when learning is more competitive.
- Provide opportunities for both girls and boys to experience active learning (visiting farms, zoos, science centers), and bring a variety of specimens into the classroom.
- Focus on girls' successes to help them become more self-confident and overcome their fears.
- Pay attention to and take advantage of gender preferences in toys, activities, and interests. For example, teachers can use housekeeping toys to give girls experience with measurement, comparison, and observational skills.

Source: Data taken from "Social Behaviors and Gender Differences Among Preschoolers: Implications for Science Activities," by J. M. S. Desouza and C. M. Czerniak, 2002, *Journal of Research in Childhood Education, 18*(2), 175–188.

SUMMARY

Since children as young as age 2 years differentiate between people of differing skin color and gender, it is important to begin a program of cross-cultural, nonsexist education as early as possible so that they learn that *different*, be it a difference in sex or race or culture, does not mean *inferior*.

Teaching this principle of equity can be achieved in several ways. First and fundamentally, we want to emphasize that every individual has the unique, treasurable gift of individuality to share with others. Second, no matter how unique the individual is, each person has some basic needs in common with the rest of the people in the world that can be satisfied in a variety of ways. Third and finally, every child of either sex or any color should be encouraged to explore the full range of his or her abilities and potential competencies.

Schools that incorporate such cross-cultural, nonsexist emphases in their programs help children learn to value the differences and similarities in themselves, their friends, and their teachers as being positive strengths. This positive valuing lies at the heart of equity in education.

Questions and Activities

1. Have you been with a young child who commented on differences in skin color or other differences related to ethnic group membership? What did the child say, and what would be an effective way to reply to these comments or questions?

2. Do you think it might be confusing or contradictory to teach children that people are alike and different at the same time?

3. Do you ever wonder whether perhaps you are unconsciously behaving in a prejudiced way by paying more attention to children from certain ethnic groups and less to members of other groups or favoring girls more than boys or vice versa? One way to check up on yourself is to ask a trusted colleague to keep track for various time periods of your contacts with the children over a week or more. All it takes is a list of the children's names and putting a check by each one for each contact made. If you wish to refine this strategy, plus and minus checks can be used, depending on the kind of encounter, whether it is disciplinary, showing positive interest, and so on. (A word of encouragement: This behavior is fairly easy to correct once the teacher is aware of it.)

4. Analyze the books in your center. Do some present both boys and girls as effective, active people? Do some appear to perpetuate stereotypes of little girl and little boy behavior? Are these books necessarily undesirable?

Predicaments

1. You are working in a school that serves many single-parent families in which mothers have primary care of the children. Many of the children, therefore, have relatively little experience with men. Suggest some practical plans that would help alleviate this deficit for the children in your care.

2. Take a few minutes and make two columns headed "What I Am Good at Doing" and "What I Am Not Good at Doing" and then analyze why you are either good or not good at those particular activities. If you answer, "Well, I never learned that," identify what prevented you from learning it, whatever it was.

3. Is it really the responsibility of schools to provide information about reproduction and gender differences? If you think it is not, how would you handle such comments as, "What happened to her wee-wee—did they cut it off?" or (from a little boy), "When I grow up, I'm gonna have six children! There won't hardly be room in my stomach I'm gonna have so many!"

Self-Check Questions for Review

Content-Related Questions

1. When incorporating multicultural and nonsexist goals into the curriculum, what are the two fundamental principles we want children to learn?

2. Are preschool children too young to notice ethnic and gender differences? Cite some examples that support your answer.

3. Name five things you can do to control your own prejudices.

4. Provide several examples of ways multicultural experiences could be consistently included in an early childhood curriculum.

5. Provide several examples of ways nonsexist experiences could be consistently included in an early childhood curriculum.

6. Why is encouraging pride in sexuality an important part of nonsexist education?

Integrative Questions

1. Can you produce examples of sexism being expressed at the college level? At the preschool level? At the elementary school level?

2. Research shows that teachers comment on girls' appearance, such as dress and hair, more than they do boys. How do you think this behavior might influence girls' concepts of their sex roles? How might the boys' sex role concepts also be influenced?

3. List some principles that cross-cultural and nonsexist education have in common.

Reference for Further Reading

Copple, C. (Ed.). (2003). *A world of difference: Readings on teaching young children in a diverse society.* Washington, DC: National Association for the Education of Young Children. A rich assortment of articles about almost every aspect of diversity and multicultural learning is included here.

Related Organizations and Online Resources

Center for Research on Education, Diversity and Excellence (CREDE). This federally funded research and development program is focused on improving the education of students whose ability to reach their potential is challenged by language or cultural barriers, race, geographic location, or poverty. Information is available at http://www.crede.ucsc.edu/.

Coalition for Asian American Children and Families (CACF). This is an advocacy organization dedicated to improving the health and well-being of Asian American children in New York City. Many resources are available at http://www.cacf.org/.

Head Start. Since its conception in 1965, Head Start has been dedicated to multicultural, nonsexist education. Many valuable and practical resources relating to bilingual, cross-cultural education are available at http://eclkc.ohs.acf.hhs.gov/hslc.

MenTeach. This organization serves as a clearinghouse for research, education, and advocacy with a commitment to increase the number of men teaching young children in early and elementary education. Many resources are available at http://www.menteach.org.

National Black Child Development Institute (NBCDI). For over 3 decades, NBCDI has worked to build family support services. Information can be found at http://www.nbcdi.org/.

National Center on Fathers and Families (NCOFF). The center is dedicated to research and practice that expands the knowledge base on father involvement and family developments. Information is available at http://www.ncoff.gse.upenn.edu.

National Indian Education Association. The mission of the National Indian Education Association is to support traditional Native cultures and values, to enable Native learners to become contributing members of their communities, to promote Native control of educational institutions, and to improve educational opportunities and resources for American Indians, Alaska Natives, and Native Hawaiians throughout the United States. Information can be found at http://www.niea.org/.

National Task Force on Early Childhood Education for Hispanics. This task force was established for the purpose of identifying major educational challenges facing Hispanic children throughout the United States from birth through the primary grades and making recommendations for actions. Information is available at http://www.ecehispanic.org/.

Tolerance.org. This is an online destination for people interested in dismantling bigotry and creating communities that value diversity. Resources are available at http//:www.tolerance.org.

CHAPTER five

Welcoming Children Who Have Special Educational Requirements

About a child who might need special help but were unsure what to say to the parent about it?

Whether you knew enough about a particular disability to admit a child with that condition to your class?

How to tell whether a child really needed help from a psychologist?

What to do with that exceptionally bright little boy who acts so bored when he comes to school?

. . . IF YOU HAVE, THE MATERIAL IN THE FOLLOWING PAGES WILL HELP YOU.

Whether they're handicapped or healthy, homeless or affluent, safe or at-risk, children need each other to grow. Children need to be together, in a safe, warm and caring environment—to play together, learn together. The rooted and the displaced, the graceful runner and the child who'll never walk, the sure-of-himself, easy smiler, and the child who's afraid to risk loving again all become part, each of the other.

Gretchen Buchenholz (in L. G. Johnson, Rogers, Johnson, & McMillan, 1993)

. . . the United Nations which recognized the inherent dignity and worth and the equal and inalienable rights of all members of the human family as the foundation of freedom, justice and peace in the world . . . has proclaimed and agreed that everyone is entitled to all the rights and freedoms set forth therein, without distinction of any kind . . . to ensure the full enjoyment by children with disabilities of all human rights and fundamental freedoms on an equal basis with other children.

The United Nations (2006)

Although all children have special educational needs at one point or another in their lives, some children require specialized attention more consistently. This group involves a wide assortment of children, including those who are physically challenged, who are emotionally disturbed, or whose intellectual development either lags behind or is markedly ahead of their peers. In short, the category of exceptionality covers children who deviate in at least one respect far enough from the typical that they are noticeable in the group because of this deviation (National Dissemination Center for Children with Disabilities [NICHCY], 2003).

The U.S. Department of Education (2006a) reports that the number of children ages 3 to 21 years identified as having disabilities continues to rise with 6.8 million children and youth receiving educational assistance for their disabilities. In the year 2003, youth receiving special education services made up 13.7% of all students between the ages of 3 and 21. Of these special education students, 75% were classified as having either learning disabilities or speech/language impairments as their primary disabilities, 9% were classified with mental retardation, 6% were classified with emotional disturbances, and 10% were classified with other health impairments or disabilities (NICHCY, 2003; U.S. Department of Education, 2006a).

The increasing attention to identifying and including children who have special educational requirements is the result of Congress enacting and revising the *Individuals with Disabilities Education Act* (IDEA) and the *Americans with Disabilities Act* (ADA). These laws mandate that such youngsters be educated in the most facilitative, least restrictive educational environments (Division for Early Childhood and the National Association for the Education of Young Children [NAEYC], 2000; Lillie & Vakil, 2002; NICHCY, 2008; Sandall, Hemmeter, Smith, & McLean, 2005; U.S. Department of Education, 2006b; Vakil, Freeman, & Swim, 2003).

Perhaps you are thinking, "It's nice these laws exist, but what does that have to do with me?" The answer is threefold. First, passage of these laws means that help for young children with disabilities is more readily available than it was in the past. This is a wonderful comfort to teachers who still come across children who need help but have escaped the notice of other professionals before entering school. Second, it means that because of certain requirements in the laws, many more children who have disabilities are attending our "regular" public or independent early childhood centers and elementary schools, and each of them will come equipped with an *individualized education program* (IEP) identifying specific skills the teacher and child are supposed to work on together. Finally, it means that we teachers are expected to become part of the treatment teams engaged in working with such children (Division for Early Childhood and NAEYC, 2000; NICHCY, 2008; Sandall et al., 2005; Sandall, Schwartz, Joseph et al., 2002; U.S. Department of Education, 2006b; Vakil et al., 2003).

These circumstances make it increasingly important for teachers to have a practical, working knowledge of the more common ways children deviate from the typical and also to understand how to work with such youngsters and the specialists who help them. Examples and resources are provided throughout *The Whole Child* in relevant chapters, but experience has shown it is also helpful for students to have a concise source of information presented all together. That is the reason this chapter is included in the text. It is important to realize, however, that the subject of exceptionality is *huge*, and *so only an introduction can be offered here. It is hoped it will pave the way to further reading and education in this important area.*

IDENTIFYING CHILDREN WHO HAVE SPECIAL NEEDS AND FINDING HELP FOR THEM: THE TEACHER AS A SCREENING AGENT

One advantage teachers have that physicians do not is that they see the same children for extended periods of time, and this makes it possible to be aware of physical, emotional, and cognitive behavior that may indicate a serious underlying difficulty. It is a mistaken notion that such difficulties are always first noticed in the physician's office or by parents. Physicians see children for brief periods of time, often under conditions quite stressful to the child. These comments are not intended to imply that a highly trained medical specialist knows less than early childhood teachers do. Rather, teachers should keep their eyes open since they have the advantage of seeing the child in a natural setting for extended periods of time, and they have seen many youngsters of similar age and background. Thus it is possible that they may become aware of difficulties that should be drawn to the attention of the family and physician or psychologist.

The sooner such potential disabilities are identified, the sooner they may be ameliorated and further formation of undesirable habit patterns and emotional reactions reduced (Sandall et al., 2005; Steele, 2004). Sometimes early diagnosis means a condition can be cleared up entirely (as when a child's hearing is restored following a tonsillectomy-adenoidectomy), and sometimes the effect of the condition can only be mitigated (as is often the case with children who have cognitive delays). But *nothing* can be done until the child is identified as needing assistance and a referral has been successfully carried out. These are points at which teachers' help is crucial because they are most likely to provide day-by-day linkage between the family and the services that can help them.

Referring Children for Special Help: Calling the Difficulty to the Family's Attention

Calling a family's attention to a special problem requires delicacy and tact on the part of the teacher since it is all too easy for parents to feel that they are being attacked or criticized and that they have failed to be good parents. This is particularly true if the teacher must raise the issue of a pronounced behavior problem. However, the teacher can do several things to reduce the strength of this understandable defensive reaction.

If Teachers Listen Carefully While Talking with the Families, They May Find That the Families Themselves Are Raising the Problem Very Tentatively

For example, the parent may ask nervously, "How did he do today?" or comment, "He's just like his older brother. Doesn't he ever sit still?" Many teachers respond to such questions by just as nervously reassuring the parent, saying brightly, "Oh, he did just fine!" (while thinking wryly "Just fine, that is, if you don't count biting Ben, destroying Julie's block tower, and refusing to come to story time"). Rather than being falsely reassuring, the teacher could use the opening the parent has provided by responding,

"I'm glad you asked. He *is* having some difficulties at school. I'm beginning to think it's time to put our heads together and come up with some special ways to help him."

It Takes Time to Bring About a Referral

It is best to raise problems gradually with parents because it takes a while for families to accustom themselves to the fact that their child may need special help. Even such an apparently simple thing as having an eye examination may loom as either a financial or emotional threat to particular families, and teachers should not expect instant acceptance and compliance with their recommendations just because they have finally worked up their courage to the point of mentioning a difficulty.

The Teacher Should Have the Reasons Why the Child Needs Special Help Clearly in Mind Before Raising the Issue with Families

The recommendation of having the reasons for needing special help clearly in mind before talking with a child's family is not intended to mean that teachers should confront families with a long, unhappy list of grievances against the child. Rather, they should be prepared to provide examples of the problem while explaining gently and clearly to the family the reason for their concern.

For example, while examining photographs taken for this book, the staff and one of the authors were surprised to notice that one child was looking at a seriation game with her eyes consistently "crossed." It was helpful to use these snapshots with the family when suggesting they have her eyes examined.

Usually, of course, one does not have anything as concrete as a picture to share, but episodes or examples of the problem can be described almost as well and are essential to have in mind when discussing such difficulties with parents.

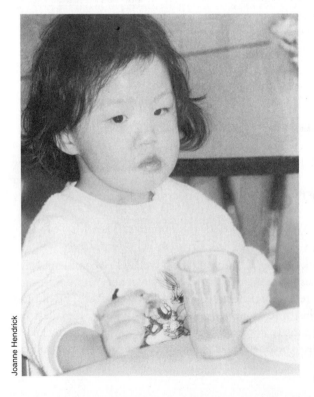

Joanne Hendrick

This youngster has the condition called lazy eye, or amblyopia. It is important for this condition to receive prompt medical attention.

It Is Not the Teacher's Place to Diagnose

A particular behavior can have many different causes. For example, failure to pay attention in story hour may be the consequence of a hearing loss, inappropriate reading material, borderline intelligence, fatigue, poor eyesight, or simply needing to go to the toilet. The teacher's role is to recognize that a difficulty exists, do everything possible to mitigate it in the group, inform the parent, and suggest a referral to an expert professional for diagnosis and treatment when necessary.

Therefore, when conferring with the family, the teacher should discuss the symptoms and express concern but avoid giving the impression he or she knows for certain what the real cause of the problem may be. Instead the teacher should become an ally with the family in a joint quest to find the answer together.

Finding the Appropriate Referral Source

Teachers need to acquaint themselves with the variety of referral sources available in their community since it is both senseless and cruel to raise a problem with families and have no suggestions about where they can go for help. When the problem appears to be serious, the foremost resource to seek out is whatever agency in your state administers IDEA. The names of these agencies vary widely; typical names are the State Health Department, Department of Human Services, or Office of Children, Youth, and Families.

Other resources include directories of community services, public health nurses, pediatricians, local children's hospitals, school counselors, county medical societies, and mental health clinics. The same resource and referral agency that provides lists of child care sources for parents and employers often knows of appropriate referrals, as does the United Way. Whenever possible, it is always desirable to list three referral possibilities so that the family has the opportunity to select the one they think suits them best. The National Dissemination Center for Children with Disabilities (NICHCY), listed at the end of this chapter in Related Organizations and Online Resources, is a very helpful resource and can offer assistance in locating the appropriate agency in each state.

Observing Professional Ethics

As already mentioned, the teacher should not assume the role of diagnostician. Often, however, the teacher possesses information that is of value to the specialist to whom the child is referred. It can be a temptation to pick up the telephone and call this person without pausing to ask parental permission, but this is a violation of professional ethics. The teacher must obtain a parent's consent before talking to the specialist. Some professional people even require that this permission be in writing before any information is exchanged. After permission is obtained, exchanges of information and suggestions from the specialist can be extraordinarily helpful and should be used whenever the opportunity presents itself.

Also, when dealing with a special case, the teacher may be tempted to discuss it with people who are not entitled to know about it, because it is so interesting and perhaps makes the teacher feel important. This gossiping is an unforgivable violation of the family's privacy, and a teacher must never indulge the desire to do this (NAEYC, 1998b).

INCLUDING CHILDREN WHO HAVE DISABILITIES

What the Laws Say

Go to MyEducationLab and select the topic "Special Needs/Inclusion." Under Activities and Applications, watch the video *Inclusion in an Early Childhood Class.* How can teachers plan for the inclusion of children with disabilities in the early childhood classroom?

Long before Congress passed laws related to children who have disabilities, many nursery schools made it a point to welcome these children into their groups and their inclusion has usually worked out quite satisfactorily. The individualized, developmentally appropriate curriculum characteristic of preschools, children's centers, Head Start, and some kindergarten and primary classrooms makes it relatively easy to incorporate a child with an IEP into the life of the school. Indeed, one would hope that every child in these schools already has at least an informal IEP developed for that child and carried in the back of the teacher's mind.

This trend toward integration has been augmented by the passage of the two pieces of legislation mentioned at the beginning of this chapter: the IDEA and the ADA. The IDEA was originally enacted by Congress in 1975 and has been revised many times over the years. Recent amendments were passed by Congress in December 2004, with final regulations published in August 2006 (NICHCY, 2008).

The IDEA basically says that every child (including infants and toddlers) with a disability is entitled to a free public education, that each of these youngsters shall be provided with an *individualized education program* (IEP) or an *individualized family service plan* (IFSP) for the youngest children, and that he or she shall be educated in the least restrictive environment. Provisions are also included for parental input and protest opportunities to ensure that the intentions of the law are carried out in fact (Division for Early Childhood and NAEYC, 2000; NICHCY, 2008; Sandall et al., 2005; U.S. Department of Education, 2006b). A wide variety of disabilities ranging from cognitive or emotional disabilities to physical problems are covered, and many

Every child with a disability is entitled to a free public education and inclusion in the life of the school.

support services such as physical therapy and speech and language training are mandated. Emphasis is on service to families and fostering family autonomy and decision making (Divison for Early Childhood and NAEYC, 2000; NICHCY, 2008; Sandall et al., 2005).

The ADA legislation is sometimes spoken of as the "civil rights bill for people with handicaps." It states that people with disabilities are entitled to equal rights in employment, state and local public services, and public accommodations. This law makes it illegal to discriminate against people with disabilities in employment, public services, and public accommodations, such as schools and early childhood programs (Division for Early Childhood and NAEYC, 2000; Sandall et al., 2005; U.S. Department of Education, 2006b).

When Planning the IEP, It Is Essential to Have a Careful Assessment of the Child's Accomplishments and Abilities Available

The assessment is usually carried out by a team of professional people versed in the areas of development in which the child's difficulties lie. Working with the family, the team does its best to identify the youngster's strengths and problem areas. Then it recommends things to do to help the child develop as well as possible. These assessments should involve a range of measures including naturalistic observations, parent reports, various standardized tests, a physical examination if it is warranted, and whatever special measures are appropriate to gain further insight into the individual youngster's disability (Cook, Tessier, & Klein, 2003; Division for Early Childhood and NAEYC, 2000; Sandall et al., 2005; U.S. Department of Education, 2006b).

Once the assessment has been accomplished, the information is pooled. A team is formed composed of whoever will be teaching the child, at least one of the parents, a representative of the school district, and—if it is a first meeting—a member of the assessment team. During this conference the IEP is developed that outlines the most important learning goals and objectives for the child and suggested ways to achieve those goals.

For example, one child's IEP might include developing muscular dexterity and social independence by pushing the bar handle of the water tap while washing his hands, whereas another child's might include paying attention to hand gestures when the teacher uses sign language. Follow-up meetings are scheduled to revise and update the IEP as needed.

Although IEPs may sound like a good deal of paperwork (and they are!), the clear intention of the law is to benefit children who have special needs and to protect their rights to a free, public education—a right sorely abused in prior times. They also have the virtue of protecting the family's right to privacy and their right to participate actively in planning what is best for their child's well-being and future.

LEARNING TO WORK AS A MEMBER OF THE TEAM

As more and more children with disabilities are placed in regular preschool and elementary school settings, there is an additional reason to be grateful for IDEA: It requires that support services be provided to children who need them. This is a blessing since early childhood educators, though strong in offering a range of developmentally appropriate activities, are likely to be weak in providing the highly specialized educational strategies some children with special needs require. We desperately need the examples and advice such specialists can provide.

Currently the trend is to incorporate these special services into the setting right along with the child and to encourage the teacher and other specialists to combine their skills. This is called the *transdisciplinary approach*. It is a desirable change from former days when the speech therapist, for example, would arrive and take the child away to a quiet place to be drilled on building language skills in isolation from ongoing classroom life. In addition to disrupting whatever the child was doing, the problem with this approach was getting the training to carry over into real-life situations (Cook et al., 2003; Guralnick, 2001; Howard, Williams, & Lepper, 2005).

myeducationlab

Go to MyEducationLab and select the topic "Speical Needs/Inclusion." Under Activities and Applications, watch the video *Early Intervention.* What are the benefits of early intervention and why is it an important component of early childhood education?

Now physical therapists, speech pathologists, and other specialists are more likely to integrate their work into the ongoing school program—seizing opportunities for the child to practice desired skills as they arise during play. This is particularly easy to do at the preschool and kindergarten level because the self-select, open-choice periods provide golden opportunities for practice to take place in a natural life setting (Cook et al., 2003; Guralnick, 2001; Howard et al., 2005).

The advantages of this activity-oriented approach are obvious, but it is up to the teacher and specialist to make it work, and this is not always easy! For example, the educational philosophies of the two people may differ considerably. Many special education teachers unfortunately have no background in early childhood. To these uninitiated people, self-select time may appear to be more like bedlam than the carefully planned array of educational opportunities the early childhood teacher perceives it as being. Nor do some of these people understand the value of play in the lives of all children.

Then, too, many special education specialists are devoted to the behavior modification approach to learning. There's no denying that approach has merit, particularly when one is working with certain kinds of severe disabilities. However, the early childhood teacher often finds the charts and reward systems this approach typically depends on to be repugnant.

Clearly both teacher and specialist will need to develop generous amounts of appreciation for each other's points of view and the unique strengths each brings to the children if the team effort is to succeed. Without that mutual appreciation, the specialist may feel so unwelcome and the teacher so irritated and threatened that the old, isolated approach to instruction will be reinstated. Unfortunately it is the child who pays the price in this ego-fraught situation.

The best way to overcome prejudices and build respect is to make certain that *regular* times are scheduled for team members to talk together; *hurried conferences at the door when the children are present are not sufficient.* Sometimes these chats can fit in during the lunch break, or they can even take place over the phone. They present invaluable opportunities for teacher and specialist to exchange concerns and ideas and to coordinate strategies. This mutual approach to problem solving, *particularly when families are included,* maximizes the child's opportunities to thrive.

GETTING STARTED WITH A CHILD WHO HAS A DISABILITY

Welcome the Child and Family

Above and beyond adapting the program to meet the needs of a child with a disability, it is crucial to extend a sincere welcome. The teacher must reflect an attitude of openness and warmth to the child and family, without labeling the child or slipping into a self-fulfilling prophesy for negative behavior (Allen & Schwartz, 2001; Greenspan, 2006; Guralnick, 2001; Odom, 2002).

In this country, we can learn from the example set in Reggio Emilia, Italy, where inclusive practices have been implemented with great success since the 1960s (Vakil et al., 2003). In observing the preprimary schools in Reggio, American teachers often note the seeming ease with which children with disabilities are integrated into the life of the classroom. Much of the success with inclusive practices in Reggio is due to the attitude of the educators there: Children with special needs are seen as having the right to the best possible education, and they are not referred to as children with special needs, but rather as "children with special rights."

It Is Important to Make It Clear to the Family That the Staff Has Great Goodwill but Also Has Certain Limitations

Few early childhood teachers have much training in working with children who have exceptional needs. In addition, it is unlikely that during the year they will be able to devote much extra time to studying this subject. They do, however, know a great deal about working with children in general and will bring to this particular child the benefit of these insights and practical, matter-of-fact treatment that emphasizes the typical rather than the exceptional.

The Staff Will Have to Come to Terms with How Much Extra Effort the Child Will Require Them to Expend Every Day

In welcoming a child with disabilities, we must be prepared to make special arrangements. For example, a child who is developmentally delayed may need to have his pants changed three or four times each morning. Some children with emotional disturbance may also require an inordinate amount of time and attention. The quandary for the staff is that they have obligations to all the children and that the time required to work with one child may eventually deprive the other youngsters of their due share of energy and concern.

Fortunately the rather extreme examples given above are the exception rather than the rule, but the possibility of overtaxing the staff must be taken into consideration. However, experience has shown that most children with exceptional needs can and should be gathered in. Usually the amount of special care is considerable during the first few weeks but gradually declines as the child and staff make the adjustment.

It Will Be Necessary for the Staff to Examine Their Feelings About Children with Disabilities

It is all too easy to succumb to a rescue fantasy and decide that what children with disabilities really need is plenty of love and they will be all right. This is, of course, untrue. Children, whether exceptional or ordinary, require a great many other talents from their teachers besides the ability to express affection, and teachers should not delude themselves that affection can overcome all problems. If they intend to work with all children effectively, they must plan on learning the best ways to help them in addition to loving them.

Information garnered from the various specialists serving the child is, of course, invaluable, but never forget that the most valuable resource the teacher can call on is *the family*.

Many Seemingly Insurmountable Problems Can Be Solved During the Trial Period If the Staff and Family Are Creatively Minded

How can seemingly insurmountable problems be overcome creatively? For example, a child who cannot negotiate a flight of stairs and who is too heavy to be carried can come to the center if the parents build a ramp over the stairs. A child who requires a good deal of extra physical care may be able to attend if he is accompanied in the beginning by a family member or, if the family needs relief, by an aide who tends to the extra chores until the child becomes more self-sufficient.

There Are Several Ways to Ease Entry Pangs

The regular practice in preschools of asking parents to stay with their children until they have made friends should be followed when welcoming a child with special needs into the group in both preprimary and primary classrooms.

Sometimes it also helps to begin with a short day and gradually extend the attendence time as the child's skills and toleration of the group increase. The shorter day means the child can go home while he is still experiencing success and before becoming overwhelmed with fatigue. For example, in a half-day program it may be easiest if the child arrives in the middle of the morning and leaves when the other children do since this means the child does not have to depart when everyone else is still having a good time.

A chat with the child's physician or other team members may also reassure the teacher and provide special guidelines that may be necessary for handling the newly admitted youngster. Children with heart conditions or asthma, for instance, occasionally require special treatment but sometimes arrive with firm instructions to let them alone so that they can pace themselves.

Many Disabilities Will Pass Unnoticed by Other Children in the Group, but Some Will Require Explanation

Children *do* notice differences and will conjure up their own explanations for the child's disability unless they are provided the correct one. Explanations need not be elaborate; they should avoid the condescension of pity and should stress matter-of-fact suggestions about how the children can get along with the child about whom they are asking (Derman-Sparks & ABC Task Force, 1989; Kemple, 2004). It may be necessary, for example, to help the children understand that a particular child uses his ears and hands in place of his eyes because he cannot see, to coach them to stand in front of a child who is hard of hearing and catch her attention before speaking to her, or to explain that another youngster has to stand at the table sandbox to keep the grit out of his leg braces.

When our school recently included a child who had severe emotional problems, we found it helped the children and us to discuss together what we could do to help him. It was heartening to see how our 4-year-olds, who were at first nonplussed by Stewart's behavior, came to ignore it in time and to brush off his panicky attacks. This was followed by a gradual shift to telling him he should say "Stop it!" (which he often did, with staff assistance), and finally, children coached him about what to say. I recall one child saying, "Tell me to stop—*tell* me to stop and I will!" There is no denying that the therapy the child was undergoing concurrently had a significant effect on his growth and development, but some credit must also go to the staff and children who worked together to understand, accept, and help Stewart.

GENERAL RECOMMENDATIONS FOR WORKING WITH CHILDREN WHO HAVE DISABILITIES

See Through the Exceptional to the Typical in Every Child

It can be easy to become so caught up in the differences of a child with exceptional needs that the teacher loses sight of the fact that the child is largely like the other children in the group and should be treated as much like them as possible. Feeling sorry for children weakens their character and ultimately does them a terrible disservice. Many children with exceptional needs have too many allowances made for them out of pity, misguided good intentions, and inexperience—and sometimes, where parents

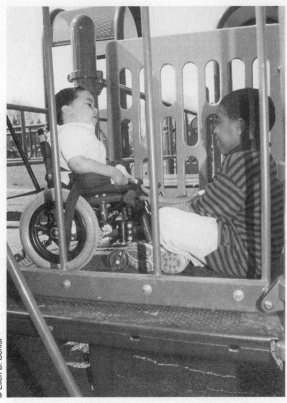

© Ellen B. Senisi

The child with exceptional needs is largely like the other children in the group and should be treated as much like them as possible.

are concerned, as a consequence of guilt. The outcome is that the child may become a demanding and rather unpleasant person to have around.

Consistency, reasonable expectations, and sound policies are, if anything, *more important* to employ when dealing with exceptional children than when dealing with typical children. Teachers should feel comfortable about drawing on their common sense and considerable experience, but they should also be able to turn freely to experts for consultation when they feel puzzled and uncertain about how to proceed.

Try to Steer a Middle Course, Neither Overprotecting nor Overexpecting

The most common pitfall in working with children who have exceptional needs is becoming so concerned for their safety and well-being that they are stifled and deprived of the opportunity to be as typical as they might be were they not overprotected. In general, the teacher should proceed on the assumption that the child should be encouraged to participate in every activity, with modifications provided only when necessary to ensure success (Guralnick, 2001; Kemple, 2004; Odom, 2002; Sandall et al., 2005; Sandall et al., 2002). Thus a child who is behind other children of the same age in intellectual development should be expected to participate in story hour but may find it more enjoyable to sit with the youngest group.

On the other hand, some families and teachers set their expectations unreasonably high and are unwilling to make any exceptions for the child with a disability. This causes unnecessary strain and even despair for the child. Teachers can be helpful here by pointing out what is reasonable to expect of 5- or 6-year-olds in general and helping the family understand what a reasonable expectation would be for their particular youngster. It is often helpful with such families to note each step as the child attains it and to discuss what the next stage of development will be so that the parents can see progress coming bit by bit. This may reduce the feeling of desperately driving toward a difficult distant goal.

Be Realistic

It is important to see the child realistically and to avoid false promises and unrealistic reassurances when talking with the parents or the child. Everyone yearns for a child with a disability to "make it," and sometimes this yearning leads to unwitting self-deceptions, which can do the family and child a disservice by delaying acceptance of the disability or by encouraging them to make inadequate future plans. For example, one of our preschoolers who is blind said to her teacher, "I can tell by feeling things with my hands what they are like; but when I grow up, then I will be able to see the colors, too, won't I?" Unfortunately, the teacher replied tearfully, "Yes, then everything will be all right."

Acceptance of the child's limitations, as well as capitalization on the child's strengths, is the balance to strive for and to model for the family. Some children will in time overcome a disability entirely, but others will not be able to do this. Helping the parents and the child accept this fact, as well as accepting it oneself, is difficult to do but valuable (N. B. Miller & Sammons, 1999).

Keep Regular Records of the Child's Development

Since progress with all children, including those with exceptional needs, occurs a little at a time, it is easy to feel discouraged and to lose sight of how far the youngster has come. If teachers keep regular written records, however brief, an occasional review of that material can be encouraging.

It is particularly important to keep records on a youngster with exceptional needs so that they may be summarized and referred to at the next IEP meeting or passed on to acquaint the next teacher with the child's interests and progress. The records should cover whatever incidents seem particularly important to the child; indications of growth or slipping backward; special interests and tastes; effective educational approaches; significant information contributed by the family, physician, and other support personnel; and any possible questions that may have come up.

Remain in Constant Contact with the Family

All families are concerned about their children and need consistent contact with teachers, but families of children who have special needs require this even more, and so do the teachers who have welcomed such children to their group (Greenspan, 2006; Odom, 2002; Stephens, 2006a).

Families can help the teacher with many details about child management. It may be as simple as explaining the easiest way to slip the arm of a child with cerebral palsy into a snowsuit or an offer of special equipment for pedals for a child with spina bifida who is eager to ride the tricycle. Moreover, families are often the intermediary between specialist and teacher, relaying information from one to the other.

Families often hang on the teacher's words about how their child with a disability is getting along at school. For this reason teachers should choose their words with care while remaining sincere and truthful. As many opportunities as possible should be created for quick, friendly chats. Even notes sent home can help, but chatting is preferred because of the direct person-to-person encounter it provides.

Benjamin La Framboise

As many opportunities as possible should be created for quick, friendly chats.

Do not limit your ideas of how families can help by thinking of them as only supplying physical labor. Always remember that families are the foremost authorities on their child. They know the child in ways the specialists never can, and they can contribute an endless amount of advice and information if only the teacher will ask for it.

Moreover, including the families in discussions and plans makes consistency in expectations and handling at both home and school more probable. This consistency of approach is very valuable and, therefore, is one of the basic tenets of IDEA.

IDENTIFYING AND HELPING CHILDREN WHO HAVE PHYSICAL DISABILITIES AND ILLNESSES

Some Specific Physical Conditions and Symptoms of Which the Teacher Should Be Aware

Speech and Hearing Problems

Various speech difficulties and symptoms of possible hearing impairment are reviewed in the chapter on language, so it is only noted here that speech and hearing problems are among the physical disorders that occur most frequently in childhood (Shelov & Hannemann, 2004; U.S. Department of Education, 2006a). Speech difficulties are likely to be noticed, but hearing loss may be overlooked as a possible cause of misbehavior, inattention, or lack of responsiveness. However, once hearing loss is suspected, it is a relatively simple matter to refer the child to an otolaryngologist for examination. Since such losses may be a result of infection, they can and should be treated promptly.

Difficulties of Vision

Another physical disability that may pass unnoticed but that occurs frequently is an inability to see clearly. Indications that children may need their eyes examined include crossed eyes, rapid movement of the eyeball, holding objects close to the eyes, squinting, sensitivity to bright lights, inattention to pictures or reading, awkward eye-hand coordination, avoidance of tasks that require close eye work, complaints about vision, and lack of normal curiosity about visually appealing objects (Kirk, Gallagher, & Anastasiow, 2003).

One defect of vision in particular requires treatment during early childhood because later attempts at correction are not so effective (American Academy of Ophthalmology, 1993; Desrochers, 1999). This is *amblyopia*, sometimes called *lazy eye*, a condition in which one eye is weaker than the other because of a muscle imbalance. Common signs of this condition include squinting with one eye or tilting the head to one side to see better, or having so-called crossed eyes. Since early treatment of this condition is important, *if there is any possible way to incorporate visual screening tests into the school program, it should be done.* Sometimes local ophthalmologic or optometric societies will sponsor this service, sometimes a public health nurse can be prevailed upon, or an interested civic group will employ a trained nurse to visit centers and nursery schools and conduct such tests.

Screening is best done at school rather than at a central clinic because coverage of children attending the school is likely to be more complete and the environment in which testing takes place is familiar to the children, so they will be more at ease. Giving the children practice before the actual examination day in holding the E according to instructions will facilitate testing and help save the examiner's sanity. Central clinics should also be offered as a service to children who do not attend school.

It is important to remember that a screening test does only that: It screens for some of the more obvious vision disabilities. For this reason, even though a youngster may have passed the screening test with flying colors, if difficulties continue, the child should be referred for further testing. Of course, when the screening test *does* pick up a possible problem, that youngster should be referred to an ophthalmologist or qualified optometrist for diagnosis and follow-up, too.

Attention Deficit Disorder

Attention deficit disorder (ADD) and its cousin *attention deficit/hyperactivity disorder* (ADHD) are terms used by experts to describe a neurobiological disorder the general public labels *hyperactivity* (Greenspan, 2006; Jensen, 2006; Wender, 2000). Because the hallmarks of this condition include impulsivity, inattention, and in some cases, overactivity, some school personnel and inexperienced parents have the tendency to misuse the term to describe every active, vigorous child. In the past this has occasionally led to overprescription of medication to control behavior that was actually within normal bounds. Almost 2 million children (approximately 4%) are on medication for ADD in the United States (Jensen, 2006).

ADHD is the most common ongoing psychiatric disorder of childhood, affecting approximately 3% to 10% of school-age children. ADHD also affects adults at a rate of 4% to 5%. By identifying and treating ADHD early, later problems can be avoided (Greenspan, 2006; Jensen, 2006; Wender, 2000). As the list in Figure 5.1 makes clear, there is a tremendous difference between normal behavior and the behavior of youngsters who fit into this category.

Predominantly inattentive type (AD/HD-I):

- Has difficulty sustaining attention
- Does not appear to listen
- Struggles to follow instructions
- Avoids or dislikes tasks requiring sustained mental effort
- Loses things
- Is easily distracted
- Is forgetful in daily activities

Predominantly hyperactive-impulsive type (AD/HD-HI):

- Fidgets with hands or feet
- Squirms in chair
- Runs about or climbs excessively, appears to be a "bundle of energy"
- Acts as if driven by a motor, is constantly "on the go"
- Talks excessively
- Has difficulty taking turns
- Interrupts or intrudes upon others

Figure 5.1
Indications of attention deficit/hyperactivity disorder (ADHD)

Source: Adapted from The Disorder Named AD/HD, *by Children and Adults with Attention-Deficit/Hyperactivity Disorder (2005). Landover, MD: CHADD.*

Of course, most young children exhibit these kinds of behaviors from time to time. What sets true hyperactivity apart is the *intensity and consistency of the behavior*. Some, though not all, of these behaviors may appear to subside by adolescence, but the years of stress and the unhappy side effects of this condition have usually taken a painful toll by then (Jensen, 2006; Wender, 2000).

The most adequate referral is one made to a child psychiatrist or a pediatrician conversant with this disorder since medication often contributes to the successful management of this condition. A child psychologist or social worker can also provide valuable assistance because behavior modification techniques and other educational strategies may be helpful to use with some of these children (Jensen, 2006). Recent research has shown that the most effective strategy for most—but not all children—is a combination of medication with behavioral therapy (Rothenberger & Banaschewski, 2005). It is important to continually assess the child's progress and focus on strengths rather than weaknesses (Greenspan, 2004, 2006).

Childhood Asthma

During the past few years the number of young children with asthma has increased alarmingly so that now it is the most prevalent of all chronic health-related disorders in childhood, affecting about 5 million children today (Shelov & Hannemann, 2004). Anyone who has ever seen the panic of a child who wheezes and gasps desperately for breath knows how serious and frightening this condition can be. Although asthma can and does affect all kinds of children, research reveals it to be most prevalent among boys, African American youngsters, and children of the poor (Centers for Disease Control and Prevention, 1996).

During an attack three things happen: (a) The lining of the bronchial tubes becomes inflamed, thus constricting airflow, (b) the muscles around them become hypersensitive, restricting airflow even more, and (c) glands begin to secrete extra mucus, which clogs the airways even further. No wonder the person with asthma dreads these attacks. Unfortunately, attacks are not always predictable, but some *triggers* such as heavy urban smog, cigarette smoke, various allergens, molds, furs, and dust mites are classic.

Although teachers can't do much about the presence of some triggers, there are some things they *can* do. Talking with the family and medical provider and being well informed about the particular youngster's condition and triggers is one of these. Doing everything possible to help the child feel in control of what is happening is another, and the most effective way to accomplish this is to make certain the child always has an inhaler available, knows where it is, and knows how to use it. Many young children also know how to use a peak flow meter that can give early warning of an attack and so use the inhaler before the symptoms become severe. Since vigorous exercise in cold, dry air is a common trigger, the teacher should also encourage the child to wrap a scarf warmly around the nose and mouth before going outside; even then it's sometimes necessary to suggest something quiet like going down the slide rather than joining the others in the more active galloping around so dear to the hearts of many 4-year-olds.

Seizure Disorders

A condition that responds particularly well to medication is epilepsy. Indeed, the *generalized tonic clonic seizures* (formerly termed *grand mal seizures*) in which the individual loses consciousness are now rarely witnessed in children's centers. Unless a major convulsive seizure occurs for the first time at school, teachers usually need not worry about referring such children because it is almost certain that they are already under treatment by their physician. Teachers should, however, report seizures to the family.

If a seizure occurs at school, it is important to remain calm and remember that a seizure is not painful to the child. Clear the area around the child, and do not try to restrain the child or interfere in any way—a seizure must run its course. It is not advised to force anything between the teeth. Once the seizure has subsided, allow the child to rest (Epilepsy Foundation of America, n.d.).

The teacher will also need to explain to the other children, who may be either curious or distressed, what happened. The explanation should be simple and matter-of-fact to make it as easy as possible for the child to return to the group with little comment.

Epilepsy is not contagious, and people who have this condition do not have a mental illness or mental retardation. The seizures are the result of disturbances to the nervous system because of inappropriate electrical activity within the brain, but the causes of such activity are largely unknown at this time. Stress and fatigue may increase the probability of a seizure, but erratic use of prescribed medication is the most common cause of difficulty. When medication is taken consistently, about 80% of all patients who have convulsive seizures experience good control (Shelov & Hannemann, 2004).

The teacher needs to be more alert to the much milder form of convulsion, formerly called *petit mal* but now called *generalized absence* (pronounced to rhyme with *Alphonse*). It is important to pay particular attention to this kind of lighter seizure since it sometimes escapes the notice of the family, to whom it may seem to be a case of day-dreaming or inattention.

These brief episodes are characterized by the child having a glazed look, blinking, and being unaware of the surroundings. The child may interrupt what he is saying and then pick up where he left off. Although this condition is uncommon, these seizures may occur hundreds of times a day and yet be undetected because they usually last less than 10 seconds. It is worthwhile to identify this behavior and refer the child for treatment to a pediatrician or neurologist since the probability of successful control by means of medication is high.

Sickle-Cell Anemia

A discussion of sickle-cell anemia is included here because it is both painful and serious for some children, and most teachers don't know much about it. It is a serious, chronic, inherited condition. Although occurring mainly among African Americans (Morse & Shine, 1998; Shelov & Hannemann, 2004), it also occurs in other populations—for example, some Turkish and Greek youngsters and those of Italian (primarily Sicilian) descent.

This serious disorder is not infectious and cannot be "caught." It is incurable at present and causes much pain and misery, but it *can* be treated. As with other anemias, the child may lack energy and tire easily. When people have this condition, their red blood cells become sickle shaped, rather than remain round (hence the name), and painful episodes occur when these red cells stiffen because of lack of oxygen and stack up in small blood vessels. Depending on where it happens, the individual may have severe abdominal pain or an enlarged spleen; or the brain, liver, kidneys, lungs, or eyes may be affected. Children under age 3 are particularly likely to experience swollen hands and feet. Young children with this condition are often characterized by a barrel-shaped chest; an enlarged, protruding abdomen; and thin arms and legs. They have little ability to resist infections. Sometimes, for unknown reasons, production of red blood cells stops altogether (aplastic crisis). Symptoms of this include increased lethargy, rapid heart rate, weakness, fainting, and paleness of the lining of the eyelids (Morse & Shine, 1998). *(If an aplastic crisis occurs at school, the family and the physician should be notified promptly because this condition requires immediate medical attention.)*

Children who have been diagnosed as having sickle-cell anemia must be under regular care by a physician. The teacher can help by encouraging families to keep medical appointments and by carefully carrying out the physician's recommendations at school. These may include prohibiting vigorous exercise since lowered oxygen levels increase the likelihood of a vaso-occlusive attack. Such youngsters tend to drink more water than most children do and so may need to urinate more frequently. Careful, early attention should also be paid to cold symptoms because these youngsters are very vulnerable to pneumonia and influenza.

Admitting Children Who Are HIV Positive to the School

According to the National Pediatric and Family HIV Resource Center (1999), AIDS is the fifth leading cause of death in children ages 1 to 4 and seventh in young people ages 15 to 21. When you add to these statistics the estimate that for every child with AIDS, another 2 to 10 children are likely to be HIV positive, the seriousness of the problem becomes clear and the probability that we early childhood teachers will encounter such children in our classes grows ever more likely.

Since that is true, it is important to know the basic facts about how HIV is transmitted (primarily through contact with semen or blood of infected people) and what the difference is between children who are HIV positive and children with AIDS. When tested, children who are HIV positive are found to be infected with the AIDS virus but do not necessarily exhibit other symptoms of that disease. The more unfortunate children are those youngsters whose bodies have been overwhelmed by the virus and have become deathly ill with AIDS. Children acquire the HIV infection primarily from their infected mothers, in utero, during delivery, or by ingestion of infected breast milk. Once a person is infected with HIV, the virus will be present for life; however, the person may not develop the symptoms of AIDS for years (Shelov & Hannemann, 2004).

Many myths surround this condition, even among people who understand the fundamental facts about transmission. For example, some early childhood staff and/or parents fear that biting will transmit this disease; however, no case of this happening has ever been reported (S. M. Black, 1999). Actually, no episodes have even been reported of children acquiring the infection from attending school with infected youngsters (Steglin, 1997). This is indeed fortunate because the Americans with Disabilities Act makes it illegal to refuse admission of such youngsters to child care centers (Steglin, 1997).

Although it may be against the law to refuse admission to children who are HIV positive, the fact remains that a great deal of uncertain and negative attitudes are

1. Wash your hands for 30 seconds after contact with blood and other body fluids contaminated with blood.

2. Wear disposable latex gloves when you encounter large amounts of blood, especially if you have open cuts or chapped skin. Wash your hands as soon as you remove your gloves.

3. Use disposable absorbent material like paper towels to stop bleeding.

4. Cover cuts or scratches with a bandage until healed.

5. Immediately clean up blood-soiled surfaces and disinfect with a fresh solution of one part bleach and nine parts water.

6. Discard blood-stained material in a sealed bag and place in a lined, covered garbage container.

7. Put blood-stained laundry in sealed plastic bags. Machine-wash separately in hot soapy water.

Figure 5.2
Recommended Universal Precaution procedures for child care centers

Source: Canadian Child Care Federation, 1999. *Reprinted with permission.*

expressed by both caregivers and parents about such admissions. The problem of stigma remains a serious one; for this reason the issue of privacy and confidentiality is important. Parents are under no obligation to inform the school or center that their child or, for that matter, anyone else in their family is afflicted with the condition. Even when they have risked confiding to the staff, this does not mean the information is common knowledge. No matter whether one agrees with the ethics of this or not, when entrusted with that information the staff *must* treat it as confidential.

The fact that the issue of confidentiality may prevent the director's informing staff when a child who is HIV positive is attending their school emphasizes how important it is for everyone to follow the guidelines for taking *Universal Precautions* whenever any bleeding occurs, no matter how minor the accident may be to a child or, possibly, to an adult. Figure 5.2 details the recommended procedures as adapted for child care centers.

Other Physical Problems

In general, the teacher should watch for pronounced changes in the physical appearance of every child and, in particular, should take notice of children who are excessively pale or who convey a general air of exhaustion or lassitude. These conditions often develop so gradually that parents are unaware of the change. It is especially important to watch a child with care during the week or two after returning from a serious illness, such as measles, chicken pox, scarlet fever, or meningitis, because potentially serious problems occasionally develop following such infections.

Further Guidelines for Working with Children
Who Have Physical Challenges

Since physical disabilities are as varied as blindness and cerebral palsy, it is, of course, impossible to discuss each condition in detail here. The suggestions already included apply to these children: A child who is physically challenged should be treated as typically as possible, and should be neither overprotected nor underprotected. Conferences with the child's physician, physical therapist, or other specialist can help the staff ascertain the degree of protection and motivation that is necessary.

The teacher who bears these guidelines in mind and approaches each situation pragmatically will find it relatively simple to deal with children who have physical disabilities. Also, families are often gold mines of practical advice about how to help their child effectively, and their information, combined with the fresh point of view provided by the center staff, can usually solve problems if they arise.

IDENTIFYING AND HELPING CHILDREN WHO HAVE EMOTIONAL DIFFICULTIES

Signs of Emotional Disturbance That Indicate a Referral Is Needed

Deciding when referral for emotional disturbance is warranted and when it is unnecessary can be a difficult problem because transitory symptoms of emotional upset are common during early childhood. A good early childhood environment can accomplish wonders with children who are emotionally upset, and many physicians routinely refer children who are having emotional difficulties to such centers because they have witnessed many happy results from such referrals.

However, the time may come when the staff begins to question whether the center environment, no matter how therapeutic, can offer sufficient help to a particular child. Perhaps after a reasonable period for adjustment and learning, the child persists in "blowing up" over relatively inconsequential matters, or insists on spending most of each morning hidden within the housekeeping corner or even crouched beneath a table. These behaviors, to name only two of a much wider list of possibilities, should arouse feelings of concern in the staff because they are examples of behavior that is *too extreme, happens too often,* and *persists too long.*

The teacher should also apply another criterion when considering the necessity of a referral: whether the number and variety of symptoms manifested by the child at any one period are excessive. We have seen that signs of upset are common and often disappear either spontaneously or as a result of adequate handling by parents and teachers. Occasionally, though, a child will exhibit several reactions at the same time. The child may begin to wet the bed again, be unable to fall asleep easily, cry a great deal, and refuse to play. When a cluster of these behaviors occurs together, it is time for the staff to admit their limitations of time and training and to encourage the family to seek the advice of a qualified psychologist or psychiatrist.

Guidelines for Working with Children Who Have Emotional Disturbance

Even though teachers may not have a child who is chronically disturbed in their school, it is certain they will have to deal with children who are at least temporarily upset from time to time. These upsets may be as minor as a child who has occasional

Benjamin La Framboise

Even though teachers may not have a child who is chronically disturbed in their school, it is certain they will have to deal with children who are at least temporarily upset from time to time.

emotional outbursts or as major as a child who weeps frantically upon arrival to school, refuses to eat anything, and is unable to participate in play.

The teacher should watch for any pronounced change in children's behavior, as well as for signs of withdrawal, inability to give or receive affection, reduced ability to play either by themselves or with other children, reduced interest in conversation, aggressive acting out, marked preoccupation with a particular activity or topic, and extreme emotional responses such as frequently bursting into tears or temper tantrums. The teacher should also notice the usual signs of tension commonly seen in young children who are upset: whining, bed-wetting, increased fretfulness and irritability, hair twisting, thumb sucking, stuttering, an increased dependence on security symbols such as blankets or toy animals, and so forth.

Teachers should realize that these behaviors are not reprehensible and that it is not desirable for them to concentrate their energy on removing these from the child's repertoire. The behaviors *are* signals that the child is suffering from some kind of stress either at home or school and that this should be looked into and mitigated.

Short-Term Techniques

First, a note of caution is in order. When a child who has been getting along well at school suddenly falls apart, it is always best to consider whether the upset could be because of physical illness. Many an inexperienced teacher has spent a sleepless night over such a child only to have the family call and report an illness the next morning. When this is *not* the case, the following techniques can help the child:

1. Make a special point of offering tension-relieving activities to the child who is upset, such as the tension- and aggression-relieving activities listed in chapter 11.
2. Relax standards somewhat to take stress off the child.
3. Talk things over with the family and work with them to identify what may be generating the upset in the child.
4. Help the child work through these feelings by furnishing opportunities to use dolls, puppets, and dramatic play to express concerns.

Long-Term Techniques with Children Who Are More Severely Disturbed

A few fortunate communities offer special care for children categorized as chronically disturbed. Because such opportunities are still rare, however, and because many of these children profit from inclusion in at least a half-day school, it is desirable for teachers to offer this special service whenever they can. Apart from treating children who are psychotic, who generally require a specialized environment that allows more one-to-one contact combined with special expertise, nothing is particularly mysterious about providing care for youngsters who are more severely disturbed. What it really takes to make such a placement turn out successfully is common sense, patience, a steady temperament, determination, faith in oneself, and faith that the child and the family will be able to change (Kemple, 2004).

Treat Children Who Are Chronically Disturbed as Much Like the Other Children as Possible, and Use Their Strengths to Bring Them into the Life of the Group.   In our school one boy who was unable to talk with either children or adults loved using the large push broom and spent many hours sweeping sand off the tricycle track. The first words he ever used at school grew out of this participation when, after weeks of sweeping, he yelled at one of the children who had bumped into his broom, "You just stay outta my way!" Once the sound barrier was broken, this child became increasingly verbal and was able to move on to kindergarten with reasonable success.

Anticipate That Progress Will Be Uneven.   Children who are chronically disturbed may move ahead in an encouraging way and then suddenly backslide. This should not be cause for despair. If they progressed once, they will do it again, and probably faster the second time. It is, of course, desirable to identify and ameliorate the reason for the regression if this can be discerned.

Provide Support for Those Who Are Working with the Child.   Staff members who make the decision to include a child who is severely disturbed will also require many opportunities to meet together and discuss the child's behavior. This is important so that consistency can be maintained in the way the child is handled, so that everyone's insights and information can be pooled together, and so that group decisions can be made about what should be done next.

Working with such children requires stamina and the ability to take a long-term perspective. It also requires enough staff so that someone can be spared as needed when the child flies off the handle. At the end of an exhausting day a touch of humor—but never in the sense of ridicule or denigration of the child—can help staff maintain perspective and provide the sense of camaraderie needed when people are under stress.

Draw on the Advice of Specialists and Encourage the Family to Continue to Do This.   Children who are disturbed often come to school because they have been referred by a specialist. A regular arrangement for calling and reporting progress to the expert, invitations to come and visit the school, and perhaps some written reports during the year should be part of the teacher's professional obligation when agreeing to enroll a youngster with chronic disturbance. Needless to say the specialists who make such referrals should be willing to discharge their responsibilities by guiding teachers when they require their help.

Autism Spectrum Disorder

From time to time the early childhood teacher is still likely to come across children who seem truly out of the ordinary. These children can generally be described in the following terms: They pay scant attention to other children or adults and seem emotionally distant and uninvolved; it is difficult or impossible to get them to look the person who is speaking in the eye; they may become very distressed when asked to change from one activity to another (e.g., they may fly into a panic when asked to stop swinging and go inside for a snack); their speech may be minimal or nonexistent; they may repeat phrases in a meaningless way; and they may show a marked interest in things that spin or twirl, such as a tricycle wheel, which they may sit by and spin absorbedly, or a spoon, which they will twirl with great skill (National Center on Birth Defects and Developmental Disabilities, 2007; Shelov & Hannemann, 2004). When several of these symptoms occur together, the child may be showing autistic behaviors. This condition typically appears during the first 3 years of life and affects the child's ability to communicate and interact with others. Autism is defined by a certain set of behaviors and is called a "spectrum disorder" because it affects individuals differently and to varying degrees. There is no known single cause for autism. Recent data indicate that autism afflicts 300,000 children in the United States, or about 6 per 1,000 American children. For reasons not fully understood it appears more so in boys, at a rate of 1 in every 94 (National Center on Birth Defects and Developmental Disabilities, 2007).

With such unusual symptoms, it may be surprising that the teacher may be the first person who realizes how unusual the behaviors are. Treatment is difficult, and *these children need highly professional help as soon as they can get it.* The Autism Society of America estimates that the cost of treatment can be reduced by two thirds with early diagnosis and intervention ("Autism Facts," 2003). Therefore, the family should be urged to seek help as soon as possible from a child psychiatrist or psychologist who specializes in treating this condition. Treatment is likely to include intensive work based on the principles of behavior modification possibly combined with medications to relieve specific symptoms such as anxiety behaviors and sleeplessness (Shelov & Hannemann, 2004).

Parents and teachers wonder a good deal about the causes of this condition since the behavior can be so extreme. Although included here in the category of emotional disturbance, research now indicates that the underlying cause of infantile autism is a disruption in the development of the brain. This has been traced to a variety of factors. Among these are rubella or other viral infections during pregnancy, phenylketonuria (PKU), genetically regulated disturbances, and many additional, yet-to-be-ascertained physiological insults or developmental anomalies (Cole & Arndt, 1998; Shelov & Hannemann, 2004). This is valuable information to remember because it takes away a lot of the mystery and the possible tendency to blame parents.

Identifying and Helping Children Who Have Delayed or Advanced Mental Ability

Children Who Have Developmental Lags

All teachers of young children need to know enough about developmental sequences and the ages at which behavioral milestones can be anticipated that they can tell when children are developing normally, when they are lagging markedly behind their peers, or when they are exceptionally advanced for their age. Lists of developmental standards have been included in many chapters in this book, not with the intention of urging developmental conformity, but in the hope that they will help the teacher be tolerant of behaviors characteristic of various ages and also alert to children who are developing so far out of phase that they require special help (Copple & Bredekamp, 2009). Appendix A also provides a chart of developmental guidelines.

Many preprimary teachers do not recognize cognitive delay when they see it. Being unaware of retardation can be an advantage in a way since it means a child is not stuck with a stereotyped reaction to the condition or burdened with an undesirable label. However, it may also mean that an undiagnosed, slow-learning 4-year-old who is actually operating at a 2-1/2-year-old level may be expected to sit with the other 4-year-olds for long stories he does not comprehend or may be criticized and disciplined for refusing to share equipment when actually he is behaving in a way typical of his developmental but not chronological age. An adequate diagnosis would enable the teachers to match their expectations to the child's real level of ability.

Behavior that should be cause for concern includes a widespread pattern of delayed development that is a year or more behind the typical in physical, social, and intellectual areas. Such lags are usually accompanied by speech that is obviously immature for the child's chronological age (Shelov & Hannemann, 2004).

The American Association on Mental Retardation characterizes mental retardation as being "significantly subaverage functioning" concurrently with related limitations in two or more of the following applicable adaptive skills areas: communication, self-care, home living, social skills, community use, self-direction, health and safety, functional academics, leisure, and work.

Causes of the condition are numerous and range from physiological causes such as chromosomal disorders to pseudoretardation induced by environmental causes such as severe malnutrition or an insufficiently stimulating environment. It is often impossible even for specialists to determine why the child is developing slowly. Particularly children whose retardation is due to physiological causes do not outgrow their condition or ultimately catch up with their peers, so it is necessary for teachers and parents to come to a realistic understanding of what can be reasonably expected of them. Knowledgeable specialists can provide many helpful, encouraging suggestions about how to maximize learning for these youngsters.

Guidelines for Working with Children Who Are Cognitively Delayed

Children who are mildly or moderately delayed are the best prospects for inclusion in early childhood classrooms. The child who is mildly delayed will probably fit so easily into a program serving a mixed-age group that no special recommendations are necessary other than reminding the teacher to see the child in terms of actual developmental level, rather than chronological age.

Children who are moderately affected will also often fit comfortably into a mixed-age group, but many teachers find it helpful to have a clear understanding of the most worthwhile educational goals for these children and of some simple principles for teaching them most effectively.

Basic learning goals for children with moderate delay should center on helping them be as independent as possible, which includes learning simple self-help skills, as well as learning to help other people by doing simple tasks. It also includes helping the child develop language skills and learn to get along with other children in an acceptable way (Kemple, 2004; Shelov & Hannemann, 2004).

These goals are only slightly different from those that are part of the regular curriculum. The only differences are that the child who is developing more slowly will be farther behind other children of the same age and will need a simpler manner of instruction. Children who learn slowly should not be confused with a lot of talk and shadings of meaning. *They need concrete examples, definite rules, and consistent reinforcement of desirable behavior.* In general, the bywords with these children are *keep it concrete, keep it simple, keep it fun,* and *be patient.* The suggestions listed in Figure 5.3 will help the teacher include a child with delays in the children's center program.

Much can be said for the value of step-by-step, prescriptive teaching for children with cognitive delays in particular. This requires careful identification of the current level of the child's skills, as well as knowledge of the appropriate next step. On going communication with the family and resource specialists is crucial in developing an appropriate educational plan for the child.

Children Who Are Intellectually Gifted

Although the child who is slow to learn has received special attention for several decades, only during the past few years have young children who are intellectually gifted received any attention at all (Rotigel, 2003). Currently, only a handful of special programs cater to their needs. A child with exceptional mental ability usually exhibits a general pattern of advanced skills, but not always. Sometimes the pattern is quite spotty, or its manifestations may vary from day to day (Jensen, 2006; Rotigel, 2003; Piirto, 1999).

In general, children who are gifted may exhibit some or all of the following skills: They learn quickly and easily; their language is more elaborate and extended than that of other children of the same age, and their vocabulary is likely to be large; their attention span may be longer if their interest is aroused; they grasp ideas easily; and they probably possess an exceptional amount of general information, which is characterized not only by more variety but also by greater detail. They often have a very good memory. These children like to pursue reasons for things, talk about cause-and-effect relationships, and compare and draw conclusions. They are particularly sensitive to social values and the behavior of those around them. They are often almost insatiably interested in special subjects that appeal to them. Some of them already know how to read. They may prefer the company of older children or adults (Jensen, 2006; Shelov & Hannemann, 2004).

Teachers who do not build their curriculum and increase its complexity sufficiently during the year may find that children who are gifted become increasingly restless and gradually get into difficulties because they have lost interest in what is happening at

1. As much as possible, treat the child as you would treat all children in the group, but exercise common sense so that you expect neither too much nor too little.

2. Know the developmental steps so that you understand what the child should learn next as he progresses.

3. Remember that children with cognitive delays learn best what they repeat frequently. Be prepared to go over a simple rule or task many times until the child has it firmly in mind. (This need for patient repetition is one of the things inexperienced teachers may find most irritating, particularly when the child had appeared to grasp the idea just the day before. Don't give up hope; if the teaching is simple and concrete enough, he will eventually learn.)

4. Pick out behavior to teach that the child can use all his life; that is, try to teach ways of behaving that will be appropriate for an older as well as a younger child to use. For example, don't let him run and kiss everyone he meets, because this will not be acceptable when he is just a little older.

5. Take it easy. Give short directions, one point at a time.

6. Allow sufficient time for the child to acquire a selected task. Complex things take longer; simpler things take less time.

7. Encourage the child to be persistent by keeping tasks simple and satisfying. This will encourage him to finish what he starts.

8. Remember that independence is an important goal. Make sure the child is not being overprotected.

9. Teach one thing at a time. For instance, teach the child to feed himself, then to use a napkin, and then to pour his milk.

10. Provide lots of concrete experiences that use as many of the senses as possible.

11. Don't rely on talking as the primary means of instruction. Show the child what you mean whenever possible by modeling it.

12. Encourage the development of speech. Wait for at least some form of verbal reply whenever possible. Gently increase the demand for a "quality" response as the child's skills increase.

13. *Remember that these children are just as sensitive to the emotional climate around them as ordinary children are.* Therefore, never talk about the child in front of him. It is likely that he will at least pick up the sense of what you are saying, and this may hurt his feelings badly.

14. Show the child that you are pleased with him and that you like him.

15. After a fair trial at learning something new, if the child cannot seem to learn it, drop the activity without recrimination. Try it again in a few months; he may be ready to learn it by then.

Figure 5.3
Suggestions for including a child with developmental delays in the children's center program

school. Teachers who meet this challenge and deal with it satisfactorily modify the curriculum so that it meets the needs of these youngsters by adding more difficult and interesting learning activities. Some suggestions for accomplishing this are offered next.

Teaching Preschool Children Who Are Mentally Gifted

The provision of an enriched curriculum does not necessarily mean that the teacher must teach the child to read, although Piirto (1999) states that one half to two thirds of gifted children read by age 5. One of the authors of this text will never forget her surprise when one of the bright lights in the preschool wandered into her office, picked up a plain bound book from her desk, and commented, "Hmmmmm, this looks interesting—*All About Dinosaurs.* Can I borrow this?" (She let him.)

What the teacher *can* do is make sure such children have plenty of opportunities to pursue subjects that interest them in as much depth as they desire. It is important to avoid the trap of thinking to oneself, "Oh, well, *they* wouldn't be able to do *that*." It is astonishing what children can do when given encouragement and materials. Children who are intellectually gifted often love discussions that focus on "What would happen if . . . ?" or "How could we . . . ?" These questions require creative reasoning, as well as transforming old information into new solutions. Asking them to evaluate the potential results of these ideas, if done sensitively so that they do not feel crushed when an idea doesn't work out, will give them even wider scope for their talents.

Children who are gifted will also relish the more difficult activities suggested in the chapters on mental development because these activities can be adjusted to their level of ability and thus sustain their interest. Perhaps a few examples of specific ways of enriching the curriculum for them will best illustrate how to accomplish this.

Investigate How Things Work, Finding Out Either by Close Observation or by Taking Them Apart and Reassembling Them. A music box, a vacuum cleaner and all its parts, a Christmas tree stand, a flashlight, an old bicycle, and so forth, can be offered. Ask the child to put into words a theory about what makes it work.

Build Additional Language Skills. Make a time to read the child books that are longer and have more detail in them than picture books do. After story time, have a special discussion. Encourage the child to expound on the stories that were just read: Were they true? Has the child ever had a similar or opposite experience?

Offer More Complex Materials or Advanced Information. A good example of this is the use of more difficult puzzles. Cube puzzles can be used to reproduce particular patterns, or jigsaw puzzles can be offered rather than only the framed wooden ones typical of preschools. On a library trip take the child to the older children's section to find books on a particular subject of interest to the child.

Offer an Enriched Curriculum in the Area of Science. Be prepared to allow for expanded scientific activities. For example, provide vinegar for testing for limestone in various materials such as tiles, building materials, and so forth. Or explore the concept of time.

Above All, Use Instructional Methods That Foster Problem Solving and Encourage Development of Creative Ideas. How can everyday items be put to new uses? How can old problems be solved in new ways? It is valuable to ask pertinent questions and provide rich opportunities for children to propose answers and test them to see whether they are correct.

SUMMARY

Teachers who work with children with special needs must seek all the information they can on each child's particular condition if they really want to be effective teachers. This chapter can do no more than scratch the surface.

Increasing numbers of courses in exceptionality are being offered by schools of education, as in-service training, and by university extension units as the general trend toward including children with exceptional needs in regular public school classes and early childhood centers gains ground. In addition to these courses, books are also available.

Unfortunately the education of very young children with special needs is still only sparsely covered in the literature, but IDEA and ADA are gradually changing this situation for the better. These laws have made a difference to early childhood teachers because their passage means that help for young children with disabilities is more readily available than it was in the past, many more children who have disabilities will be attending "regular" early childhood centers, and teachers will become part of the treatment teams responsible for working with such children.

Early childhood teachers owe two main responsibilities to children who have special needs. First, they must serve as screening agents and help identify possible problems (physical, emotional, or mental) that have escaped the attention of the physician. Following identification of a difficulty, teachers should attempt to effect a referral to the appropriate specialist.

Second, they must do all they can to include these children in their group. This requires careful assessment before admission and flexibility of adjustment following entrance to school. It is vital that they treat the child as typically as possible and encourage independence without demanding skills that lie beyond the child's ability. Specific suggestions for working with children who are physically disabled, emotionally disturbed, cognitively delayed, or intellectually gifted conclude the chapter.

Questions and Activities

1. Do you think it is generally wise to suggest medication as a means of controlling hyperactivity in children? Why or why not?
2. This chapter makes a strong case for the early identification of potentially handicapping disorders. What are the real disadvantages of labeling children as being *different*? What are some ways to obtain help for such youngsters without stigmatizing them at the same time?
3. What do you think accounts for the fact that children who are intellectually gifted are often overlooked at the early childhood level? Might the provision of a special curriculum for them result in precocity and overintellectualization, thereby spoiling their childhood?

Diversity Question

1. What is sickle-cell anemia? Is it contagious?

Predicaments

1. A 4-1/2-year-old boy attending your school is cognitively delayed and functions at about the 2-1/2-year-old level. He hangs around the housekeeping corner and the blocks a lot, but the children push

him aside. One of them in particular makes a point of saying, "He can't play here. His nose is snotty, and he talks dumb." What would you do?
2. A 6-year-old girl in your group has a heart condition. In addition to looking somewhat pale, she is not supposed to exert herself by climbing or other vigorous exercise, which she yearns to do. She is well liked by the other children, who invite her frequently to climb around and play with them. What would you do?

Self-Check Questions for Review

Content-Related Questions

1. List three reasons why the passage of IDEA and ADA are making a difference in what teachers of young children need to know and do.
2. What is one of the most important services early childhood teachers can provide for young children?
3. What basically sets the child who is hyperactive apart from other young children?
4. What are the guidelines for deciding when to refer a child who seems to be emotionally disturbed for outside help? What behaviors might signal that the child has possible autistic

tendencies? What are some guidelines teachers may use when working with children who are emotionally disturbed?

5. What kinds of behaviors might alert a teacher to the possibility that a child could be developing more slowly than normal? What are some practical pieces of information to remember when teaching such a child?

6. Explain some important steps in making a referral when a child has a special problem.

7. What are IDEA and ADA? How do they affect the welfare of exceptional children?

Integrative Questions

1. The book states that teachers should "see through the exceptional to the typical in every child." Explain how doing this could be an antidote for expecting either too much or too little from the youngster with a disability.

2. It is important for teachers and parents of all children to remain in close contact. Using the example of a disability, give an example of something a parent might share with the teacher that would be helpful. Now give an example of something the teacher could share with the parent. Be as specific as possible.

Reference for Further Reading

Guralnick, M. J. (Ed.). (2001). *Early childhood inclusion: Focus on change*. Baltimore: Brookes. This is an excellent place to start learning about including children with disabilities in ordinary classrooms since it provides a discussion of implications of relevant laws and a discussion of practical aspects of child inclusion.

Related Organizations and Online Resources

Division for Early Childhood (DEC) of the Council for Exceptional Children (CEC). This nonprofit organization advocates for individuals who work with or on behalf of children with special needs, birth through age 8, and their families. The DEC home page includes an index for the *Journal of Early Intervention and Young Exceptional Children*. It also includes information on publications, position statements, and conferences at http://www.cec.sped.org.

Head Start Bureau. Head Start is a nationwide early childhood program for preschool children from families of low income, designed to provide comprehensive services in preparation for public school. Since 1972, the Head Start program has operated under a congressional mandate to make available, at a minimum, 10% of its enrollment opportunities to children with disabilities. For information about Head Start visit http://www.nhsa.org or http://www.acf.hhs.gov/programs/ohs/.

National Dissemination Center for Children with Disabilities (NICHCY). This organization provides information on disabilities in children; and IDEA, the law authorizing special education. A wealth of resources and information is available at http://www.nichcy.org.

CHAPTER six

Using Standards and Assessment in Early Childhood Education

How to tell what the children are really learning?

What the No Child Left Behind Act is and how it effects early childhood programs?

How to adhere to mandated standards and still have time for play?

. . . IF YOU HAVE, THE MATERIAL IN THIS CHAPTER WILL HELP YOU.

To use early learning standards effectively, teachers must be intentional about what they teach, how they teach, and how they know if children are learning.

Catherine Scott-Little, Sharon Lynn Kagan, and Victoria Stebbins Frelow (2006, p. 32)

The presence of standards will not free parents from the constant need to monitor their children's education to ensure they have opportunities to learn. Standards do provide parents with a guide to what they should expect teachers to teach and children to learn.

Barbara T. Bowman (2006b, p. 43)

Experience has taught us that we must never remove ourselves from the process of assessment to rely on tests alone to make important decisions about children's lives. Testing is not a natural environment, particularly for young children. Whenever possible, we should use the test data in conjunction with information from parents, teachers, other professionals, and firsthand observations of children.

Samuel J. Meisels and Sally Atkins-Burnett (2005, p. 3)

Today,   standards-based education is the rule for many early childhood educators, particularly those who work in public elementary schools and Head Start programs. Since the passage of the No Child Left Behind (NCLB) Act of 2001, academic testing is required in all U.S. public elementary through high schools beginning in third grade. Although NCLB focuses on primary-age children and older, it has influenced early education for younger children as well. Standards—and assessment to see if the standards are met—are common in many types of preschool programs today. Head Start, for example, adopted the Head Start National Reporting System in 2003 and now tests all its enrolled 4-year-olds twice a year (Meisels & Atkins-Burnett, 2005; Grisham-Brown, Hallam, & Brookshire, 2006; Yell & Drasgow, 2005).

WHAT ARE EARLY LEARNING STANDARDS?

Standards are called many different things: *developmental benchmarks,* and *learning guidelines, educational goals, and objectives*. Whatever they are called, standards say that teachers are responsible for organizing the educational program so that children learn—and they specify precisely what that learning involves. Early learning standards outline the expectations for children's learning and development. There is no denying that standards can be misused, such as when teachers are more concerned with "teaching the test" than with the quality of the educational experience. However, when correctly employed, standards can also help teachers think seriously about which objectives have the greatest value and how to tell when they have been accomplished.

Standards can and should cover many areas of learning rather than only the cognitive domain (Bodrova & Leong, 2008; Bodrova, Leong, & Shore, 2004; Meisels & Atkins-Burnett, 2005). Figure 6.1 shows examples of learning standards that are taken from the Head Start Child Outcomes Framework, which includes 8 domains of learning and development, 27 specific domain elements, and 100 examples of more specific indicators of children's skills, abilities, knowledge, and behaviors. These are among the standards that all Head Start programs must work toward (Head Start Bureau, 2001) and are an example of comprehensive learning goals for 4-year-olds.

It is important to note that there is no universally accepted or mandated set of early learning standards. An analysis of educational standards from 38 states found great variation among the states' standards. The domains of language and communication, and cognition and general knowledge—particularly logico-mathematical thinking—were focused on most. Some of the least often addressed categories included physical fitness, relationships with adults and peers, imagination, questioning, and understanding of social groups, relationships, and rules (Scott-Little, Kagan, & Frelow, 2006).

One criticism of the educational standards movement is that there has been increased emphasis on the achievement of academic and cognitive skills while other developmental tasks are deemed less important (Noddings, 2006). In a study of public schools for the 2005–2006 school year, the majority of educators reported spending more time teaching test-taking strategies and focusing more narrowly on the topics covered on the state tests (Viadero, 2007). A nationwide study of 299 public school districts in 50 states concluded

Language Development Domain

Listening and Understanding

1. Demonstrates increasing ability to attend to and understand conversations, stories, songs, and poems.

2. Shows progress in understanding and following simple and multiple-step directions.

Speaking and Communicating Domain

1. Progresses in abilities to initiate and respond appropriately in conversation and discussions with peers and adults.

2. Uses an increasingly complex and varied spoken vocabulary.

Literacy Domain

Phonological Awareness

1. Shows increasing ability to discriminate and identify sounds in spoken language.

2. Shows growing awareness of beginning and ending sounds of words.

Book Knowledge and Appreciation

1. Shows growing interest and involvement in listening to and discussing a variety of fiction and non-fiction books and poetry.

Early Writing

1. Develops understanding that writing is a way of communicating for a variety of purposes.

2. Begins to represent stories and experiences through pictures, dictation, and in play.

Alphabet Knowledge

1. Shows progress in associating the names of letters with their shapes and sounds.

2. Identifies at least 10 letters of the alphabet, especially those in their own name.

Mathematics Domain

Number and Operations

1. Demonstrates increasing interest and awareness of numbers and counting as a means for solving problems and determining quantity.

2. Develops increasing ability to count in sequence to 10 and beyond.

Figure 6.1
Example of early learning standards

Continued

Source: From the Head Start Child Outcomes Framework *(Head Start Bureau, 2001).*

Geometry and Spatial Sense

1. Begins to recognize, describe, compare, and name common shapes, their parts, and attributes.

2. Progresses in ability to put together and take apart shapes.

Science Domain

Scientific Skills and Methods

1. Begins to use senses and a variety of tools and simple measuring devices to gather information, investigate materials, and observe processes and relationships.

2. Develops increased ability to observe and discuss common properties, differences, and comparisons among objects and materials.

Scientific Knowledge

1. Expands knowledge of and abilities to observe, describe, and discuss the natural world, materials, living things, and natural processes.

2. Expands knowledge of and respect for their body and the environment.

Creative Arts Domain

Music

1. Participates with increasing interest and enjoyment in a variety of music activities, including listening, singing, finger plays, games, and performances.

2. Experiments with a variety of musical instruments.

Art

1. Gains ability in using different art media and materials in a variety of ways for creative expression and representation.

2. Progresses in abilities to create drawings, paintings, models, and other art creations that are more detailed, creative, or realistic.

3. Develops growing abilities to plan, work independently, and demonstrate care and persistence in a variety of art projects.

Movement

1. Shows growth in moving in time to different patterns of beat and rhythm in music.

Dramatic Play

1. Participates in a variety of dramatic play activities that become more extended and complex.

Figure 6.1
Example of early learning standards—*Continued*

142

2. Shows growing creativity and imagination in using materials and in assuming different roles in dramatic play situations.

Social and Emotional Development Domain

Self-Concept

1. Begins to develop and express awareness of self in terms of specific abilities, characteristics, and preferences.

2. Develops growing capacity for independence in a range of activities, routines, and tasks.

Self-Control

1. Shows progress in expressing feelings, needs and opinions in difficult situations and conflicts without harming themselves, others, or property.

2. Develops growing understanding of how their actions affect others and begins to accept the consequences of their actions.

3. Increases abilities to sustain interactions with peers by helping, sharing, and discussion.

Cooperation

1. Develops increasing abilities to give and take in interactions, to take turns in games or using materials, and to interact without being overly submissive or directive.

2. Shows progress in developing friendships with peers.

Social Relationships

1. Progresses in responding sympathetically to peers who are in need, upset, hurt, or angry; and in expressing empathy or caring for others.

Knowledge of Families and Community

1. Develops ability to identify personal characteristics including gender and family composition.

2. Progresses in understanding similarities and respecting differences among people, such as gender, race, special needs, culture, language, and family structures.

Approaches to Learning Domain

Initiative and Curiosity

1. Chooses to participate in an increasing variety of tasks and activities.

2. Develops increased ability to make independent choices.

3. Approaches tasks and activities with increased flexibility, imagination, and inventiveness.

Figure 6.1
Example of early learning standards—*Continued*

Continued

Engagement and Persistence

1. Grows in abilities to persist in and complete a variety of tasks, activities, projects, and experiences.

2. Demonstrates increasing ability to set goals and develop and follow through on plans.

Reasoning and Problem-Solving

1. Develops increasing ability to find more than one solution to a question, task, or problem.

2. Grows in recognizing and solving problems through active exploration, including trial and error, and interactions and discussions with peers and adults.

3. Develops increasing abilities to classify, compare and contrast objects, events, and experiences.

Physical Health and Development Domain

Fine Motor Skills

1. Develops growing strength, dexterity, and control needed to use tools such as scissors, paper punch, stapler, and hammer.

2. Grows in hand-eye coordination in building with blocks, putting together puzzles, reproducing shapes and patterns, stringing beads, and using scissors.

Gross Motor Skills

1. Shows increasing levels of proficiency, control and balance in walking, climbing, running, jumping, hopping, skipping, marching, and galloping.

2. Demonstrates increasing abilities to coordinate movements in throwing, catching, kicking, bouncing balls, and using the slide and swing.

Health Status and Practices

1. Progresses in physical growth, strength, stamina, and flexibility.

2. Participates actively in games, outdoor play, and other forms of exercise that enhance physical fitness.

Figure 6.1
Example of early learning standards—*Continued*

that in response to the NCLB Act "narrowing the curriculum" has become common practice and subjects such as history, language, and the arts have been dropped by many schools in favor of more classes in math and reading (Dillon, 2006). In addition, many elementary schools have eliminated recess and outdoor play since physical development is not assessed in the NCLB tests (Cleaver, 2007a).

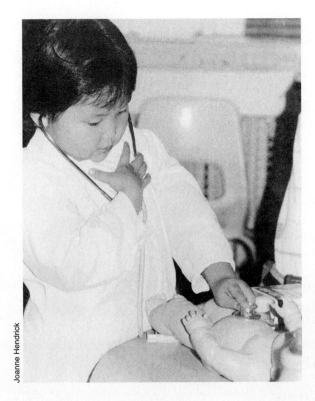

Joanne Hendrick

Standards can and should cover many areas of learning rather than just the cognitive domain. This child "shows growing creativity and imagination in using materials and in assuming different roles in dramatic play situations."

WHERE DO STANDARDS COME FROM?

Program and School Standards

Program and school standards are not new in early childhood education. As every child care center director knows, there are many requirements or standards that a program must meet in order to be licensed. Various state agencies see that program standards are met and usually perform inspections before issuing a license. These standards range from the type of training teachers and directors must have to the number of children allowed in a group of preschoolers to the number of square feet of outdoor space required per child. There is no universally accepted or mandated set of program standards in the United States, and each state agency determines the licensing requirements as well as inspection schedule for early childhood programs.

NAEYC Program Accreditation Standards

In 1985 the National Association for the Education of Young Children (NAEYC), the nation's largest organization for early childhood educators, established a voluntary accreditation system to set standards for early childhood programs. To attain NAEYC accreditation, programs serving young children from birth to age 8 volunteer to be measured against the NAEYC Early Childhood Program Standards. In 2008, there were over 11,000 early childhood education programs that were NAEYC accredited.

The process of NAEYC accreditation can be accomplished in about a year. Once a licensed facility applies for candidacy, it begins a rigorous process of self-assessment. Programs must conduct a formal assessment that involves families, teaching staff, and program administration. They must observe, record, survey, and document what the school does and how. The programs must provide evidence that all NAEYC program standards are met through program and classroom portfolios. Site visits are conducted by NAEYC staff to ensure that standards are met, and each year the program must submit a report to maintain its accreditation. There are 10 NAEYC Early Childhood Program Standards Topic Areas:

Standard 1: Relationships

Standard 2: Curriculum

Standard 3: Teaching

Standard 4: Assessment of Child Progress

Standard 5: Health

Standard 6: Teachers

Standard 7: Families

Standard 8: Community Relationships

Standard 9: Physical Environment

Standard 10: Leadership and Management

State Early Learning Standards

States are the largest source of public preschool education: More than a million children were enrolled in state-funded early childhood programs in 2006–2007 (Barnett, Hustedt, Friedman, Boyd, & Ainsworth, 2007). Recent federal legislation known as "Good Start, Grow Smart" requires that states develop early learning guidelines in order to qualify for Child Care and Development Funds. This initiative was designed to improve the quality of early childhood programs across the nation. Forty-eight states and the District of Columbia have developed early learning guidelines specifying what preschool children should know and be able to do, and the other two are in the process. In addition, several states are developing standards for infants and toddlers. Thirteen states are engaged in assessing preschoolers and 17 states assess kindergartners (Scott-Little et al., 2006; Scott-Little, Lesko, Martella, & Milburn, 2007; Schultz & Kagan, 2005). The creation of early learning standards by states has been a rapid development: In 1999 only 10 states had documented expectations for preschool children's development compared to the 48 states with early learning standards in place today (Scott-Little et al., 2007).

There is no national set of standards and each state is left to create its own criteria and forms of assessment. Teachers who work in state-sponsored programs must be aware of the learning standards in their state and be able to assess how well the children are learning the content included in the standards. State agencies, state branches of NAEYC, and local resource and referral agencies provide training and assistance to teachers in order to use early learning standards in their classrooms. See Related Organizations and Online Resources at the end of this chapter to find specific state standards.

Federal Early Learning Standards

The federal government develops outcome standards for programs that receive funding, such as Head Start (see Figure 6.1) and the public school system. In addition, recent legislation mandates the inclusion of children with disabilities into typical school settings, including preschool settings. Additional legislation also requires these children be equipped with individualized education programs (IEPs) that specify what each child is supposed to learn next. These expectations are typically written in the form of educational objectives—another term for learning standards. Teachers who welcome children with disabilities into their classrooms will find they are often expected to help formulate such objectives for the children in their care or, at the very least, understand what they are and be able to translate the stipulated behaviors into reality (Vacca, 2006).

The Individuals with Disabilities Education Act (IDEA—Public Law 105-17)

As discussed in chapter 5, IDEA mandates that increased services be made available to young children who have disabilities. Among these is the requirement that an early childhood teacher—preferably the child's classroom teacher—is included in the conferences where the IEP is developed outlining what the child with the disability should learn next.

The first step in creating the IEP involves a thorough investigation to find out what services will be needed to help the child develop to full potential. This process is based on the child's apparent needs and may involve everything from a neurological or psychological evaluation, to a hearing test or an eye examination, to gathering information from the teacher and parents about how the child is functioning at school and home.

Once that information is obtained, a meeting is scheduled to discuss the results and reach agreement about what should be done next to enhance the child's development. An IEP is stated as a series of goals and objectives identifying behavior that exemplifies those goals—these are the specific early learning standards for that particular child. It will be up to teachers to design curriculum activities and practice opportunities that enable the child to reach those objectives.

But how do teachers do that? When planning curriculum, how do they find out what particular children are good at doing, what their potentials are, and who is interested in learning what next? The answer is that teachers need to have a systematic procedure of *assessment* for collecting information about the individual children to make those plans fit them well. Appropriate assessment methods are an integral component of the IEP process—as well as standards-based education in general—and will be discussed at length in the second half of this chapter.

No Child Left Behind (NCLB) Act

Since the year 2002, NCLB has been a federal mandate for all public schools in the United States. The NCLB Act focuses on improving students' academic performance and on improving the performance of those schools with low levels of student achievement. In order to do this, states and school districts must identify enrolled children, test their progress, and report the results to the parents and to the U.S. Department of Education. In this way, the assessments are used to hold schools accountable for their students' achievement. To receive federal funding, states must submit their accountability plan and assess students' skills in reading and math in grades 3 through 8. States must also set proficiency standards that detail what children are expected to know and learn in the areas of reading, language arts, math, and science in each grade. The goal of NCLB is that all children enrolled in U.S. public schools will be proficient on state-defined standards in the four academic areas by the end of the 2013–2014 school year (Yell & Drasgow, 2005).

Developmentally Appropriate Practices and Standards Recommended by National Organizations

Many states have worked in cooperation with various national organizations to determine which standards will be used in early education programs. NAEYC has been the main organization to form linkages with other organizations in the development of early learning standards for early childhood programs across the country. NAEYC position statements have been created jointly with the National Association of Early Childhood Specialists in State Departments of Education (NAECS/SDE) to guide states in adopting standards (see Related Organizations and Online Resources at the end of this chapter). In addition, NAEYC has worked with other national organizations to create joint position statements with regard to standards in particular learning areas such as math, reading, and science. These position statements as well as the NAEYC publication *Developmentally Appropriate Practice in Early Childhood Programs Serving Children Birth Through Age 8* (Copple & Bredekamp, 2009) offer educators comprehensive and appropriate early learning standards for children. The position statements are accessible through the NAEYC Web site referenced at the end of this chapter in Related Organizations and Online Resources. It would behoove teachers to review the NAEYC joint position statements to see what the major organizations in the fields of the different learning domains deem to be appropriate early learning standards. They can help novice teachers establish learning goals for children that are grounded in years of research and experience.

WHAT IS ASSESSMENT?

Assessment is "observing, recording, and otherwise documenting work that children do and how they do it, as a basis for a variety of educational decisions that affect the child" (NAEYC & NAECS/SDE, 1991, p. 21). Observing children is a natural activity for most early educators; we probably wouldn't be teachers if we weren't interested in seeing what the children do and learn, and how they change over time. Assessment is a process of gathering our observations and the various demonstrations of the child's learning, interpreting the information, sharing it with others involved in the child's learning, and making educational and curriculum decisions based on that information.

Effective, Appropriate Assessment in Early Childhood Education

According to NAEYC and NAECS/SDE, appropriate assessment starts with an understanding of what is to be assessed (i.e., the desired outcomes of the early learning standards). We want to know if the goals that we had set earlier for the child were accomplished. The measures used to assess children's development must be appropriate in terms of addressing the standards as well as appropriate for the child's developmental level. In other words, is the test *valid*—does it really test the standard we are

Leslie Gleim

Assessment is a process to gather our observations and demonstrations of the children's learning.

interested in? Is it developmentally appropriate? If we are assessing 4-year-olds, is the test something most 4-year-olds can typically handle or is it too advanced or too easy?

Because so much developmental change occurs during the early childhood years, assessments must never be a "one-shot deal." Assessments must also include observations by knowledgeable adults in real-life early childhood situations, with multiple and different types of opportunities for assessment over time. It is also crucial that when developing standards-related assessments, the needs of culturally diverse children and children with disabilities are taken into account. In addition, the information yielded by these assessments must be useful to educators and families so that, ultimately, the children benefit from the assessments (NAEYC & NAECS/SDE, 2002).

In effective early childhood programs, assessment is closely linked to standards as well as to the curriculum. Assessment measures the objectives set forth in the early learning standards, and the assessment is then used to inform teachers about appropriate next steps to take in developing the curriculum. Teachers assess children in relation to the curricular goals of the early childhood program and with attention to each individual child's needs and interests in relation to those goals (NAEYC & NAECS/SDE, 1991, 2002, 2003).

Assessment is an important part of curriculum planning: It tells us what the children know, what their skills are, where their interests lie, and how they behave and relate to others. Based upon information gleaned from the assessments, we can provide them with the experiences that will best support their learning and development. In order to accomplish this, our assessments must be ongoing, well planned in a systematic way, and conducted collaboratively with others involved in the children's learning—including parents and families.

Above all, "Information gained from assessments *must benefit* children. Assessment and accountability systems should improve practices and services and should not be used to rank, sort, or penalize young children" (NAEYC/NAECS/SDE, 2004, p. 2). The information from assessments should be used to support children's strengths, interests, and development rather than used to try to speed up their learning.

TYPES OF ASSESSMENT

Developmental Screening

Screening is a brief, quickly administered assessment to determine if a child needs further, more extensive assessment due to a disability or learning problem. Tests are used to identify children who may be in need of special services and are a first step in identifying children in need of further diagnosis.

Only staff with sufficient training should conduct developmental screening tests, using instruments that meet strict technical requirements for test construction and that are linguistically and culturally appropriate. These instruments focus on the child's ability to acquire skills in language, reasoning, gross motor, fine motor, and emotional/social development. It is good practice to include hearing and vision assessments as part of the screening procedures.

Assessment of children's development and learning in the context of identifying special needs should be related to standards in all domains and give adaptations or special attention to young children's developmental, cultural, and linguistic variability. We must be careful in jumping to conclusions about a young child's mental capacities, particularly when the child does not speak English as a first language. Additionally, initial developmental screening is only the first step and should not be used to determine if a child has special needs—further professional assessment is needed and a referral should be made. The standardized screening tests should be used in conjunction with other sources of information such as medical exams, hearing and vision tests, and family communication (Meisels & Atkins-Burnett, 2005).

Assessment to Support Learning and Development

There is more to assessment than simply administering tests. This is especially true in early childhood, when so much development takes place so quickly and is hard to measure. Imagine trying to sit a classroom of 4-year-olds down at their desks to take a pencil-and-paper test for an hour! In order to assess young children as accurately as we can, we must use more than one measure and make sure that it is appropriate for their developmental level. Fortunately, early childhood educators have been using a range of assessment methods since the beginning of kindergarten. Appropriate early childhood assessments include observation, the documenting and collection of children's work, checklists and rating scales, portfolios, and standardized tests.

Authentic Assessment

Authentic assessment refers to observing and assessing children in a situation that is as close to their real-life context as possible. Rather than the ridiculous notion of sitting a young child down to take a written exam, you might observe the child during play or in the art studio or at the lunch table. "Throughout our day, we observe many rich learning moments that reveal the children's thinking to us. Many of these are short moments, so we must be sensitive so that we can capture them. However short they are, they can be monumental within a child's learning process" (Gleim, 2007, para. 1).

Through anecdotal observations, child interviews and conversations, and checklists identifying specific skills and accomplishments, we can assess the child's concepts and skill development as well as the important foundational skills such as listening and paying attention.

Informal anecdotal observations are the notes made by teachers that record events and behaviors they think are particularly important to remember about individual children. This is a relatively easy method of assessment to use regularly. All that is required is the discipline to sit at the computer once a week and add notes for each child or keep records on individual cards. Be sure to head each file with the name, birth date, and date of admission to the center. Also, include the name or initials of the observer and the date of each entry.

Authentic assessment should be used in alignment with early standards and in planning appropriate curriculum activities. Figure 6.2 illustrates how one preschool teacher uses authentic assessment to determine which early learning standards are being met and how the child's development can be supported.

Using Conversations to Gather Information About the Child.

Notice how the teacher in Figure 6.2 uses conversations with the child to gain further insight into the child's thinking. Nothing beats sitting down and talking with people to find out what they know and what's on their mind. When talking with children in an open and engaging way—not grilling them on "correct" test answers—we find out what they are thinking and what sorts of theories they are constructing about the world.

It is a valuable practice to record the actual discussion either by having someone take notes on the spot or by transcribing an audio- or videotape later—a strategy frequently employed in Reggio-inspired settings (Cadwell, 2002). Teachers who take this amount of time and effort are often astonished at comments they initially overlooked that were actually of great significance. This kind of detailed recording makes it possible to use the records when sharing insights with other adults about the children's knowledge as well as providing a precise record of their language skills.

Using Checklists to Gather Information About the Child.

Checklists are another practical way to keep track of what the children have or have not learned. Because the items on such lists tend to be precise and single out specific accomplishments, they lend themselves particularly well to measuring behaviors the teacher can actually see happening such as physical attributes—for example, measurements of weight and height—and physical accomplishments—hopping on one foot, for example, or catching a ball. It is a simple matter to compile such checklists by referring to readily available charts of physical development. But checklists, while particularly useful for evaluating the status of the physical self, need not be limited to these kinds of items; they can also be useful for identifying social abilities and emotional behaviors.

Each school has its own philosophies about what is most important. The checklists should be designed to fit these objectives. It is astonishingly easy to become trapped into evaluating children on skills that have not been emphasized in the curriculum. Results of such mismatched evaluations can only be disappointing. The teacher should be as explicit and clear as possible when describing the behaviors that will be evaluated.

PEARSON
myeducationlab

Go to MyEducationLab and select the topic "Observation and Assessment." Under Activities and Applications, watch the video *Observing Children in Authentic Contexts.* How does the observation of children in authentic contexts differ from giving them a test?

Throughout our day, we observe many rich learning moments that reveal the children's thinking to us. Many of these are short moments, so we must be sensitive so that we can capture them. However short they are, they can be monumental within a child's learning process. We would like to share a brief but important moment of learning, the moment when K revealed to us that a shift in her thinking had occurred.

During a shared morning of work between the 4s and 3's classrooms, we observed the children who were engaged in the message area. Initially the children were creating jewelry, using paper and what the children call the rainbow string. It was interesting to watch one of the 3's interacting and following the work of the 4's with great intensity. While observing the dynamics of this play, I watched as K left the jewelry-making process and shifted toward writing on small pieces of paper. Wondering why she had made this shift, I realized that the other girls in the classroom were busy preparing for a hula performance outside. Had she overheard the other girls? I speculated that this could be the case, for in the past we have observed her writing on small pieces of paper. When asked about this, she explained that the writing was for everybody to come to the performance. Was she perhaps making tickets for everyone? This piece of the performance was of great interest to her. Is this what she was doing?

Continuing to watch her work, I saw a sudden change in what she was doing. She abandoned the ticket-making process for the creation of a list of who was coming to the performance. What happened next was unexpected. I heard her asking, "What's your name, Ms. Leslie?" I said, "Ms. Leslie." K: "No, what's your *name*, Ms. Leslie?" Her emphasis on "name" led me to look closer at her work and to pause for a moment and think about the context of her question. In doing so, I noted the change in materials that she was using.

I asked, "Do you want to know how to spell my name?" K replied, "Yeah."

For each letter of my name that I shared with her, she created a symbol/letter. This was not in a hurried or whimsical fashion; each mark was made with great intention and thought. To the casual viewer, these would seem to be "merely" marks. However, something far more had occurred and was being revealed in this moment. As she ran out of space, she made her symbols smaller to try to keep them together rather than putting them on another line. Why was that?

When K finished, she showed my name to me. A moment later, I heard K talking out loud.

K: "H's name." When I looked toward K, I found her looking toward the message boxes, copying H's name. She would look at the message box, write a letter/symbol, and look over again, repeating the process until she was satisfied that she had all the letters/symbols from H's name represented on paper. Once again, we found K assigning a letter to a corresponding symbolic form.

Teacher Reflections Children are constantly trying to make meaning of their world. During ages 4 and 5, we find them shifting from making meaning from verbal thinking to making meaning from written symbols. This is a complicated yet powerful experience for children. In our learning community, we continuously are supporting the child's learning processes by allowing them to experience the powerful functions of print. One way we do this is through our ongoing plan-making for our day. This process has had a major impact in many areas of our learning community, from literacy to the work in the atelier [art studio] to the organization of thinking processes and expression of thoughts.

This moment with K allowed us to see into her theories about the printed word. K clearly knew that a spoken name is different in representation than a written name. We also saw K's confidence as she realized that each person has their own set of graphic symbols or representations that must be grouped in a particular arrangement in order for it to be called a name.

Figure 6.2
Example of authentic assessment

Source: A Moment of Learning *by Leslie Gleim. Posted on October 23, 2007, on the Mid-Pacific Institute, Honolulu, HI Web site. http://www. midpac.edu/elementary/PG/2007/10/an_ordinary_moment_of_learning.php*

K seems to be in the midst of a huge leap into the world of literacy and the written word, for we found that she had developed a theory around "names." This was evident in her question, "What's your name, Ms. Leslie?" When I responded, "Ms. Leslie," she said, "No, what's your *name*, Ms. Leslie?" Clearly she wasn't after the verbal spoken name; she wanted the symbols that would turn the spoken "Leslie" into the written "Leslie." Her theory became visible as she assigned a graphic symbol to each letter that I told her. Again, each mark was purposeful and intentional.

During this learning moment, K was making her thinking visible to us through her spoken and unspoken actions. We found K to be beginning to grasp the value of words/names in her world and environment. K nailed down the meaning or intentions of her work a few moments later when we observed her using the message boxes to scaffold and support her as she added H to the list of those coming to the performance.

She could have easily asked me for the information to spell H, but instead we found K solving this dilemma using her own resources—looking at the message boxes nearby. This moment demonstrated to us a shift from relying on others to solving her own problems. K clearly is learning how to learn.

We have since observed K connecting and cycling through this theory of hers around names. Today she created a bracelet for Ms. Leslie that included a name tag. She again asked me for my name. As I said each letter to her, she repeated the letter and assigned a symbol. Earlier she constructed a book in which she began writing symbols and letters that were close approximations of actual letters. She clearly has emerged into the powerful world of words as she now is formulating theories about the function of words and the graphic representations that are assigned to make up words.

After observing this moment, how might we support K with future provocations for learning? Seeing K's interest in the written word now beginning to unfold, it is important for us to continue connecting this new knowledge in meaningful ways for her. Perhaps in her plan-making, we could have her make lists for us. Perhaps at home, her parents could make a list of a couple of items that are needed from the store, such as milk (which has two letters from her name in it), etc. We will also be watching for her to make more closer approximations of how the letters look.

In this learning moment of K's, we captured only one small slice of the thinking that is occurring in our classroom learning processes each day. These small moments will impact K's (and each of the children's) future learning for a lifetime.

Figure 6.2
Example of authentic assessment—*Continued*

When composing such lists, the teacher also must keep them within reason in terms of developmental levels. It can be frustrating and discouraging to both a child and teacher if the teacher expects behavior that lies beyond the child's developmental ability to achieve. For this reason, it cannot be recommended too strongly that developmental charts, such as the one included in Appendix A, be consulted.

Portfolio Assessment.   A portfolio is a "purposeful collection of evidence of a child's learning, collected over time, that demonstrates a child's efforts, progress, or achievement" (McAfee, Leong, & Bodrova, 2004, p. 52). The observations, conversations,

myeducationlab

Go to MyEducationLab and select the topic "Observation and Assessment." Under Activities and Applications, watch the video *Portfolios* and notice how the child is included in the portfolio process. How does the child benefit from this type of assessment?

and checklists discussed previously are good examples of teacher-produced records that are typically included, but the ingredients of the child's portfolio should never be limited to only that kind of material. Suggestions of what to include are limited only by the teacher's imagination and energy (and available storage space). For example, the following items might be included:

Teacher-Produced Records

Informal observations

Conversations and investigations

Checklists

Photographs

Video- and audiotapes

Health records—vaccinations, height, weight, possibly attendance

Summaries of parent interviews

Evaluation of achievements defined by IEPs

Results of standardized commercial tests

Child-Produced Material

Photographs of block structures

Self-expressive efforts such as paintings, drawings, collages, and so forth

Dictated stories

Interviews with the child—favorite books, pets, things to do

Parent-Produced Material

Questionnaires about child's development, preferences, and health

Summaries of conferences

Noteworthy family events

List of family members who are emotionally significant to the child

Emergency contact list

Anecdotes and other information the parent wants to include

Records from Community Resources

Physician reports: immunizations, allergies, other relevant information

Information from the child development team and IEPs, if the child uses these services

Documentation Boards.   The early childhood educators in Reggio Emilia have developed the collection and documentation of children's work literally into an art form (the exhibit, *The Hundred Languages of Children* is composed of such documentation and is on tour in North America). Rather than creating a portfolio of the children's work and other materials that document their learning, the Reggio teachers create documentation panels that line the classroom and school walls. In this way, there is ongoing visible communication with all the participants in the school (children, families, and teachers) about what the children are thinking, doing, creating, and learning. The use of

Leslie Gleim

Documentation panels are a wonderful way to draw parents and families into the school.

documentation panels is more than simply a display of the children's artwork. It is used to document the path of the children's thinking and development, usually including conversations about their theories and ideas that form the basis for their creations. Teachers in the United States who have used documentation panels have found it to be a wonderful way to draw parents and families into the school, as well as heighten the educational experience for the children.

Standardized Tests

Standardized tests are developed according to scientific guidelines and conform to high standards of reliability and validity. These tests have strict procedures for administration, and they have a numerical scoring system based on comparison to others who have taken the test (this is called *norm referencing*). Standardized tests present the same task the same way to every child; they are scored the same way and provide comparison tables that reveal how other children performed on the same items (McAfee et al., 2004). This quality of sameness is the reason they are referred to as being "standardized," and it often reassures the public they are "fair."

Since the tests themselves do not vary, their use makes it possible to compare the performance of the tested group or individual with a larger, national sample. Although this practice is often criticized because it may encourage teachers to teach to the test instead of to the needs of the children, many school systems require this kind of numerical data as part (or all) of their accountability procedures. Public schools must use standardized tests beginning in the third grade as mandated by the NCLB Act.

Using a standardized test also makes it possible to compare the performance of one child with that of a group of children of similar age, gender, and so forth. Such comparisons can be quick and helpful assets in screening situations where pronounced deviations from the average can identify youngsters who will benefit from being offered whatever special help that deviation requires.

However, there are drawbacks to using standardized tests with such young children. Early childhood is a time of rapid developmental change and it is hard to "capture it" at one moment in time, with just one test. Young children are active and hands-on, and they represent what they know by showing. In general, experts urge great caution in the use of standardized tests to assess young children's development and they should never be used as the sole means of assessment (Bodrova et al., 2004; McAfee, Leong, & Bodrova, 2004; NAEYC & NAECS/SDE, 2002, 2003).

Because these kinds of tests require individual administration and special training when used with young children, they are typically administered by someone the child doesn't know in an unfamiliar setting performing unfamiliar tasks—hardly circumstances under which a "best" performance can be expected. Additional objections cited by the National Association for the Education of Young Children (2005, 2006) and NAEYC and the State Departments of Education (NAEYC & NAECS/SDE, 2001) in their position papers on testing include the statements that such tests provide extremely narrow assessments of skills, the form of the tests and methods of administration are often developmentally inappropriate, people put too much trust in the results, tests tend to label children unfairly or prematurely, and the testing situations are unrealistic.

A report from the National Research Council (Bowman, Donovan, & Burns, 2000) cautions, "The first five years of life are a time of incredible growth and learning, but the course of development is uneven and sporadic. The status of a child's development as of any given day can change very rapidly. Consequently, assessment results—in particular, standardized test scores that reflect a given point in time—can easily misrepresent children's learning" (p. 9).

IMPORTANT PRINCIPLES ABOUT ASSESSMENTS

Children's Records Are Private and Should Be Kept Confidential

Children's records must never be left lying around for someone to pick up and read even while the teacher is working on them. The competence of individual children should never be discussed with people outside the school or with other parents who do not have a right to know about it.

Use Assessment to Connect with Families

Families have the right to be informed about the assessment of their child. In addition, families provide important information about the child's interests and development that may not be apparent at school or in a testing situation. Both informal and formal assessment results should be shared with the family in a respectful and culturally responsive way.

Carry Out Assessments More Than One Time

Sometimes teachers employ measures of evaluation only at the end of the year. This provides a summing up for the family and for the next teacher (who may or may not read it) but is of little value to the teacher who has done the work. It is more useful to employ evaluative measures shortly after the child enters the program and again later on. Early assessment helps the teacher quickly become acquainted with the child and plan around the child's needs and interests. It also provides a record to be used as a comparison at the middle and end of the year. Without this measurement at the beginning, there is no way to show how much the child has learned during the time at school.

Take Varying Ethnic/Cultural Backgrounds into Account

Assessments should occur with ongoing communication with families and with sensitivity to the child's cultural context (NAEYC & NAECS/SDE, 2003). There are many cultural factors, such as inability to understand the test language or *poverty*, that can lead to erroneous conclusions about the child's development. If educational decisions are based on culturally biased assessment results, the child's future opportunities might be limited.

Make Sure Assessments Are Comprehensive and Include Measures for All Five Selves

The purpose of keeping track is to help the teacher see the whole child, not just the problem areas. For this reason, it is important to look at the child's abilities for all five selves so a balanced picture of the child can be obtained. In this way, the teacher can identify and build on current strengths to mitigate some possible weaker areas of development.

Put Assessment to Good Use in Planning Curriculum

Assessment and curriculum are closely tied. Assessment indicates what the children are interested in and allows teachers to modify the curriculum to meet the children's needs.

Use Assessment to Benefit Children with Disabilities

Children with disabilities can benefit from appropriate assessment by using a range of assessments to ensure their needs are being met and to individualize the curriculum accordingly. When using assessments that were developed for typically developing children, it is important to adapt measures and interpretation of results with respect to the child's developmental level.

Interpret Assessment Results Cautiously

There are two reasons for remembering this recommendation. The first is that every form of assessing children has limitations and weaknesses. The second is that it is very possible the teacher may have reached an incorrect conclusion about what the results mean—all our assessments are subjective interpretations about the child's visible behaviors, not absolute objective fact.

SUMMARY

Since the passage of the No Child Left Behind (NCLB) Act of 2001, standards and assessment are required in public elementary schools and are common in many types of preschool programs today. Early learning standards outline the expectations for children's learning and development. It is left up to each state or program to determine the learning standards to be applied and the types of assessment to be used. Teachers should familiarize themselves with their state and program standards.

Early learning standards should be comprehensive, address all areas of development, and include measures for all five selves of the whole child. It is unfortunate that many schools have narrowed the curriculum to focus only on academic domains that are included on standardized tests. IDEA is federal legislation mandating that children with disabilities have regular assessments and IEPs conducted so as to best meet their individual needs.

Assessment is closely linked to standards as well as to the curriculum. Assessment measures the objectives set forth in the early learning standards, and the assessment is then used to inform teachers about appropriate next steps to take in developing the curriculum. Keeping track of the children's development is a valuable process that early childhood teachers can use for describing children and measuring changes in their behavior. However, great care must be taken when selecting such measures. Teachers must not place too much confidence in any one measure and must interpret all results with caution.

Early childhood teachers must serve as screening agents to help identify possible problems (physical, emotional, or cognitive). Following identification of a difficulty, teachers should attempt to effect a referral to the appropriate specialist.

Practical, informal methods of recording and evaluating behavior include the use of observations, conversations, interviews with children and families, and developmentally relevant checklists. These are often compiled into documentation boards and individual portfolios.

Standardized tests provide more formal methods of assessment. Although they have some important strengths, such tests also have many significant weaknesses when used to measure the abilities of preschool children. They should be carefully evaluated and used with great discretion.

Ultimately, the child assessment process should benefit the child.

Questions and Activities

1. Using the Related Organizations and Online Resources at the end of this chapter, determine if your state has early learning standards. What are they? Are they comprehensive in addressing the five selves of the whole child, or are they weighted in favor of certain domains?
2. Look up the early learning standards for your (or another) state for 4-year-olds. How would you assess the children to see if the standards have been met?
3. What is the difference between authentic assessment and standardized tests?

Diversity Question

1. Why is it important to take linguistic and cultural variation into account when assessing young children?

Predicament

1. A 4-1/2-year-old boy attending your school is cognitively delayed and functions at about the 2 1/2-year-old level. He hangs around the housekeeping corner and the blocks a lot, but rarely speaks to the other children or joins in at group time. How would you use standards and assessment to benefit this child?

Self-Check Questions for Review

Content-Related Questions

1. List three reasons why the passage of IDEA has made a difference in what teachers of young children need to know and do.
2. List three reasons why the passage of NCLB has made a difference in what teachers of young children need to know and do.
3. Why is it important to align assessment with early learning standards and curriculum development?

Integrative Questions

1. How can standards and assessment be used to benefit children?
2. It is important for teachers and families to remain in close contact. Describe how you can use the assessment process to communicate with families. What specific techniques would you use to include families in assessment?

Reference for Further Reading

McAfee, O., Leong, D. J., & Bodrova, E. (2004). *Basics of assessment: A primer for early childhood educators*. Washington, DC: National Association for the Education of Young Children.

Related Organizations and Online Resources

Beyond the Journal. This is the online resource for articles published in *Young Children*. The January 2004 issue is devoted to assessment. A wealth of resource information is available at http://www.journal.naeyc.org/btj/200401/.

Culturally and Linguistically Appropriate Services (CLAS). Descriptions of assessments, screening tools, and appropriate practices for children with and without disabilities from culturally and linguistically diverse backgrounds can be found at http://clas.uiuc.edu/special/evaltools/.

Head Start Performance Standards. These standards are available at http://www.ehsnrc.org/Information Resources/HeadstartPerfStandards.htm.

National Association for the Education of Young Children (NAEYC) and the National Association of Early Childhood Specialists in State Departments of Education (NAECS/SDE). The joint position statement on early learning standards can be accessed at http://www.naeyc.org/about/positions/early_learning_standards.asp. Additional NAEYC joint position statements can be accessed at http://www.naeyc.org.

National Institute for Early Education Research (NIEER). A state data bank with regard to standards and assessment for early childhood education is available at http://www.nieer.org/yearbook/states.

U.S. Department of Education. Many resources about the NCLB Act, standards and assessments in the public schools, and state-by-state information are available at http://www.ed.gov.

CHAPTER seven

Handling Daily Routines

How to stop nagging the children through transition times?

Why Miguel won't eat his lunch?

How to get Rosie off the climbing gym when it's time to go indoors?

. . . IF YOU HAVE, THE MATERIAL IN THE FOLLOWING PAGES WILL HELP YOU.

Think for a moment about how you ate as a child. Unless you have worked very hard to change your childhood habits, chances are that the way you ate then closely resembles the way you eat now. It's true: The older we get, the harder it is to change. So the earlier you start children on the right eating track, the easier it will be for them to stay the course.

Bridget Swinney (1999, p. 13)

Sure, a nutritious diet helps power a child's busy day and all that growing that's going on. But also on the menu is learning—that bringing a cup to mouth without spilling half the juice takes a steady hand, that the oat circles don't stay on the spoon when you turn it over, that the shape those sandwiches are cut in is called a square. What's more, mealtime is a time for fun (applesauce makes a great dip for chicken fingers . . . and baby fingers!) and for socializing (who cares if all the milk drips down my face when I smile back at you?) Bon appetit!

Heidi Murkoff (2003, p. 37)

Routines, those omnipresent recurring sequences of behavior, constitute the backbone of the early childhood day and serve as landmarks that divide the day into different sections. They typically include the activities of arriving, departing, eating, diapering or toileting, washing up, resting, cleanup, and the transitions between them and the other daily activities of the center and school life. Physical health is vital to children's well-being, and they need these routines to help them build strong bodies as well as stable personalities. For infants and toddlers, routines are the basis of the curriculum. Caregivers who respond in a sensitive and consistent manner to our youngest children's needs (rather than rushing through diapering, for example) help create a sense of security that allows the child to bond with others and feel safe in the world (Gonzalez-Mena & Eyer, 2006; Honig, 2002; Lally et al., 2003).

One note of caution about routines: If the teacher is unwise enough to go to war with a child on the subject of routines, the child, if so inclined, can always win. Thus children who absolutely will not eat, will not use the toilet, or refuse to go to sleep can win any time they want to; there is little the teacher can do about it. Fortunately teachers and children rarely reach this kind of impasse, but it is important to understand that such power struggles *can* happen and *have* happened and that the most common way to bring about such a disaster is to reduce oneself to attempting to force children to comply with any routine absolutely against their will. It just does not work.

The best way to prevent conflicts from developing is to realize that children usually find comfort in reasonable routines that contribute to their physical well-being. It also helps if the teacher determines the most important learnings to be derived from each routine and then works toward achieving those goals, rather than becoming caught up in "winning for its own sake." For example, it is more important that children enjoy food and take pleasure in mealtimes than it is that they clear their plates, wait until everyone is served, or not rap their glasses on the table. Bearing this primary goal in mind will reduce the amount of criticism and control that may otherwise mar snack and lunch times.

Schedules and Transitions into Routines

Schedules

Routines and transitions are best understood when seen in the perspective of the overall schedule, so a sample full-day preschool schedule is provided (Figure 7.1). Teachers in elementary schools have less flexibility in scheduling the day and must adhere to the curriculum guidelines required by their school and state standards. However, the areas addressed in the sample preschool schedule should also be included in primary classrooms. Elementary school teachers should make use of the standards recommended by their school, state, and national organizations to help determine the schedule (see Related Organizations and Online Resources at the end of chapter 6).

Remember that a schedule should be regarded as a guide, not as dogma. Allowance should always be made for deviations when these are desirable. Perhaps it took longer

7:00–7:30	Some teachers arrive, set out materials, and ready the environment for children.
7:30	Children begin to arrive. One teacher or the director is specially assigned to greet children and parents, chat, and carry out the health check. If possible, another staff member provides a cozy time reading books with those who desire it. Self-select materials are also available.
8:30–9:15	Breakfast available for children who want it. Breakfast area set up near schoolroom sink to facilitate hand-washing before and after eating. Self-selected activity continues until 9:15 for those who are not hungry.
9:15–9:45	Small- or large-group time: this often continues quite a while for 4-year-olds, less time for younger children. Its length should vary each day in order to adapt to the changing needs of the group.
9:45–10:00	Transition to activities.
10:00–11:40	Mingled indoor-outdoor experience or outdoor followed by indoor activity, depending on staffing and weather. Small-group experiences and field trips occur during this time. Self-selected activities, changed from the ones available in the early arrival period, are also provided.
11:40–12:00	Children help put things away, prepare gradually for lunch. Children go to toilet; children and teachers wash hands.
12:00–12:35	Family-style lunchtime; children are seated with adults in groups as small as possible.
12:35–1:00	Children prepare for nap: toilet, wash hands, brush teeth, snuggle down.
1:00–3:00	Nap time; children get up as they wake up, toilet, and move out of nap area. Snack ready as they arrive and desire it.
By 3:30	All snacks completed. Indoor-outdoor self-select continues, again with special activities planned and provided for.
4:40	Children begin to put things away, freshen up (wash hands and faces, etc.), and have quiet opportunities to use manipulatives or sit with teacher for songs, stories, and general quiet, relaxing time as parents call for them.
5:30	Children picked up (except for the inevitable emergencies of course!)

Figure 7.1
Daily schedule for a full-day program for 3- and 4-year-olds

than anticipated for the bread to rise, or perhaps dramatic play is involving most of the group in an intensely satisfying way. Schedules need give and stretch to accommodate these kinds of possibilities. This is why overlap times and approximate times are listed in the schedule. Even a modest amount of latitude allows children to proceed gradually from one activity to the next without being hassled by the teachers (Hemmeter, Ostrosky, Artman, & Kinder, 2008; K. Miller, 2003).

It can also happen that some schedules do not match what actually takes place in the classroom. Studies of early childhood curricula reveal how some scheduled times were consistently short-changed—particularly times allotted for free play (Wiltz & Klein, 2001; Zigler et al., 2004). This is a shame because play is overwhelmingly (98%) the favorite activity of young children, regardless of quality or program type. In addition, despite teachers' good intentions, researchers found the activity children cited as their *least* favorite was circle time, because, as one child phrased it, "It always takes too long" (Wiltz & Klein, 2001, p. 225). Teachers would do well to keep these studies in mind when planning the day for children. We must ensure that adequate time is allotted for free play—in actuality and not just on paper—and that there are not so many lengthy, teacher-directed activities that the children dislike.

The Research Study in this chapter demonstrates the value of offering self-selected, child-initiated activities and small-group activities over large-group, teacher-directed activities to increase later academic skills. Preprimary and elementary school teachers can use these findings to support a play-rich curriculum and explain to families how free-choice time and play can enhance children's cognitive growth.

Note that the schedule in Figure 7.1 allows for breakfast to be served only to those children who desire it. For years our center was plagued with the problem of having some children arrive at 8:30 or 9:00 stuffed to the gills, whereas others were clearly famished. If we waited for snack until 10:00, when everyone had at least a little appetite, then they were not hungry for lunch! We finally decided to solve this problem by offering breakfast on a self-select basis, with food kept appetizing on warming trays and with a friendly staff member sitting in the breakfast corner at all times to assist the children and welcome them for a quiet personal chat as they ate. This solution, though unconventional, has done a much better job of meeting all the children's needs by freeing more of the staff to work with the youngsters who are not hungry and by providing a homey, comfortable, slow-paced beginning of the day for children who are just waking up and do want breakfast. It also helps settle down children who may have been rushed off to school in too much of a hurry to have had more than a bite to eat before departure.

The same policy of eating by choice is followed after nap since children drift out of the nap area a few at a time. Almost all of them at that point, of course, are ready for something good to eat, but it is still a matter of self-decision for them. This not only prevents wasted food but also is part of our effort to encourage children to be aware of what their bodies are saying to them. Are they eating just because it is the thing to do, or are their bodies telling them they are really hungry?

The primary rule that applies to both breakfast and snack time is that, once seated, the children stay until they are finished eating. No one walks around with food in their hands, and a staff member is always seated at the table to keep the children company.

Transition Times

Transitions (the time spent in moving from one activity to the next) occupy a large part of activity time in early childhood education, depending on the school, the particular day, and the skill and planning contributed by the teacher. Transitions are worth thinking about and managing well so that children can move as smoothly as possible from one activity to the next. It is necessary to plan for enough time when shifting, for instance, from music to lunch or from lunch to nap so that children are not unnecessarily harried in the process. Infant and toddler caregivers need to be sensitive about moving from one activity to the next, as this is the time our youngest children can become most anxious. Additionally, teachers must pay particular attention during transitions to students with behavioral problems; this is often a confusing time when directing their own behavior becomes especially difficult (Hemmeter et al., 2008; McIntosh, Herman, Sanford, McGraw, & Florence, 2004). "Children's challenging behavior during transitions may be related to how program staff structure, schedule, and implement transitions" (Hemmeter et al., 2008, p. 19).

If you find yourself continually nagging and urging the children to hurry through their paces, you may want to try the following suggestions to make transitions easier for you and them. In addition to allowing a realistic amount of time for transitions to take place, it always helps to warn *once* in advance when a change is in the offing, saying, "It's almost story time," or, "You can have a little more time with the beads, but then we'll have to put them away." This gives the children a chance to finish what they are doing and makes their compliance more likely. It also helps to remember that transitions do not usually present an opportunity for a real choice (the child is supposed to come, not linger in the yard), so it is best not to ask, "Would you like to come?" or, "It's time to come in, OK?" but to say more definitely, "In just a minute it's going to be time for lunch, and we will go indoors. What do you suppose we're having to eat today?" Occasionally singing a simple song will also help get children moving in the desired direction, and singing is especially effective with babies and toddlers during transition times. Avoiding situations in which all the children have to do something at once is the best help of all because this avoids the noisy, crowded situations that seem to happen with particular frequency in the toilet room (Hemmeter et al., 2008).

ROUTINES OF ARRIVAL AND DEPARTURE

It is natural for young children to feel anxious when their fathers or mothers leave them at school. This feeling, called *separation anxiety*, appears to be strongest in American children between the ages of 10 and 18 months (Honig, 2002). When working with children at this age, it is a good idea to prepare yourself for separation anxiety by reading up on it and openly discussing it with parents and coworkers. It can be very emotionally draining to care for a child who is experiencing intense separation anxiety—and you will need all the support you can get! An excellent resource is *Secure Relationships: Nurturing Infant/Toddler Attachment in Early Care Settings,* by Alice Sterling Honig (2002). Even beyond this age, however, separation requires time and tactful handling by the staff so that the child and the family come to feel comfortable about parting.

Introduce the Child to School Gradually

It is common practice and good sense to recommend a visit by parent and child for the first day, then another short stay while the parent leaves for a brief period, followed by a gradual extension of time as the child's ability to endure separation increases. With infants and toddlers, the more the family can stay in the beginning, the better (Honig, 2002). A transitional object brought from home can help ease a young child's anxiety, as does making sure the children each have their own space for the safekeeping of their belongings. It is also important to maintain a positive atmosphere for the child during separation and to find things that make the child feel comfortable and interested in the new environment.

Another way of helping children become comfortable is by having an open house during which families can come and go at their convenience. Some schools begin the term with half the children coming on one day, and the other half coming on the next. At our center we send each child a personal letter with a name tag, an invitation to the open house, and a short description of what we will be doing at school. The children love these letters, and this preliminary contact does seem to overcome some of their initial apprehension.

These suggestions about gradual adaptation to the new environment are fine for many families whose schedules can be somewhat flexible, but they do not work for parents whose jobs demand that they appear promptly at 8:00 a.m. no matter what the teacher recommends or how hard the child is crying. If at all possible, special arrangements should be made for such families when their children begin attending. A grandfather or aunt might be pressed into service and stay while the child makes friends. Sometimes the parent can bring the child by for a visit around lunchtime, the teacher can make a Saturday visit to the home, or the child can come to school with a friend. Any of these arrangements, though not ideal, are preferable to allowing the child to walk in and simply be left in a strange place with strange people for 9 hours on the first day (Honig, 2002).

Handle Outbursts of Emotion with Care

It helps to recognize that children must often deal with three feelings when their loved one leaves: (a) grief (the emotion that seems most obvious and logical), (b) fear (also not very surprising), and (c) anger (the emotion the teacher is least likely to recognize in these circumstances) (Bowlby, 1973, 1980). It is often necessary not only to comfort and reassure children but also to recognize with them that they feel angry about being left at school. At our center, one forthright 3-year-old took real pleasure in biting the mama doll with our toothy rubber hippopotamus as soon as her mother departed. The teacher may also see this angry reaction at being left behind come out at the end of the day when the child insists (with just a touch of malice) that he or she wants to stay at school "for ever and ever" and does not want to go home. If the teacher interprets this reaction to the family as being a way of relieving angry feelings, it will help maintain friendly relations all around.

Actually it is the children who make a forthright fuss as their families leave who seem to work through their feelings of loss with the greatest expedition, whereas the children who apparently make an easy adjustment by becoming instantly involved in activities often become downcast a few weeks later as they lower their defenses. If this happens 3 to 4 weeks after entry to school, the parent is likely to assume something has happened there that makes the child want to stay home. The best protection against this conclusion is to explain casually to the parent *before the child's facade crumbles* that the child may show grief at a later time and that most children feel some sadness and loneliness when left at school.

Learning to let go is part of becoming mature. A nice balance of comfort combined with a matter-of-fact expectation that they will feel better soon usually gets these children started on the day. Having something at hand that they especially enjoy will help, too. Holding a distressed baby is essential in reducing separation anxiety, as well as rubbing the back and using soothing words and song to reassure the baby that "Mommy (or Daddy or Nana) will come back." Teachers must take care to permit the older child

Benjamin La Framboise

Learning to separate is part of becoming mature.

to form a relationship with them as a bridge to the other children yet at the same time not encourage this relationship so much that the youngster droops around longer than necessary or becomes a careerist hand-holder. Wise elementary school teachers encourage friendships within the classroom and can use peers to lure a reluctant child into the wonders of the classroom.

ROUTINES THAT CENTER AROUND EATING

Adequate Nutrition Is Important

In these days of imitation foods and casual eating habits it is important to emphasize the value of good food for young children. Too many schools depend on artificial juices and a cracker for a snack, supposedly on the grounds that the children are well fed at home. But the underlying reason for serving this kind of food is that it is convenient and cheap. Yet studies continue to accumulate that indicate good nutrition combined with other environmental factors is associated with the ability to pay attention and learn (Center on Hunger, Poverty, and Nutrition Policy, 1999).

Although nutritional problems are most severe among families of low income, not only the children in compensatory programs are "orphans of wealth." Less than 1% of U.S. children consume the balanced diet recommended by the U.S. Department of

Agriculture (American Dietetic Association [ADA], 1999). Instead researchers found that 40% of children's diets came from fat and added sugars (Association for Childhood Education International [ACEI], 2004). Even infants and toddlers are not free from poor feeding habits. According to a recent study, almost a quarter of toddlers ages 19 to 24 months consumed hot dogs, french fries, and sweetened beverages on a daily basis (Gerber Products Company, 2003). Not surprisingly, the number of overweight children has skyrocketed in the last decade: Ten percent of children ages 2 to 5 years and 15% of school-age children are overweight, representing an 11% increase since the 1990s (American Heart Association, 2005). This is why, no matter the income level of the families of children served by the program, careful planning of nutritious meals is so important and why so much attention is devoted to it in the following pages.

Planning Appealing and Nutritious Meals

One fortunate fact about teaching at the preprimary level is that teachers and directors usually have opportunities to participate in planning what the children will eat. Even when the menus are decided at a "higher" level, it can still be possible to influence the planning if this is attempted with tact and persistence! Teachers in public elementary schools are encouraged to work with families and school staff to support healthy eating habits in the children.

A useful way to begin such planning is to become acquainted with the preschool lunch pattern required by the U.S. Department of Agriculture (USDA; Table 7.1) since so many children's centers use funding from that agency to support their food services. The USDA also publishes recommended feeding patterns for infants, and those who work with this age should become familiar with the guidelines. It should be noted that caregivers must never give juice in a bottle as it can cause severe damage to developing teeth long before they appear. One can also use the MyPyramid for Kids published by the USDA as an overall guide for what to feed young children. Note the emphasis on complex carbohydrates, fruits, and vegetables (Figure 7.2).

These standards can serve as basic guidelines, but some additional points should be considered as well. Variety, particularly as the year progresses and the children feel at ease, should be a keynote of the food program. Snacks should be different every day and can be based on seasonal fruits and vegetables to help keep budgets within reason.

Dessert should be unsugared fruit and should be regarded as a nutritional component of the meal, not as a reward to be bargained for.

If the food is plain and familiar and a lot of it can be eaten with the fingers, children will eat more. As a general rule, young children are deeply suspicious of casseroles and food soaked in drab-looking sauces and gravies. They prefer things they can recognize, such as carrot sticks, hamburger, and plain fruit.

Table 7.2 provides some sample lunch menus that show how appealing plain, relatively inexpensive food can be. Even if all the children are from one particular ethnic group, it is desirable to vary the suggestions in Table 7.2 by incorporating food from many cultures bit by bit. For example, menus might include black-eyed peas with ham or pinto beans with melted cheese. Introduction of such foods at this time of the child's life is particularly desirable for two reasons. First, good-tasting food that is identified as coming from a particular culture helps children feel friendly toward that culture.

Table 7.1

U.S. Department of Agriculture Child Care Food Program required meal program

Breakfast

AGES*	1–2	3–5	6–12
MILK Must be fluid milk	1/2 cup	3/4 cup	1 cup
VEGETABLE or FRUIT or JUICE	1/4 cup	1/2 cup	1/2 cup
GRAINS/BREADS A serving is a bread or bread alternate and/or cereal:			
Bread, enriched or whole-grain	1/2 slice	1/2 slice	1 slice
Cereal, enriched or whole-grain			
Cold dry cereal	1/4 cup	1/3 cup	3/4 cup
or			
Hot cooked cereal	1/4 cup	1/4 cup	1/2 cup
Cooked pasta or noodle products	1/4 cup	1/4 cup	1/2 cup

Supplement (Snack)

	1–2	3–5	6–12
MILK Must be fluid milk	1/2 cup	1/2 cup	1 cup
MEAT or MEAT ALTERNATE			
Meat, poultry, or fish (cooked, lean meat without bone)	1/2 oz	1/2 oz	1 oz
Cheese	1/2 oz	1/2 oz	1 oz
Egg (large)	1/2	1/2	1/2
Cooked dry beans or peas	1/8 cup	1/8 cup	1/4 cup
Peanut butter or other nut or seed butters	1 Tbsp	1 Tbsp	2 Tbsp
Nuts and/or seeds**	1/2 oz	1/2 oz	1 oz
Yogurt, plain or sweetened	2 oz	2 oz	4 oz
VEGETABLE or FRUIT or JUICE*	1/2 cup	1/2 cup	3/4 cup
GRAINS/BREADS A serving is a bread or bread alternate and/or cereal:			
Bread, enriched or whole-grain	1/2 slice	1/2 slice	1 slice
Cereal, enriched or whole-grain			
Cold dry cereal	1/4 cup	1/3 cup	3/4 cup
or			
Hot cooked cereal	1/4 cup	1/4 cup	1/2 cup
Cooked pasta or noodle products	1/4 cup	1/4 cup	1/2 cup

Lunch or Supper

	1–2	3–5	6–12
MILK Must be fluid milk	1/2 cup	3/4 cup	1 cup
MEAT or MEAT ALTERNATE			
Meat, poultry, or fish (cooked, lean meat without bone)	1 oz	1 1/2 oz	2 oz
Cheese	1 oz	1 1/2 oz	2 oz
Egg (large)	1/2	3/4	1
Cooked dry beans or peas	1/4 cup	3/8 cup	1/2 cup
Peanut butter or other nut or seed butters	2 Tbsp	3 Tbsp	4 Tbsp
Nuts and/or seeds**	1/2 oz	3/4 oz	1 oz
Yogurt, plain or sweetened	4 oz	6 oz	8 oz
VEGETABLE or FRUIT or JUICE* Serve two different vegetables and/or fruits to equal	1/4 cup	1/2 cup	3/4 cup
GRAINS/BREADS A serving is a bread or bread alternate and/or cooked cereal:			
Bread, enriched or whole-grain	1/2 slice	1/2 slice	1 slice
Cooked cereal grains, enriched or whole-grain	1/4 cup	1/4 cup	1/2 cup
Cooked pasta or noodle products	1/4 cup	1/4 cup	1/2 cup

*For required serving amounts for infants up to age 1 year, refer to program regulations.

**CAUTION: Children under 4 years of age are at the highest risk of choking. For this age group, USDA recommends that nuts and/or seeds be ground or finely chopped and served to children in prepared foods.

***If you are serving juice: Try not to serve juice to meet the fruit/vegetable requirement too many times throughout the day. It may fill up the children and take the place of other needed nutrients.

Source: United States Department of Agriculture, Food and Nutrition Service, Fall 2001.

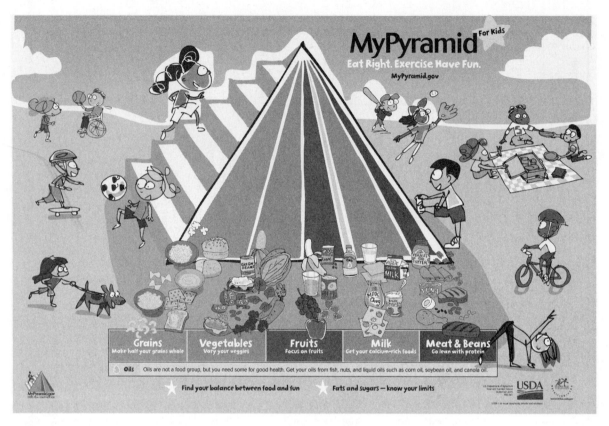

Figure 7.2
MyPyramid for Kids

Source: U.S. Department of Agriculture, Food and Nutrition Service, 2005 (http://www.mypyramid.gov).

Second, research indicates that learning plays a big part in developing food preferences and that the preschool years may be a particularly sensitive period. If we wish to extend the range of children's food preferences, this is a good time to begin.

When there are children at the center of various ethnic and cultural backgrounds, it is even more crucial to include foods that they like and that are familiar. It is important to discuss food preferences with each child's family, and encourage the sharing of family recipes. It is also good practice to invite family members in to cook with the children.

Some Basic Principles Having to Do with Eating

Perhaps no area in our social life (except sex) has as many restrictions and regulations attached to it as eating does. One class counted up the rules enforced by their families about mealtimes. They thought of 43 rules within 10 minutes. They ranged from "no dessert until you clear your plate" to "wait until the men are fed before you sit down." We will content ourselves here with enumerating only the principles the majority of early childhood teachers have come to feel are important as they work with young children.

Table 7.2
Sample lunch and snack menus for preschoolers

Menus for Preschoolers: Lunch and Snack				
Day 1	**Day 2**	**Day 3**	**Day 4**	**Day 5**
Beef/vegetable stew	Stir-fry chicken with celery, carrots, and bok choy	Lean roast pork	Baked chicken	White beans and ham
Molded salad with orange sections	Orange slices	Sweet potato	Broccoli	Cooked greens
Whole-wheat bread	Spinach salad with fat-free dressing	Baby lima beans	Cooked tomatoes and pasta	Fresh broccoli with fat-free ranch dressing
Margarine	Whole-wheat bread	Carrot sticks	Whole-wheat bread	Apple slices
2% milk	2% milk	Whole-wheat bread	Margarine	Cornbread
		Margarine	2% milk	Margarine
		2% milk		2% milk
Snack:	**Snack:**	**Snack:**	**Snack:**	**Snack:**
Hard-cooked egg	Pineapple chunks	Grapefruit sections	Dried fruits—peach slice, apricot slice, dates	Grapes (green)
Blueberries	2% milk	2% milk	2% milk	2% milk
2% milk				
Day 6	**Day 7**	**Day 8**	**Day 9**	**Day 10**
Soy-enhanced chicken patty	Chili with tomato sauce, beans, and hamburger	Roast turkey	Vegetable burger with tomato, pickle, lettuce	Seafood chop suey with bean sprouts, bamboo shoots, water chestnuts, and green pepper
Baked potato	Spinach salad with fat-free dressing	Sweet potatoes	Oven-baked potatoes	Brown rice
Fresh cantaloupe	Grapefruit	Cranberry salad	Baked beans in tomato sauce	Fresh fruit salad
Brussels sprouts	Whole-wheat crackers	Whole-wheat bread	Apricots	Whole-wheat bread
Whole-wheat bread	2% milk	Margarine	Whole-wheat bun	Margarine
Margarine		2% milk	2% milk	2% milk
2% milk				
Snack:	**Snack:**	**Snack:**	**Snack:**	**Snack:**
Pineapple	Sliced peaches	Citrus cup	Apple slices	Strawberries
2% milk	2% milk	Toasted wheat germ	Peanut butter	2% milk
		2% milk	2% milk	

Source: From Food, Nutrition, and the Young Child *(5th ed.), by J. B. Endres, R. E. Rockwell, & C. G. Mense, 2004. Upper Saddle River, NJ: Merrill/Prentice Hall. Reprinted by permission of Pearson Education, Inc., Upper Saddle River, NJ.*

Eating Should Be a Pleasure, but Food Should Not Be Used as a Reward

Most of us are shocked when we hear of parents punishing their children by sending them to bed with no dinner, but how many of us would feel equally concerned about the adult who habitually rewards a child with a cookie or other desired food for being good? Yet this tying food together with behavior is one link in developing eating disorders in later years. Certainly eating should be (and is!) a satisfying pleasure, but that pleasure needs to be kept within bounds; it should not become the primary source of gratification in life. Food should not be used to punish or to bribe or to reward.

Eating Together Should Convey a Sense of Happy Family Life to the Children

There should be time both to eat and to chat. Discipline situations should be avoided whenever possible. Mealtime can also be a time to enjoy each other and to help the group by going for seconds, passing food to each other, and group cleanup.

Eating Should Help a Child Be Independent

When food is passed around the table, the children can take what they desire; it is up to them to choose. They know how hungry they are, and they know their preferences far better than the teacher does. Then, too, by serving themselves, children have the opportunity to learn the social rule "Take some and leave some."

Having sponges close at hand also helps children become independent because they can mop up their own spills. Advertisements that stress the joys of carpeting to the contrary, it is much easier to clean up food from uncarpeted floors, so it is best to eat over a linoleum floor or even outdoors when possible.

Another way to help children retain independence is to make sure they do not have to wait to be fed. When children are hungry and their blood glucose level is low, they

Benjamin La Framboise

Eating should help a child become independent.

are in poor control of themselves, so food should be ready to be served as the children sit down. If it is placed on a low table or nearby shelf, the teacher can start passing around the serving bowls as soon as everyone has arrived.

Eating Can Be a Learning Experience

Although the most important goal of the eating situation is to furnish nourishment and pleasure, this experience can provide many opportunities for intellectual and social learning, too (Hemmeter et al., 2008; Martini, 2002). The lunch table is a fine place for conversation and the development of verbal fluency. Children can be encouraged to talk about their pets, what they did on the weekend, what they like best to eat, and what was fun at school during the morning. The opportunity can also be taken to talk about foods, textures, colors, and more factual kinds of information, but some teachers seem to do this to excess and forget to emphasize the more valuable goal of fluency. No matter what kinds of learning experiences go along with the meal, the teacher should always remember that eating should, first and foremost, be pleasurable and satisfying.

Special Eating Concerns

Allergies and Other Food Restrictions

Children who have allergies can have a difficult time at school, particularly at the lunch table, and so deserve special mention. The allergies that occur most frequently are the ones requiring a restriction on milk, milk products, eggs, soy, wheat, shellfish, and most especially *peanuts*. According to Aronson (1997), peanuts are responsible for more allergic reactions than any other food. Sometimes even being in the same room with a smidgen of peanut butter can trigger a serious physiological crisis.

Allergic reactions can happen right away or take several hours to show up. Whichever is the case, they must not be ignored since some of them are actually life threatening. It is important to discuss the situation with parents and to develop a plan for dealing with a possible reaction *before* it happens. This plan should include arrangements not only for avoiding the food but also for storing medications or injections and for determining who will administer them should the necessity arise.

At the same time it is necessary to consider the feelings of the child involved because other children may be curious about why they cannot share a cookie with him or why he isn't allowed to eat macaroni and cheese. It is wise to be as matter-of-fact as possible to avoid making the child feel regretful or persecuted about the restriction. Usually a simple explanation that it is a physician's orders is sufficient.

Choking

Teachers must take care that food is cut into small enough pieces for children to avoid choking. Even grapes should be cut in half, as these are among the most dangerous choking hazards. All early childhood teachers should be trained in proper first aid and be prepared to handle a choking emergency. Certainly, rules about sitting while eating must be explained to the children and enforced.

THE PROCESS OF TOILETING IN PREPRIMARY CENTERS

Diapering and Toilet Learning

In many family child care homes and infant/toddler centers, the processes of diapering and toilet learning are extemely important. It is crucial that programs have clear policies and that these are discussed at length with family members. The more families and care-givers can align their practices, the easier it will be on the child. Proper sanitation and hand-washing—even for babies—is essential to reduce the spread of germs. Those who work with young children at this age should avail themselves of the developmentally appropriate practices guidelines developed by NAEYC (Copple & Bredekamp, 2009).

Taking Children to the Toilet

In general, preschools use the same toilet rooms for boys and girls. However, this rule always has exceptions such as some schools that serve mostly Mexican American youngsters, where families may feel strongly that open toileting violates the modesty of the little girls.

One benefit of toileting together is that children learn to treat sexual differences quite casually. They will ask or comment about differences from time to time, and this provides golden opportunities to give straightforward, simple explanations. (Refer to chapter 4 for a more detailed discussion about sex education.) Open toileting has the advantage of reducing the peeking and furtive inspections that may go on otherwise. It promotes a healthier attitude toward sexual differences and therefore should be encouraged.

The majority of children of preschool age can be expected to go to the toilet when they feel the need, but an occasional child will have to be reminded. Rather than lining up everyone at once and insisting they use the toilet, it is better to remind

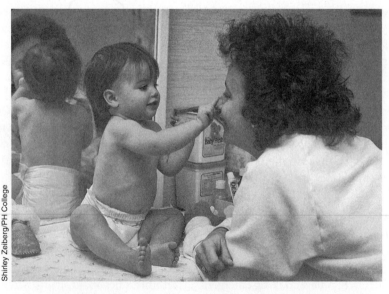

Shirley Zeiberg/PH College

Diapering can teach a baby her needs will be met by a loving adult: The world is good!

children while washing up for lunch or before nap that they will be more comfortable if they use the toilet first.

It will encourage children to take this responsibility for themselves if their parents dress them in pants with elastic tops or other easily managed clothing. It is also sound to remark to children that it certainly feels good to go to the toilet, a point of view with which most of them will concur.

Thorough hand-washing—with soap and a disposable towel—should be a consistent part of the toilet routine. Children generally enjoy it and will gladly slick their hands with soap when they are reminded. An effective technique is to teach children to sing an entire song, such as "Yankee Doodle," while lathering up with soap. *Teachers should always take time to wash their hands, too.* Although this takes a little extra time, the reduction in colds and diarrhea that results for everyone is well worth the effort (Kendrick, Kaufmann, & Messenger, 2002). Due to the intimate and close contact that children and teachers have in preschool programs, frequent and thorough hand-washing cannot be emphasized enough. The immune systems of young children and especially infants are just developing so they easily become ill when exposed to the many germs found in group care. Hand-washing and sanitizing procedures are discussed in more detail in chapter 8.

Handling Mishaps

When children wet themselves or have a bowel movement in their pants, they should be changed without shaming or disgust, but without an air of cozy approval either. Such loss of control often happens when children are new to the school, are overly fatigued, or are coming down with an illness, as well as when they have not yet acquired the rudiments of control. Many children are humiliated by wet or soiled

Benjamin La Framboise

Frequent hand-washing cannot be emphasized enough.

underwear, and the teacher should be sensitive to this and help them change in a quiet place. Theoretically, the children should always have dry pairs of pants stowed in their cubbies, but actually these are often not there when needed; so it is necessary to have some extras on hand. Should this happen in elementary school, the teacher should be particularly aware of the reaction of other children and do everything possible to avoid social humiliation for the child.

HANDLING NAP TIMES

If eating in a strange place with unknown people is disturbing to young children, going to sleep under such circumstances can be even more so. Releasing oneself into sleep is, among other things, an act of trust, and it is not surprising that this can be difficult for a young child to allow during the first days at school. Fortunately there are some things the teacher can do to make this task easier for the child.

Go to MyEducationLab and select the topic "Health, Safety, and Nutrition." Under Activities and Applications, watch the video *Napping Routine: Preschoolers.* How do naptime routines enhance children's development? What do children learn from naptime routines?

Regularize the Routine

Keep daily expectations and the order of events the same when approaching the nap period. That is, try to do things the same quiet, steady way every day. One pattern that works well is to send the children one by one as they finish lunch to use the toilet, wash their hands, and brush their teeth. Remember that this is the only time some children ever brush their teeth. Then they are expected to settle down on their cots or mats with a book to look at quietly until all the children are ready to begin resting. Next the room is darkened, and the teacher moves quietly about, helping children take off their shoes; find their blankets, stuffed rabbits, and so forth; and set their books aside. This process should be accomplished with quiet affection combined with the clearly projected expectation that the youngster is going to settle down.

When the children are all snuggled in their blankets, some teachers prefer to read a story, whereas others sing softly or play a soothing recording. It helps to have the children spread out as far from each other as possible and to have them lie head to toe; this reduces stimulation and also keeps them from breathing in each other's faces. Restless children should be placed in out-of-the-way corners.

Benjamin La Framboise

Releasing oneself into sleep is an act of trust.

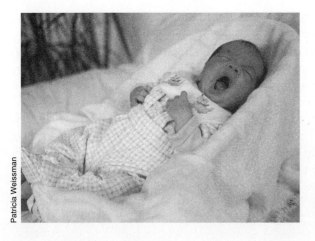

Give babies a nap whenever they need it!

Teachers need to be quiet and not talk among themselves, and other people must not be allowed to tiptoe in and out.

It takes at least two teachers to settle a roomful of children, and it may take as long as 30 to 45 minutes before all the children go to sleep. Some children will need their backs rubbed in a monotonous way to soothe them into slumber.

Infants have their own individual needs for sleep; therefore a set nap time for babies is unrealistic. Babies should be put to sleep (always on their backs and never with a bottle in the crib!) *as they need it* throughout the day (Gonzalez-Mena & Eyer, 2006; Lally et al., 2003).

Allow the Children to Get Up as They Wake Up

Usually after about an hour some of the children will wake up by themselves and begin to stir about. This gradual awakening is convenient because it means that each child can be greeted and helped to dress one by one, and it presents a nice opportunity for friendly, quiet chats with the teacher. Children are more likely to wake up in a good mood if they are wakened gradually by the activity around them, rather than by having the teacher wake them up. They need time to collect themselves and to regain awareness before they begin their afternoon activities. It often works well to have a few staff members getting children up while the rest of the adults are in the play area, with snack being available as the children desire it and some quiet, attractive activity also available that the children may select when they feel ready for it.

How Long Should Children Sleep?

It is unfair to the family to allow a child to sleep all afternoon—unless, of course, the child does not feel well. A sleep of an hour or so is about right for most youngsters, but this does not include the time it takes for them to settle down.

Should All Children Nap?

All children of preschool age should be expected to lie down and relax for a while in the middle of the day. The need for sleep itself varies considerably among different children, and this difference needs to be taken into consideration. Some youngsters, though, particularly older children who are approaching kindergarten age, never go to sleep during the daytime. They should not be expected to lie stiffly on their mats for 2 hours. Instead, after a reasonable rest period, they should be permitted to go outdoors or to another room and play under the supervision of a staff member. These more mature children often greatly enjoy helping prepare the afternoon snack; it makes them feel important and pays tribute to their own grown-up status.

Occasionally a child may need to rest but is so high-strung and active that everyone is disturbed at nap time. Our staff has concluded that it is more satisfactory to take these youngsters out of the nap room and give them something quiet to do in the director's office than to become involved in angry, usually noisy confrontations, which upset all the children as well as frighten the restless one.

Summary

Routines, which consist of arriving and departing, eating, diapering and toileting, cleaning up, and resting, are an important part of a child's day. If they are handled well, they can contribute to both the physical health and emotional well-being of young children.

Teachers will experience greatest success in handling routines if they avoid trying to win for the sake of winning, but work instead toward the more worthwhile goals of helping the children become competent, independent people who have healthy attitudes toward their bodily needs and who look forward to eating, toileting, and resting because of the comfort and pleasure associated with these activities.

Questions and Activities

1. List all the rules you can think of that applied to eating, sleeping, or toileting in your own family as you grew up. After recalling the stated rules, think of some of the deeper, unspoken ones that were also observed.

Diversity Question

1. Why is it important to introduce young children to foods from cultures other than their own? How would you do this if your class had little cultural diversity?

Predicaments

1. You are the staff teacher delegated to greet children at the door every morning, and one little boy always begins to whimper as he arrives. At that point the father gives him a smack on the bottom, telling him firmly, "Little boys don't cry!" You have learned in your student teaching days that it is important for children to express their feelings. How would you handle this situation?

2. Although you never meant to arrive at such an impasse, you have inadvertently made such an issue of a child's going to the toilet that she has become balky about it and will not use the toilet anymore, wetting her pants instead. At this point, what approach would you try next to solve this difficulty?

Self-Check Questions for Review

Content-Related Questions

1. Why is it wise to avoid "going to war" with a child about conforming to a particular routine?

2. Describe some sound procedures for helping children adjust to the new situation during their first days at a children's center.

3. What basic principles can you think of regarding the management of routines such as eating, naps, and toileting?

Integrative Questions

1. Identify two different transition times that take place at the school where you teach. Which one of the two goes more smoothly? Analyze why that is the case. Can procedures that are effective in managing that transition be applied to the less effective one?

2. What would you do to introduce a variety of ethnic foods that also meet the requirements of the USDA guidelines in Table 7.1?

Reference for Further Reading

Appleton, J., McCrea, N., & Patterson, C. (2001). *Do carrots make you see better? A guide to food and nutrition in early childhood programs*. Beltsville, MD: Gryphon House. So much useful information is packed into this book, including food selection, recipes, nutritional information, information about special food needs and allergies, and cultural diversity in foods.

Related Organizations and Online Resources

American Academy of Pediatrics (AAP). A database full of useful information for teachers and parents, and brochures that can be downloaded, are available at http://www.aap.org.

Centers for Disease Control. Another good source for downloads on topics ranging from children's dental health, vaccinations, injury prevention, nutrition, and exercise is found at http://www.cdc.gov.

Child Care Nutrition Resource System, USDA. Many useful resources in addition to information about guidelines for child care centers to receive assistance can be found at http://www.healthymeals.nal.usda.gov/.

CHAPTER eight

Promoting the Development of the Physical Self

How to send a sick child home without hurting the child's feelings?

Whether it's really all right to admit a child to school whose parents are "going to get her booster shots just as soon as they can"?

What in the world you can do to encourage physical fitness in children?

. . . IF YOU HAVE, THE MATERIAL IN THE FOLLOWING PAGES WILL HELP YOU.

Birds gotta sing, fish gotta swim, and kids gotta MOVE AND TOUCH. Moving and touching are how children first learn about the world. Feeling the sun and grass on their skin, throwing and catching balls, stretching their arms to the ceiling, climbing jungle gyms, and running in great circles are examples of ways that children gain the important information they require to function well. Nature's plan is for young children to absorb sensory knowledge through their skin, muscles, and joints as a foundation for more complex learning.

Carol S. Kranowitz (1994, p. 37)

Good food, reasonable toilet procedures, and adequate rest are important factors in maintaining the physical and emotional well-being of young children. Additional factors that affect the physical development of children include health and safety and the provision of maximum opportunities for their bodies to grow and develop in the healthiest way.

PROMOTION OF HEALTH AND SAFETY IN THE CHILDREN'S CENTER

Providing Safe Transportation to School Is a Must!

As information continues to indicate that safety seats and seat belts help save lives, it becomes clear that teachers *must* encourage their consistent and correct use (American Academy of Pediatrics [AAP], 2008). Preprimary teachers have a unique opportunity to foster automobile safety because they meet families as they deliver their youngsters to school.

Many schools now insist that any child delivered to their premises be transported there "buckled up," and it is a policy that *every* school should institute. Since some children do not like these restraints, teachers should also support the parents' efforts by discussing the value of safety restraints during large-group times, explaining in a matter-of-fact, nonalarmist way how lucky we are that we have this practical way to keep us safe. Teachers and families should be informed about proper car seat usage; an excellent source of information is the American Academy of Pediatrics, referred to as AAP (see Related Organizations and Online Resources at the end of the chapter).

Basic Ways to Protect and Foster the Physical Health of Children

It is so important that teachers work with families to make sure their children have health checkups and immunizations. Since the first edition of this book, some encouraging progress has been made in the area of immunization, although much remains to be done. According to UNICEF (2003), about 2 million children worldwide under age 5 years still die every year from six vaccine-preventable illnesses: diphtheria, measles, pertussis, polio, tuberculosis, and tetanus. We are fortunate that in the United States recent federal legislation has made free vaccines more available than formerly. By 2002 just over 90% of American children had actually received their full series of shots, as compared with 10 years previously, when only 55% had been immunized. Even more encouraging is the news that, following an epidemic of measles in 1990, a special effort was made and now 91% of U.S. toddlers are immune to its potentially serious aftereffects (UNICEF, 2003).

Despite this rise in child immunity it is still necessary to caution adults that *rubella* (often called 3-day *measles*) remains a menace to many women who were not protected from it during childhood—a circumstance that may have deadly implications for the fetus, should a woman become pregnant. In particular, teachers of young children must take special care that they are vaccinated against rubella as well as hepatitis A and B, and it is wise to get an annual flu shot, also.

Benjamin La Framboise

Teachers must insist on proper car safety at all times.

Although immunization shots are more available now, still not all states require vaccination checks at the preschool level. To make matters worse, even when these regulations exist they are often only laxly enforced. For these reasons all preschools and centers, including family child care homes, should establish their own policies and be *adamant about requiring up-to-date immunization records from parents.* Such certification protects not only the child in question but also all the other children and adults in the school. Anything short of full enforcement of this policy is inexcusable. (Appendix D provides a childhood immunization schedule recommended by the AAP.)

Early childhood professionals should also encourage families to vaccinate their children each year for the flu. Nationwide, only 4.4% of children between the ages of 6 months and 2 years were fully vaccinated for the 2002–2003 flu season, when 152 children died of complications of the virus (Centers for Disease Control and Prevention [CDC], 2004). It is appalling that children today are dying from illnesses that, in many cases, are preventable.

Physical Examinations Should Be Required Before the Child Enrolls

Because the preschool or kindergarten is often the first institution that comes into contact with families of young children in a formal way, it is particularly valuable for each school to require pre-entry physical examinations, as well as inoculations. Careful evaluation of potential vision and hearing problems should be a part of this process.

The Teacher Should Be Prepared to Help Families Find Health Care During the Year Whenever Possible

In addition to the free or low-cost health insurance now more available for families of low income throughout the United States (U.S. Department of Health and Human Services, 2008), a variety of other free health services and examinations are also available that teachers should be acquainted with so they can refer families who need help. These services are as varied as university-sponsored speech and hearing clinics and free asthma checkups. Sometimes arrangements can be made with training schools to supply health services in return for the opportunity to work with young children. Dental hygienists in training, for example, may be willing to clean children's teeth to obtain experience with preschoolers. A good way to locate information about such services is to contact the public health nurses in your community. These people are gold mines of practical information about sources of assistance.

The Teacher Should Act as a Health Screener

An alert teacher can often spot problems that have been overlooked by families and even by pediatricians, who though expert, lack the teacher's opportunity to see the child over an extended period of time. The teacher should particularly watch for children who do not seem to see or hear well, who are very awkward, who seldom talk, who are unusually apathetic, or who are excessively active. The behavior may be only an idiosyncrasy, or it may require professional help, and the sooner help is sought the better. (See chapters 5 and 11 for further details on identification of special problems.)

The teacher should make a health check of the children as they arrive at school each day. This ensures a personal greeting for each child and provides a quick once-over so that a child who is not feeling up to par may be sent home before the parent departs. Although some standard signs should be checked for, such as faces that are flushed or "sickly looking," rashes, and marked lethargy, the most important symptom to be aware of is any significant change in the child's appearance. Teachers who see the same children every day get to know how they usually look and behave and can often spot such variations promptly; then they can take the appropriate steps to avoid exposing other children in school to the condition.

Providing care for sick children is a particularly difficult problem for families when both parents work outside the home. Centers and preschools need very clear, firm policies concerning contagious diseases and how they are handled and at the same time do everything they can to make compliance as easy as possible for the families. Since a youngster can seem perfectly healthy in the evening yet turn up green and pale the next morning, it is important to encourage families to have backup care planned—relatives or a friendly neighbor to be relied on. Sometimes schools maintain lists of home caregivers who specialize in sick child care. A plan for sick child care is especially important in infant and toddler centers, as well as family child care homes, where immature immune systems and the intimate setting lead to increased illness.

The Teacher Must Know What to Do When a Child Becomes Ill at School

No matter how careful the teacher and how conscientious the family, an occasional child will come down with some illness during the day. Ideally the child should be sent home immediately, but in practice this can be very difficult to do (Baker & Manfredi/Petitt, 2004; Cohen, 1998). Even when parents have been asked to make alternative arrangements for emergency care, these arrangements sometimes fall through, and the school and youngster have to make the best of it. Reputable schools try to keep children who are ill apart from the rest; usually the center office serves this purpose fairly well. Children who are ill should have a place to lie down located as close as possible to a bathroom, and they will need to be comforted and reassured so that they do not feel bereft and lonely.

Because sending a child home from school often embarrasses and angers the family and hurts the child's feelings as well, it is desirable to be firm but gentle when doing this. Sending something home along with the child, such as a book or perhaps an impromptu card made by the children, will help ease the sense of rejection and make returning to school easier when the child is feeling better.

General Health Precautions Should Be Observed Consistently by Children and Staff

The most effective action teachers can take to protect themselves and the children from illness is to reduce the spread of germs in the child care center. Blowing noses in disposable tissue, washing hands before handling food and after toileting and diapering, and not allowing children to share food, cups, utensils, or teethers and baby toys they have had in their mouths are basic precautions that must always be observed. If teachers form the habit of washing their hands whenever they have children participate in that routine, it not only sets a good example but also helps maintain the teachers' good health (Kendrick et al., 2002).

Benjamin La Framboise

Teachers can maintain a healthy center by washing their hands frequently, too.

The AAP (2002) recommends that caregivers and children in child care settings wash their hands with soap and water (not alcohol-based hand rubs) at the following times:

- Upon arrival for the day or when moving from one child care group to another
- Before and after eating, handling food or feeding a child; giving medication; or playing in water that is used by more than one person
- After diapering; using the toilet or helping a child use the toilet; handling bodily fluids from noses, mouths, or sores; handling uncooked food, especially meat and poultry; handling pets and other animals; playing in sandboxes; and cleaning or handling the garbage

In addition to frequent and thorough hand-washing, teachers must sanitize the children's center areas and toys with a sanitizing bleach solution (1 tablespoon per quart of water, made fresh daily) to reduce the number of germs. Any surface that has been contaminated with body fluids must be sanitized immediately. Food preparation surfaces, anything that has gone in a child's mouth (toy, pacifier, spoon, etc.), and changing tables need sanitation after each child's use. And finally, cleaning with soap and water, followed by sanitizing, must be done on a daily basis for counters and tabletops, floors, sinks, faucets, soap dispensers, toilets, and doorknobs (Kendrick et al., 2002).

Another routine that should be maintained is regular toothbrushing. Dental disease is preventable in early childhood and yet 1 in 5 preschoolers has untreated dental decay which can lead to chronic pain, the inability to eat, and distraction from learning and play (Finn & Wolpin, 2005). To reinforce the importance of toothbrushing, teachers can invite a friendly dentist to the class for a brief demonstration and hang posters about toothbrushing on a parent bulletin board.

Sometimes a child who is well enough to return to school must still continue taking medicine during school hours. A word of warning is in order here: To avoid the possibility of lawsuits most schools make it a practice *never to administer any kind of medication (including nonprescription pain relievers)* without the express written request of the physician and parent.

Maintaining the Physical Safety of Children

Teachers must never forget that the children in their care are not their own and that supervising them carries with it a special responsibility.

Even though insurance costs are high, it is very important for all schools to carry it both to protect themselves against lawsuits and to provide accident coverage for the children. One solution for financing such protection is to include a one-time insurance fee when the child is first enrolled.

In addition, the entire school needs to be checked continually to make sure it is maintained in a safe condition. Broken equipment such as tricycles without pedals and wobbly jungle gyms *must be removed or repaired promptly*. Safety precautions such as using only swings with canvas seats should be observed. The danger area around swings must be clearly marked, and children should be taught to wait on the bottom step (which can be painted red to make it easier to identify) of the slide.

PEARSON myeducationlab)

Go to MyEducationLab and select the topic "Health, Safety, and Nutrition." Under Activities and Applications, watch the video *Fire Safety.* How can teachers help protect young children from fire?

Joanne Hendrick

Another routine that should be maintained is regular toothbrushing.

Disinfectants, ant poisons, scouring powders, bleaches, and antiseptics, which are all commonly found in centers and schools, should be kept on high shelves where children are not permitted, or better yet in locked cabinets. Even a bucket with a small amount of water left in it can prove deadly to a curious toddler. It is good practice for teachers to survey each and every indoor and outdoor area that is accessible to children *from a child's point of view* with a special eye for dangerous attractions.

One sensible rule of thumb is that teachers should stop an activity if it looks dangerous to them rather than permit an accident to happen. One other safety rule has proved to be generally helpful: The teacher should never lift children onto a piece of play equipment if they cannot manage to get on it by themselves (swings are an exception to this rule). Of course, children sometimes climb up on something, feel marooned, and must be helped down; but that is different from lifting them onto the top of the jungle gym or boosting them onto a tippy gangplank before they are really able to cope with these situations.

It is particularly important to remember that high places such as slides and monkey bars are dangerous for young children. Of the 280,000 children treated during 1 year in hospital emergency rooms for playground injuries, two out of three were injured by falling from equipment, often onto hard surfaces ("Check Playgrounds for Safety," 1996). For this reason it is vital to maintain soft, deep surfaces such as sand, rubber, or bark mulch beneath such equipment. *Grass is not suitable.* Cushioning must also be used underneath indoor climbing structures—a protection that is often overlooked at many centers.

The concern for safety has to be moderated by the teacher's good sense and self-control. Children must be protected, but they also need the chance to venture and try things out. This venturesomeness is a hallmark of 4-year-olds in particular. Occasional small catastrophes are to be expected, and teachers should not become so overly protective that they hover over the children and remind them constantly to be careful. Instead they should try to maintain a generally high level of safety combined with the opportunity for the children to experiment with the mild risks that build feelings of competence as they are met and mastered.

BASIC PRINCIPLES OF PHYSICAL DEVELOPMENT

Before reading about specific ways to foster psychomotor development, it is necessary to understand some developmental principles that have important implications for education.

Development Occurs in Predictable Patterns and Sequences

It is generally agreed that children progress through a predictable sequence of physical developmental stages (Gallahue & Ozmun, 2001; Shelov & Hannemann, 2004; Wood, 2007). The examples provided in Table 8.1 illustrate this clearly. (In addition, Appendix A provides a more comprehensive chart of normal development from infancy to 8 years of age, organized according to the various selves.) Children usually sit before they stand, stand before they walk, and walk before they run. In addition specific skills such as running, jumping, throwing, and climbing progress through a series of substages of competency before they emerge as mature physical abilities (S. W. Sanders, 2002; Wood, 2007).

Teachers need to be able to recognize the stages of development so that they can adjust their curriculum offerings to provide a good balance between opportunities for practice to consolidate the skill and opportunities for accepting the challenge of a slightly more difficult activity to go on to next.

The Course of Development Moves from Head to Tail

That development moves from head to tail is the *cephalocaudal* principle. It means that children are able to control the region around their head and shoulders before they can control their hands and feet. This is an easy principle to remember if one recalls that babies can sit up and manipulate playthings long before they are able to stand on their feet and walk. Quite simply, children are able to reach, grasp, and use their hands with considerable skill before they are able to master the art of skipping or kicking accurately. The curriculum in early childhood education should be planned accordingly.

The Course of Development Moves from Large- to Fine-Muscle Control

Large-muscle activities include static balance, dynamic precision, gross body coordination, and flexibility. Examples of *fine-muscle activities* include finger speed, arm steadiness, arm and hand precision, and finger and hand dexterity. Development from large- to fine-muscle control means that children gain control over their larger muscles first and then gradually attain control over the finer muscle groups. Thus children are able to walk long before they are able to construct a tabletop house of small plastic bricks.

myeducationlab

Go to MyEducationLab and select the topic "Child Development." Under Activities and Applications, watch the video *Physical Development*. In observing these two children, which developmental differences are apparent?

Table 8.1
Age at which most children perform locomotor skills

By the End of the 1st Year, the Child:	By the End of the 2nd Year, the Child:	By the End of the 3rd Year, the Child:	By the End of the 4th Year, the Child:	By the End of the 5th Year, the Child:	By the End of the 6th Year, the Child:	By the End of the 7th Year, the Child:	By the End of the 8th Year, the Child:
Reaches sitting position independently	Walks independently	Climbs well	Hops and stands on one foot up to 5 seconds	Balances on one foot for 10 seconds or longer	Is more aware of using fingers as tools	Has improved coordination and physical abilities	Has good visual focus on both near and far objects
Crawls forward on stomach	Climbs stairs (sometimes needs support)	Walks up and down stairs using a rail	Goes upstairs and downstairs independently and alternating feet	Walks backward	Is always in a hurry—speed is the hallmark of 6s	Enjoys playground games such as jump rope and four-square	Is full of physical energy
Pushes up into hands-and-knees position	Enjoys climbing structures (and climbing on furniture)	Jumps off steps or structures	Kicks ball forward	Hops	Has learned "left" from "right"	May enjoy organized sports	Has a high need for active play indoors and outdoors
Creeps on hands and knees or crawls	Carries objects while walking	Throws, kicks a ball	Throws ball overhand	Jumps rope	Has good visual tracking from left to right	Can keep eyes focused on a small area	Loves group games such as tag and soccer
Pulls self up to standing, may stand alone for a short time	Trots and runs	Runs easily	Catches a bounced ball	Somersaults		Can hold pencil with 3-finger grasp	Experiences growth spurts
Walks while holding onto something, may take a few steps alone	Stands on toes	Pedals a tricycle	Jumps rope	Swings		Can produce small and tidy printed letters, numbers, and drawings	Holds pencil using grasp like an adult
	Throws, kicks a ball	Bends over without falling	Moves forward and backward easily	Climbs			Has well-developed eye-hand coordination; can form cursive letters
		Engages in physical play with full energy, then gets tired, sometimes cranky		Rides a bike			
				Swims			
				Skips			
				Usually is independent in toileting			
				Has a high level of physical energy			

189

The educational implication of this developmental principle for early childhood teachers is that young children need ample opportunities to use their large muscles in vigorous, energetic, physical play. It can be torment for young children to remain confined too long at chairs and tables. Since the finer muscle, eye-hand skills are also developing during this period, activities that stimulate children to practice these skills should also be offered—but not overdone to the point that excessive demands are made on the children's self-control.

FOSTERING LARGE-MUSCLE DEVELOPMENT IN YOUNG CHILDREN

Use of Apparatus to Promote Large-Muscle Skills

In general the school should furnish a large assortment of big, sturdy, durable equipment that provides many opportunities for all kinds of physical activity. It should also provide a teacher who values vigorous large-muscle play and encourages children to participate freely in this pleasure.

Equipment good for crawling through, climbing up, balancing on, and hanging from should be included. Children need things they can lift, haul, and shove around to test their strength and use to make discoveries about physical properties the equipment possesses. They need things they can use for construction, and they need equipment that provides opportunities for rhythmic activities, such as bouncing and jumping and swinging. In addition, they need places of generous size for carrying out the wonderful sensory experiences that involve mud, sand, and water. Finally, they need plenty of space in which to simply move about.

Equipment need not be expensive to provide sound play value. It is wise to remember, though, that poorly constructed, cheap equipment can be the poorest kind of economy in the long run. Children are hard on things, and it does not pay to buy or make playthings that are flimsy—better to have a fund-raiser for better quality equipment than be stuck with buying two cheap swing sets 2 years in a row.

In general, the more movable and versatile the equipment is, the more stimulating and interesting it will remain for the children. It is vital to have plenty of boards, sawhorses, large hollow blocks, ropes, rubber tires, and barrels lest the children feel frustrated when they cannot complete their more ambitious projects. Schools should budget for more of this kind of equipment every year; there is no such thing as owning too much of it.

Role of the Teacher in Fostering Large-Muscle Play

In addition to providing equipment to enhance large-muscle play, teachers can do much to encourage this kind of activity. Probably the most important thing they can do is provide enough uninterrupted time for satisfying play to transpire. Children need time to develop their ideas and carry them through, and if they build something, they need time to use it after they build it.

It is vital to provide plenty of opportunity for unrestricted outdoor play to support children's physical development. Almost 13% of public schools have no recess for children (Cleaver, 2007a). Studies have shown that even in preprimary schools and Head Start programs, children spend "far too little time engaged in vigorous physical activity during the hours they attend the center" (Thigpen, 2007, p. 20).

Playtime requires active involvement of the teacher with the children—not by participating as a companion in their play, but by observing and being alert to ways to make the play richer and by offering additional equipment or tactfully teaching an intrusive child how to be more welcome to the group. Because the teacher's function is to encourage the continuation of play, it is important to be as facilitative yet unobtrusive as possible. Achieving this balance takes considerable practice and skill. For example, one novice teacher tried so hard to involve herself in the child's play that she actually seemed to annoy the child. When told by 4-year-old Tony, "You be the dog," the teacher began barking and jumping around so enthusiastically that Tony stopped what he was doing, watched the teacher for a moment, and remarked, "You can stop barking now." Teachers should remember that their role is to encourage the child's play, not dominate or control it.

Fostering Play in Children with Special Needs

It is especially important for teachers to be aware of children with special needs during outdoor playtime. Studies have shown that although maturation plays a major role in children's physical development, other factors such as the environment, opportunities to practice, and teacher direction come into play as well. For children with developmental delays, these factors become even more important (Doctoroff, 2001; Gallahue & Ozmun, 2001).

Some ways in which teachers can help children with disabilities enjoy playtime include letting these children become familiar with the play area without having other children around to overwhelm them, making certain such youngsters understand outdoor safety rules, encouraging them to take part in large-motor activities, encouraging them to play with or at least nearby other children, and encouraging them to try out things within their abilities while keeping a sensible balance between overprotection and poorly judged risk taking.

If teachers keeps their eyes and minds open to possibilities, they can adapt outdoor equipment in many ways to make it accessible to everyone (Doctoroff, 2001). Large-muscle play offers excellent opportunities for children with disabilities to play with the other children if equipment is included that requires two or more youngsters to make it work: rocking boats, trikes with wagons, and tire swings can all help meet this need.

Finally, the teacher should keep on the lookout for children who are at loose ends and involve them in activities before they begin to run wildly and aimlessly about. Teachers need to be comfortable with a good deal of noise, though, and welcome the vigorous activity so characteristic of young children because they need this opportunity for boisterous assertion and movement to develop fully.

TEACHERS' SUPPORT OF CHILDREN'S FITNESS

Programs Should Encourage Physical Activity—and Plenty of It!

Reports concerning the general level of physical fitness in young children are not encouraging. Children are more sedentary today than ever before (Cleaver, 2007a; National Association for Sport and Physical Education, 2002). This is due in large part to children's increasing use of electronic media, such as television and computers. A recent study found that children under the age of 6 spent as much time with TV,

RESEARCH STUDY

Is Early Television Viewing Associated with Later Attentional Problems?

Research Question: Is early television exposure, at ages 1 and 3 years, associated with attentional problems at age 7?

Research Method: Data from the National Longitudinal Survey of Youth-Child from 1986 to 2000 were analyzed and included findings for 1,278 children from age 1 and 1,345 children from age 3. Information about the child was collected biennially from the mother regarding developmental assessment, family background, home environment, and health history. The Behavioral Problems Index was used to determine if the child at age 7 had attentional problems, including difficulty concentrating, confusion, impulsivity, obsessiveness, and restlessness.

Research Results: Of the 2,623 children studied, 10% had attentional problems at age 7. A 1–standard deviation increase in the number of hours of television watched at age 1 was associated with a 28% increase in the probability of having attentional problems at age 7.

Implications for Teaching: Although this study was not of an experimental design and therefore does not show that early television viewing *causes* attentional problems, it does suggest there is an interaction. Since the young child's brain is still forming at that age, the authors caution that exposing children to hours of daily television viewing before the age of 3 might lead to changes in their brain development. More research is necessary since so many young children are watching TV at ever younger ages. In addition, this study did not determine which programs children were watching. We need to investigate further to see if the type of programming, such as children's educational shows, has a different effect. In the meantime, it is probably wise to discuss children's television viewing with parents and caution against it for children under the age of 2.

Source: Data taken from "Early Television Exposure and Subsequent Attentional Problems in Children," by D. A. Christakis, F. J. Zimmerman, D. L. DiGiuseppe, and C. A. McCarty, 2003, *Pediatrics, 113*(4), 708–713.

computers, and video games as playing outside. According to the 1,051 parents surveyed in the study, children began using electronic media at a very young age: In any given day, 61% of the babies age 1 and under used screen media for over an hour and 90% of 4- to 6-year-olds watched screen media for about 2 hours. A third of children age 6 years and younger live in homes where the television is on all or most of the time, and 33% have a television in their bedroom (Kaiser Family Foundation, 2006). These data are even more alarming given the AAP's warning that children under the age of 2 should not watch television because of concerns it affects brain growth and developmental skills (Mistry et al., 2007). The Research Study for this chapter cautions that early television viewing may be associated with attention problems later in the elementary school years.

Another reason to limit children's television viewing is that hours of TV watching have been associated with overweight (American Dietetic Association [ADA], 1999; Sorte & Daeschel, 2006). Childhood overweight and obesity is becoming an increasingly prevalent problem (Association for Childhood Education International [ACEI], 2004; American Heart Association, 2005). When a recent national study compared the number of 2- to 5-year-olds who were overweight in 1980 with the number in 2000, researchers found that the percentage of overweight preschoolers had doubled to just over 10%. In addition, the obesity rates have tripled since the 1980s for school-age children and teenagers, indicating that 15% of 6- to 19-year-olds are obese (CDC, 2000).

Early childhood teachers must help children develop healthy bodies. Health professionals do not recommend dieting for young children; therefore, we must encourage lots of physical activity in early childhood programs. Children who are overweight suffer from social and emotional impacts (ADA, 1999; Sorte & Daeschel, 2006) and are prone to develop other physical health risks, such as high blood pressure, heart disease, arthritis, and diabetes (ACEI, 2004; American Heart Association, 2005; Sorte & Daeschel, 2006).

Physical fitness itself and the satisfaction that feeling of fitness provides must not be overlooked. Children should be encouraged to play vigorously and to *sustain* their efforts while avoiding overfatigue so that they increase their level of endurance while playing. Just as wholesome eating habits contribute to better lifelong health, so, too, does the establishment of healthy habits of exercise in early childhood (S. W. Sanders, 2002; Sorte & Daeschel, 2006; Thigpen, 2007).

One way we can help children even more to establish lifelong health habits is by offering fitness information to their families and by encouraging them to promote the healthy physical development of their child. We can support families' efforts to curb television viewing and increase physical and cognitive activity by sending home lists of alternative activities to TV viewing, such as the list shown in Figure 8.1. It is easier for families to try out these suggestions when the children have an active part in brainstorming the ideas. Field trips are a great way to include family members in the life of the school, and also to support family fitness. Visits to parks, nature centers, arboretums, farms, and even pumpkin patches provide educational experiences as well as plenty of walking and exercise for both children and adults.

Despite studies that make the value of plentiful exercise so evident, many teachers are still inclined to turn the children loose during outdoor play and content themselves with just supplying an assortment of equipment such as swings and slides, hoping the children will seek out the experiences they need by using this apparatus in a variety of ways (Pica, 2003). But we now know that outdoor activities should go beyond this

---

- Take a walk.
- Challenge your child to invent different ways to move about your home or outside: go to the kitchen as slowly as you possibly can, then crawl back, then hop back again, and so on.
- Read a book together.
- Do a puzzle together.
- Write down your child's words in a letter to a loved one, then decorate it together.
- Find something you use every day in your house and make it fancy—how about a toothbrush with a glitter handle?
- Go outside to rake leaves, shovel snow, or gather interesting objects that you find.
- Get down on the floor and build something with blocks, tangrams, or Legos.
- Ride bikes with your child.
- Swim at the local Y.
- Brainstorm ideas with your child about what would be more fun than watching TV.

Figure 8.1
Suggested family activities to replace TV viewing

Leslie Gleim

Field trips provide opportunities for children and their families to engage in outdoor explorations and fitness activities together.

without requiring children to be regimented and drilled. We really must offer them a broader selection of physically developmental activities than we formerly did if we wish to enhance the full range of their skills and developmental potential.

USE OF PERCEPTUAL-MOTOR ACTIVITIES TO ENHANCE PHYSICAL DEVELOPMENT

By perceptual-motor, we mean "the child's developing ability to interact with the environment, combining the use of the senses and motor skills" (Frost et al., 2008, p. 123). This includes such things as body awareness, sense of space, sense of time, and sense of rhythm. The teacher can approach the area of planned perceptual-motor activities in two ways: The first is to provide opportunities for practice in specific skills; the second is to use physical activity to promote creative thought and self-expression. Both approaches have merit.

Planning for Specific Perceptual-Motor Activities

An effective way to go about teaching motor skills is to divide motor tasks into the following eight categories that apply to preschoolers:

1. *Locomotion:* Rolling, crawling, climbing, jumping, running, and so forth
2. *Balance:* While still, such as balancing on tiptoes, or on one foot, or on one's side
    While moving, such as on a balance beam or walking on stones
    or
    Using objects to balance, such as beanbags
3. *Body and space perception:* Dancing, shadow play, experiments in moving (How big can you be? How can you move to the other side of the room without using your feet?)
4. *Rhythm and temporal awareness:* Any moving in time to music or using a rhythmic beat

5. *Rebound and airborne activities:*   Bouncing, swinging, hanging
6. *Projectile management:*   Using balls or other objects to throw, kick, strike, and bounce
7. *Management of daily motor activities (including many fine-muscle tasks):*   Self-help skills (buttoning, zippering, tying, etc.) as well as fine-motor tasks including the use of tools (paintbrushes, beads, scissors, woodworking tools, etc.) and self-select fine-motor materials (small blocks, puzzles, manipulatives) and
8. *Tension releasers:*   Guided relaxation, deep breathing, and so forth (Frost et al., 2008)

It is easy to think of motor activities in relation to these headings once they have been identified and to make certain that opportunities for repeated practice in each of the categories are included in curriculum plans. The trick lies in concocting ways of presenting them that appeal to children. Obstacle courses, simple want-to-try-this kind of noncompetitive games, and movement activities can all be used effectively if only the teacher will keep in mind the diversity of action that should be incorporated. Fortunately the mere challenge of having such possibilities available often provides attraction enough because youngsters are almost irresistibly drawn to physical activities that are just challenging enough without being too difficult. As a matter of fact, if children are encouraged to experiment, they will often develop the next hardest task for themselves following mastery of its simpler elements, a nice illustration, incidentally, of children moving toward the growing edge of their zone of proximal development (Vygotsky, 1978).

Fostering Fine-Muscle Development (Daily Motor Activities)

Although this chapter has stressed the importance of large-muscle involvement, fine-muscle (eye-hand) skills are just as important. Examples of these skills are feeding oneself, buttoning sweaters, sewing, and working with pegboards, puzzles, beads, and put-together materials (often termed *manipulatives*). Block building (which taps stacking and balancing skills), pouring and spooning in their many forms, and manipulating art materials (most particularly pencils, brushes, scissors, and crayons) also require careful coordination of eye and hand, as does woodworking; it takes a good deal of skill to hit a nail with something as small as a hammerhead.

Things to Remember When Presenting Fine-Muscle Activities

Offering a range of challenge in levels of difficulty is particularly important in a group of mixed ages, but even in a relatively homogeneous group of 3-year-olds provision must be made for the fact that the level of fine-muscle skill—not to mention the amount of emotional control and ability to concentrate—will vary considerably from child to child. Rather than setting out three or four puzzles of 16 pieces each, the children's range of abilities will be better met if one or two inset puzzles and perhaps 7-, 15-, and 22-piece puzzles are set out and changed as they become boring.

Fine-muscle activities should be of reasonably short duration. It is difficult for young children to hold still for very long, much less sit and concentrate on a fine-muscle task that requires considerable self-control. For this reason several activities should be available at the same time, and children should always be free to get up, move around, and shift to more or less taxing experiences as they feel the need. Quiet periods such as story hours or snack times should not be followed by additional quiet, fine-muscle play but by more vigorous large-muscle activity.

Relaxation and Tension-Relieving Activities

Sometimes we do not think of relaxation as being a motor skill but rather as the absence of one, because "all the child has to do is hold still!" However, the ability to relax and let go can be learned (P. Thomas, 2003) and the ever-increasing stress of life as people mature in our culture makes acquiring these techniques invaluable. Moreover, since full-day centers invariably include naps as part of their routine, knowledge of relaxation techniques is doubly valuable there. Tension, of course, is intimately tied to emotional states, as well as to activity level. We all know that children who are emotionally overwrought find it more difficult to relax. It is worth taking extra time and pains with such youngsters to teach them relaxation skills because of the relief they experience when they can let down even a little.

Children can be encouraged to sense their own bodies and purposefully relax themselves by pretending to be floppy dolls or boiled noodles or melting ice cream. Relaxation should be contrasted with its opposite state of intense contraction. Even young children can learn to make their bodies stiff and hard and then become limp and soft. Stretching, holding the stretch, and then relaxing are also easily understood by children of preschool age, and it does feel wonderful. As we come to understand more about meditation, it becomes evident that some of these techniques can be used with children, too (P. Thomas, 2003).

Using Physical Activity to Promote Creative Thought and Self-Expression

Using Movement Exploration

An interesting aspect of creative physical education is termed *movement education* (Pica, 1998, 2003). It is a blend of physical activity and problem solving that can be considerable fun for children. The teacher may ask a youngster, "Is there some way you could get across the rug without using your feet?" and then, "Is there another way you could do that?" Or the teacher might question, "What could you do with a ball with different parts of your feet?" or, "Can you hold a ball without using your hands?"

Using Creative Dance as a Means of Self-Expression

Dancing can be the freest and most joyful of all large-motor activities. For young children, dancing usually means moving rhythmically to music in a variety of relatively unstructured ways. The quandary beginning teachers often feel is just how unstructured this should be. On the one hand, it is rarely effective just to play a recording, no matter how appealing, and expect the children to "dance." On the other hand, the teacher who sets out to teach specific patterns, often in the guise of folk dances, surely limits the creative aspects of this experience. Besides that limitation, patterned dances are usually too complicated for young children to learn unless these are stripped to very simple levels.

What works best is to have an array of recordings on hand with which the teacher is very familiar and that provide a selection of moods and tempi. Creative props, such as colored scarves, laminated pictures of moving animals, streamers, bubbles, and so forth, can enhance dancing and encourage otherwise reticent children to participate. As the session moves along, more and more ideas and movements can be drawn from the children themselves—an approach that makes the activity truly creative and satisfying for them.

FOSTERING SENSORY EXPERIENCE

Teachers should remember to use *all* the senses as avenues of learning. Children should be encouraged to make comparisons of substances by feeling them and smelling them, as well as by looking at them. Science areas should be explored by handling and manipulating, rather than by looking at bulletin board pictures or observing demonstrations carried out by the teacher. Stress should be placed on developing auditory discrimination skills (telling sounds apart), as well as on paying attention to what is said by the teacher. Learning through physical, sensory participation should be an important part of every early education day.

The Sensory Experience of Close Physical Contact Is Important to Children

The handful of sensational court cases concerning sexual abuse in children's centers has made some teachers of young children uneasy about touching or cuddling youngsters lest they, too, be accused. They feel torn between the desire to protect themselves and the knowledge, well substantiated by practical experience, that young children require the reassurance and comfort of being patted, rocked, held, and hugged from time to time.

Research, as well as experience, supports the value of close physical contact (R. T. Johnson, 2000). There are beneficial effects of being touched, and tactile experience is an essential component to healthy physical and emotional development. Investigations documenting the link between touching and the development of attachment have confirmed how important it is for children to be touched.

Yet staff members must realize that parents are understandably concerned about the possibility of sexual abuse. Centers need to do everything they can to reassure them. No one, teachers included, wants children to be molested, and parents worry about this particularly when their children are away from home. To allay these fears, centers should have clearly stated policies encouraging parents to drop in for unannounced visits, and they should create opportunities for families and teachers to become well acquainted so that a climate of trust develops between them. If the center is staffed so that more than one person is with the children at all times, so much the better.

When such openness is the case, parents are reassured, and children and staff are more comfortable, too. In these circumstances the children will grow and thrive, and Cornelia Goldsmith's statement will prove as true today as when she said it over 40 years ago: "The teacher's most important piece of equipment is her lap!"

SUMMARY

The promotion of health and safety is vital to the physical well-being of young children. During the hours when children are at school, it is the teacher's responsibility to see that they follow good health practices and to keep the children as safe as possible without nagging them or being overprotective.

In addition, it is desirable to offer equipment and activities that foster large- and fine-muscle development. Attaining competence in these physical areas enhances children's self-esteem and provides opportunities for children to gain social expertise as they develop wholesome feelings of vigor and good health.

Benjamin La Framboise

"The teacher's most important piece of equipment is her lap!"

Teachers should encourage physical fitness to combat the epidemic of overweight and obesity in children, as well as the trend for young children to remain sedentary as they engage in electronic media.

Equipment for large-muscle activities should be versatile, sturdy, safe, and well maintained. Teachers can encourage active play by tuning in on what is happening and being alert to ways to add to its richness, rather than by regarding large-muscle playtime as a recess period when they can sit down and relax.

Fine-muscle activity is also valuable to offer, but it is important to provide an assortment of levels of difficulty and to be sure such activities do not continue for too long a time without relief.

Increasing knowledge of perceptual-motor development has made it necessary for preprimary teachers to broaden the range of activities offered to young children and so provide opportunities for practice in specific motor skills: locomotion, balance, body and space perception, rhythm and temporal awareness, rebound and airborne activities, projectile management, management of daily motor activities (fine-muscle activities), and tension relievers. Movement activities that encourage creative thinking and self-expression should also be included. Use of all the senses is important in education. Encourage children to touch, taste, and listen, as well as look to make the fullest use of these potential pathways for learning.

By using this comprehensive approach involving large- and fine-muscle skills and various sensory abilities, teachers can assure themselves that the physical development of the child is brought to its fullest potential.

Questions and Activities

1. Suppose you were beginning a new school and had a budget of $5,000 for large-muscle equipment. In your opinion, what would be the most satisfactory way to invest this money? What would you buy and why?
2. What conditions, if any, in the school where you are teaching are particularly well handled in terms of safety precautions? What possible hazards, if any, warrant attention?

Diversity Question

1. What steps would you take to encourage physical activity for a child who is blind? A child with developmental delays? A child who uses a wheelchair?

Predicament

1. A little boy has just fallen out of a swing and is brought into the office, bleeding heavily from the mouth. Examination reveals that his front tooth is still whole but has cut entirely through his lower lip. As the teacher in charge, how would you handle this emergency? Remember to think about both short- and long-term aspects of the situation.

Self-Check Questions for Review

Content-Related Questions

1. Explain why it is so important for schools to insist that children be immunized and have a physical examination before attending school.
2. List some general health precautions teachers should follow when caring for children.
3. List three principles of physical development.
4. What are some typical fine-muscle activities offered to young children in preprimary schools? Why is it important not to keep children doing these activities for overly long periods of time?
5. Discuss some effective ways to help children learn to relax.
6. What are some effective policies that schools might follow to reassure parents their children are safe from sexual abuse?

Integrative Question

1. The teacher in the room next door, who is very interested in promoting physical fitness, usually organizes the 4-year-olds into teams and has them compete to see which team can get through an obstacle course fastest. Explain whether you would include that kind of activity in your plans for the children in your room. Be sure to include reasons why you would or would not do this.

Reference for Further Reading

Sanders, S. W. (2002). *Active for life: Developmentally appropriate movement programs for young children.* Washington, DC: National Association for the Education of Young Children. This is good overview of children's developing physical skills and how to apply developmentally appropriate principles in a preschool program.

Related Organizations and Online Resources

American Academy of Pediatrics (AAP). The AAP provides many resources for parents and teachers, and an excellent Web site with many useful downloads at http://www.aap.org.

American Alliance for Health, Physical Education, Recreation, and Dance (AAHPERD). The alliance offers many publications and media materials with an astonishing range of physical activities. Information is available at http://www.aahperd.org/.

Child Health Alert. This organization is committed to the health and well-being of all children by helping parents and teachers understand health news that affects children. Good online resources and information about their monthly newsletter are available at http://www.childhealthalert.com/.

Division for Early Childhood of the Council for Exceptional Children (DEC). This is an international membership organization for individuals who work with or on behalf of children with special needs, birth through age 8, and their families. DEC publishes *Young Exceptional Children*, an outstanding resource for all early childhood teachers. It provides information on ways to adapt teaching strategies that enable more children to fit in comfortably to the school environment. Information can be found at http://www.dec-sped.org.

P.E. Central. The latest information about developmentally appropriate physical education programs, with a good section on preschool, is provided at http://www.pecentral.com.

CHAPTER nine

Strengthening the Development of the Emotional Self

How to get children to say what they're feeling instead of hitting somebody?

What to do for a child who just won't stop crying?

How to tell whether a child is mentally healthy?

. . . IF YOU HAVE, THE MATERIAL IN THE FOLLOWING PAGES WILL HELP YOU.

Children of all ages need an atmosphere of warmth in which to thrive, the warmth of close, honest human contacts. They need the feeling that adults, teachers, and parents like them, are interested in them, enjoy them, and feel ready to be responsible for them, to protect them even from themselves when occasion demands.

Barbara Biber (1984, p. 5)

Until your child can express her feelings in words, she doesn't really picture her feelings as you do. The idea is difficult for adults to grasp since we are all so familiar with feelings, but until your child has negotiated this stage she lives in an action- and body-oriented state. She experiences her feelings as impulses in her body—a sudden urge to strike out, for example, or a tightening in her chest that causes her to fall on the floor in tears. The sensation is concrete, as is the rest of her experience. Until she grows into the world of ideas, she doesn't have the capacity to understand the very abstract idea of feelings.

Stanley I. Greenspan and Serena Wieder (1998, p. 219)

The valuable contribution early childhood programs can make to fostering mental health was emphasized as long ago as 1970, when the Joint Commission on the Mental Health of Children repeatedly pointed out that child care centers, nursery schools, and compensatory programs present outstanding opportunities for carrying out preventive and remedial work in this area.

The potential value of these programs to children's mental health continues to be recognized today because the incidence of mental illness remains high (Elias, 2008; Greenberg, Domitrovich, Graczyk, & Zins, 2005; Knudsen, Heckman, Cameron, & Shonkoff, 2006; National Education Goals Panel, 1999). The *Report on Mental Illness* by the surgeon general of the United States (U.S. Department of Health and Human Services, 2000) summarizes studies of mental illness in the United States documenting that 1 in 10 children and adolescents suffer from mental illness severe enough to cause some level of impairment. The report goes on to state that only about 1 in 5 of such children receive mental health services, concluding, "The nation is facing a public crisis in mental healthcare for infants, children and adolescents. . . . Unmet need for services remains as high now as it was 20 years ago" (p. 1). The report agrees that some mental illnesses are the result of genetic factors but also emphasizes that some are the result of malign environments and life experiences.

One outcome of the increase in mental health problems for children is the use of medication even in the early childhood years. The number of children under the age of 9 who were prescribed powerful antipsychotic drugs increased by 57% between the years 2001 and 2005 (Elias, 2008). Although these drugs have been shown to help those with severe mental illness such as schizophrenia, diagnosis is difficult particularly in children. Additionally, these drugs have not been tested or approved for use with children and it is unknown what effect they will have on a child's developing body and brain.

Early childhood teachers can be of real help—in part by providing information, support, and good examples for the children's families, and in part by providing wholesome, emotionally healthy environments while the children are at school.

IMPORTANCE OF DEVELOPING BASIC ATTITUDES OF TRUST, AUTONOMY, INITIATIVE, AND INDUSTRY IN YOUNG CHILDREN

PEARSON
myeducationlab

Go to MyEducationLab and select the topic "Child Development." Under Activities and Applications, watch the video *Emotional Development: Infancy*. What does the adult do to support the infant's emotional development?

The most fundamental thing the teacher can do to foster mental health in young children is to provide many opportunities for basic, healthy emotional attitudes to develop. As noted in chapter 1, Erikson (1959, 1963, 1982) made a significant contribution to our understanding of what these basic attitudes are. He hypothesized that during the life span an individual passes through a series of stages of emotional development wherein basic attitudes are formed. Early childhood encompasses four of these stages: trust versus mistrust, autonomy versus shame and doubt, initiative versus guilt, and industry versus inferiority.

In the stage of trust versus mistrust, babies learn (or fail to learn) that other people can be depended on and that they can depend on themselves to elicit needed responses from other people. The need to experience trust and to have it reaffirmed remains with people throughout their lives.

Therefore it is vital that the basic climate of the school encourages the establishment of trust between everyone who is part of that community. If teachers think of establishing trust in terms of letting the children know they can depend on them, it will be fairly easy to implement this goal. For example, consistent policies and regularity of events in the program obviously contribute to establishing a trustful climate. Being reasonable also makes it clear to the children that they can depend on the teacher. In addition, if the teacher is sensitive to the individual needs of the children and meets these as they arise, this confirms the message that they are worthy of love and thus further strengthens trust and self-esteem.

In our society the attitudes of autonomy versus shame and doubt are formed during the same period in which toilet training takes place. During this time the child is acquiring the skills of holding on and letting go. This fundamental exercise in self-assertion and control is associated with the drive to become independent and to express this independence by making choices and decisions. According to Erikson, children who are overregulated and deprived of the opportunity to establish independence and autonomy may become oppressed with feelings of shame and self-doubt, which result in losing self-esteem, being defiant, trying to get away with things, or in later life developing various forms of compulsive behavior.

The desirable way to handle this strong need for choice and self-assertion is to provide an environment at home and school that provides many opportunities for the child to be independent and to make decisions. This is the fundamental reason why self-selection is an important principle in curriculum design. At the same time, the teacher must be able to establish decisive control when necessary since young children often show poor judgment and can be tyrannized by their own willfulness unless the teacher is willing to intervene.

Gradually, as children develop the ability to act independently, they embark on building the next set of basic attitudes. Around the age of 4 or 5 they become more interested in reaching out to the world around them, in doing things, and in being part of the group. At this stage they want to think up things and try them out; they are interested in the effect their actions have on other people (witness their experimentation with profanity and "bad" language); they formulate concepts of appropriate sex roles; they enjoy imaginative play; and they become avid seekers of information about the world around them. This is the stage Erikson so aptly named initiative versus guilt.

To feel emotionally satisfied, a child of this age must be allowed to explore, to act, and to do. Preprimary schools are generally strong about meeting children's needs to explore and create, but they often underestimate the ability of children to participate in making plans and decisions for their group or to attempt challenging projects. Encouraging the ability to initiate plans and take action will enhance the child's feeling of self-worth and creativity, as well as the ability to be a self-starter—all highly desirable outcomes necessary for future development and happiness.

In the early grades of primary school (approximately age 6 to 11 years), healthy children develop a sense of industry versus inferiority. At this age children pay more attention to those around them and want to know how they stand in relation to others. Children seek recognition in school and from peers, and feel inferior if they experience failure. School teaches them the "tools" of the culture, such as reading, writing, arithmetic, and social skills, and it is crucial that each child experience success in order to be socially well adjusted.

To feel emotionally satisfied, a child must be allowed to explore, to act, and to do.

HALLMARKS OF AN EMOTIONALLY HEALTHY YOUNG CHILD

To determine whether the child is in good emotional health, the teacher should ask the following questions. If the majority of them can be answered affirmatively, chances are good that the child is emotionally healthy.

Is the Child Working on Emotional Tasks That Are Age Appropriate?

We have already talked about the fundamental need for planning a curriculum that provides many opportunities for children to exercise their autonomy and initiative. When looking at individual children, the teacher should consider whether they are taking advantage of these opportunities. The teacher will find that the majority of them are achieving independence, choosing what they want to do, and generating their own ideas with zest and enthusiasm; but there will be a handful of children who will need sensitive help to venture forth. This usually involves taking time to build a strong foundation of trust between these children and the teacher and then helping them advance to increased independence as their confidence grows (Edwards & Raikes, 2002; Honig, 2002; Pianta & Stuhlman, 2004).

Is the Child Learning to Separate from the Family Without Undue Stress and to Form an Attachment with at Least One Other Adult at School?

In chapter 7 considerable space was devoted to handling separation anxiety in a constructive way because the ability to separate from significant others and form additional relationships is an important skill (Honig, 2002; Landy, 2002; National Research Council and Institute of Medicine, 2000). The teacher should realize that most children, particularly shy ones and those who are very young, make friends with a teacher at school before they branch out to make friends with other children. This link between teacher and child is, of course, not so strong as the bond between parent and child (Honig, 2002; Landy, 2002; Swick, 2006). It seems reasonable to propose, however, that in a milder way a wholesome attachment between teacher and child encourages the child to explore and venture out in the center setting, just as it has been demonstrated by Ainsworth and her colleagues (Ainsworth, Blehar, Waters, & Wall, 1978; Pianta & Stuhlman, 2004) that toddlers who are well attached to their mothers are more likely to venture and explore new experiences when that parent is present. The teacher who is aware that this is a typical and valuable pattern can relax and enjoy this process without fretting about the child's dependency. In time most children will leave the teacher's side in favor of being with other children.

Several studies have highlighted the importance of early teacher-child relationships in child care settings (Kauffman Early Education Exchange, 2002; Peisner-Feinberg et al., 1999; Pianta & Stuhlman, 2004; National Research Council and Institute of Medicine, 2000; National Institute of Child Health and Human Development [NICHD], 2000). Children who have good relationships with their teachers in preprimary school fare better in elementary school—not just academically, but socially and emotionally as well. The impact of the early childhood teacher is long-lasting: The teacher helps the child learn how to form positive relationships with others, a skill that will be retained later in life. These studies indicate that the emotional connection a child has with the caregiver in the child care center is a major predictor of later success in school. Indeed, as the Kauffman Early Education Exchange concludes, "How children feel is as important as how they think in ensuring learning" (p. 2). The child who feels loved, cared for, and respected will grow into a person who can express those same feelings toward others.

Is the Child Learning to Conform to Routines at School Without Undue Fuss?

Of course, conforming to routines varies with the child's age and temperament, and teachers anticipate some balkiness and noncompliance as being not only inevitable but healthy. Two-year-olds are particularly likely to be balky and at the same time insist that things should be done the same way every time. Self-assertiveness appears again rather prominently between the ages of 4 and 5. The quality of the behavior seems different, though: The assertiveness of age 2 comes across as being more dogmatic and less logical, whereas the assertiveness of age 4 seems to be more of a deliberate challenge and trying out of the other person. However, consistent refusal to conform differs from these healthy behaviors because it goes beyond these norms. When this is the case, it should be regarded as a warning sign that the child needs help working through the behavior.

Sojin Yi

Is the child able to become deeply involved in play?

Is the Child Able to Become Deeply Involved in Play?

One characteristic of children who are seriously disturbed in mental institutions is that they cannot give themselves up to the experience of satisfying play. Indeed, when they become able to do so, it is encouraging evidence that they are getting ready to be released from the hospital. Being able to play is also important for more typical children. As the child grows older, the ability to enjoy participating in play alone or with other children not only is a hallmark of emotional health but also contributes to maintaining mental health.

Is the Child Developing the Ability to Settle Down and Concentrate?

Children may be distractible or restless for a variety of reasons, and no child is able to pay attention under all circumstances. Excitement, boredom, the need to go to the toilet, fatigue, interesting distractions, hunger, or not feeling well can all interfere from time to time with any child's ability to concentrate. But occasionally the teacher will come across a child who never seems to settle down. These children flit continually from place to place and seem to give only surface attention to what they are doing. There are a multitude of reasons for this behavior, ranging from attention deficit/hyperactivity disorder (ADHD), to subtle birth injuries, to just plain poor habits, but a common cause of distractibility that is often overlooked is tension or anxiety due to some family crisis.

Is the Child Unusually Withdrawn or Aggressive Compared to Other Children the Same Age?

One of the great advantages teachers have is that by becoming acquainted with hundreds of children over a period of time, they are able to develop some norms for behavior that make it relatively easy to identify children who behave in extreme ways. Very withdrawn behavior is more likely to be overlooked than aggressive behavior since it is much less troublesome to the teacher. However, either response is a signal that the child is emotionally out of balance and needs some extra thought and plans devoted to helping resolve whatever is causing the child to cope in that manner.

Does the Child Have Access to a Full Range of Feelings and the Ability to Deal with Them in an Age-Appropriate Way?

Some children have already learned by the age of 3 or 4 to conceal or deny the existence of their feelings, rather than to accept and express them in a tolerable way. Early childhood teachers can help children stay in touch with the full repertoire of their emotions by showing them that they, too, have all sorts of feelings and that they understand that children have feelings as well, whether these be anger, sadness, or affection. Healthy children should also begin to learn during their early years to express their feelings to the people who have actually caused the feelings and to do this in a way that does not harm themselves or others. Learning to do this successfully takes a long time but has its roots in early childhood (Novick, 2002).

PERSONAL QUALITIES THAT WILL HELP THE TEACHER ESTABLISH AN EMOTIONALLY POSITIVE CLIMATE IN THE CHILDREN'S CENTER

Early childhood teachers should use their personal qualities, as well as what are commonly referred to as "teaching techniques," to foster a growth-enhancing climate for young children. Such a climate consistently favors the active development and maintenance of an atmosphere conducive to emotional health. It frees people to develop to their fullest potential as balanced, happy individuals, and the personal qualities of the teacher have a lot to do with establishing this desirable climate. For this reason they are discussed next.

Consistency

One way to build a sense of trust between teacher and children is to behave in ways children can predict and to be consistent about maintaining guidelines and schedules—a very basic form of being "trustworthy" and dependable. Thus, the children know what to expect and do not live in fear of erratic or temperamental responses to what they do. For this reason, emotional stability is a highly desirable trait for teachers of young children to possess. Of course, consistency does not mean that rules must be inflexible, but their enforcement should not depend on the whim of the teacher or the manipulative power of various children.

Reasonableness

Coupled with the steadiness of consistency should go the trait of reasonableness, which can be defined as "expecting neither too much nor too little from children."

One practical way to increase reasonableness is to learn the characteristics of the developmental stages when these are discussed in child development courses. The brief developmental summaries presented in this book are intended to remind you of general developmental characteristics. Knowledge of these characteristics prevents inexperienced teachers from setting their standards too high or too low.

Another excellent way to help children (and adults, too) see that the teacher is reasonable is to really listen when people try to tell you something. Walter Hodges (1987) describes this kind of active listening to perfection:

> Active listening requires giving undivided attention to children and accepting what they say without blame, shock, or solving their problems for them. Giving undivided attention is signaled by positioning squarely in front of a child, getting close to the child's eye level, and leaning forward without crowding. Active listening enables us to reflect the feelings of the child, respond appropriately, and check to see if we understand. Active listening communicates respect, warmth, and empathy. Children know that they are important and that they belong when they are heard. (p. 13)

Courage and Strength of Character

Particularly when dealing with outbursts of anger, the novice teacher will find that courage and the strength of character commonly called "fortitude" are required to see such outbursts through. Understandably, the embarrassment and insecurity of fearing that the scene may not turn out all right may make it easy to placate angry children or, more usually, to allow them to run off or have their way. But the problem with allowing this to happen is that the child will repeat the behavior and feel contemptuous of the adult who permits it. Therefore, being courageous and seeing a problem through are worth the struggle when coping with the strong emotional reactions so common in children at this age.

Being Genuine

Teachers also promote confidence between themselves and the children by being honest about their own feelings. Thus a teacher might level with one child by saying, "I don't want you to kick me again; I feel really angry with you when you do that to me," or with another by saying, "I'm glad to see you today. I've been looking forward to hearing about your new kittens."

However, a note of caution is in order. Children should not be subjected to outbursts of temper or angry attacks by adults in the name of honesty. Uncontrolled outbursts are too disturbing to children because they know they are relatively helpless and at the mercy of the teacher.

Empathy

Empathy is the ability to feel as other people feel, to feel *with* them, rather than *for* them. Empathy is valuable not only because it allows teachers to put themselves in the child's place but also because it helps them identify and clarify how the child is feeling. In order to respond to the child's feelings with empathy, the caregiver must interpret the emotional cues and respond appropriately. An empathic teacher is essential for children's healthy emotional development and will have an impact on their later social and academic success (Dettore, 2002; Fox & Lentini, 2006; Swick, 2006).

Patricia Weissman

A warm lap . . . a warm teacher . . . so important for healthy development!

Warmth

Warmth is so important and deserves special emphasis since its presence has been linked with the development of positive self-concepts in children (Gonzalez-Mena & Eyer, 2006; Honig, 2002; Lally et al., 2003; Swick, 2006). Warm teachers let the children and staff know that they like them and think well of them. Both children and adults flourish in this climate of sincere approval and acceptance. But being warm and accepting does not mean the teacher just sits around and smiles at the children no matter what they do. There is a difference between expressing warmth and being indulgently permissive, and there are times when the teacher must exert control because a child is unable to. But when teachers do this for a child, they must make it plain that they are taking control because they truly care for the child and not because they want to obtain power for its own sake or have the satisfaction of winning.

Appreciation

Teaching must be unbearable, or at least much less satisfying, for those who fail to take time to relish and enjoy the children in their care. What a shame it would be to overlook the comment, "That little cat is licking her sweater!" or not sense the impact for a 2-year-old who bids her mother adieu and then says stoutly, "I'm my own mommy, now!" Such precious moments can be a major reward of teaching if only teachers take the time to savor and appreciate the children and their reactions.

However, *appreciation* should not be interpreted to mean "be amused by" the children. Appreciation is not the same thing as amusement. Appreciation is composed of perceptive understanding and empathy—with a dash of delight thrown in! When children sense this attitude, they blossom since they feel the approval it also implies. Perhaps it feels to them as if a generous sun were shining in the room.

Good Health

It is necessary to emphasize the significance of valuing and taking care of oneself if one wishes to facilitate health in others.

We all experience times when we seem to have no other choice than to operate on the ragged edge of energy. Some teachers, however, appear to accept this as being a continuing, necessary style of life. Teachers who wish to do their best with children, as well as with their other personal relationships, need to recognize what their bodies and spirits need and make certain they honor these needs to remain physically and emotionally healthy. The prescription includes adequate rest, exercise, wholesome food, and someone to care about who cares in return. Providing oneself with these requisites should be viewed as being part of one's own basic self-respect, as well as being plain good sense.

PRACTICAL WAYS TO HELP YOUNG CHILDREN ACHIEVE HEALTHY EMOTIONAL DEVELOPMENT

Remember That Children Have Different Temperaments

As anyone who has ever visited a nursery of newborns can attest, children respond differently to their environment right from the moment of birth. This disposition to respond in a characteristic way or style is called *temperament*. Some babies wince at every loud noise, some are fretful, and some are more placid. As children develop, temperamental differences become even more apparent. One child can be crushed by a look, whereas another seems impervious to all but the most explicit expression of displeasure from the grown-up. Some children are excitable or lose their tempers easily. Some are so emotionally expressive that the teacher is rarely left in doubt about the child's feelings; others seem impassive, and feelings (which may be just as intense internally as that of the more outwardly expressive child) are not sensed as easily by the caregiver.

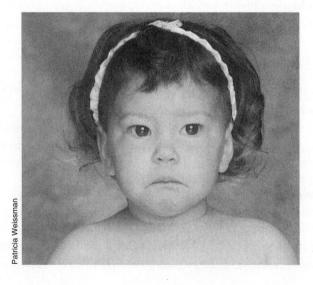

Patricia Weissman

Each child has a unique temperament.

Teachers have temperaments, too, and so may find they are more "in tune" with some children than they are with others. This sense of being in tune with a child has been referred to by researchers as "goodness-of-fit," and it has been found to be very important for the child's healthy adjustment (Ainsworth et al., 1978; Churchill, 2003; Kristal, 2005). A child who does not fit the always-smiling, happy-go-lucky image that we see in advertisements (a child with a more difficult temperament) fares much better when the caregiver is respectful of and sensitive to the child's temperamental disposition—rather than judgmental toward it. Years of research on the mother's goodness-of-fit with her infant has borne this out, but only recently has the importance of goodness-of-fit with the child's preschool caregiver been studied. As the Research Study in this chapter shows, temperament has an impact on the child's well-being in the center. The author concludes that teachers of young children should gain knowledge about temperament and goodness-of-fit in order to improve their skills for coping with children who have a more difficult temperament (Churchill, 2003; Kristal, 2005).

RESEARCH STUDY

Temperament and Goodness-of-Fit in Child Care Settings

Research Question: Churchill asked if a "good fit" between a child's temperament and the teacher's expectations for the child's behavior was associated with better social skills in the preschool classroom.

Research Method: Churchill assessed 45 children from three Head Start programs with regard to their temperamental characteristics by having parents and teachers complete questionnaires about the child's behavior. In addition, the parents and teachers completed a test to measure their expectations for the child's behavior. An index score composed of the two questionnaires was used to determine goodness-of-fit between the child's temperament and the adults' expectations. Finally, the children were observed in their classrooms and assessed for social skills, including self-esteem, following rules, helping, making friends, and so on.

Results: A significant correlation was found between child–teacher goodness-of-fit and the child's social skills. When the child's temperament was in alignment with the teacher's beliefs about appropriate behavior, the child had more positive social interactions than children whose temperaments were not in accordance with teacher expectations.

Implications: This study shows the importance of the child's temperament and relationship with the teacher in developing positive social interactions. Goodness-of-fit between the child and teacher has important developmental consequences that should be taken into account in early childhood programs. It is especially important that children with disabilities or behavioral problems be matched with a teacher whose view of appropriate behavior can accommodate different temperaments. Teachers should evaluate their relationships with each child in the classroom to determine if there is goodness-of-fit. In cases where a teacher has strong negative feelings toward a child, the child's temperament should be taken into account. Since temperament cannot be changed (or only minimally so), the teacher must make efforts to accommodate the child or find a better fit with another teacher.

Source: Data taken from "Goodness-of-Fit in Early Childhood Settings," by S. L. Churchill, 2003, *Early Childhood Research Journal, 31*(2), 113–118.

The interplay and mix of temperaments is one reason that working with young children is so interesting—and so challenging. Although it would be much easier if only "one size fit all" and we could treat all children alike, particularly when working with the emotional self, we must remember to be sensitive to these variations and adjust our responses accordingly.

A valuable way to increase that sensitivity is to ask families about their children: How do they see their children, and what would they like you to know about them? What do their children care about most intensely? What is most likely to hurt their feelings—or to bring them joy? How is each child best comforted when feeling sad?

Another way to gain insight is to quiet oneself inside and be as open and receptive as possible to what a child might be feeling before jumping to conclusions. Wait a little and widen the frame of possibilities through which you can see the child; for example, what might that scowl on Carmen's face mean: Is she angry? Or is she thinking very seriously about something? Or could she be squinting because she needs glasses?

Reduce Frustration for the Children When Possible

Children should not have to spend time waiting for things to happen when this can be prevented. Children's needs are *immediate, intense,* and *personal,* and the longer they are kept waiting the more irritable and out of hand they become. A snack should be available as the children sit down, and someone should be outside for supervision as the children are dressed and ready to go outdoors to play. Duplicates of equipment mean there is generally enough to go around; two or three toy trucks are much more satisfactory than just one. A good assortment of developmentally appropriate activities must be available so that 3-year-olds are not expected to stack tiny plastic blocks and 6-year-olds do not have to make do with eight-piece puzzles. The day should be planned so that few and moderate demands are made on children at points when they are likely to be tired and hungry.

Learn to Couple Language with Emotion by Identifying and Describing Children's Feelings to Them and by Helping Them Express These Feelings to Relevant People in an Acceptable Way

Many in our society seem to have reached the conclusion that it is dangerous to allow some emotions to be expressed. The assumption is that if they are expressed they will become stronger or the person will act the feeling out but that if we ignore them or deny their presence they will vanish. Actually, the opposite of this premise is psychologically true. Research supports the principle that if negative emotions are recognized, accepted, and expressed, they usually fade; but if they are not expressed, they seem to generate pressure that ultimately causes the person to relieve them in a more explosive or veiled yet hostile way. Also, if children are *not* provided with ways of telling someone else how they feel, they are almost inevitably driven to *show* how they feel by acting the feelings out (Fox & Lentini, 2006).

It is not easy for such young children to put their feelings and impulsive intentions into words instead of actions. As we will see in chapter 10, learning to self-regulate aggression requires a lot of experience and practice, but teaching children to recognize what they are feeling inside and to say "outside" what that feeling is instead of acting it out is a crucial step toward acquiring self-regulation (Novick, 2002). Identifying feelings is one of the first steps children must acquire in order to regulate their behavior and get along with others (Fox & Lentini, 2006).

Teach Children the Difference Between Verbal Attack and Self-Report

When teaching children to express their feelings, we must teach them gradually to understand the difference between saying how one feels about something (self-report) and telling another person what he or she is (verbal attack). There's a big difference between allowing a child to attack by shouting, "You meanie! Gimme that shovel now or you can't come to my birthday party!" and teaching the child to say instead, "I need that shovel now! I can't wait another minute!"

Admittedly this is a sophisticated concept for young children to grasp. Sad to say, even some adults seem unable to make this distinction and say something nasty about the other person, rather than explain their own feelings. Nevertheless, self-report is such an extraordinarily valuable emotional and social skill to acquire that teachers should begin to model and teach children the rudiments of self-report very early. Acquisition of this skill will benefit them all their lives.

There are many additional ways to express feelings through play and through the use of expressive materials (which are discussed later), but *the ability to recognize and acknowledge feelings openly* is the soundest and most fundamental therapeutic skill to use to foster mental health.

Go to MyEducationLab and select the topic "Guidance." Under Activities and Applications, watch the video *Managing Challenging Behavior: Discussing Choices.* How does the teacher help the children identify and give words to feelings?

Joanne Hendrick

The ability to recognize and acknowledge feelings openly is the soundest way to foster mental health.

Learn to Recognize Signs of Stress and Emotional Upset in Children

Children give many signals besides crying or fussing that indicate emotional stress. Reverting (regressing) to less mature behavior is a common signal. We are all familiar with the independent 5-year-old who suddenly wants to be babied while recovering from the flu or the child who wets the bed after the baby arrives.

Various nervous habits such as hair twisting, deep sighing, nail biting, or thumb sucking also reveal that the child is under stress. Increased irritability, sometimes to the point of tantrums, is another indicator, as are lethargy and withdrawing from activities. Sometimes children suddenly begin to challenge rules and routines, sometimes they cry a lot, sometimes expressions of tension or stress are subtler and conveyed only by a strained look about the eyes or a tightened mouth, and sometimes stress is expressed in the more obvious form of excessive activity and running about.

In addition to this knowledge of common symptoms, as the year progresses and the teachers get to know the children well, they will have the additional advantage of knowing how each child usually behaves. This makes it easier to spot changes and identify children who are signaling for special help.

Know What to Do for Children Who Are Emotionally Upset

Emotional upsets have to be handled on a short-term basis and sometimes on a long-term basis as well. (See also chapter 5.)

Short-Term, Emergency Treatment

The first thing to do for children who are upset to the point of tears is to comfort them. But the manner of comfort will vary from child to child: Some children need to be held and rocked, whereas others do best when they are allowed to reduce themselves to hiccuping silence while the teacher putters about nearby. Children who are using emotional outbursts as a means of controlling the adult's behavior require still a third response—mildly ignoring them until they subside. When in doubt, it is better to err on the side of comfort than to ignore unhappiness.

No matter why children are crying hard, it is a waste of energy to try to reason with them until they have calmed down. However, it can be helpful and soothing to repeat something in a quieter and quieter tone of voice so that the child gradually quiets down to hear what is being said. This may be as simple a sentence as, "When you've stopped crying, we'll talk things over," or, "I'm waiting to help you when you've stopped crying." Occasionally it can also be helpful to remark matter-of-factly if the occasion warrants, "You know, I will keep on holding you, even when you've stopped crying."

As the child calms down, getting him a drink of water or wiping his eyes may also soothe him. It is often effective at this point to talk over the difficulty, but sometimes it is better to wait and discuss it in a casual way later in the day to clarify how the child felt or why he broke down. Each situation has to be judged in its own context.

Finally, the teacher should either help the child return and resolve the problem in the group or, if it is deemed wiser, help the child get started on another satisfying activity. Activities that are particularly helpful at such times include swinging, water play, and messy activities such as finger painting or working with clay. Water play generally seems to be the best choice.

Long-Term Treatment

It is always wise, before deciding that an emotional upset represents a serious long-term difficulty, to wait and see whether the child is coming down with something; incipient illness is a frequent source of loss of emotional control. It is also wise to consider whether an approaching holiday could be causing the disturbance. If the symptoms of stress do not subside, it is necessary to find out more about what is causing tension in the child. The behavior may be caused by something going on at home or by something going on at school or by a combination of these circumstances.

One helpful way to locate the cause is to think back to the point when the signs of stress appeared and then to confer with the family about what else changed in the child's life at about the same time. Perhaps the child was moved to another room at school, or a close friend was absent because of chicken pox; perhaps the child's grandmother died, or the father was away, or houseguests were visiting. Once the cause has been discovered, steps can be taken to help the child feel more at ease. Sometimes just recognizing the source helps a lot, without doing anything more.

Other signals of disturbance can be traced to continuing environmental situations. Perhaps discipline policies are erratic at home, or affection is lacking, or the child is excessively fatigued from watching television until late at night. Another major source of stress on both children and adults is poverty. Teachers should be aware of the effects that poverty can have on children and help families to counteract these effects. These are more difficult situations to deal with, but even they can often be resolved successfully by working together with the family.

If the situation is too complicated or difficult to be quickly eased by the teacher's intervention, the family must be encouraged to seek counseling from a psychologist or psychiatrist. The area of guidance and referral is such an extensive one that it cannot be treated in detail here. To pursue the subject further, refer to chapters 2 and 5.

PROMOTE EVERY CHILD'S SENSE OF SELF-ESTEEM

Unconditional Positive Regard

The most effective way to help a child build a basic feeling of self-esteem is, unfortunately, also the most elusive for some teachers to achieve: It is the ability to feel and project what Carl Rogers (1961) termed *unconditional positive regard*. This kind of fundamental acceptance and approval of all children is not contingent on their meeting the teacher's expectations of what they should be; it simply depends on their being alive, being themselves as individuals, and being in the group. A good test of being accepting or not is to become aware of what one is usually thinking about when looking at the children. Ask yourself, "Am I taking time to enjoy the children, or am I looking at each one with a critical eye—noting mainly what behavior should be improved?" If you catch yourself habitually noting only what should be changed, then this is a sign you are losing sight of half the pleasure of teaching, which is to appreciate the children and enjoy who they are right now, at this particular moment in time—no strings attached.

This ability to be uncritical implies a kind of faith in the way children will turn out, an attitude that subtly makes them aware that the teacher has confidence they will grow in sound directions. There is no substitute for these underlying feelings of trust and confidence in the child. Some teachers are fortunate enough to have developed optimism about people as a result of their own trust-building childhood experiences, some gain it from long experience with children themselves, and some acquire it by means of psychotherapeutic treatment, which helps restore their own confidence as well as their faith in others.

Acceptance of all children as they are also includes accepting each child's right to be different from the teacher and from other children. Here again, ethnic and cultural differences and various disabilities come particularly to mind. Teachers can make a significant contribution to increasing the self-esteem of such children by unconditionally valuing them and by using themselves as models to influence the attitude of the other children and their families (Swick, 2006).

Honest Recognition and Praise

Rewarding a child with praise is usually the first way teachers think of to build self-esteem. Unfortunately, sometimes praise is the *only* method they think of. Actually it is only one of several and perhaps not one of the better ways to enhance a child's feelings of self-worth (Cleaver, 2007b; Kohn, 2001; Marano, 2008).

Alfie Kohn points out in the article "Five Reasons to Stop Saying 'Good Job!'" (2001), "Does praise motivate kids? Sure. It motivates kids to get praise" (p. 27). Even the effects of praise vary quite a bit (Kohn, 1999). If you do use praise, remember that to be an effective esteem raiser and motivator, praise should include information about something specific a child has achieved; that is, praise should be based on performance. Used in that context, it can heighten the inner *intrinsic* satisfaction of the child. For example, it is better to say to a 4-year-old, "Thanks for letting Keiko play; it cheered her up," than to say, "You sure are a nice little boy!" Erikson (1963) was right when he said, "Children cannot be fooled by empty praise and condescending encouragement."

Using encouragement rather than praise is another effective way of building self-esteem while recognizing what a child is accomplishing. Such comments as, "I bet you can do it if you try," or, "Look how much work you've done," encourage children without passing judgment on what they've done.

Children also need to learn that failing at something is not the end of the world. For this reason it is also important to appreciate the effort of children when they have not been successful. They particularly need encouragement at this point since the reward inherent in successful accomplishment has not been realized. The teacher can say, "I see how hard you've worked on that," or, "I'm proud of you; you really tried," or, "It takes a while to learn to do that. You've really stuck with it; it's *hard* to learn things sometimes, isn't it?"

Then the teacher might follow up that comment by asking a question coupled with an offer of support if needed; for example, "I guess that didn't work. How can we fix it?" or, "Want to try again? I'll stand here and see if I can help you balance," or, "Tell you what. Why don't I hold the box for you? Then I bet you could get all those crayons back in." Responses like these are worthwhile because they encourage the child to persist—to continue trying—and persistence is a valuable part of achieving mastery. Note also that these responses illustrate ways of encouraging children to move closer to the growing edge of their abilities à la the zone of proximal development so beloved by Vygotsky.

Respect

Respecting the child is such a high-minded phrase that examples of behavior must be provided in order to see how respect can be implemented when working with young children. One basic way to show respect is to abide by children's decisions when they have been given a valid choice. By doing this, the teacher is really saying, "What you want is important. I have confidence that you know yourself better than I do, and I count on you to choose what will enhance your existence most." Children also sense respect when the teacher asks their opinion and listens carefully to their replies. Even young children can answer "Do you think we should . . ." kinds of questions.

Another way to show respect and thus sustain the child's self-esteem is to avoid humiliating a child in front of other people. It is best to carry out disciplinary measures as unobtrusively as possible. Belittling a child's behavior at any time is, of course, fundamentally disrespectful as well as destructive of self-esteem.

A third valuable way to show respect is to pay the child the compliment of explaining the reason behind the rule. Such reasoning confers respect since it assumes that the child is important enough to be entitled to an explanation and intelligent enough to comprehend it.

Finally, we must never lose sight of the fact that children are intensely aware of how teachers feel about their families. Teachers who truly respect and value the child's family show this each day in the way they welcome them to the classroom, by the way they avoid making derogatory remarks about them, and by the way they really listen to a family member who has something to say (Swick, 2006).

Helping the Child Achieve Competence

Positive regard, respect, and merited praise are sound in that they help build positive self-pictures for children, but they have one weakness in common: *They all depend on the goodwill of another person for implementation.* Yet the ultimate goal should be the internalization of esteem so that the individual will not remain permanently dependent on others to supply feelings of self-worth (Cleaver, 2007b; Marano, 2008).

But how can children be helped to shift from relying on external praise or other supports to experiencing *intrinsic* satisfaction from within themselves? The most effective answer is that helping children achieve competence is the surest way to instill internal feelings of self-worth. Every time a child does something that works out well, be it standing up for his rights in the trike area or writing the letter "A" for the first time, the reward of success is inherent in the act, and the child feels competent because of what he *did*, not because of what someone said. This knowledge of capability makes children (and adults, too, for that matter) feel good about themselves, feel that they are worth something—*and in that knowledge lies the foundation of inner self-esteem.*

Allow Children to Experience Mastery by Making Their Own Choices and by Being as Independent as Possible

Making choices and being independent are two ways to encourage competence that have already been discussed. Maccoby (1980) has referred to this as keeping the *locus of control* as much within the hands of the child as possible. She has cited several studies that support the value of encouraging children to feel that they are in control of their environment at least part of the time. Of course, this should not be interpreted as meaning that the teacher or parent should submit unquestioningly to every passing whim. Rather, it does mean that encouraging children to make choices and decisions and to do things for themselves is worth doing whenever reasonable and possible. Granting them such "power" reduces their feelings of helplessness and increases their feelings of mastery by placing the locus of control within rather than outside themselves (Cleaver, 2007b; Marano, 2008; Noddings, 2006).

Provide Opportunities That Are Challenging but Not Excessively Difficult to Give Children the Chance to Test Themselves Against Difficulties

The derring-do of 4-year-olds is a prime example of this desire to make things a little bit harder every time they attempt them. In general, children should always be allowed to attempt more difficult feats as they think of them unless it is evident they have not anticipated any serious dangers that may be involved.

Something else first-time teachers may forget is that it takes practice to acquire a new skill. A novice teacher might offer an activity once and assume that one opportunity would be sufficient for the children to learn how to do it. Be it using the scooter or cutting around a circle or playing lotto, other things being equal, repeated practice increases competence. It is therefore important to provide chances for children to do something more than once if you want them to become skillful.

Emphasize the Value of Building Cross-Sex Competencies of Various Kinds

It is still the case that girls often grow up unable to use power saws or drills or lacking even a rudimentary understanding of the combustion engine and that boys are sometimes described as limited in their ability to express emotion. Most women (and many men) have only to recall the last time they dealt with a garage mechanic to realize the sense of inferiority such incompetence produces. Methods of remedying these deficiencies are discussed at greater length in chapter 4, so it is only noted here that broader and more various educational experiences for both sexes should be encouraged.

Make Certain That Children with Disabilities Experience Opportunities to Build Competence, Too

Although opportunities to achieve success are important for all children, they are particularly important for children who have special difficulties they must overcome. It's so easy to underestimate and overhelp these youngsters with disabilities in the interests of kindness or, more realistically, saving time. Perhaps it is as simple a thing as handing the child a crayon instead of waiting for him to reach for it, or answering for him when another child asks him a question. It isn't just one tiny episode that makes a difference; it's when many episodes are added together that children get the message they cannot be effective or competent. Then the fragile balloon of self-esteem begins to deflate.

Although we often speak of the *child who has special needs*, perhaps in these circumstances it would be better to think of the *teacher who has special needs* and identify what a few of these are if the child is to prosper. When working with such a youngster, some of the teacher's special needs include the need to know what the child is able to do *and* what the child can probably do next, the need to feel and project confidence that the child wants to attempt something independently, and the need to have patience and wait that extra minute it may take for the child to experience success.

Offer Many Opportunities to Accomplish Meaningful Work

One of the most effective yet often overlooked ways to generate feelings of mastery and self-worth is to provide many opportunities for children to do meaningful work. This work should not be limited to tedious chores such as putting all the blocks back on the shelves. Many jobs such as washing the finger-painting aprons, dying eggshells to crush for collage, or mixing paint are fun, are not too difficult, and provide valuable opportunities to do something that helps the group. What's more, they all have tangible results—accomplishments that can be viewed with satisfaction and that help children see doing work in a positive light. This is a very healthy attitude to instill since working is a cornerstone of so much adult existence and satisfaction.

Offer Creative Activities Because They Provide Excellent Opportunities for Experiencing Competence

There is so much latitude for individual abilities and differences to be expressed in creative activity areas that they must be singled out as avenues for building self-esteem. Indeed, as the work from Reggio Emilia demonstrates, the very essence of a child's ideas and being can be revealed through paint or clay or collages. What adult has not experienced the satisfaction and boost in self-esteem that came from attempting a new art or craft? Children feel the same way. It feels good to make something attractive generated by oneself. Therefore, the value of creative self-expression is an avenue to building self-esteem that must not be overlooked.

Help Children Connect with Nature to Soothe the Soul

Richard Louv (2005) coined the phrase "nature deficit disorder" to describe the current state of childhood in which children are disconnected from the natural world. While the average child spends almost 6 hours a day sitting in front of an electronic screen, schools have cut back recess and outdoor time. In addition, childhood obesity, attention deficit disorder, and childhood depression are on the rise (Louv, 2008; White, 2008).

The effects of outdoor education have been summarized in a policy action report published by the National Wildlife Federation (White, 2008). Studies have shown that:

- Outdoor play increases creativity, reduces stress, and increases physical fitness.
- Viewing nature reduces stress, increases levels of attention and interest, and decreases feelings of anger and aggression.
- Contact with nature has a positive effect on mood and reduces feelings of anxiety.
- Outdoor time has improved the behavior of children diagnosed with attention disorders.

Early childhood educators should provide outdoor play and nature education for children as much as possible. Elementary teachers often struggle in schools that emphasize academics and eliminate physical education and outdoor play from the curriculum altogether. Primary teachers can find support from a coalition of educational and health organizations called "No Child Left Inside" that is listed in the Related Organizations and Online Resources. As the National Wildlife Federation suggests, "Children should have access to and time for play in nature. A right for unstructured play. A right to create and explore. A right to experience the sense of wonder of being outside" (White, 2008, p. 1).

SUMMARY

Growth-enhancing early education seeks to create as many opportunities as possible for young children to develop their sense of autonomy and initiative in a setting that is reasonable, consistent, trustful, empathic, warm, and appreciative. Children who are mentally healthy are working on emotional tasks appropriate for their age. They are learning to separate from their families and to conform to school routines without undue stress. They can involve themselves deeply in play, and they are developing the ability to settle down and concentrate. Emotionally healthy children are not excessively withdrawn or aggressive; they have access to the full range of their feelings and are beginning to learn to deal with these feelings in appropriate ways.

Teachers can help the children in their care develop in emotionally healthy ways by supporting each child's temperament, reducing frustration for the children when possible, identifying and describing the children's feelings for them and helping them express these to the relevant people, recognizing the signs of stress that signal that help is needed, handling emotional problems on a short-term and long-term basis as necessary, and promoting a healthy sense of self-worth in each and every child—without resorting to the overuse of meaningless praise. Providing soothing nature experiences also leads to the emotional well-being of children.

Questions and Activities

1. What are some matter-of-fact ways to express warmth and liking to young children?
2. Looking back on your own education, give an example of a teacher who had unreasonably high expectations of you as a pupil. What was the effect on your learning?
3. With other members of the class, set up some role-playing situations that provide opportunities for "children" to express their feelings and "teachers" to practice phrasing responses that would help children identify how they feel and show that the teacher understands them. Practice this a lot!
4. Describe some examples in which you have seen adults ignore, suppress, or mislabel a child's

feelings. Could you see how the child was immediately affected by this kind of response? What would you predict might be the long-term effects of a child's experiencing many such responses?

Diversity Question

1. What are some warning signs that a child's emotional development may need a referral or outside intervention?

Predicaments

1. A child in your class seems very shy and stays mostly to herself, neither playing with other children, nor interacting with you very much.

What specific steps would you take to help support her healthy emotional development?

2. Two 4-year-olds are fighting over possession of a very beautiful doll (of which there is only one). One child screams at the other, "I hate you! You're mean and ugly and I'm never going to play with you!" What would you do to remedy this situation in a way that is emotionally supportive of both youngsters? What could be done to prevent situations like this in the future?

Self-Check Questions for Review

Content-Related Questions

1. Name the first four stages of emotional development identified by Erikson and list some actions early childhood teachers can take to foster the successful mastering of each stage.
2. Identify the hallmarks of an emotionally healthy child.
3. Select four personal qualities of teachers that would help foster emotional health in the children, and explain why each is important.
4. What common behaviors of children might alert you to the fact that they are experiencing stress?

Integrative Question

1. What is goodness-of-fit and why is it important in the preschool environment? Provide examples of two different types of temperament and how

the caregiver would respond to each one in a sensitive, health-promoting manner.

Reference for Further Reading

Koplow, L. (2002). *Creating schools that heal*. New York: Teachers College Press. This wonderful book is filled with examples of how teachers can construct therapeutic learning environments for all children.

Related Organizations and Online Resources

Caring for Every Child's Mental Health Campaign. The goal of this education campaign by the Center for Mental Health Services (CMHS), U.S. Department of Health and Human Services, is to increase awareness about the emotional problems of America's children. Information is available at http://www.mentalhealth.org/child/default.asp.

National Institute of Mental Health (NIMH). NIMH is part of the National Institutes of Health (NIH), the principal biomedical and behavioral research agency of the U.S. government. Information and many resources are available at http://www.nimh.nih.gov.

National Mental Health Association (NMHA). NMHA promotes mental health through advocacy, education, research, and services. A section of this Web site is devoted to children and families: http://www.nmha.org.

No Child Left Inside. This coalition of over 500 education and public health organizations advocates environmental education. Information can be found at http://www.nclicoalition.org.

The Social Self: Encouraging Social Competence in Young Children

Thought that young children were just naturally selfish and that nothing could be done about this?

Wondered whether children felt generous *inside* when you made them share and take turns?

Wanted to know how to get children to help each other and work together?

. . . IF YOU HAVE, THE MATERIAL IN THE FOLLOWING PAGES WILL HELP YOU.

This point was brought home to me by the comments of a distinguished Soviet psychologist, an expert on development during the preschool years. He had been observing in an American day-care center for children of working mothers. The center was conducted under university auspices and reflected modern outlooks and methods in early childhood education. It was therefore with some concern that I noted how upset my colleague was on his return.

"I wouldn't have believed it," he said, "if I hadn't seen it with my own eyes. There were four children sitting at a table, just as in our nurseries. But each was doing something different. What's more, I watched them for a whole ten minutes, and not once did any child help another one. They didn't even talk to each other. Each was busy in his own activity. You really are a nation of individualists."

Urie Bronfenbrenner (1969, p. 5)

Individuals can realize their potential only within a community. Participation in any community requires knowledge and understanding of its norms, rules, and values and mastery of the skills necessary to interact effectively within it. The learning processes involved in such mastery begin at birth and must be well under way during the early years of childhood.

Lilian Katz and Diane McClellan (1997, p. vii)

Early childhood is a time that can be rich in social learnings; it is a dynamic period characterized by many beginnings but few completely attained learnings in the development of social skills and interactions. Although the home is profoundly influential in this area, early childhood teachers can also make a valuable contribution to social development (Hyson, 2008; Ray, Bowman, & Brownell, 2006; Swick, 2006).

THE IMPORTANCE OF HELPING YOUNG CHILDREN DEVELOP SOCIAL COMPETENCE

Teachers should know that children who succeed in elementary school tend to do so not because of previous academic training in subjects such as reading and writing, but rather primarily because of their social skills. A number of recent research studies have indicated how important social development is for the child in attaining later success in school. Social development includes the ability to form caring relationships with other people, to cooperate with others, to share, to listen to others, to use self-control, to pay attention, and to follow directions. These social skills develop when children attend high-quality early childhood programs—and these are the same qualities that lead to later success (Bronson, 2006; McClelland & Morrison, 2003; National Research Council and Institute of Medicine, 2000; National Institute of Child Health and Human Development [NICHD], 2000; Peisner-Feinberg et al., 1999, 2001; Rimm-Kaufman, Pianta, & Cox, 2000).

The Research Study in this chapter highlights the positive effects good early childhood programs can have on reducing children's problem behaviors in school and on enhancing their ability to interact with others.

As the Research Study indicates, children with good social competence do better in school. But what about the children who have less developed skills in interacting with others? This is an important question since another study found that kindergarten teachers reported at least 50% of the children entering their class did not have the basic social skills necessary to succeed in school. The teachers stated that the most difficult problem is children who lack emotional and social competence: those who are not interested in learning, lack confidence, or are incapable of cooperation and self-control (Rimm-Kaufman et al., 2000).

Once again it is apparent that early care and education can have a positive impact on children's development—this time on their social skills and future success in school. There is a lot early childhood teachers can do to enhance children's social learnings. But before pursuing important social goals for the young children in their care, teachers should review the developmental theories of social growth discussed here to help them understand what social behavior to expect from the children.

RESEARCH STUDY

How Does High-Quality Child Care Impact Later Social Development?

Research Question: Peisner-Feinberg et al. wanted to learn how high-quality child care experiences affected later performance in school.

Research Method: The researchers examined child care centers and children's development from preschool through second grade in order to find the relationship between high-quality care and later development. A random sample of 401 full-day children's centers, half for-profit and half nonprofit, were studied in California, Colorado, Connecticut, and North Carolina. From those programs, 733 children were followed from their next-to-last year in preschool through second grade. Researchers used a variety of measures to establish "high-quality" child care, including the Early Childhood Environmental Rating Scale, the Caregiver Interaction Scale, and the UCLA Early Childhood Observation Form. The Adult Involvement Scale and Student-Teacher Relationship Scale were used to determine the quality of teacher-child relationships in early care settings. Finally, to assess the children's social behaviors in second grade, two measures were administered: the Classroom Behavior Inventory and the Teacher Assessment of Social Behavior.

Research Results: A correlation was found between the quality of the child care center and children's social skills: Children who were in higher quality centers had better interactions with other children and fewer problem behaviors in school. High-quality care was also associated with better school readiness skills such as paying attention and following classroom rules. Additionally, it was found that children who had close relationships with their preschool teachers had more positive social interactions with teachers and other children when they were in second grade. Children who attended lower quality preschool centers (where the social-emotional climate was more negative and teachers did not establish close relationships with the children) showed more aggression, disruptive behavior, and social withdrawal in elementary school.

One additional result found by Peisner-Feinberg et al. was that children who are typically "at risk" for school difficulties, particularly those whose mothers had lower levels of education, were the most affected by the quality of their child care experience. Poor-quality child care seemed to compound these children's problems of getting along in school, whereas high-quality care seemed to enhance their social and cognitive abilities, leading to higher levels of school success.

Implications for Teaching: This study highlights the importance of providing high-quality early care and education for all children—particularly those who have fewer advantages when they enter school. The research supports what early educators have known all along: Children who develop close relationships with their caregivers and have positive social experiences early in life seem to develop the necessary social and emotional skills that will support their success later in school. Early childhood educators have the responsibility to make sure they are providing high-quality care, in large part by developing close, caring relationships with each child. The researchers also call for teachers to advocate on behalf of children and lobby for local, state, and federal support for high-quality child care programs.

Source: "The Relation of Preschool Child-Care Quality to Children's Cognitive and Social Developmental Trajectories Through Second Grade" by E. S. Peisner-Feinberg et al., 2001, *Child Development, 72*(5), 1534–1553.

DEVELOPMENTAL TRENDS IN SOCIAL GROWTH

In the past, many people tended to view young children as generally self-centered human beings who were insensitive and uncaring about others. However, recent research now supports a more encouraging view of young children's nature. Prosocial behavior—behavior intended to help or benefit someone else—begins at an early age and can be encouraged in high-quality early education programs (Cavner, 2008; Landy, 2002; Levin, 2003; Swick, 2006).

Swick (2006, p. 279) suggests that early childhood education should foster "caring and peaceable children" by addressing six goals to model and teach young children:

1. Value each person's integrity (each child, each family member, each educator).
2. Reach out to people in caring ways; model altruism.
3. Respect human differences.
4. Demonstrate how to serve and care for others.
5. Engage in charitable behavior; teach children it feels good to give.
6. Develop and express a belief in the goodness of people.

It is never too early to infuse these goals into the educational program. As each infant, toddler, and young child feels cared for and nurtured at school, they begin to develop caring and nurturing for others.

How Do Children Become Socialized?

Although opinion remains divided about how children learn to be like other people in their society—that is, become *socialized*—most experts agree it is a complex process that depends on the interaction of numerous factors. Among these are biological, cultural, and family influences; personality traits; intellectual ability; developmental level; and situational influences (Bowman, 2006a; Hyson, 2008; National Research Council and Institute of Medicine, 2000; Ray et al., 2006; Swick, 2006).

Not only are a great many factors involved, but there are also complex interactions that go on among them. For example, initial analyses of socialization stressed the influence of parents on children's behavior and paid scant attention to the way children influenced their parents' behavior, but we now understand that this is very much a two-way street (Hyson, 2008; National Research Council and Institute of Medicine, 2000; Parke & Buriel, 1998).

Several theories attempt to explain how factors achieve this influence. It is useful to understand the most important of these theories because each of them provides a helpful way to think about how to foster positive social growth in young children. One of these is *social learning theory*. It proposes some matter-of-fact explanations of the way socialization comes about that are helpful for teachers to understand. That theory emphasizes that children learn to become like other people and to get along with them as a result of identifying with and imitating them, and by experiencing reinforcement for desirable social behaviors.

Considerable evidence indicates that children do learn by observing grown-ups and other children and that, particularly if they are nurturing and powerful, children will seek to be like those models and imitate their behavior (Bandura, 1977; Center on the Social and Emotional Foundations for Early Learning [CSEFEL], 2004; Hyson,

2008; Kostelnik, 2004). Evidence also indicates that although children may be somewhat influenced by how people tell them they should behave, they are even more strongly influenced by actual modeling of desirable behavior (Elkind, 2004b; Katz & McClellan, 1997; Kostelnik, 2004; Levin, 2003). So it behooves teachers to model the behavior they wish to encourage, rather than just talking about it or, worse yet, preaching something they don't do themselves.

Research indicates that children also learn socially acceptable responses as a result of reinforcement either by adults or by peers (Choi & Kim, 2003; CSEFEL, 2004; Kemple, 2004). This can be negative reinforcement in the form of punishment that may suppress behavior, or positive reinforcement in the form of recognition, praise, approval, admission to the group, or other positively reinforcing responses and satisfactions that come from without or within themselves. Although scholarly discussions of socialization processes currently pay scant attention to the value of this theory, it must be noted that many adults continue to rely on punishment or gold stars to produce good behavior and put this theory into daily practice.

A differing point of view about how children become socialized has been contributed by the developmental interactionists typified by Piaget (1948), DeVries and Zan (1996), and the sociocultural theorist Vygotsky (1978). Supporters of this theory contend that, to exist successfully in the social world, the intricacies of learning require explanations that go far beyond the simplicities of reinforcement and modeling theory. They maintain that social development occurs as a result of interaction among people. The cognitive, intellectual learnings that result from the experience of that interaction—coupled with maturation—produce the widening range of social knowledge and skills necessary for social survival (Katz & McClellan, 1997; Kemple, 2004).

It is not only interaction between adults and children, of course, that enhances such learning. Child-child interaction becomes of ever-increasing importance during the early years as groups of children make it clear to their members that they favor positive, friendly behavior and dislike aggression and selfishness (CSEFEL, 2004; Katz & McClellan, 1997; Kemple, 2004). Such groups rate socially competent children highly, and these attitudes, which are often frankly expressed, help shape the behavior of the children in the group. Then, too, as children become 4 or 5 years old, they turn to their peers more frequently for help than they turn to adults for it. This aid seeking promotes additional opportunities for positive social interactions and learning to take place.

The quality of emotional attachment between mother and child is an additional important influence on socialization. Children who are closely attached to their mothers tend to be more compliant—that is, conform more readily to the wishes and instructions of their families (Honig, 2002)—and are better liked and accepted by their peers. Securely attached children also tend to be more sensitive to other people's feelings (Honig, 2002).

Implications for Teaching

As far as teachers of young children are concerned, social learning theory, developmental interactionist theory, and Vygotsky's sociocultural theory all have merit because they make it plain that teachers need to do more than sit idly by while the children grow and develop. Since one way that children acquire social behaviors is by

Pam Oken-Wright

Social learning occurs as a result of interaction with others.

identifying with models and imitating their behavior, obviously teachers should provide good examples (Elkind, 2004b; Katz & McClellan, 1997; Kostelnik, 2004; Levin, 2003; Swick, 2006; Swick & Freeman, 2004). In addition, the relationship between themselves and the child should be based on mutual liking and warmth to encourage imitation of positive behavior (Gonzalez-Mena & Eyer, 2006; Honig, 2002). Because young boys may tend to imitate male models more readily than they do female ones, it is also desirable to include male teachers and volunteers in early childhood classrooms whenever possible.

Since children also learn as a result of positive reinforcement, teachers need to be sure that children receive satisfaction from acting in socially desirable ways. Sometimes this reinforcement will be in the form of a pleasant comment or expression of affection, but a more desirable approach is for the teacher to point out to the child that it feels good to help other people so that the pleasure stems from this inherent reward rather than from a calculated external one (Elkind, 2004b; Kohn, 2001; Levin, 2003; Marano, 2008; Swick, 2006).

In addition to these teacher-child interactions, plentiful opportunities for the children to interact together must also be included during the day because so much social learning takes place during play (Elias & Berk, 2002; Elkind, 2006; Isenberg & Jalongo, 2006; Klein et al., 2003; Koralek, 2004). As Isenberg and Jalongo (2002) state, "play enables children to make sense of their world, develop social and cultural understandings, [and] allows children to express their

PEARSON
myeducationlab

Go to MyEducationLab and select the topic "Social Studies." Under Activities and Applications, watch the video *Social Studies*. In what ways does the early childhood program support children's social learning?

thoughts and feelings" (p. 59). This, then, furnishes us with yet another reason for including ample opportunities in the day for children to play together.

The Development of Social Skills

In addition to providing plenty of play opportunities for the child's social self to develop fully, the early childhood teacher must be aware of typical patterns of development in order to provide experiences that foster growth. So many factors ride on the healthy development of social skills—from academic success to cognitive skills to language development—that keeping an eye on each child's social development in relation to the norm is crucial. Table 10.1 summarizes social behaviors characteristic of children at various ages.

HELPING CHILDREN BECOME SOCIALLY COMPETENT: SUGGESTIONS FOR TEACHING APPROPRIATE SOCIAL SKILLS

When young children want something, be it attention, assistance, or possession of an article, *their need is immediate, intense, and personal.* Their reactions, therefore, to having to wait or to consider the rights of others can be very strong, and it takes patient teaching backed by fortitude to help them develop the ability to wait a little, to control their feelings to a degree, and to consider the rights and desires of others when necessary. All these skills are central to the process of getting along in a social world. If teachers remember to take into account the strength of these immediate, intense, and personal needs as they read about specific social learnings, they will gain an added appreciation for the magnitude of the child's task in learning to become a socialized human being.

It will, of course, take years and years for children to reach these goals in their maturest and most desirable form, but it is also true that socialization begins at the moment of birth as attachment develops between families and children. Therefore, early childhood is

Encourage role playing so children learn what it is like to be in someone else's shoes.

Table 10.1
Age at which most children develop social behaviors

By the End of the First Year, the Child:	By the End of the Second Year, the Child:	By the End of the Third Year, the Child:	By the End of the Fourth Year, the Child:
Plays peek-a-boo	Engages in imaginary play	Observes adults and playmates and imitates them frequently	Enjoys playing with friends in imaginary games such as "House"
Exhibits anxious behavior, such as crying when primary caregiver leaves	Observes adults and older children and likes to imitate their behavior	Uses imaginary play often, especially with dolls, animals, and people	Is intrigued by new situations
Likes to "test" adults and see their reactions; might drop food repeatedly or tip over a cup	Is excited to be around other children	Is comfortable hugging familiar playmates	Knows how to interact with friends in a cooperative manner
Shows signs that primary caregiver(s) are preferred over all others; will hold arms out to primary caregiver	May use aggression to achieve goals; will be possessive of toys	Is able to take turns	Is beginning to use own words to resolve conflicts
Gets attention by repeating sounds and making gestures	Shows signs of independence; tries to put on shoes without help	Knows the concept of "mine" and "his/hers"	Becomes increasingly more independent
Likes to play with adults and will initiate interaction	Shows increased interest in adult language	Demonstrates that signs of empathy are present; will hug a friend who fell down	Is becoming more detailed and creative in fantasy play
		Enjoys participating in small-group activities	Gains more control of intense feelings like anger, but still needs adult guidance
		Knows how to show more self-control	Has an awareness of what is expected
		Is able to express feelings such as fear, anger, and affection	Is increasingly more confident with self-help skills like dressing and eating

certainly not too early to begin instilling these important, positive values as long as they are worked on in an appropriate way (Copple & Bredekamp, 2009; Elkind, 2004b; Katz & McClellan, 1997; Kostelnik, 2004; Swick, 2006). There are also many more social goals than the seven listed in this chapter. These particular goals have been chosen for discussion because they are frequently listed by teachers and families of young children in the United States as being important and as having long-term social value.

Goal I: Help Children Develop Empathy

Being able to feel what another person is feeling is a valuable social skill for many reasons. It helps us anticipate how someone will react to what we do, it helps us understand possible motives for other people's behavior, and it may encourage prosocial behavior (acting to benefit someone else when we realize how they feel).

By the End of the Fifth Year, the Child:	By the End of the Sixth Year, the Child:	By the End of the Seventh Year, the Child:	By the End of the Eighth Year, the Child:
Has friends and wants to please them	Is ready to take on personal and social responsibility	Is interested in friendships and who is friends with whom	Has developed the ability to work effectively with peers
Feels the importance of being accepted by friends	Is developing prosocial skills of cooperation, caring about others, and resolving conflicts with peers	Frequently changes friends	Works best in small groups
Recognizes rules and is compliant with them		Usually prefers to work alone or with one other	Has developed more mature sense of morality; is intensely interested in fairness
Likes to engage in movement, acting, and singing	Is very sensitive to criticism	Has more developed sense of self-control	Enjoys learning about different cultures
Continues to display more independence	Likes to test own relationship to authority	Finds classroom and social changes upsetting	Has mastered the basic academic and cultural skills (reading, writing, social behavior, etc.)
Is likely to have a best friend because social life is important	Wants to fit in with regard to others' skills and friendships	Has a more developed sense of humor; uses humor to mediate social situations	
Has a very strong sense of right and wrong	Pays attention to the wider social world	May use teasing and exclusion as a form of aggression—is aware of ability to inflict pain with insults or ganging up behavior	
Engages in elaborate pretend play with friends	Is curious about the adult world and occupations		
Has an understanding of rejection and the powerful feeling it creates, i.e., "You aren't my friend."	Learns social skills through imaginary play with friends		
Uses words to express angry feelings, rather than aggression			

Young children are just beginning to learn to separate themselves and their feelings from the feelings of other people. Indeed, Piaget (1926, 1959) long maintained that young children are egocentric and unable to put themselves in the place of another. But research, as well as the experience of many early childhood teachers, indicates that this egocentrism is not an all-or-nothing condition. As children grow from age 2 to 5, they become increasingly able to assume roles and to perceive complex feelings. With training they can also become more sensitive to other people's feelings and to the effect their actions have on these feelings (Cavner, 2008; Elkind, 2004b; Kostelnik, 2004; Landy, 2002; Novick, 2002; Swick, 2006).

Encourage Role Playing

The teacher can do several things to increase the awareness of how it feels to be some-one else. One of the most obvious of these is to provide many opportunities for dra-matic and imaginative play involving taking roles about what people do (Bodrova, Leong, Henson, & Henninger, 2000; Elias & Berk, 2002). Most preprimary centers maintain housekeeping corners, which facilitate the role playing of family life so dear to 3- and 4-year-olds. We have seen that as children reach 4 and 5 years of age, their interest in the world around them increases and extends beyond the family and the school. For these young children enriched role opportunities can be offered with acces-sories for doctors and nurses, bus drivers, preschool teachers, or anyone else whose work is familiar to the children. The costumes need not be complete. Indeed, it seems wise to leave some things out to exercise the children's imaginations. In the primary grades, children become aware of the wider world around them and begin to learn the skills appropriate to their culture. Elementary classrooms should support children's explo-ration of the wider world through role-play opportunities and props.

Help the Child Understand How the Other Person Feels

Teaching children how other people *feel,* in addition to what they *do,* is more difficult than simple role playing but is not impossible. One virtue of encouraging children to tell each other what they want or how they feel is that in addition to relieving the speaker's feelings, it informs the other child about someone else's emotions and desires. The other important reason for doing this, according to Piaget, is that children are freed of egocentrism by experiencing interactions with other people. He maintained that social conflict and discussion facilitate cognitive growth and the accompanying ability to put the self in another's place (Piaget, 1926).

Teachers can increase empathy for another's feelings by explaining how a child is feeling in terms that are personal to the observing child, relating the feeling to one they, too, have experienced. Katz and McClellan (1997) provide an example of how teach-ers can arouse feelings of empathy in children through common, daily interactions:

> Many situations provide an opportunity to evoke and reinforce children's empathic and al-truistic dispositions. Suppose, for example, that a child has been waiting a long time for a turn on a piece of outdoor play equipment. . . . The teacher . . . can say calmly, "Robin has been waiting a long time, and you know how it feels to wait." The second part of the state-ment is made in a straightforward manner that conveys no attribution of meanness, shame, or other negative implication. (p. 85)

During group time, showing pictures of people expressing strong emotions is yet an-other way to build awareness and sensitivity. Children can often identify the feeling (remember that it can be a positive as well as a negative one) and talk over what might have made that person happy or sad and how they might offer help or comfort if that is deemed necessary (Levin, 2003; Novick, 2002; Zeece, 2004).

Teaching children to appreciate others' feelings need not involve intensive inter-vention and planning—although sometimes that is worthwhile also—but can be done through simple day-by-day modeling. David Elkind (2004b) provides us with an ex-ample he observed at the Children's School at Tufts University:

> One morning while I was observing, a child asked to join two others who were building in the block corner. They said, "No," he could not join them. The teacher who witnessed the

episode sat down on the floor next to the rejected boy and helped him build a tower of his own. When the other boys noticed what the teacher was doing they had second thoughts and invited the other child to join them. Without saying anything, the teacher, by being fair, made the other boys aware they had been unfair. (p. 47)

Goal II: Help Children Learn to Be Generous, Altruistic, and Able to Share Equipment, Experiences, and People with Other Children

It is worthwhile to do what we can to develop children's ability to feel empathy since it appears that this ability to sense someone else's feelings is related at least in younger children to a second prosocial skill as well: the development of altruistic behavior—behavior a person performs with the unselfish intention of making another person feel good or happy (Cavner, 2008; Novick, 2002; Swick, 2006; Swick & Freeman, 2004).

Research on social development indicates that when affection from the teacher is combined with verbal comments about what is happening, the greatest number of charitable responses is produced in children. Modeling generosity also increases this behavior (Levin, 2003; Swick, 2006; Swick & Freeman, 2004), and paternal nurturing facilitates generosity in boys of nursery school age. Thus we again find support for the recommendation that *teaching a prosocial behavior is accomplished most effectively by a teacher who sets a good example and expresses affection while at the same time clarifying what is happening by discussing it with the children* (Hyson, 2008; Landy, 2002; Levin, 2003; Swick, 2006).

Help Children Learn to Share Equipment

Teaching a specific aspect of generosity such as sharing (a social skill of real concern in children's centers and classrooms) requires more than nurturing and setting a good example. It requires following through with clear-cut policies directed toward building the generous impulse within the child, rather than relying on externally enforced generosity supervised by the teacher. As one student teacher put it, "I want him to share from his heart, not because I make him do it."

Many teachers try to teach sharing by regulating turn taking ("You can have it for 2 minutes, then he can have it for 2 minutes"). They seem to interpret sharing as meaning that children have to hand over anything they are using almost as soon as another child asks for it. Teachers who enforce taking turns on this basis find they are constantly required to monitor and referee the turn taking themselves. This not only is tiresome but also *puts the locus of control and decision making outside, rather than within the child*. It also means that a child may not be permitted to have enough of an experience to be filled up and truly satisfied by it. Such deprivation builds a kind of watchful hunger and avarice that should be avoided. It is still true that one doesn't cure hunger by snatching away the bread.

Rather than struggling to institute the police-like control of the previous procedure, the teacher can establish a climate of generosity by making sure each child has enough of most experiences. Therefore, the teacher does not limit the children to two paintings or allow them to ride the trike around the course only three times because another child is waiting. Instead the rule is that children may keep what they have or do what they are doing until they have had enough of it. This means that children do not have to be calculating and defensive about hanging on to things. It also makes settling arguments easier since it is relatively simple to base decisions on who was using it first and then to state the rule "Whoever had it first may keep it until they're done with it."

Once assured their own rights and desires will be protected, it becomes much easier for children to share. When another child is waiting, the teacher can point this out, perhaps saying, "Will, when you're done with the swing would you remember to tell Ashley? She'd like a turn when you're through." The final step in this process is recognizing when he *does* remember to tell Ashley he is through by commending him and pointing out, "Look how happy she is that you remembered. She's really smiling at you. I guess you're her friend."

It helps in such situations to have enough equipment available so that children do not have to wait and wait. Several easels are better than one, and feeling free to improvise to meet peak demands will help, too. For example, if painting is suddenly very popular, setting out paint tables might help, or giving children cans of water and old brushes to paint the fence could satisfy their need and reduce waiting.

Help Children Learn to Share the Teacher

Children not only have to learn to share equipment but also have to learn to share the teacher's attention with other children. Again the best model is the generous one, in which the children each get what they need, rather than each getting an identical, metered amount. This may mean that only one child is rocked while several others play nearby in the block corner, rather than that every child is rocked a little. As long as each child receives comfort when needed, teachers do not have to worry about whether they are being "fair." They can explain to the children that different people get different special things according to what they need. To remind the children that this policy applies to everyone, teachers can cite examples of times when those children received special attention.

Benjamin La Framboise

Have enough equipment and materials available so children don't have to wait and wait. In this way socialization flourishes and conflicts about who gets a turn are avoided.

Sometimes individual satisfactions have to be put off because it is not possible for one child to monopolize the teacher's attention throughout lunch or story time. To handle such demands the teacher might say, "You know, lunch is for everyone to talk together, but I can see you really want to talk just to me. I promise we'll have time for that while I'm getting you ready for nap."

Goal III: Help Children Learn That Being Kind to Other People Feels Good

Helping Other People Is One Way of Expressing Kindness

Providing opportunities for children to experience the satisfaction and pleasure that come from helping someone else appears to be a sound way to generate willingness to take prosocial action because the resulting good feeling reinforces the behavior. Sometimes helping others takes the form of comforting another child; sometimes it is as simple as passing the cups at snack; sometimes it is as sophisticated as thinking of an excursion everyone will enjoy (Levin, 2003; Vance & Weaver, 2002).

Children should be encouraged and expected to help each other. The teacher should emphasize that helping other people is a worthwhile, important thing to do (Cavner, 2008; Kostelnik, 2004; Landy, 2002; Elkind, 2004b; Swick, 2006). Here are some simple examples furnished by student teachers* of how this can be clearly and consistently taught at the preschool level when teachers are sensitive to incorporating these values.

This episode took place in the hollow block area with some cardboard blocks that have foam packing glued to their insides. Janelle, Timothy, and Jenny were all climbing around on them.

Timothy: Look, I can climb out of here by myself. (He proceeds to do so.)
Me: Boy, Timothy, you sure can. I wonder if it's just as easy to climb in?
Timothy: Yeah, I can. I got to put my leg over first. (He climbs in the box, accidentally putting his foot on Janelle's shoulder.)
Janelle: Watch out, Timothy!
Me: Whoops! He accidentally hit your shoulder, huh?
Janelle: Yeah. Watch me hide in this corner. (She does so and almost gets stuck between the layers of foam. She finally gets herself out.) I almost got stuck!
Me: Yeah, you finally slipped your way out.
Jenny: (who has crammed herself in more firmly, shrieks) Help me, teacher. I can't get outta here!
Me: Uh oh! Now Jenny's stuck in there. (Jenny continues to twist and struggle.) Janelle, do you remember how you got out?
Janelle: Yeah! Here, Jenny, I'll help you. (With Janelle pulling and Jenny pushing, Jenny manages to get out.)
Me: Good, you guys! She sure needed you, Janelle!
Jenny: Yeah, I was stuck! I woulda spent the night in there! (She laughs.)

My thanks to Mary Kashmar, Lauran Davis, Sandi Coe, and the children for the following episodes.

Or sometimes helping takes the form of one youngster teaching another.

Roe (age 4 years, 8 months) is washing and drying some toy animals when Yvonne (age 2 years, 3 months) walks up, takes up the other towel, and wants to play. Roe takes the towel away from Yvonne and looks at me.

Roe: Will you dry?

Me: Yvonne looks like she really wants to play. Why don't you ask her to dry them for you? (Roe is agreeable to the suggestion.)

Roe: Yvonne, will you dry? (Yvonne nods her head yes. She begins to dry but is having difficulty.)

Roe: (snatching the towel away impatiently) She's too slow. You dry.

Me: I think you should give Yvonne a chance. Maybe you can show her how to do it.

Roe: Here, Yvonne, do it this way. (Yvonne catches on quickly and squeals with delight.)

Roe: Wow, now she's waiting for me. I better hurry up.

Me: You girls work well together. Thanks, Roe.

(Soon all the toys are washed and dried.)

Note that it is necessary to handle these situations carefully to avoid the undesirable effect of comparing children with each other. For example, rather than saying, "Why don't you do it the way Naima does; she's a big girl," it is better to say, "Naima just learned how to zip her coat. Why don't you ask her to show you how it goes together?" Children are often generous about teaching such skills to each other as long as it does not take so much time that they lose patience.

The Presence of Children Who Have Disabilities Presents Special Opportunities for Children to Be Kind and Considerate

Although it is desirable to treat children who have disabilities as much as possible as we treat all the other children, it is also true that sometimes these children require special consideration (Guralnick, Neville, Hammond, & Connor, 2007; Harper & McCluskey, 2002; Kemple, 2004). For example, a child who is hard of hearing benefits from having others around who know at least some sign language just as a child who has Down syndrome benefits from frequent repetition and enforcement of simple social rules.

Experience has shown that other children in the group can be quick to offer practical help in a kindly, matter-of-fact way if they are encouraged by the teacher to do so. The problem is helping them understand the difference between kindness and pity and the difference between offering help that empowers the child with the disability and overwhelming the child by being too solicitous. Although it is definitely worth encouraging such simple acts of thoughtfulness as moving the crayons within the reach of a child who uses a wheelchair, the best, kindest thing the children can do is include the child with the disability in their play. The teacher cannot force them to do this but *can* encourage it by pointing out a practical way the child can participate and by subtly expressing approval when that takes place.

Teachers should keep in mind that children with developmental delays tend to initiate interactions with other children less frequently than those without delays, and they tend to play more by themselves (Harper & McCluskey, 2002; Odom, 2002). Teachers are advised to observe the children with disabilities in their classrooms to see how much social interaction they engage in, and encourage the children to play with those who are less sociable (Guralnick et al., 2007).

Not Doing Something Can Also Be a Way of Being Kind to Someone

Children also need to learn that kindness goes beyond doing something nice for somebody else. Sometimes it means *not* doing something you feel inclined to do. Although we cannot expect young children always to anticipate when their comments may be tactless or even hurtful, many times they know unequivocally that they are saying something with the intention of being mean. For example, the child who says with a sneer, "You can't come to my birthday party," or, "You talk funny," is saying those words with the deliberate intention of hurting the other child.

Teachers should not tolerate this kind of deliberately hurtful behavior any more than they would permit a child to hurt an animal. Instead, they should take the speaker aside and explain that what was said was unkind and made the other child feel bad. While acknowledging that nobody has to play with everybody, the teacher should tell the child that causing pain that way is not permitted in the group and that she is not to do it again. Then, of course, the teacher must also deal with the feelings of the child who has been hurt, perhaps by saying, "I'm sorry she was feeling mean and wanted to hurt your feelings. Everybody has stuff to learn at school, and she's just learning to be kind. Let's see what we can find that you'd like to do in case it doesn't work out for you to play here right now."

Goal IV: Teach Children That Everyone Has Rights and That These Rights Are Respected by All

As mentioned earlier, children have individual needs and teachers should not hesitate to meet these on an individual basis; that is, they should not interpret fairness as meaning that everyone gets exactly the same thing. But children do, in general, have to conform to the same rules. This impartiality of rule enforcement will help children gradually understand that everyone is respected as having equal rights.

Many early educators find it effective to ask the children to help establish the classroom rules (Kostelnik, 2004; Noddings, 2006). This not only models respect for the children's ideas but also opens up the ongoing discussion about what is fair and just to the children. Regular class meetings are an excellent way for children to experience the social give-and-take that is necessary to create a caring, peaceful, and democratic society (Levin, 2003; Noddings, 2006; Vance & Weaver, 2002).

Go to MyEducationLab and select the topic "Curriculum/Program Models." Under Activities and Applications, watch the video *Emergent Curriculum Built on Children's Interests: A Hospital Project in Preschool.* How does this teacher use emergent curriculum and group discussion to convey respect for the children's ideas?

Teach Children That Rules Apply to Everyone

A good example of this may be seen in handling sharing problems. At the beginning of the year there always seems to be one or two children who seize possession rather than asking and waiting for turns. Of course, the teacher often has to restrain such children from doing this. It is particularly important with these children that the teacher also watch carefully and almost ostentatiously protect their rights when someone tries to take their possessions away, so that they see that everyone has their rights of possession protected. This is an effective way to teach fairness and to help the children see what the rule is and that it applies to every child. The message is "You may not intrude on their rights, and they may not intrude on yours, either." As the year progresses and the children learn to know and apply these rules themselves, they will become increasingly able to enforce them without the teacher's help and thus be able to stand up for themselves in social interaction situations.

Goal V: Emphasize the Value of Cooperation and Compromise Rather Than Stress Competition and Winning

Competition and winning are so much a part of American life that it hardly seems necessary to emphasize them with such young children, and yet many teachers do so because appealing to children's competitive instincts is such an easy way to get them to do what teachers want. Examples include, "Oh, look how well Kendra's picking up the blocks; I bet you can't pick up as many as she can!" or, "It's time for lunch! Whoever gets to the bathroom first can sit by me. Now, remember, no running!" The trouble with these strategies is they reward children for triumphing over other children and neglect the chance to teach them the pleasure of accomplishing things together (Cavner, 2008; Katz & McClellan, 1997; Swick, 2006).

In Place of Fostering Competition, Model Cooperation and Helping Behavior Yourself

One effective way for the teacher to substitute cooperation for competition is to model it by helping the children. Thus when it is time to put away the blocks, the teacher warns in advance and then says, "It's time to put the blocks away. Come on, let's all pitch in. I guess I'll begin by picking up the biggest ones. Kelvin, would you like to drive the truck over here so we can load it up?" Kelvin may refuse, of course, but after a pause he will probably join in if the teacher continues to work with the group to complete the task, meanwhile thanking those who are helping.

Teach the Art of Compromise

Being able to compromise is another basic part of learning to cooperate. Four-year-olds love to strike bargains and are often able to appreciate the fact that everyone has gained some of what they want when a fair bargain or agreement is reached. Primary children can articulate their "game plan" for a successful bargain and are adept at lobbying for their position.

Teach Children to Work Together

The teacher should also be on the lookout for opportunities for which it takes two children (or more) to accomplish what they want. Perhaps one child has to pull on the handle while the other shoves the wagon of sand from behind, or one must steady the juicer while the other squeezes. When these circumstances arise, encourage the children to help each other, rather than hurrying too quickly to help them yourself.

A few pieces of play equipment also require cooperation for success, and a point should be made of acquiring these. Double rocking horses, for example, just will not work if the children do not cooperate and coordinate their efforts; neither will tire

Pam Oken-Wright

Encourage children to experience the pleasure of accomplishing things together.

swings that are hung horizontally. Some kinds of jump ropes also need at least two people participating for success, as does playing catch.

Goal VI: Help Children Discover the Pleasures of Friendship

Children become more and more interested in having friends as they grow older. By age 5 they are likely to spend more than half their playtime with other children, and friendship bonds between particular children are generally much stronger at this age than they are in younger children. By second grade it is almost intolerable to be without a friend.

As early as the preschool years, research reports that friendships occur typically between children of the same sex, race, age, and activity preference and that those friendships persist over longer periods of time than was previously thought. Ways of demonstrating friendship pass through developmental stages, moving from a 6-year-old's interpretation of showing friendship by means of sharing toys and material items, through the stage of playing together as a primary indication, and going on to showing friendship by offering psychological assistance such as giving comfort when needed (Copple & Bredekamp, 2009; Bronson, 2006; Guralnick et al., 2007; Thompson, 2006).

One list compiled by a group of 4-year-olds at the Institute for Child Development at the University of Oklahoma included the following ways of showing friends they liked them: hug them, kiss them, play with them, have a party, celebrate Valentine's Day, run to them, mail them a letter, sing a song to them, tell a secret, give them a present, and let them spend the night.

Friendships formed in early childhood create valuable opportunities to learn and practice skills essential to the child's social, emotional, language, and cognitive development. Friendless children, in contrast, do not get along well in interactions with peers, demonstrate less ability to resolve conflicts, and are less verbal and more physically aggressive than children with friends. Having no friends in early childhood often has a lasting impact. It results in poor attitudes and performance in elementary school and later, increased feelings of isolation and depression, frequent discipline problems in school and in the legal system, and increased psychological problems as an adult (Bronson, 2006; Choi & Kim, 2003; Guralnick et al., 2007; Thompson, 2006).

Facilitate Friendliness by Using Reinforcement to Reduce Isolated Behavior

Social interaction between children can be increased by the judicious use of reinforcement. This is a particularly helpful technique to employ with shy, isolated children. Using this approach, the teacher provides some kind of social dividend whenever the child approaches a group or interacts with them but withholds such recognition when the child withdraws and plays alone. (It is hoped that over a period of time the pleasure the child finds in being part of the group will replace this more calculated reward.) Note that this approach is just the opposite of the pattern that often occurs, in which the teacher tends to "try to draw out the child" who has retired from the group, thereby rewarding with attention the very behavior it is desirable to extinguish.

Increase the Social Skills of Friendless or Excluded Children

Another way to foster friendships among children is to teach less likable youngsters social skills that make them more acceptable to the other children. For example, children who have learned to ask for what they want are generally more welcome than those who rush in and grab whatever appeals to them (Katz & McClellan, 1997).

Identifying just which skills a child needs in order to fit in with a group can require careful observation and analysis if it is to be truly helpful. However, it is well worth the time and trouble it takes to do this. Consistent social rejection can really dishearten and discourage a child, as well as have an unfortunate effect on self-esteem unless someone lends an effective hand.

This kind of social instruction can sometimes be best accomplished on a one-to-one basis whereby children are coached by the teacher in more successful ways to behave. Sometimes, for example, it really clarifies the situation when the teacher simply points out, "You know, when you knock their blocks down, they don't like you. It makes Carmen and Hannah really mad, and then they won't let you play. Why don't you try building something near them next time? Then maybe they'll gradually let you join them and be your friends."

Pair Children Together

Pairing children sometimes helps them make friends. Coming to school in a car pool or going home from school to play together can cement a friendship, as can doing jobs together or sharing an interest in common. In the elementary grades, when who is "in" becomes a lively topic of discussion, teachers can help friendless children by assigning them projects in partnership with more socially accepted children. In order for the strategy to succeed, a classroom climate of mutual respect must already be in place, and the teacher must keep a close eye on the interactions. In the long run, though, it is up to the children to form the friendship; all the teacher can do is make such possibilities available to them, and help the less socially successful child learn the specific skills necessary to make friends.

Help Children When a Friend Departs or When They Are Rejected

Sometimes teachers underestimate what it means to a child when a friend moves away, or makes a new friend and rejects the former one, or is transferred to another room. Children often feel quite despondent and adrift when this occurs.

When someone is transferring rooms or leaving school, everyone needs to be prepared for the change. This should include the child and the parents and the other children as well. When a child is transferring, we have often prepared everyone by inviting the child for a "visit" to the new room once or twice before making the total switch. And if we have warning, then we often serve a festive snack when a child is moving away. Allowing the departee to choose it and having the other children help make it adds to the fun.

As in working through any other kind of separation, the leaver's and the left-behinds' feelings of grief, apprehension, and sometimes anger need to be recognized and honored. There is no shame in feeling saddened when a friend has departed, and children should be allowed to mourn this without being ridiculed. They should also be assisted, in an unpushy way, to strike up a new friendship at the right moment.

Rejection by a former pal hurts, too, as does rejection by an entire group. It is not uncommon for 4-year-olds and 7-year-olds to form tight little cliques, part of whose "joy" is excluding as well as including other children. Teachers of young children need to be on the lookout for these happenings and ease the ache of rejection when they can. Sometimes the exclusion is only temporary, but sometimes the rejection is more lasting. When this happens, it takes sensitive analysis to determine the reason for the rejection and possible teaching of needed skills to both the rejectors and the rejectee. Sometimes the only alternative is to face reality, acknowledge the child's feelings, and encourage a new beginning with another friend or group.

Goal VII: Help Children with Special Needs Fit into the Life of the Group

The primary advantage of including children with special needs in typical early childhood classrooms, often cited by proponents of inclusive early education, is that all the children derive social benefits from that inclusion, and research supports this suggestion (Guralnick, 1999; Kemple, 2004; Taylor, Peterson, McMurray-Schwarz, & Guillou, 2002).

This chapter has already pointed out that one of many social benefits typical children receive is learning matter-of-fact kindness from that experience, but there are other benefits as well. While learning to accept and adapt to those with special needs, the group also learns that all children are more alike than different and, ideally, to feel comfortable rather than uneasy around such youngsters.

The other side of the coin is that the child with the disability has the opportunity to learn to fit in with a group of ordinary peers and get along with them (Kemple, 2004). The child sees typical behavior modeled, including various strategies the children employ for getting what they want and playing together. These can be emphasized quietly by the teacher, showing how the child with a disability might use the same strategies (Guralnick et al., 2007).

Chapter 5 discusses many things the teacher can do to help all the children get along together, and many helpful resources are included at the end of that chapter. It is also helpful to remember the 5 Ps when teaching social skills to children with special needs: *Don't pity* or over*protect* these children. *Do* be *patient*, *persistent*, and *practical*.

SUMMARY

It is important for teachers of young children to foster the development of social competence because it plays such a crucial role in later school success. Social competence develops at a rapid rate during the years of early childhood, and several theories have evolved to explain how this complex process takes place. Children become socialized in part as a result of identifying with and emulating models they admire; in part as a consequence of reinforcement that encourages or suppresses various kinds of social behavior; and in part by other kinds of interactions among themselves and with adults that foster cognitive, intellectual learnings conducive to the development of social skills.

Although children begin to attain many social skills during this period, seven of them were selected in this chapter as being particularly important: (a) developing empathy, (b) learning to be generous, (c) understanding that everyone has rights that must be respected, (d) learning that it feels good to help other people, (e) discovering the value of cooperation and compromise rather than stressing competition, (f) discovering the joys of friendship, and (g) helping children with special needs fit into the life of the group.

Questions and Activities

1. During the next week watch for situations in which a child could be helped to understand another person's feelings or point of view. Using the situations you observed, discuss possible ways that genuine feeling for another person could have been developed from these situations.

2. Have you witnessed examples at your school of children seeking to comfort each other? Share the situation with the class and explain what the comforter did to help the other child.

Diversity Question

1. Imagine you are teaching in a classroom that includes a child with developmental delays who tends to not speak unless spoken to and generally plays alone. What would you do to encourage the child's interactions with other children?

Predicament

1. You are working as a teacher in a Head Start center. One volunteer is supervising the trike area and is firmly telling the children that they can ride the trike around the track three times and then must give a turn to the next child who is standing in line (several children are standing there already, making plaintive noises about wanting turns). What would you do to handle this situation on both a short- and long-term basis?

Self-Check Questions for Review

Content-Related Questions

1. What are some typical social behaviors of 2-year-olds? How does the social behavior of 3-year-olds differ from that of 6-year-olds?

2. After reviewing the processes by which children become socialized, discuss what the implications are for teachers. Basing your comments on what is known about the process of socialization, explain how teachers can apply that knowledge to further socialize the young children in their care.

3. Review the seven social learning goals and then list some practical pointers you would give a new teacher about how each of those goals might be accomplished.

Integrative Questions

1. Review the equipment in the school where you are teaching or have taught and identify which equipment facilitates social interaction between children. Do any items, for example, require two people using them at once to make them work effectively? Suggest additional activities you could offer that would be more successful if two or more children worked together to accomplish them.

2. The chapter discusses three theories about how children become socialized. What do these theories have in common and how do they differ? Do these differences mean that only one of them is correct and the others are wrong?

3. Propose two or three brief skits or episodes the staff might act out that demonstrate social situations and/or social problems for the children to discuss. For example, two people might act out a problem at the snack table where two children both want to get refills. Be sure to think of at least one situation that demonstrates positive social interaction.

4. The woodworking table is very popular this morning; everyone wants to hammer and saw. Carpentry is offered several times a week. Which of the following solutions for regulating participation would you favor? Be sure to explain the pros and cons for following each of the four policies: (a) Allow each child to make one item and then let the next child have a turn; (b) have the teacher keep a list and have the children sign up for turns; (c) tell requesters the table is full right now and to please come back later; (d) suggest to children as they finish that they alert waiters there is space for them.

Reference for Further Reading

Gartrell, D. (2004). *The power of guidance: Teaching social-emotional skills in early childhood classrooms.* Clifton Park, NY: Delmar. This compilation of articles is a valuable aid in understanding and managing classroom behaviors.

Related Organizations and Online Resources

Center on the Social and Emotional Foundations for Early Learning. The center designs projects to strengthen the capacity of Head Start and child care programs to improve the social and emotional outcomes of young children. Information can be found at http://www.vanderbilt.edu/csefel/.

Committee for Children. This organization promotes the safety, well-being, and social development of children. Information is available at http://www.cfchildren.org/.

Educators for Social Responsibility. This organization helps educators work with children to develop the social skills, emotional competencies, and qualities of character they need to succeed in school. Resources are available at http://www.esrnational.org/home.htm.

National Center for Early Development & Learning. This research project is supported by the U.S. Department of Education's Institute for Educational Sciences. Much of its research has involved children's social development and how to improve opportunities for children through positive early social experiences. Abstracts and full research reports are available at http://www.fpg.unc.edu/~ncedl/index.cfm#.

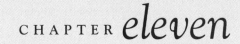

CHAPTER eleven

The Social Self: Fostering Self-Discipline and Conflict Resolution Skills

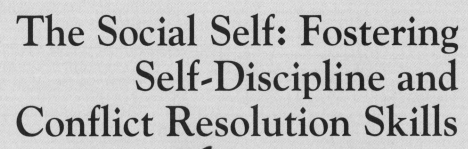

How to help children control themselves instead of depending on other people to control them?

How to make it easier for children to behave in acceptable ways?

What "time-out" really teaches children?

. . . IF YOU HAVE, THE MATERIAL IN THE FOLLOWING PAGES WILL HELP YOU.

It is insanity to believe that if we get children to feel bad, they will behave better.

Becky Bailey (1997, p. 73)

Traditional classroom discipline too easily slides into punishment. . . . Guidance teaches children to solve their problems, rather than punishing them for having problems they cannot solve. Guidance teaches children to learn from their mistakes rather than "disciplining" children for the mistakes they make.

Dan Gartrell (2004, p. 65)

DISCIPLINE OR GUIDANCE TOWARD SELF-DISCIPLINE?

Since discipline worries beginning teachers the most, it is usually the subject they want to discuss first when they begin teaching. Sometimes this is because they fear physical aggression or that the children will not like them, but more frequently they fear losing control of a situation because they do not know what to do next. So when teachers say fervently that they want to discuss discipline, what they usually have in mind is how to control the children or, as one forthright young student put it, "how to get the kids to do what I want." Although "getting the kids to do what I want" is undeniably part of the package, should it be all that is encompassed by the concept of discipline? The teacher should also have in mind the higher goal of instilling inner self-controls in the child in place of teacher-maintained external ones. As Dan Gartrell points out in the preceding quotation, there is a difference between *discipline* and guidance. Therefore, every guidance situation should not only achieve a workable solution to the current conflict but also seek to internalize self-control (Blair, 2003; Chen, 2003; DeVries, Hildebrandt, & Zan, 2000; Elkind, 2001; Gartrell, 2004, 2008; Howes & Ritchie, 2002; Kaiser & Rasminsky, 2003; Levin, 2003).

It is necessary for teachers to make a subtle shift in attitude for true guidance (which encourages the development of *self*-discipline in the child) to take place. Although it can be trying for teachers to deal with aggressive or disruptive behavior in young children, we must start to view those interactions not as difficulties, but rather as prime learning times. If we view children's unacceptable actions as mistakes that they make while learning how to manage their feelings (just as children make mistakes when they learn other skills like writing—we don't lecture or make them say they are sorry then!), it will be easier to maintain a sense of calm and caring that is so necessary for the child to develop self-control (Elkind, 2001; Gartrell, 2004, 2008; Levin, 2003).

Young children are just beginning to experience emotions as they attempt to understand what they are and express them to others. At the same time children find

Benjamin La Framboise

Create a classroom climate where people cooperate and treat each other with respect.

themselves immersed in a new social world filled with people who continually provoke intense reactions—feelings that range from friendly delight and love to utter frustration and anger. Sorting out the vast array of emotions is quite an undertaking for children. (This is a big task for many adults, too; let's not underestimate how confusing or overwhelming our own feelings sometimes can be.) If we jump in to discipline or control children when they have trouble managing their feelings, we ignore their place in the developmental continuum (i.e., just beginning to sort it all out) as well as deny them the rich educational experience of learning to control their own behavior.

This is not to say that teachers should sit back and let children pummel each other whenever they feel like it! On the contrary, the teacher has a very active role in creating a peaceable classroom where children are cooperative and behave in a respectful, caring way toward others. Approaches that foster the development of self-discipline and the ability to resolve conflicts are discussed at length in the rest of this chapter.

ESTABLISHING INNER CONTROLS: EGO STRENGTH, MORAL DEVELOPMENT, AND SOCIAL AWARENESS

Why Does Self-Control Matter?

Self- rather than "other"-control is desirable for numerous reasons. People who can control themselves are trustworthy and responsible. They can be counted on to do the right thing whether or not a police officer is standing on the corner watching. A number of recent research studies have shown that preschool-age children who are able to self-regulate have a significantly greater chance of later social and school success (Blair, 2003; Bronson, 2006; Chen, 2003; McClelland & Morrison, 2003; C. Raver, 2003). Figure 11.1 indicates the important self-regulation skills children need to develop before entering kindergarten in order to be academically and socially successful.

Granted that internalization of control is desirable, the question that remains for early childhood teachers to answer is, How can I help such young children begin to establish inner control? Teachers must realize that this is a long process taking many years, and it rests on the gradual development of ego strength, moral judgment, and social awareness. A strong ego (see Freud in chapter 1) enables children to control

The following competencies have been linked to school and social success in later years. By the time they enter kindergarten, children can:

- Use language to communicate with others what they are thinking and feeling
- Manage angry feelings in a way that causes no harm
- Control themselves from acting on every impulse
- Pay attention to adults and other children
- Follow directions
- Take turns
- Acknowledge that others have feelings, too

Figure 11.1
Important self-regulation skills for preschool children

Joanne Hendrick

Children learn how to resolve conflict through their interactions with others. Is this conflict an exasperating problem for the teacher to fix or a rich opportunity for the children to learn?

their impulses, moral judgment (telling right from wrong) enables them to decide which impulses they must control, and social awareness enables them to understand there are expectations for their behavior as well as other points of view.

Ego strength, moral judgment, and social awareness begin to develop during early childhood (Copple & Bredekamp, 2009; Bronson, 2006; Hyson, 2008; Shelov & Hannemann, 2004). As many theorists have pointed out, the child's interactions with others, both adults and children, have a powerful impact on the way these developments progress (Dewey, 1916; Erikson, 1963; Freud, 1922/1959; Piaget, 1932; Vygotsky, 1978). Early childhood educators are in a prime position to enhance children's development by creating a classroom climate that fosters positive interactions for each child. Such a classroom is rich in warm, caring relationships, respect, cooperation, and peaceful resolution of conflicts. In such a classroom, where the child constructs a sense of self, moral values, and social awareness through experiences with others, the child is given ample opportunity to practice and learn through interactions with other children. Developing self-control and conflict resolution skills are seen as an important part of the curriculum, not problems to be controlled by the teacher. The following suggestions will help you create a peaceable, caring classroom where the child's ego is strengthened, moral development is enhanced, and awareness of others grows—all of which lead to the child's ability to control behavior and resolve conflicts.

Suggestions for Creating a Peaceable, Caring Classroom in Which Children Develop Self-Discipline and Conflict Resolution Skills

Create a Sense of Trust and Safety

The importance of forming attachments has been discussed in chapters 9 and 10 with regard to its effect on emotional health and social success for the child. In addition, attachment is important for the development of the child's conscience (Bronson, 2006; Honig, 2002; Howes & Ritchie, 2002; Levin, 2003). When children feel an attachment toward their caregiver, they then want to adopt the social and moral rules that the caregiver embraces. Once attachment is established, children then feel safe and secure enough that they can start to think about other people, not just themselves and their own needs. If the essential basic need for attachment is not met in the early years, the ability to trust and care for others is stunted (Erikson, 1963; Hyson, 2008; Kristal, 2005; National Research Council and Institute of Medicine, 2000; Prince & Howard, 2002). Therefore, the first goal in creating a caring, peaceable classroom is to develop and sustain a close relationship with each child. As Loris Malaguzzi (1993), the Reggio Emilia philosopher, emphasized, it is crucial that we create an "education based on relationships."

The next step is to establish trust and safety in the classroom at large. This can be done in several ways: through conflict resolution, "guidance talks" with individual children, and class meetings. In all types of situations, the teacher makes clear that the classroom is a safe place for all children so actions that hurt others in any way will not be allowed. Classroom rules can then be generated by the children during class meetings and ways for maintaining peaceable behavior discussed. The child can more readily understand the reasons behind classroom and social rules—and has had an active role in making them—which makes it easier for the child to put them into practice (Gartrell, 2004; Hyson, 2008; Marion, 1998; Stone, 2001; Vance & Weaver, 2002). These three techniques form the basis for establishing trust and security in the classroom as the children come to trust that their safety is ensured and their needs will be treated fairly by all. When used together in a conscious way, these methods for promoting social awareness and collaboration are quite effective in creating a peaceable classroom (Gartrell, 2004, 2008; Levin, 2003). Instituting these practices takes care and devotion, but it is well worth the effort. The focus of the teacher becomes much more positive as the children's prosocial skills evolve and the teacher is freed from having to maintain external control for negative behavior.

Go to MyEducationLab and select the topic "Guidance." Under Activities and Applications, watch the video *Classroom Rules.* How does this teacher establish trust and safety in the classroom?

Teach Conflict Resolution Skills

It is important to establish a consistent and developmentally appropriate approach for helping children negotiate and resolve their conflicts (Copple & Bredekamp, 2009; Gartrell, 2008; Stone, 2001). The teacher's role in helping children develop these skills is not to stop the conflict and impose a solution (unless there is the immediate threat of real harm—which usually is not the case), but to help the children articulate their feelings, listen to other people's viewpoints, and collaborate in finding possible solutions (Chen, 2003; DeVries et al., 2000; Gartrell, 2004, 2008; Levin, 2003).

This brings up the provocative topic of "time-out," where the teacher directs a disruptive child to sit off by himself, sometimes "to think about what he did," sometimes until a timer goes off, and sometimes until whenever the teacher feels like it! Although this method is certainly an improvement over spanking or saying hurtful things, there are some drawbacks to its use that must be considered. Basically what is happening when the time-out chair is used is that the child is sent to the corner; all that is lacking is the old-fashioned dunce cap. Sent off to sit alone, the child is emotionally abandoned. Besides that, teacher and child frequently become involved in secondary struggles when the child tries to sneak away and the teacher catches him. Finally, many time-out episodes go on way too long, either because it's such a relief to the teacher to have the child removed or because the teacher forgets the child is there.

In situations where it is clear that the teacher must step in to manage an out-of-control child, it is better to give what David Elkind refers to as a "time in," that is, keeping the child with you to help calm his feelings and trying to find out why he is so upset:

> It might be the case that the child had a right to be angry. . . . Once we have an idea of why the child was troubled, we have a much better chance of helping him to calm down and rejoin the group. In the *time out*, a child learns that her feelings are ignored, and therefore of no value. A child given a *time in*, on the other hand, learns that his feelings are important and will be attended to. Which child is more likely to act out again? (Elkind, 2001, p. 8)

After the child has calmed down, it is important to help him reenter the social world of his peers in a positive way and without too much fanfare. The following steps should help the child learn from the situation and strengthen the ability for self-control:

1. *Recognize and discuss feelings and rules after a reasonable degree of calm has prevailed.*   This is a very important part of guidance. Even if the child is saying such things as, "I hate you—you're mean! I'm going to tell my mother, and I'm never coming back!" it is possible to show you recognize the child's feelings by describing them, replying, "You're really mad at me because I made you stop throwing blocks. [Pause] But the rule here is that we keep our classroom safe for everyone." If more than one child is involved, it is vital to help each of the children put their feelings into words as best they can. The virtue of doing this is that when children know you understand what they feel, even though you don't agree, they don't have to keep *showing* you how they feel.

Once feelings have been aired and everyone is calmer, this is also a good time to state whatever rules apply and discuss alternative ways of solving the conflict. If the children are mature enough, they should be able to contribute their own ideas, as well as hearing what the teacher and others have to say.

2. *Have children take the responsibility of deciding when they can control themselves and return.* At this step many teachers say something on the order of, "Now you sit here with me until lunch is ready," thus shifting the responsibility for the child's behavior to the teacher instead of putting the child in command. But if the long-term goal of internalizing self-control is to be reached, it is much wiser to say, "Now tell me when you can control yourself, and then we will go back," or, more specifically, "When you've decided to keep the sand down, tell me, and then you can go back and play." Some children can actually say they are ready, but others need help from the teacher, who can ask them when they look ready, "Are you ready to go back now?" (Perhaps the child nods or just looks ready.) "Good, your eyes tell me you are. Let's make a plan. What would you like to do for fun there?"

3. *It is important to help children be successful when they do go back so that they have the experience of substituting acceptable for unacceptable behavior.*   It will probably be necessary to take a few minutes and get the child really interested. Be sure to congratulate the child for acceptable behavior, perhaps saying, "Now you're doing the right thing. I'm proud of you!"

4. *Follow through with suspending privileges if children repeat unacceptable behavior.* Occasionally the teacher will come across a glibber customer who says hastily when removed from the sandbox, "I'll be good, I'll be good!" but then goes right back to throwing sand when he returns. At this point it is necessary to take firmer action. Have

1. Establish a sense of calm.
Sometimes this might mean directly intervening by separating children or removing a toy, but it is only for the purpose of cooling off—not punishment—to allow for discussion and mediation.

2. Determine what the conflict is about and convey that each child will have a role in finding a solution.
Help the children state what the conflict is and help them see how it involves more than just their own feelings. Encourage children to express their feelings in words and listen to each other.

3. Ask for solutions.
Challenge the children to consider everyone's perspective and generate possible ways for solving the conflict without fighting.

4. Reach agreement in a solution.
Guide the children toward agreement. Sometimes you may need to have quieter guidance talks with a particular child or children, but the idea is to get them to take social responsibility. Help the children put the solution into practice.

5. Discuss how the solution worked.
Be sure to discuss the conflict and solution with the children afterward, either in a guidance talk or class meeting. This helps them see that mistakes are okay and that they can get better at negotiating their own conflicts through this process. Point out how they have contributed to creating a "safe and caring classroom community."

Figure 11.2
Steps to resolve conflict in the classroom

the child sit beside you until he can think of something acceptable to do, but do not permit him to go back to the sandbox. You might say, "What you did [be explicit] shows me that you haven't decided to do the right thing, so you'll have to come and sit with me until you can think of somewhere else to play. You've lost the privilege of playing in the sandbox for now."

But our goal here extends beyond switching from time out to time in. What we are really aiming for is that children learn to express their emotions and control them in a socially acceptable way. Figure 11.2 details a positive method for guiding children to do so and learn to resolve their own conflicts.

Use Guidance Talks to Promote Self-Control

Gartrell (2004, 2008) recommends using guidance talks with one or two children to reinforce positive social learning after a conflict has occurred. This is not an opportunity for the teacher to lecture or to instill guilt, but to find out how the children are processing the experience, where they are in terms of developing self-control, and what help they need for future success. It is a good time to air feelings about classroom rules and make plans for dealing with conflict in the future.

Use Class Meetings to Promote Social Awareness and Collaboration

Class meetings are an effective way to help children understand and process social expectations and responsibilities (Gartrell, 2004, 2008; Harris & Fuqua, 2000; Hyson,

2008; Levin, 2003, Noddings, 2006). They allow children to feel they are part of a larger community, one based on democratic principles and respect for each child's feelings and opinions. Class meetings can be held weekly, daily, even several times a day. The teacher is responsible for leading the discussion about relevant topics (e.g., "Today Dillon got hurt playing wrestlers. What can we do to make our classroom a safe place for everyone?") in a way that encourages the sharing of ideas and group discussion. Class meetings should not be used for group punishment or, worse, singling out a particular child.

Involve the Families in Creating a Peaceable Classroom

Encourage families to learn about and discuss the ways you are helping their children learn self-control and conflict resolution skills. Convene a community meeting to discuss these issues as well as such things as time-out, home discipline, punishment, and so on. Have plenty of materials and information available as this is an area many families feel confused and overwhelmed by. Remember your goal is not to judge but to get everyone on board in fostering peaceable behavior in the children.

Increase Children's Feelings of Mastery by Giving Them Many Opportunities for Making Decisions

Of course, the choices offered must be appropriate and not too difficult. Fortunately, the school day abounds with opportunities for decisions well within the ability of most children to handle. The catch is that *the teacher must be prepared to honor the choice once the child has made the decision*. Such questions as "Do you want dessert?" "Would you rather finger-paint or play with the blocks?" or "Would you like to erase the board today?" are examples of valid choices because it is all right if the child chooses to refuse. Unfortunately many teachers use "Would you like . . . ?" or "Would you please . . . ?" or "OK?" as a polite camouflage for conveying an order. Thus they inquire, "Let's get on the bus, OK?" or, "Would you like to put on your sweater?" Young children are likely to retort, "No!" when asked such questions, and then the teacher is really stuck. It is better not to ask, "Let's get on the bus, OK?" if the child has to get on the bus anyway, but to try saying, "The bus is here, and it's time to go home. Where do you want to sit?" or, "It's cold today. If you want to go out, you will have to put on your sweater." In short, honor choices when given, *but give no choice when there is no valid opportunity to make one*.

It is also important to see to it that children experience the consequences of their decisions. Perhaps you will recall the example in the chapter on routines (chapter 7) in which children who elect to skip snack are not permitted to change their mind at the last minute. Abiding by decisions once they are made teaches children to make responsible choices.

Increase the Child's Feelings of Being a Competent, Worthwhile Person

The feelings of self-esteem generated by competency also make the ego stronger. Children who think well of themselves because they are competent are in a favorable position to assume command and control of themselves because they see themselves as being effective and strong (Bronson, 2006; Elkind, 2004b; Gartrell, 2004; Hyson, 2008; Marion, 1998).

Unfortunately some children are noticed only when they do something wrong. This continual negative relationship with the teacher does not enhance the children's feelings of self-worth, especially when other children begin to type the child as "bad." This sometimes happens with a child who has special needs and whose development of social skills may be delayed. Remember that the child who needs the most help in learning self-discipline is the one who will benefit most from your continued patience and effort. Remember, too, there is no such thing as a "bad child" and that a considerable part of each child's day is spent in acceptable activities. If children's self-esteem and self-mastery are to remain intact, it is vital that they receive credit for their good behavior as well as that they feel a sincere, positive connection with the teacher (Kristal, 2005; Landy, 2002; Levin, 2003; National Research Council and Institute of Medicine, 2000; Peisner-Feinberg et al., 1999, 2001).

However, the most desirable source of self-worth stems not from the opinion of the teacher but from the acquisition of skills. These may be as diverse as being able to walk the balance beam or knowing effective strategies for worming one's way into a play group. It does not really matter what the competency is as long as it contributes to the child's self-perception of being an able person who is in command of herself or himself.

The most desirable source of self-esteem stems from acquiring competency and skills.

Benjamin La Framboise

Foster a More Social, Less Egocentric Orientation

Piaget (1932) described the young children as being egocentric, that is, viewing the world from their own perspective. Piaget also stated that through interaction with others, and often through conflict, the children are confronted with other points of view that challenge their egocentricity and force them to readjust their perspective to adapt to a larger world. Recognizing and appreciating the perspective of others lays the groundwork for moral development and the sort of positive social behavior we are trying to promote.

There are many things a teacher can do to encourage the development of the child's social awareness. The first has been touched upon already: As much as possible allow children to resolve their own conflicts (Bronson, 2006; Chen, 2003; DeVries et al., 2000; Gartrell, 2004, 2008; Hyson, 2008; Levin, 2003). Unfortunately, teachers often have a hard time doing this and feel a need to jump in at the first sign of discord. These "cessation strategies" focus on teacher control of the children's behavior and include redirection, issuing warnings, separating the children, removing a toy, removing a child to time-out, and so on. In these and similar instances, it is up to the teacher to solve the conflict, and children are not involved in negotiating a resolution. On the other hand, "mediation strategies" focus on helping the children express their feelings, listen to others, identify the problem, brainstorm solutions, and attempt to come to an agreement about a resolution (Chen, 2003). The steps to resolve conflict listed in Figure 11.2 represent a mediation strategy that helps children become more socially aware.

Another way to foster social awareness is by giving children a reason why they should or should not do something. For example, you might say, "I can't let you hit Max with the block; it hurts him too much." This encourages children to think of other people's well-being.

Teachers often try to use this person-oriented/victim-oriented approach by saying to a child who has just tossed sand into another child's face, "Stop that! How would *you* like it if *you* were Derek and someone threw sand into *your* eyes? How would *you* feel then?" This what-if-*you*-were-him approach may work with older children but is too complicated and involves too much role reversal for 3- or 4-year-olds to understand. It just leaves them bewildered.

The same lesson can be taught much more effectively by making a simple change in approach that is still other-person-oriented but related more directly to the sand-thrower's own experience. This teacher might begin by saying, "Be careful with the sand! Throwing sand hurts too much when it gets in Derek's eyes. Remember when Michael threw sand in *your* eyes? Remember how that hurt? Well, that's how Derek's eyes feel now." Even better would be to bring Derek over and ask him to tell the child how he feels. Of course this goes beyond Derek saying, "You're mean!" but it is amazing how quickly children learn to report their feelings honestly and without insult when they are consistently encouraged to do so in your peaceable classroom using the conflict resolution process described in Figure 11.2. It is well worth your effort because it really does help children learn to think about how their actions affect other people's feelings.

Stop Conflict Situations Before They Start

When Trouble Repeats Itself, Analyze the Situation and Try Changing It, Rather than Nagging the Child.   When something happens over and over, the teacher should think about changing the situation instead of the child. For example, instead of telling a restless child to be quiet all the time, it might be better to let him leave after hearing one story, to ask a volunteer to read to him alone, or even to let him play quietly nearby during story time until he becomes more interested and can be drawn gradually into the group.

Consistently Position Yourself So That You Are Able to See a Large Area of the Room or Play Yard at the Same Time.   All too often beginning teachers focus on only a small group of children at a time. Learning to position yourself close to a wall or fence instead means you have a clear view of a larger area, just as sitting at a table so that you face most of the room makes it easier to scan the larger space. Teachers who circulate within the supervision area instead of remaining planted in one place are more likely to be aware of what is going on and to be available to help children when they need it to mediate conflict resolution.

Warn Ahead of Time to Make Transitions Easier.   The teacher should anticipate transitions with the children a few minutes before the activity is due to change. For example, the teacher might say, "It's going to be lunchtime pretty soon. I wonder what we're going to have?" Or, "There's just enough time for one more painting. Then you can help me wash the brushes, and we'll have a story." Warning ahead gives the children time to wind up what they are doing.

Arrange the Environment to Promote Positive Interactions.   Interest is continuing in studying the ecological relationship between children and their environments (Edwards, Gandini, & Forman, 1998; Greenman, 1998, 2005), and some of these findings about the interconnections are helpful to know when planning ways to promote socially cooperative behavior.

Many children in a small space (a high density of children), combined with few resources, leads to more aggression and more destructive and unoccupied behavior. Experienced and wise teachers know: If enough space is provided for the children to use, conflicts will be reduced accordingly.

One area that illustrates this situation is the block area of many schools. Although interest can run high in this activity, all too often blocks are crammed into a corner where there is no possibility for play to expand as interest dictates.

Another matter-of-fact suggestion about room arrangement that decreases the necessity to restrain children is separating areas with high levels of activity from each other to provide protection. In one school, only one large open area was available for block and large-muscle activity. Noisy chaos was often the result in winter weather when children tried to use the same space for both activities at the same time. Students and staff dreaded working there.

With some rearranging, two widely separated areas were created. The result was that block play and the wonderful social-cognitive learnings that accompany it increased dramatically. The second area was then available for large-muscle activities and for dance and group time. The entire tone of the group of 4-year-old children became calmer and more pleasant.

Attention to traffic patterns can also increase constructive participation and reduce conflicts. When the large rooms frequently used in child care situations are broken up with dividers so that children are physically detoured around activity centers, the temptation to disrupt what other children are doing is reduced. Such dividers can be low bookcases, bulletin boards, or even a Japanese futon.

A final facet of environmental planning that will help children achieve self-discipline is the provision of quiet places to which children can retreat when they feel the need for such refreshment. We adults know that constantly being with large numbers of people is tiring, but we tend to forget that it is tiring for children, too. Cozy corners for books, a quiet retreat with some simple manipulative activity, or simply an area in which to stretch out and do nothing can meet this need and reduce the fatigue and irritability that so often lead to loss of self-control.

Have As Few Rules As Possible, but Make the Ones You Do Have Stick.   Unless the teacher is watchful, rules will grow up like a thicket around each experience. But if situations are reviewed from time to time, unnecessary restrictions can be weeded out.

Some rules are genuinely necessary, however, and their enforcement is desirable. Research shows that establishing firm limits, coupled with warmth and a simple explanation of the reason behind the rule, enhances children's self-esteem and increases their ability to establish inner controls (Bronson, 2006; Hyson, 2008).

The problem is to decide, preferably in advance, which rules are really important. Student teachers in particular seem to have trouble in this area—sometimes treating relatively minor infractions such as not saying "please" or "thank you" as though they were major transgressions, while dealing indecisively with more serious misbehavior such as tearing up picture books or running out the front door without an adult. In general the most serious infractions of rules are those related to *hurting other people, hurting oneself,* or *destroying another person's property.* If a reason for a rule is not easy to come up with, it may be a sign that the rule is not important and could be abandoned.

When Supervising Children, Plan Ahead.   Try to anticipate the point at which the children will lose interest or the play will fall apart; have alternatives ready to propose that will help the play continue to flourish. An insightful teacher might think, "Now, if I were that child, what would I like to do next with those blocks and cars?" Perhaps it would be getting out the arches or the wood strips to make a garage, or maybe it would be constructing ramps for the cars to run down. Tactfully posing several possibilities to the children will serve to continue play and lengthen concentration, as well as keep the children happily occupied and out of trouble.

Mediate Conflict Resolution When Necessary

Be Decisive; Know When to Step In and Control Behavior.   Inexperienced teachers are often unsure of when they should interfere and when they should let children work the situation through between themselves. As mentioned earlier, the general rule of thumb is that children should not be allowed to hurt other people (either children or grown-ups), to hurt themselves, or to destroy property. This policy leaves considerable latitude for noninterference, but it also sets a clear line for intervention.

When Trouble Brews, Take Action Yourself Before the Child Does.   It is a mistake for teachers to sit on the sidelines and let a situation go from bad to worse until it explodes, and then step in to pick up the pieces. If the situation is one that will have to be stopped at some point, *it is much more effective to step in before trouble starts,* rather than a minute after blood has been shed.

Prompt intervention makes it more probable that the teacher can use a rational guidance approach with the children; indeed, this is a better environment for teaching any

Joanne Hendrick

Be decisive; know when to step in and control behavior.

skill. Intervening before the fight occurs also prevents either child from receiving gratification from the attack. For example, stepping in before one child bites another takes preternatural quickness but is vital to do since biting feels so good to the biter that no amount of punishment afterward detracts sufficiently from the satisfying reward of sinking teeth into unresisting flesh.

Accept the Fact That Physical Restraint May Be Necessary. In the unusual emergency situation in which it is necessary to prevent physical attack, the most effective thing to do is hoist the child on your hip, with his head forward and his feet stuck out behind. This unglamorous pose, known as the *football carry*, works very well to stave off attack and permit the teacher to carry the child someplace if necessary. Although it is rarely necessary to resort to such measures, it helps to know what to do in a real emergency.

Sometimes the teacher must move swiftly and take hold of a child before he can strike someone else again. Let's keep in mind, though, that the need for this type of intervention is not so frequent. Research has shown that conflict between children does not usually result in violence, and much of the time children are able to resolve the conflict themselves (Chen, 2003; Hyson, 2008). However, there are those times when it becomes clear that your quick action is needed and that you must stop the aggression so no one is harmed.

When doing this, it is important to be as gentle as possible and yet be firm enough that the child cannot slip away. Usually just catching an arm is enough, although sometimes it is necessary to put both arms around the obstreperous one. As soon as the child is calm enough to hear the teacher, it will help bring the situation under control if the teacher says something on the order of, "As soon as you calm down, I can let go of you, and we can talk."

When a situation has deteriorated to the extent that physical restraint is needed, it is usually best to draw the child or children away from the group so that they do not continue to disrupt it. It is seldom necessary to take them out of the room, and it is more desirable to remain where the other children can see that nothing too terrible happens to the offenders. Otherwise anxious children fantasize too much about what was done to the fighters. In addition, the purpose of your intervention is to halt the aggression so that the children can calm down enough to be able to negotiate the conflict peaceably—*not to punish*. Every instance where teacher restraint is used should be followed by a guidance talk with those who were involved so that the children can process the high emotion that just took place and figure out ways to manage their behavior in the future (Gartrell, 2004, 2008).

Keep Your Own Emotions Under Control.   One way children learn attitudes is by observing models (Bronson, 2006; Hyson, 2008; Kostelnik, 2004; E. M. Thomas, 2004). Teachers need to control their own tempers because by doing so they provide a model of self-control for the children to copy, as well as because intense anger frightens children. Also when conflict situations arise, it is not just one child and the teacher who are involved: Every child in the room is covertly watching what is happening and drawing conclusions from it. Therefore, it is often valuable for the teacher to talk over what happened with various children afterward to help them deal with how they felt about it and to clarify and consolidate what they learned from it. For example, the teacher might explain to a worried-looking 3-year-old, "Jacob was crying because he wanted that car, but Rafael had it first so Jacob had to let go. He was pretty upset, wasn't he? Did he scare you?"

Sometimes, of course, it is simpler to advocate self-control in the teacher than to achieve it. Things that can help teachers retain control include remembering that one is dealing with a child, deliberately keeping control of oneself, and acknowledging the feeling by saying to the child, "Let's wait just a minute until we're both a little calmer. I feel pretty upset about what you did." The biggest help, though, comes from analyzing scenes and upsets after they have occurred and planning how best to handle them the next time they happen. This experience and analysis build skills and confidence, and confidence is the great strengthener of self-control.

Remember That You Don't Have to Make an Instantaneous Decision.   Not only does admitting to a child that you need time to control your feelings help you regain control of them, but it also models self-control and provides time to think about what to do next.

Once the physical action has been halted, it is not necessary to render instant justice. Waiting a minute and thinking before speaking gives you time to remember that the child is not deliberately misbehaving to annoy you but more likely is simply unable to control such powerful emotions at that time—and the child needs guidance, not anger from the teacher, to do so.

Knowing Where Your Flash Points Are Is Helpful, Too.   Different behaviors make different teachers (and parents) angry, and it is helpful to take time to analyze what your particular flash points are because this awareness can help you control your response to them. Although knowing the origin can be helpful, it is not essential to understand why you become especially angry when such behavior occurs. Just *knowing* that you are vulnerable can be sufficient since the knowing can be linked to reminding yourself to make a special effort to keep your temper under control and be fair and reasonable when a child behaves in that particular way.

Practice Restitution.   When a child has gone so far as to hurt another youngster, he should be allowed to help remedy the injury. Perhaps the child can put on the bandage or hold a cold towel on the bump. This constructive action helps the child see the consequences of his act, relieve his guilty feelings, and show concern by doing something tangible. Whether children should be asked to say they are sorry is debatable. Often they are not sorry, and even if they are, it is not helpful to teach the lesson that glib apologies make everything all right. Making restitution is a more developmentally appropriate approach since children understand the relatively concrete notion of restitution (doing something to right a "wrong") before they understand the abstract meaning of apology.

Whenever Possible, "Let the Punishment Fit the Crime."   Teachers (and enlightened parents) avoid doling out punishment in its usual forms. Teachers do not spank children, shut them in closets, take away their television privileges, or deny them dessert because they have not been good. But they *do allow* another form of "punishment" to happen when it is appropriate: This is simply permitting the child to experience the natural consequences of inappropriate behavior (Elkind, 2001). Thus the child who refuses to come in for snack is permitted to miss the meal, the child who rebelliously tears a page from a book is expected to mend it, and the youngster who pulls all the blocks off the shelf must stay to help put them away. Even young children can appreciate the justice of a consequence that stems logically from the action. It is not necessary to be unpleasant or moralistic when any of these results transpire; it is the teacher's responsibility only to make certain that the child experiences the logical outcome of inappropriate behavior.

When the Encounter Is Over, Forgive and Forget; Don't Hold a Grudge.   Inexperienced teachers sometimes dread confrontations because they fear that the child will be hostile afterward or actively dislike them for keeping their word and enforcing their authority. However, such confrontations almost invariably build a closer bond between the teacher and the child.

It is very important for a child's sense of self-esteem to be seen in a generally positive light. If teachers allow a few negative encounters to color their perception of the child so that he or she is seen as a "bad kid," it is difficult for the child to overcome this image and establish a more positive relationship. For this reason, particularly with "difficult" children, teachers need to call upon all their reserves of generosity and maturity and make every effort to concentrate on the youngster's positive qualities (Gartrell, 2008; Honig, 2002; Hyson, 2008; Katz & McClellan, 1997; Levin, 2003).

Most Important, Notice When Children Do the Right Thing, and Comment Favorably.   Fortunately most of the center day does not revolve around high-intensity conflicts; many days go smoothly and we all get along happily. When the day is a good one, when the children are obviously making progress, when they mostly talk instead of hit each other, when they share generously and enjoy the opportunities to help each other, let them know that you are pleased. They will share your pleasure in their accomplishments, and this recognition will help perpetuate the growth and self-discipline they have displayed.

Benjamin La Framboise

Always focus on the child's positive behavior—every child, every day!

A Final Thought

No teacher (or parent, for that matter) in the world handles every situation perfectly! When one of those less-than-perfect situations happens between you and a child, it is all too easy to spend energy on feeling guilty or regretful about how things went. Rather than doing that, it is wiser to think over what happened and learn from it, since every interaction provides opportunities for *two* people to learn something. When things have not turned out well, think about what the child learned and what you learned, and consider possible alternatives. Then resolve to use a different approach the next time a similar situation comes up. Perhaps it will be rearranging the environment, or perhaps stepping in sooner, or perhaps firmly seeing a struggle all the way through. Taking positive steps to analyze difficulties and improve your skills is infinitely more desirable than agonizing over past mistakes.

REDUCING AGGRESSION IN THE CLASSROOM

Now that the general subject of guidance and fostering self-discipline has been discussed, it is time to talk about dealing with aggressive behavior in particular. When we work with young children, we must consider two kinds of aggression. The first, and by far the most common kind of aggression, is *instrumental aggression*. This aggression occurs without basic hostile intent. For example, a child reaches over and takes away another child's felt-tip pen because she or he wants to draw, or a 2-year-old pushes another child aside so that she or he can reach a book.

Although these actions may require arbitration, explanation, and protection of the second child's rights, they differ from the hostile types of aggression toward other children. According to Mussen, Conger, and Kagan (1969), *hostile aggressive* behavior refers to "actions that are intended to cause injury or anxiety to others, including hitting, kicking, destroying property, quarreling, derogating others, attacking others verbally and resisting requests" (p. 370). Aggression is the result of anger—anger being the feeling, and aggression being the expression of that feeling.

In early childhood we see examples of this kind of behavior manifested when children barge through the room, leaving a bedlam of smashed blocks or ravaged housekeeping corners behind them, or when they spend most of their time whooping wildly about being tigers or monsters, or when they deliberately seek to injure other children by destroying what they are doing, teasing them, or physically hurting them.

Undesirable Ways to Cope with Aggression

Teachers and parents deal with this acting-out behavior in both useful and not-so-useful ways. Descriptions of some of the more undesirable methods of responding to such behavior follow.

The Authoritarian Teacher

Tightly controlling teachers intend to shape, control, and evaluate the way their children behave according to absolute standards of what is right. Such teachers value obedience and favor taking punitive, forceful measures when children's behaviors conflict with those standards. The result of such intensive overcontrol is generally an increase in aggression. Additionally an authoritarian teacher sets the stage for children's dislike of school and future academic problems (Bronson, 2006; Hyson, 2008).

The Overpermissive Teacher

At the other extreme are teachers who believe that "anything goes." Such teachers are often confused about the difference between freedom and license, and they fail to see that true freedom means the children may do as they wish *only as long as they do not interfere with the rights and freedom of other people*. This extremely permissive teacher is fairly rare in preprimary centers because the pandemonium that results quickly makes everyone uneasy. What the children really learn in such overpermissive circumstances is that "might makes right." This is a vicious circle because the aggressors are often rewarded by getting what they want and so are more likely to behave just as aggressively next time.

The Inconsistent Teacher

The third undesirable way to deal with aggressive behavior is to be inconsistent. Teachers may be inconsistent because they are unsure that it is really all right to control children, or they may be uncertain about how to control them, or they may be unaware that consistency is important; hence, they deal erratically with out-of-hand behavior, sometimes enforcing a rule when they think they can make it stick and other times sighing and letting the children run off or have their own way.

Inconsistent handling may sound merely weak; however, its effect is strong in that it increases aggressiveness in children. The probable reason for this result is that the reward for aggressive behavior is intermittent rather than continuous, and this leads the child to test the behavior over and over again.

Conclusion

It is fairly easy to see that teachers who are overcontrolling (authoritarian) or under-controlling (extremely permissive) or very inconsistent bring special difficulties upon themselves when dealing with aggressive behavior. It is less easy to determine what constitutes a reasonable balance between aggression and control and to decide how to handle this problem in an effective and healthy way. We want to harness and direct this energy, not abolish it.

The problem is how to channel the expression of hostile aggressive feelings into acceptable ways at school and in society. The remainder of this chapter provides some basic approaches that will help the teacher solve this problem.

Desirable Ways to Cope with Aggression

Assess the Underlying Causes of Aggression, and Ameliorate Them When Possible

First, it is helpful to remember that pronounced self-assertiveness is part of the developmental picture for young children. It is important to realize that this sometimes out-of-hand phase serves a healthy purpose for these children who are busy finding out who they are by asserting their individuality.

Besides the influence of the developmental stage, native temperament may have a lot to do with the expression of aggression (Blair, 2003; Hyson, 2008; Kristal, 2005). Some children can stand more frustration than others can without exploding. Sex-linked characteristics also affect its expression. Maccoby and Jacklin (1980) and Mercurio (2003) summarized many studies indicating that in our culture more direct physical aggression is expressed by boys than by girls, whereas girls are more likely to employ indirect means of expressing aggressive feelings. How much of this behavior is attributable to biological differences and how much to culturally instilled values, however, has yet to be determined (Froschl & Sprung, 2008).

In extreme cases of aggression, particularly when it is combined with hyperactivity, outside referral is in order. In addition, it is especially important to be in close contact with the child's family and work together with them for successful intervention to occur (Froschl & Sprung, 2008; C. Raver, 2003; Warner & Lynch, 2003).

Never Allow Bullying

Bullying is defined by Froschl and Sprung (2008, p. 12) as:

> . . . acts that occur over time, or a single unprovoked act in which physical, verbal, or exclusionary behavior is used by one child or children to intimidate, make fun of or intervene in what another child or children are doing.

Studies reveal that consistent bullying has bad results for both victim and perpetrator: Children who are unduly aggressive as young children have been found to remain unduly aggressive as they mature and often get into trouble as a result (Coie & Dodge, 1998; Garbarino, 2001; Hyson, 2008). Victims also pay a heavy price—often remaining diffident and unsure of themselves in later years (Froschl & Sprung, 2008; Gartrell, 2004; Smith et al., 1999). But we really do not need research to understand that outcome; many of us have only to recall episodes from our own childhood to understand the misery such treatment produces. For these reasons it is important to understand how to discourage teasing and stop bullying by using a combination of conflict resolution, direct intervention, ongoing guidance talks, and classroom meetings to discuss the issue effectively.

Teach Children Alternative Ways of Getting What They Want

We cannot expect children simply to stop seizing what they want or to stop attacking other children when they are angry unless we teach them other effective ways of getting what they want in place of those behaviors. Previously we have talked about helping children substitute words and talk about their own feelings in place of verbally or physically attacking other children.

The other important thing to teach is how to get what you want without hurting somebody else. The strategies teachers usually use are either trying to distract or redirect the "wanter" ("There's room at the easel. Let's see what colors we have today."), offering the child something else as a substitute ("Here's another truck. Why don't you use it? See, it has a bell you can ring."), or explaining that the child has to wait for a turn ("Jorge's using it now; you'll have to wait.").

Although all of these strategies work some of the time, it is a shame for teachers to limit themselves and the children to so few alternatives. This is particularly true because none of these three strategies provides ways for the wanter to learn negotiation skills.

Additional approaches that *do* encourage negotiation and interaction include coaching the wanter to play beside the group and, if possible, to begin to contribute to what they are doing in some way. Encouraging cooperation by pointing out to both children how doing something together can enhance the pleasure of the activity is yet another way to foster interaction ("If she holds the bowl while you whip the egg whites, it won't slide around so much."). Or sometimes the wanter can figure out how to strike a bargain to facilitate getting what he wants ("I'll let you see my sore knee if you'll let me be the patient.").

Whatever alternative is employed, the teacher should make certain the children clearly understand that hurting others is not allowed but that this need not mean they must swallow their anger and knuckle under; instead they can use a variety of both effective and acceptable alternative ways to get what they want.

Provide Substitute Opportunities for Socially Acceptable Expressions of Aggression

The cathartic (emotionally relieving) value of substituting socially acceptable expressions of aggression is emotionally satisfying to children. These substitute opportunities are safe for those around them, and they provide chances to be assertive in a harmless way for youngsters too immature to resist the need to express aggression in some physical form.

These activities are best offered, however, *before* the child reaches the boiling point. It is generally unsatisfactory to march a youngster over to a punching bag after he has hit someone and say, "It's all right to pound this!" By the time this happens, a lot of the flavor has gone out of the experience. It is better to offer acceptable aggressive activities as part of each day, as well as to make sure they are available when the teacher anticipates that the day will be especially tense either for an individual child who is upset or for the entire group (e.g., on Halloween). Fortunately a great many activities will help. The idea here is to supply plenty of material, plenty of time, and as few restrictions as you can tolerate.

Large quantities of dough (not tiny, unsatisfying dabs) are fine aggression expressers. We encourage the children to stand at the table so that they can work forcefully, using their hands to pound and squeeze and pinch and punish the dough to their hearts' content.

In finger painting and other types of smearing techniques such as soap painting, emphasis should be placed on richness of color and lots of gooey paint base, be it liquid starch, wallpaper paste, or homemade and very thick cooked starch.

Noise is an excellent outlet for expressing aggression. The aggression-expressing possibilities of sheer noise (at least on the days when the teacher does not have a headache) should not be overlooked. It is wise to remember that noise has an infectious effect on the entire group and may accelerate activity too much. However, on the many occasions when things are in good order, noise can be very helpful! Drums are an all-time, satisfying "best" for noise, but pounding on the piano is good, too. Real music and dancing can be added for those who enjoy it. Sitting on top of the slide and kicking one's heels hard makes a wonderful, satisfying noise. Yelling, playing loudly, and crying (the louder the better) also serve to express feelings harmlessly.

Opportunities for dramatic play can also help children come to terms with aggressive feelings, and dramatic play has the added benefit of helping children learn to self-regulate their feelings (Elias & Berk, 2002). Direct participation by dressing up and playing house will let youngsters work through situations that may be troubling them. Anyone who has ever watched an irate young "mama" wallop her "naughty" baby doll will understand the merit of providing this kind of play material as an aggression reliever.

The best thing for out-of-hand children to play with is water. It is deeply relaxing in any form. Washing doll clothes or plastic cars, playing with soap bubbles, or playing with water in the housekeeping area is beneficial. Even when it is squirted, it does no lasting harm.

Whenever weather permits, the best thing of all is a running hose and lots of sand and mud. This combination has led to some of the calmest, happiest days we have ever had in our school, but pouring and playing with water in tubs or basins can also be satisfying. At home a warm bath can work miracles.

Stopping Some Activities Before They Start Saves Aggression Later

Many teachers have learned, for example, to keep an eye out for "angry monster" games or Wrestling Federation or Power Rangers. When such a game gets too high pitched, the quickest way to bring it under control is to get the ringleader involved in something else particularly enjoyable.

Our staff discourages toy-gun play at our center because we believe that children should be encouraged to use more desirable play themes than killing each other. Moreover research by Watson and Peng (1992) has revealed that toy-gun play was one of the two strongest predictors of real aggression observed in the children's center. (The other predictor was the use of physical punishments by the parents.) Therefore, when toy guns are brought to school, our staff insists they be stored in the cubbies until it is time for the children to go home.

Keep in mind, though, that when children show an interest in guns or other types of aggressive play, they are using play to work through their feelings and fears. Simple

Susan Windle

Whenever weather permits, the best thing of all is a running hose and lots of sand and mud.

rules and bans on guns won't address the children's needs, whereas discussion, both privately and in class meetings, will. For some very practical examples and discussion about the issue of aggressive play, see Diane Levin's (2003) *Teaching Young Children in Violent Times: Building a Peaceable Classroom*, which is the Reference for Further Reading at the end of this chapter.

Finally, Plan, Plan, Plan!

Plan to provide interesting activities that children really like, and plan the daily program with specific children in mind ("John is coming today; I'd better get out the hammers and saw"). The program must not make undue demands on their self-control and should include acceptable outlets for their energy. As a general principle, consistent opportunities that allow children to achieve mastery and competence in acceptable areas should be provided. Every time a youngster can do something well, whether it's building with blocks, doing meaningful work, creating a painting, or learning to pump on the swing, the child's aggression has been channeled into accomplishing something constructive.

SUMMARY

Discipline should be more than just "getting the kids to do what I want." The real goal should be the development of self-control within the children. This is accomplished, in part, by strengthening the ego, by fostering the beginning of conscience, and by encouraging social awareness. The best way to foster these developments in young children is by creating a caring and peaceable classroom. Several strategies were discussed, including developing warm, nurturing relationships between child and adult, helping children learn to control their emotions, teaching children skills for resolving their own conflicts, encouraging mastery and competence, and setting up the classroom in a way that reduces frustration, among others. Three strategies in particular will help create a peaceable classroom: conflict resolution, guidance talks, and classroom meetings.

Aggressive behavior is defined in this chapter as action intended to cause injury or anxiety to others. This kind of behavior needs careful handling and guidance so that children are not forced to suppress such feelings completely but learn instead to channel these impulses into socially acceptable activities.

Questions and Activities

1. Give three examples of choices you could encourage the children to make for themselves the next time you teach.
2. Select an activity, such as lunchtime, and list every rule, spoken and implicit, you expect children to observe in this situation. Could any be abandoned? Are any really for the teacher's convenience, rather than for the purpose of fostering the children's well-being?
3. List several alternative approaches children can be taught that will help them get what they want without hurting other people.
4. Do any conflict situations in your school seem to recur? For example, are the children always being told not to run inside the building? Suggest several ways the situation could be changed instead of continuing to "teach the children to behave."
5. Everyone seems to have different "breaking points" in tolerating aggression. For example, one person sees red if a child is insolent, whereas another finds it more difficult to cope with a child who deliberately hurts another child. Compare notes among the people in class about what they feel constitutes acceptable ways to express aggression, where their breaking points are, and what they do to control themselves when they reach that point.

Diversity Question

1. A small group of children gangs up on Hashim, a boy of Iraqi descent. They tell him he's bad because his family "dresses funny and people who dress like that kill people." How would you handle this situation in a way that promotes the development of conflict resolution skills in all the children?

Predicaments

1. A child is throwing sand in the sandbox, and you want him to stop. What should you say to put your statement in positive form, rather than tell him what not to do—that is, rather than saying, "Don't throw the sand"?
2. Marcy, who is 7, is playing with a puzzle and keeps slipping little pieces of puzzle into her pocket. No one except you sees her doing this. You have already told her twice to keep the puzzles on the table so the pieces won't get lost, but she continues to challenge you by slipping them into her pocket. What should you do next to handle this situation?
3. As you enter the room, you see Zack and Jordan hanging on to a truck, both shouting, "I had it first!" and, "I can keep it until I'm done with it!" How would you cope with this crisis?

Self-Check Questions for Review

Content-Related Questions

1. Explain the five steps for conflict resolution.
2. List the self-regulation skills preschoolers need to develop, and explain why it is important that they do so.

Integrative Questions

1. The book discusses self- versus "other"-controlled behavior. Using a college-age student as the example, explain how that student who is "other controlled" might behave, compared with one who has established inner controls. Give an example of potential behavior in a group social situation and one involving taking a class.
2. Explain several principles teachers can follow that will help foster self-discipline and conflict resolution skills in the children.

Reference for Further Reading

Levin, D. E. (2003). *Teaching young children in violent times: Building a peaceable classroom* (2nd ed.). Washington, DC: National Association for the Education of Young Children (NAEYC) and Educators for Social Responsibility. This book addresses the difficult issues in classroom management straight on. Information, strategies, and examples of creating a peaceable classroom are offered.

Related Organizations and Online Resources

Collaborative for Academic, Social, and Emotional Learning (CASEL). CASEL works to create a world where schools, families, and communities work together to nurture the social and emotional development and academic performance of all children. Many online resources and a free newsletter are available at http://www.casel.org.

National Association for the Education of Young Children (NAEYC). NAEYC offers several resources related to guidance (free) at http://www.journal.naeyc.org/btj/ 200307/. These include:

"Further Readings on Preventing and Responding to Behaviors That Challenge Children and Adults," by Lise Fox.

"Democratic Discipline in Your Classroom: A Roadmap for Beginners," by Elizabeth Campbell Rightmyer.

"Love and Learn: Positive Guidance for Young Children," excerpted from *Love and Learn: Positive Guidance for Young Children*, by Alice S. Honig.

National Network for Child Care (NNCC). NNCC unites the expertise of early childhood professionals from many universities to share knowledge about children and child care. Many articles about discipline and behavior guidance are available at http://www.nncc.org.

CHAPTER twelve

Fostering the Development of Language Skills

What are some practical things teachers can do to foster language development?

How to encourage children to talk with you and with other children?

Whether or not you should insist a Mexican American child speak English at school?

. . . IF YOU HAVE, THE MATERIAL IN THE FOLLOWING PAGES WILL HELP YOU.

The specifically human capacity for language enables children to provide for auxiliary tools in the solution of tasks, to overcome impulsive behavior, to plan a solution to a problem prior to its execution, and to master their own behavior.

Lev Vygotsky (1978, p. 28)

Learning a native language is an accomplishment within the grasp of any toddler, yet discovering how children do it has eluded generations of philosophers!

Jerome S. Bruner (1978)

In the past few years we have become increasingly aware of the value of developing language skills in early childhood. This emphasis is the result of research findings indicating that a close association exists between language competence and cognitive development (Jalongo, 2008; Kalmar, 2008; National Research Council and Institute of Medicine, 2000; Tekene, 2008), that differences exist between the speech of middle- and lower-income children (Moore & Barbarin, 2003; National Institute of Child Health and Human Development [NICHD] Early Child Care Research Network, 2000; Peisner-Feinberg et al., 1999, 2001), and that most children acquire most of their language skills, though not most of their vocabulary, by age 4 or 5 (Epstein, 2007; Jalongo, 2008; Shelov & Hannemann, 2004).

Well-documented findings such as these emphasize how crucial it is that we teachers and parents of young children do all we can to enhance language learning and use. We must do so because, whether one sees language as being related but separate from thought, as did Piaget (Piaget & Inhelder, 1969), or as ultimately bound together by means of social transmission, as did Vygotsky (1978), there is general agreement that the development of language abilities goes hand in hand with the development of mental ability and academic success (Epstein, 2007; Jalongo, 2008; Kalmar, 2008; National Research Council and Institute of Medicine, 2000; NICHD, 2000; Rafanello, 2000). For this reason we devote considerable attention to methods of fostering language development as we begin study of the child's intellectual self.

THE COMPONENTS OF LANGUAGE

Language is a set of tools that we use to express our feelings and communicate our thoughts with others. In our society, children must develop their skills as listeners, speakers, readers, and writers. This chapter focuses on the first two elements of language learning which lay the foundation for literacy: listening and speaking. The development of reading and writing is discussed in chapter 13.

Kalmar (2008) defines oral language as "a cognitive tool used to construct meaning, internalize the language used in print, and regulate thought and activity" (p. 88). She points out that the quality of the language children hear is crucial for later language development and school performance. Early childhood teachers must come to grips with the problem of how to foster language development to maximize the child's potential for both comprehension and expression. To bring this about, teachers must understand how the ability to use language is acquired and how it develops; above all, they must determine what they can do to foster its growth.

HOW CHILDREN DEVELOP LANGUAGE

As Tabors (1997) has pointed out, learning any language is a complicated business that involves putting together "a variety of interlocking pieces" (p. 7). Children (or other learners) must master five aspects to be successful: (a) the sounds of the language (*phonology*), (b) the words (*vocabulary*), (c) how the words are put together to make sentences *(grammar)*, (d) how sentences are used for different purposes such as story-telling, giving directions, and asking for something *(discourse)*, and (e) how language is used to affect other people's behavior *(pragmatics)*.

One school of thought emphasizes the role of inborn, innate mechanisms, whereas other theories dwell on the significance of environmental influences. Each of these theories has something to recommend it, although none of them offers a totally satisfactory explanation. The *nativist theory*, as described by and originally championed by Chomsky (1968) and more recently by Maratsos (1998), maintains that human beings are born with an inherent, innate ability to formulate language, an ability that sets humans apart from almost all other animals. This ability or mechanism is then triggered into use by exposure to people speaking whatever language is specific to their culture.

At the other extreme is the *behaviorist* approach, which emphasizes the importance of imitation, modeling, and reinforcement as playing the most significant role in language acquisition (Bandura, 1977; Rafanello, 2000). Particularly in vogue during the heyday of behaviorism, this theory is currently criticized as offering insufficient explanations for how children are able to generate novel sentences they have never heard and therefore could not have learned by means of copying someone else. Still, reinforcement *does* play a significant role in language acquisition, and anyone who has lived through a child's learning to talk can cite numerous examples of mothers and babies imitating each other's speech, as well as many additional later episodes of imitation.

Like the purist behaviorist approach, the third theory or model, sometimes termed the *sociolinguistic* or *social communicative theory*, also emphasizes the role environment plays in how children learn to talk. These theorists (Bruner, 1983) believe that children learn about linguistic forms and rules by interacting with the people in the environment around them. Unlike the behaviorists, who see the child as being mainly acted upon by the environment, they picture the child as being an active participant in the learning process (Vygotsky, 1962, 1978). Many proponents of this point of view also acknowledge the possible existence of an inborn predisposing mechanism for language acquisition (Epstein, 2007; Jalongo, 2008; Strickland, 2006).

Contributions by Adults to the Child's Acquisition of Language

"Motherese"

Language learning is no easy task, but adults make the child's work somewhat easier by using a special form or style of language when they speak to infants and very young children. Although this has been called *Motherese*, in actuality this adjustment of form is used by most adults and even older children when talking with little ones (Carroll, 1999; Caulfield, 2002). The style includes such characteristics as using a higher pitch and a wider range of pitch, speaking more slowly and distinctly, repeating words and phrases, using limited vocabulary, and coining words such as "goney-gone" and "tum-tum."

Maternal responsiveness—that is, how much attention a mother pays to her 1- and 2-year-old's attempts at talking—also makes a significant difference in the size of the child's vocabulary. The more responsive the mother, the greater the child's number of words (Kalmar, 2008; National Research Council and Institute of

Medicine, 2000). This implies that teachers, too, should be careful to be attentive when children want to talk with them. Indeed, recent research indicates that the more high-quality language interactions the teacher has with a child, the more adept the child will become in language skills (Jalongo, 2008; Kalmar, 2008; Kauffman Early Education Exchange, 2002; Peisner-Feinberg et al., 1999, 2001; NICHD, 2000).

Valuing Listening

Listening is more than simply hearing what is said. Listening forms the foundation for language learning as infants begin to distinguish the sounds that are used in their native language. It is by listening to the sounds or *phonemes* of "m" and "d" that English speakers learn the names for "Mommy" and "Daddy." It is through this process of listening to the phonemes around them and comparing them that Spanish-speaking babies learn to produce the rolling "r," whereas English-speaking babies do not. This explains why the English-speaking baby will probably have difficulty pronouncing the rolling "r" as an adult learner of Spanish.

Go to MyEducationLab and select the topic "Emergent Literacy and Language Arts." Under Activities and Applications, watch the video *Matching Sounds.* In what ways does this activity support children's language learning?

Although listening is one of the earliest and most frequently used communication skills to develop, it is also taught the least in school (Jalongo, 2008). One need only think back to one's own education and compare the amount of time that was spent learning to write compared to specific training in learning to listen to see why "listening has been referred to as the neglected or forgotten language art" (Jalongo, 2008, p. 3).

Good listening skills do not develop automatically and these skills should be taught in the early childhood curriculum—as intentionally and thoughtfully as we teach children how to "use words" and write letters.

Valuing Children's Talking

Children's receptive language, that is, their ability to understand words and meaning, precedes their language production. Children understand more words than they are able to say. However, in order to produce language, children need to go beyond listening and practice, practice, practice! Any adult who expects young children to be quiet most of the time is not only asking for a lesson in extreme frustration, but is also imposing unrealistic expectations that are detrimental to the child's development of language and literacy skills. Because school success is affected by the child's ability to listen, speak, read, and write, it is crucial that teachers allow ample time and opportunity for children to express their ideas, questions, feelings, and hypotheses about the world through speaking with others. Early childhood teachers must address with parents how important it is for the child to practice speaking and to feel comfortable doing so.

DEVELOPMENTAL MILESTONES

Teachers should become acquainted with the developmental milestones of children's language acquisition so they can identify children who show marked developmental lags and have a clear idea of what is reasonable to aim for when establishing goals for language development. The teacher may find Table 12.1 ("Age at Which Most Children Develop Language Abilities") quite helpful; but remember that the checkpoints represent averages and that children who are developing well may often be either ahead or behind the suggested time listed. If you are concerned about a child's language development, contact the American Speech-Language-Hearing Association (ASHA) for more information and referral resources (listed in Related Organizations and Online Resources at the end of this chapter).

When assessing language competence, the teachers in our center have also found it helpful to determine whether English or some other language is the child's dominant language and to determine whether the child appears to possess "the habit of verbalness." For whatever reason, be it temperament, age, level of intelligence, cultural pattern, or socioeconomic status, it is evident to our center teachers that some children use language to meet their needs more frequently than others do. We always try to note this behavior and use the techniques described in the following section to encourage the less verbally oriented children to increase their language abilities while attending school. It should also be noted that African American children from low economic groups tend to score significantly lower on standardized language skills tests. Horton-Ikard (2006) suggests that often these children are learning another form of communication known as African American English (AAE). AAE has its own complex developmental pattern but it is not assessed when standardized tests (such as vocabulary or word counting tests) use Standard American English.

BASIC WAYS TO FOSTER LANGUAGE DEVELOPMENT

I. Listen to the Children

Many adults are so busy talking themselves that they drown the children out. But children learn to talk by being heard. Paying attention to what they say and listening both to the surface content and to the message underneath offer the most valuable inducements to children to continue making the effort to communicate (Edwards, Gandini, & Forman, 1993, 1998; Jalongo, 2008; Kalmar, 2008; Rinaldi, 2001).

Of course, it is not always easy to understand what children have to say. If a comment is unintelligible, it is all right to ask a child to repeat it; and if the message is still unclear, it may be necessary to admit this and say, "I'm sorry, I just can't tell what you're saying. Could you show me what you mean?" At least this is honest communication and shows children that the teacher is really interested and is trying. Occasionally another child can be prevailed on to clarify what a companion is saying.

II. Give the Children Something Real to Talk About

Children's talk should be based on solid, real, lived-through experience. Sometimes inexperienced teachers want to begin at the other end and set up group experiences wherein the children are supposed to discuss planting seeds or thinking about what will sink and float before they have been exposed to the experience itself. This means they are expected to use words that have few actual associations for them and to talk

Table 12.1
Age at which most children develop language abilities

By the End of the First Year, the Child:	By the End of the Second Year, the Child:	By the End of the Third Year, the Child:	By the End of the Fourth Year, the Child:	By the End of the Fifth Year, the Child:	By the End of the Sixth Year, the Child:	By the End of the Seventh Year, the Child:	By the End of the Eighth Year, the Child:
Recognizes primary caregiver by voice	Follows simple instructions	Can tell someone their age, sex, and name	Talks in sentences of five to six words	Speaks in more complex sentences	Has developed good conversational skills	Enjoys explaining things in detail	Typically has about 20,000 words
Smiles at the sound of a familiar voice	Begins to combine simple words	Understands concepts such as "on," "in," "under"	Imitates behaviors of older children and adults, such as hand gestures to express emotion	Takes turns in a conversation and interrupts others less frequently	Speaks in small groups and before the class	Listens well	Engages in reciprocal, interactive, back-and-forth conversations with peers and adults
Babbles, repeating consonants such as "bababa"	Identifies the names of body parts, familiar people, and objects	Speaks clearly enough so that strangers can understand most words	Shows mastery of basic rules of grammar	Enjoys verbally sharing experiences	Listens with attention	Enjoys one-to-one conversations	Tells jokes with enthusiasm
Turns head in the direction of sound	Uses words heard in conversation	Speaks in four- and five-word sentences; begins to use compound sentences	Has a vocabulary of 4,000 to 6,000 words	Uses inflection and pitch in communication	Can use complex sentence structure	Is interested in words and their meanings, interested in more complex forms of communication	Can use language to communicate ideas, reason and solve problems, and convince others of point of view
Enjoys using various types of sound; "plays" with sound of her own voice	Speaks several single words (15–18 months)	Points to and identifies most common objects and pictures	Claims many things by using verbal commands	Speaks in future tense when appropriate	Pays attention to the different sounds in the environment	Loves jokes, word play, puns, tongue twisters, and guessing games	Understands the power of language, might use words to tease, exclude, or hurt others
Begins to recognize language as a two-way process	Can use simple phrases or two- to four-word sentences (18–24 months)	Understands and will follow a two- or three-part command, such as, "Go to the kitchen and bring back a napkin and a spoon"	May use language to tease others; understands words can hurt	Enjoys telling stories and can recall parts of a story	Asks and answers questions readily	Speaks precisely; will seek out correct word to express self	Has developed a more sophisticated sense of humor

Responds to own name	Identifies or points to an object or picture when it is named	Begins to use plurals and pronouns	Enjoys singing simple songs and fingerplays	Can say own name and address	Uses vocabulary learned from books	Has rapidly increased vocabulary and number of words used in sentences
Can understand adults' emotions by the tone of their voice	Has a 200-word vocabulary	Makes up words to fit needs and may overgeneralize meaning	Recognizes the concepts of "same" and "different"	Recites simple poems	Speaks with attention	Enjoys codes and word puzzles
Understands and responds to "no"	Speaks words overheard in conversation	Tells simple stories	Enjoys storytelling	Demonstrates increasing speech fluency in expressing ideas	Understands the relationship between letters and the sounds they make	
Shakes head for "no"	Is able to use words such as "me," "you," and "I" correctly	Begins to ask questions with "who," "what," "why," and "when"	Speaks clearly so that people can understand what is being said	Uses facial expressions when communicating	Enjoys playing with sounds in music, singing, and poetry	
Uses inflection with simple words like "oh-oh"	Enjoys looking at picture books and identifies objects by pointing to them	Engages in songs and simple fingerplays	Attempts to speak more than vocabulary allows			
Imitates words	Understands more words than actually can be produced	Begins to use language to organize thought and can recall the events of the day	Uses more advanced sentence structures, such as, "That dog is nice, isn't she?"			
Understands simple verbal requests such as "Give me the ball"		Expresses fantasy in language	Continues to learn new vocabulary weekly or even daily			
Says "Dada" and "Mama" and possibly some other familiar names or words						

Pam Oken-Wright

Give children something real, something interesting to talk about.

about something vague and relatively meaningless. No wonder their attention wanders. It is much more satisfactory to provide the opportunity to live through the experience and to talk about what is happening while it is going on, as well as after it has been completed. At this point the child can really associate "sink" with "things that go down" and "sprout" with the pale green tip that poked its nose out of the bean.

Note also that talk and questioning are advocated as an accompaniment to experience. In former years some teachers of young children seemed to assume that mere exposure to interesting materials in the presence of a warm adult would automatically produce growth in language and mental ability. However, children develop language best when they are required to use words to express concepts and thoughts about what is happening, has happened, or will happen; this kind of activity produces the greatest gains (Jalongo, 2008; Kalmar, 2008; National Research Council and Institute of Medicine, 2000; NICHD, 2000; Walsh & Blewitt, 2006).

III. Encourage Conversation Between Children

Encouraging children to talk with each other has many benefits as varied as teaching them to use words to negotiate disagreements in place of physical attacks and providing them with effective ways of entering a group. Besides these obvious advantages, as the children of Reggio Emilia consistently demonstrate, talking together can help children put ideas into words, increase their abilities to use language to explain to someone else what is happening, repeat an interesting experience, or make cheerful social contact with another youngster (Edwards et al., 1993, 1998). Most important of all, such encounters help persuade them that talking is satisfying and important—a valuable attitude to inculcate as a foundation for later interest in other language strategies related to literacy. (These strategies are discussed in more detail in chapter 13.)

Because talking between children is so valuable, the teacher should avoid being the constant center of attention, whether the situation is dramatic play or participating at the lunch table. Instead, it is important to think of oneself as seeking to increase the amount of talk *among the children whenever possible*. Such comments as, "That's really interesting. Why don't you tell Mikhal about that?" or, "Have you talked that over with Maxine? She was talking about that just yesterday," provide openings for the children to relate to each other and focus attention on the relationships among them, rather than keeping attention focused on the teacher.

IV. Encourage Conversation and Dialogue Between Teachers and Children

Much more is involved in language development than teaching the child to name colors or objects on demand, although learning the names of things has undeniable value. The skills involved in discussion and conversation are vital, too, and the ability to conduct such dialogues develops rapidly throughout early childhood (Bredekamp & Copple, 1997; Jalongo, 2008; Kalmar, 2008; Shelov & Hannemann, 2004).

To develop these conversational interchanges, teachers must relax and stop seeing their role as one of instructor and admonisher. *Always supplying a fact or rendering an opinion in reply to a child's comment kills conversation very quickly.* Teachers should seek to prolong the interchange whenever they can. Tossing the conversational ball back and forth is a sound way to build fluency and to establish the habit of being verbal.

The value of the one-to-one situation cannot be overestimated in this regard. It is not necessary to put this off and wait for a special moment; indeed, this is impossible to do if the teacher wants to talk specially with every child every day. Instead of waiting, the teacher can seize many little interludes to generate friendly talk with a child or between two children. One teacher in our center maintains that some of her best opportunities for such chatting occur while she is helping children go to the toilet. Another capitalizes on brief moments while putting on shoes or while greeting children as they arrive at school. And certainly, let us never forget the value of play in providing rich opportunities for conversations with children.

Teachers should monitor themselves regularly to make certain they are not talking mainly to the most verbal children, because teachers tend to talk most to children who are the best talkers to start with. Some children have a knack for striking up conversations with adults, whereas others do not. It is the children lacking this ability who are often overlooked and therefore receive the least practice in an area in which they need it the most. If teachers make a checklist of the children's names and review it faithfully, they will be able to recall which children they have talked with and which they have not and then make a particular effort to include in conversation the ones who have been passed over.

Besides these one-to-one conversations, two classic, larger group opportunities occur each day in school when it is particularly possible to generate conversation. These occur at the snack or lunch table and during group time. (Group-time conversation is discussed in the following chapter.) In full-day preschool programs where children nap, nap time provides a wonderful opportunity to talk quietly and connect with each of the children before they get ready for sleep (Soundy & Stout, 2002).

Benjamin La Framboise

Play provides rich opportunities for conversation.

Developing Conversation at Mealtimes

There are several practical ways the teacher can encourage conversation during meals.

Keep Lunch and Snack Groups as Small as Possible.   It is worthwhile to keep the mealtime group down to five or six children if possible. Anyone who has ever sat at a banquet table knows how difficult it is to get conversation going under such circumstances, and yet an occasional children's center persists in seating 12 or 15 children all around one table. This kills interchange, as well as makes supervision difficult.

Adults need to plan their activities so that they are free to sit with the children during meals. Surprisingly often at mealtime, staff can be seen roaming restlessly around, passing food, running back and forth to the kitchen, or leaning on counters, arms folded, simply waiting passively for the children to eat but not being part of the group at all. Good advance planning on food delivery should make it possible for staff to sit with the children, and a clearer understanding of the potential educational value of such participation should make them willing to do so. Sitting with the children fosters the feeling of family time that young children need and encourages the relaxed chatting that makes mealtime a pleasure.

It is wise, though, to avoid putting two adults together at one table. The temptation to carry on a grown-up conversation over the heads of the children can be too great when two adults eat lunch together. It is better to add more tables when more adults are present, thereby seizing this golden opportunity to reduce group size and making it more likely that individual children will join in the talk.

Think of Good Conversation Starters.   Such questions as, "Who's your favorite superhero?" or, "Would you rather be a cat or a dog?" will lead the children into talking about things that really interest them and that they can all share together. It is also fun to talk about brothers and sisters, new clothes, birthdays, what their parents' first names are and how old they are, what they call their grandfathers, or what they did over the weekend. In addition, their memories can be developed by asking them whether they can remember what they had for lunch yesterday or what they saw on the way to school.

It takes tact to ensure that one ardent talker does not monopolize the conversation under these circumstances. The teacher may need to make a deliberate effort to draw all the children into the discussion lest someone be consistently drowned out. But the half hour or so that lunch requires is really ample opportunity for everyone to converse.

Use Mealtimes as an Opportunity to Build Children's Vocabulary and Concepts. All too often teachers permit pointing and saying "give me" to pass for language. This is just not enough. Children need to acquire commonly used vocabulary, and mealtime is an effective place to teach this. It is easy for the teacher to make sure the children say the real name of the food they are requesting and then give it to them promptly. There is no quicker way to teach them that talking pays off!

Mealtimes are also good opportunities to teach certain concepts. For example, the teacher might start by talking about the food: "What are we having today? Did any of you look in the kitchen to see what dessert is?" and then go on to ask, "What does this tortilla taste like? Is it hard or soft? Hot or cold? Can you think of anything else that's like that?"

A word of warning is in order here. Mealtimes should remain basically social occasions, in which verbal fluency and fun are the keynote, not opportunities for continuous dull inquisitions. Vocabulary and concept building should not be allowed to dominate the occasion, and such a delightful event as lunch should never be permitted to degenerate into a boring mechanical drill in which the talk centers on naming each food and discussing where it came from.

myeducationlab

Go to MyEducationLab and select the topic "Emergent Literacy and Language Arts." Under Activities and Applications, read the strategy *Saying Words Aloud*. Note how the activities encourage children to generate speech and develop language.

V. Use Questions and Answers That Generate Speech and Develop Language

Once again, the value of questions must be highlighted as we discuss effective ways of encouraging the development of language.

Ask Questions That Require More Than One-Word Answers

In chapter 14, asking questions that are open-ended is advocated because doing this encourages children to see that many questions have more than one answer. Asking these kinds of questions has an additional virtue we should think about in this chapter: It also fosters language development by promoting conversation.

One important rule of thumb will help you to elicit children's conversations: Make it a habit to ask questions that you don't already know the answer to. In this way, you ensure that the answer will be something interesting to you, not a simple fact that is already quite clear to you as an adult. It's the difference between asking a child, "What color is the sky?" and "Why do you think the sky is blue?" Which answer from a young child will probably be more interesting? That interest is an important element in generating true conversation.

When Replying to a Child's Questions or Statements, Elaborate

With younger children, about 18 months to 3 years of age, simple elaborations of their statements suffice. Thus when a child comments, "Train, bye-bye," the teacher replies, "Yes, the train is going bye-bye." With older children, more elaboration is required. The teacher responds to an older child's statement, "There goes the train," by saying, "Yes, the engine is pulling the train out of the station. Where do you think it is going?" When working with older preschoolers or grade school children, this kind of enrichment is superior to simple expansion in fostering language progress. When teachers use more suggestions, open-ended questions, and elaborative statements with children, the children exhibit higher levels of social and cognitive developmental competence (Jalongo, 2008; Wilcox-Herzog & Ward, 2004).

The way in which a teacher enriches older preschoolers' language is evident in the following example. Sojin, the teacher, opened the conversation in group time after several days of investigations into caterpillars:

Sojin: Who would like to share a story about caterpillars?
Leah: Maybe they like to make friends with bunnies.
Ethan: I've seen it at my grandma's and grandpa's. And when it becomes a "bacoon," I'll bring it to school. Then, we can watch it. . . .
Alex: Then, it'll be a butterfly!
Ethan: . . . we can watch it be a butterfly. THEN, when it's a butterfly, we can go outside and let it go!
Jack: I saw prickly kinds of caterpillars.
Sojin: Where did you see these caterpillars?
Jack: On my trees. Sometimes they're red or orange kind. Some are white.

Use questions and activities that inspire children to talk. "Look at this strange thing—what do you think it does?"

Benjamin La Framboise

Go beyond simple yes-or-no questions. "Wow—what happened to that apple?"

Sojin: Ethan, do you remember what color your caterpillars were?
Ethan: I think they are yellow.
Rachael: I went to grandma's—and I saw a caterpillar in a tree. It was yellow.
Logan: I saw a green one at my mommy's house. She almost ran over it.
Sojin: It must have been on the ground, huh?
Logan: Yeah—she almost ran over it.
Leah: My mom saw one when she went on vacation . . . a caterpillar. It was on the ground and she went right beside it.

From this small snippet of conversation, we can see how the teacher's good use of elaborative questioning—and listening—inspired significant language learning, including a sense of conversational give-and-take, as well as a rich variety of vocabulary words.

This conversation comes to us courtesy of the White Oak School in Monticello, Illinois.

VI. When Necessary, Seek Professional Assistance Promptly

Every once in a while a teacher will come across a child who speaks rarely, if at all, or one who has a pronounced speech problem. These disabilities are discussed in more detail at the end of this chapter, but as a basic principle it is important to seek professional help for these children promptly. Too often both teacher and parent let the year pass, hoping the child will somehow outgrow the difficulty. Although this does happen occasionally, it is generally wiser to refer such children for professional help after 2 or 3 months at most. Children who have pronounced developmental lags or other speech disorders and who do not show signs of improvement by that time generally need consultation from a qualified speech therapist or psychologist, and a referral is definitely in order (see Related Organizations and Online Resources).

LANGUAGE AND DIALECTICAL DIFFERENCES

Which Language Should the Teacher Encourage?

In the chapter on cross-cultural education (chapter 4), a good deal of time was spent discussing ways to honor the cultural background the child brings from home. Although there is no finer way to do this than by welcoming and encouraging children to use their native language or dialect at school, teachers are often torn between two directions on this question. On the one hand, they want to make all children welcome and to facilitate their learning in every possible way; this makes the use of their dominant language essential. On the other hand, the teacher cannot help looking ahead and knowing that as schools function today, each of the children will soon move on to elementary school, where they will have to speak Standard American English, the dominant language of the United States (ASHA, 2004a; Hickman-Davis, 2002; Horton-Ikard, 2006; Tabors, 1997).

This dilemma shows no signs of dissipating. Recent trends in population statistics make it plain that the question of bilingualism and dialects and what teachers should do about them will remain an important aspect of language education because the population of so-called minority groups is rising steadily. For example, in 2004 the U.S. Bureau of the Census reported that over 34 million people were born in other countries, representing 12% of the total U.S. population. In addition, 11% of the U.S. population has one or both parents who were born in another country. Of the foreign-born population, 53% are from Latin America, 25% are from Asia, 14% are from Europe, and 8% represent other regions including Africa and Oceania (U.S. Census Bureau, 2005). By the 2030s, it is estimated that students who speak a language other than English as their primary language will account for 40% of the school-age population in the United States. That rate is exceeded already in California, where over 60% of schoolchildren do not speak English as their primary language. In addition, for the period 1995 to 2005, the Asian population had the most growth in the United States, with the Hispanic population having the second most growth (Roseberry-McKibben & Brice, 2004).

Statistics such as these are at least partially the reason for the storm of political controversy that arises from time to time over the value of bilingual education and the use of African American English in the classroom. Pro-English advocates argue that all Americans should "melt in" and speak Standard American English. Perhaps as a result of our own typically inadequate foreign language instruction in the United States, these advocates seem to assume it is impossible to speak two (or more!) languages with proficiency and therefore English must prevail entirely. Of course, common sense makes it plain it is essential that residents of this country be fluent in Standard American English, but it is also true that speaking Standard American English well need not obliterate the ability to speak another language, too (ASHA, 2004a; Hickman-Davis, 2002; Horton-Ikard, 2006; Jalongo, 2008; NAEYC, 1995; Roseberry-McKibben & Brice, 2004; Tabors, 1997).

Some resistance to providing a bilingual approach in classrooms also stems from early studies that concluded bilingualism has a negative effect on developing language and possibly mental development as well (Ellis, 1994; Imhoff, 1990). However, these results were complicated (confounded) by the presence of additional variables that we know affect learning and behavior, such as poverty. When such a mixture of possible causes is included in research findings, sorting the effects of one from another is next to impossible.

More sophisticated studies suggest that when the effects of poverty are statistically controlled, bilingualism is not a deterrent to development. In addition, bilingualism is associated with higher cognitive skills. The more proficient children are in their first language, the more adept they are at picking up a second language (ASHA, 2004a; Jalongo, 2008; Roseberry-McKibben & Brice, 2004).

Another continuing debate centers on when and how best to teach non-English-speaking children English. Common sense argues against the folly of insisting that children try to learn important new concepts in a language they are only beginning to acquire. Imagine having to learn geometry by means of first-year French, which you are learning simultaneously—that's the stuff nightmares are made of. Yet in essence we expect this degree of expertise from young semibilingual children when we teach them "all the important things" only in their second language (Gonzalez-Mena, 2007; Jalongo, 2008). Children who are coming to school for the first time are undergoing a complicated enough set of adjustments without the teacher's expecting them to function entirely in a new language at the same time.

Probably the best we can do at present, since children are expected to speak English in grade school and beyond, is to follow the bilingual model wherein young children are taught concepts first in their dominant language and then in English (ASHA, 2004a; Jalongo, 2008; Roseberry-McKibben & Brice, 2004). This approach has been shown to be successful with children speaking a variety of languages and coming from varied cultural backgrounds. Moreover, it has the virtue of helping maintain the child's ability to remain bilingual, rather than pushing toward proficiency in English only.

Make It Clear to the Families That You Value the Child's Native Language and Cultural Background

The following discussion uses Spanish and Mexico for the sake of brevity, but Navajo, French, Vietnamese, or any other language could be used to make the same points.

The most important thing for children to learn about school is that it is a place where they feel welcome and comfortable (Gonzalez-Mena, 2007; Hickman-Davis, 2002; Kirmani, 2007). Including songs and stories in Spanish, using multiethnic pictures, and observing Mexican customs honor the family by using the language and customs of the home at school. Asking children for the Spanish equivalents of English words will help clarify that there are two languages and, if done with respect and enthusiasm, emphasizes that the Spanish-speaking child has a special ability and skill.

It is also valuable to form close bonds of mutual concern with the families of the children (R. M. Barrera, 2001; Gonzalez-Mena, 2007; Hickman-Davis, 2002; Kirmani, 2007). Not all families want their children to continue to learn in Spanish. This attitude varies a good deal from family to family, and teachers should discuss this subject with them, help them weigh the pros and cons, and respect their preferences in every way they can. Most families are realistic about the value of learning English and are almost too eager to have their children gain this skill. It may even be necessary to explain why Spanish is being included as a major component in the curriculum. Other families, rarer in number, will welcome the bicultural emphasis to such an extent that they may be reluctant to include English at all.

Sometimes school values in language development run counter to deep-seated cultural values in the home. For example, it may be necessary to explain to families the positive relationship between language competence and academic success. Such explanations may encourage families to overcome their traditional view that children should be seen and not heard, and the parents may make greater efforts to encourage their children to talk more at home.

Sometimes, of course, the teacher, rather than the family, needs to make the cultural adjustment. Some teachers, for instance, in their eagerness to promote verbalness in the children, fall into the habit of allowing the children to interrupt adult conversations whenever they please. This is frowned on in Mexican American homes. In such cases the teacher would do well to encourage participation by the children while seeing to it that they continue to observe the basic good manners taught by their own culture (Gonzalez-Mena, 2007; NAEYC, 1995).

When Teaching Bilingual Children, Do Not Attribute All Verbal-Expressive and Comprehension Difficulties to Bilingualism

Many children who come to school speaking only a little English are quite fluent in their native language, and for them the transition to English is not too difficult. *It is very important to distinguish between these children and those who do not talk very much in*

The most important thing for the children to learn about school is that it is a place where they feel welcome and comfortable.

either language. These nontalkers need all the help they can get in developing the habit of verbalness. For such children the goal is to increase fluency and participation in whichever language they feel more at ease; teaching English to them is of secondary importance to gaining fluency and the habit of talking (ASHA, 2004a; Jalongo, 2008; Roseberry-McKibben & Brice, 2004).

What to Do When You Do Not Speak a Child's Language

Although it's all very well and good to discuss bilingual education on a remote level, the problem that ordinarily confronts the teacher is the young child who arrives at school unable to speak any English at all.

Despite the language barrier, somehow a bridge of understanding must be built between that child and the teacher. It may help you to remember the sage advice of one head teacher, Clevonease Johnson. At that center we had many youngsters who came to us from Vietnam and Cambodia. There they would stand, alone and bewildered, struggling not to cry as their parent and the interpreter walked out the door.

Although it wasn't possible for the teacher to acquire the child's language (at one time Clevonease would have had to have known eight languages to meet that standard), there were two phrases she said it was essential for her to know, and she never allowed the interpreter to leave without writing these down in phonetic English. The first was "Your mother (or father or grandparent) will be back soon" and the second was "Do you need to go to the bathroom?" With these phrases tucked in her pocket, combined with warm smiles and many gestures, Clev felt she could handle anything!

Actually, of course, we found many additional language-related strategies useful to employ when working with a child who spoke another language, and several suggestions are included below. Even more valuable than these strategies, however, is the overall attitude toward cultural differences that must prevail in the school. There is no substitute for providing newcomers with the warm welcome and appreciation of their background advocated in chapter 4, "Providing Cross-Cultural, Nonsexist Education." Figure 12.1 lists some helpful suggestions for supporting communication with a child who speaks little or no English.

What to Do About the Child Who Speaks a Dialect

It is also vital for teachers who form this language bridge to acquaint themselves with research indicating that many African American children speak a dialect whose value, before the work of Labov (1970), went largely unassessed and unappreciated. As our understanding about African American English (the term often used in place of the former *Ebonics* or *Black English*) grows, it is evident that its grammar has definite rules and that there is a real sophistication to its structure (Connor & Craig, 2006; Horton-Ikard, 2006; Labov, 1970). Indeed, some theorists are already asserting that the variation in language skills between social classes or ethnic groups may ultimately turn out to be more a question of difference than defect or deficit (Horton-Ikard, 2006).

The best recommendation for working with African American English appears to be that teachers should respect the African American child's dialect just as they respect the Mexican or Puerto Rican child's Spanish, yet also make it possible for the

1. First of all, remember to talk to the child. Sometimes teachers give up speaking to her just because the child does not respond. However, it's obvious that if she isn't spoken to in English, she won't have much of a chance to learn it.

2. Encourage the child to say something right from the start if he is comfortable doing this, but remember that many children require a considerable "quiet period" before they are ready to venture into an unfamiliar language (Tabors, 1997). This hesitancy can sometimes be overcome if other children are encouraged to talk freely to the newcomer (Hickman-Davis, 2002). Children are less shy talking with each other than with the teacher.

3. When possible, pair the child with another youngster who speaks the same language. This can help her feel she has someone to turn to when feeling blocked.

4. When speaking to the child, keep your voice natural and not too loud. Talking louder does not help children understand any better, and sometimes it makes them think you are angry with them.

5. Use the child's name when you speak to him, and take care to pronounce it as accurately as you can. Never deny the child her identity by giving him an "American" name instead (R. M. Barrera, 2001; "Profiles in Culture," 2004).

6. If you can pick up a few basic, frequently used words in the child's language it will be helpful—words like *outside, jacket,* and *lunch.* Activity nouns like *blocks* and *tricycle* will help a lot in smoothing the child's way (R. M. Barrera, 2001).

7. Be visually expressive. Use gestures, smiles, encouraging looks, and friendliness to help the child understand and feel at ease.

8. Demonstrate what you mean as you speak. For example, ask, "Would you like to paint?" Then pick up the brush, gesture toward the paper, and repeat, "Would you like to paint?" (Hickman-Davis, 2002).

9. Link language to objects and real experience whenever possible. Teach nouns and verbs first; they are some of the most meaningful and useful words (except for *yes* and *no*).

10. Don't try to teach too many words at once, and be careful to repeat words many times until they become familiar (Hickman-Davis, 2002).

11. Offer some short, easily repeated rhymes and songs each day so that the child can join in with the group without being self-conscious about speaking out on her own.

12. Be careful not to overwhelm the child with attention. Too much pressure is as bad as no attention at all.

13. Encourage other children to include the newcomer in their play. Explain that he needs special help; encourage them to name things for her as they use them (Hickman-Davis, 2002).

14. And, finally, be aware yourself of how limited you feel because you speak only one or perhaps two languages. Encourage the child's family to help her retain her ability to be (ultimately) bilingual. In this way she will always retain the advantage we might lack—the advantage of being able to communicate in two languages.

Figure 12.1
Suggestions to foster communication with a child who speaks little or no English

child to learn Standard American English because many African American families as well as teachers agree it is a valuable tool for the child to possess.

This ability to switch from one form of English or even from one style of address to another is termed *code switching*. It may turn out that the most desirable skill to teach children is facility in being able to shift from one dialect to another as the situation warrants, just as speakers of Spanish, German, or French learn to code-switch from their language to English to make themselves understood (ASHA, 2004a; Connor & Craig, 2006). While acquiring this skill, it is hoped that children have the opportunity to learn Standard American English in an atmosphere that values and appreciates their already present linguistic strengths, rather than in one that smacks of disrespect.

CHILDREN WHO HAVE SPECIAL DISABILITIES RELATED TO SPEECH AND HEARING

Several kinds of speech and hearing disabilities are seen quite commonly in early childhood. Indeed, the teacher may be the first person to be aware that the child has a speech problem, because the family may be too accustomed to it to notice or too inexperienced to identify it as deviating markedly from normal speech. Speech and language disorders can affect the way children talk, understand, analyze, or process information. An estimated 6 million children under the age of 18 have a speech or language disorder, and boys make up two thirds of this population (ASHA, 2004b). The four problems the teacher is most likely to come across are articulation disorders, delayed speech, hearing disorders, and stuttering.

With all these conditions, if the difficulty is pronounced or continues without positive change for 2 or 3 months after the child enters the center, the teacher should discuss the problem with the family and encourage them to seek professional evaluation and help. Such referrals usually require both time (for the family to become used to the idea that their child needs extra help) and tact (so that they do not feel blamed or accused of neglecting the child). (For more information on how to make a successful referral, refer to chapter 5.)

What are some appropriate referral resources for such children? Colleges and universities often maintain speech and hearing clinics supervised by highly trained professionals. Moreover, often little or no cost is involved because the clinics also serve as training experiences for beginning speech clinicians. Children's hospitals usually have speech clinicians on their staffs, and public schools almost always have a speech therapist available. These people are always glad to suggest appropriate referrals for speech therapy if the youngster does not qualify for help directly from the hospital or school. The American Speech-Language-Hearing Association can also help with referral information (see Related Organizations and Online Resources).

Children with Disorders of Articulation

The teacher's problem with articulation disorders is deciding which ones are serious and which ones should be overlooked. To make this decision, the most important thing the teacher must know is that children do not acquire accuracy in pronouncing certain sounds until they are in the first or second grade. At the preschool level, therefore, many distortions, substitutions, and omissions can be treated with a combination of auditory training and benign neglect. *Referral is warranted, however, when the child's speech is generally unintelligible and the child is older than 3 or 3-1/2*, because it is probable that special help from a professionally trained clinician will be needed to learn to speak more plainly.

Besides knowing when to refer and when to overlook the articulation disorder, the teacher should realize there is a lot more to correcting an articulation problem than just reminding the child, "Don't say 'wed,' say 'red.'" Traditional speech therapists usually proceed by (a) using auditory discrimination games to help the child hear the error and tell it apart from other sounds, (b) eliminating the cause of the disorder if possible (e.g., encouraging the parents to raise their speech standards at home so that the child no longer gets by with infantile speech patterns), (c) teaching the child to make the correct sound by itself, and (d) finally incorporating it into familiar words.

The problem with this kind of isolated work is getting it to carry over into everyday speech. To make carryover more likely, newer approaches are coming into use (Justice, 2004). Rather than pulling children out of their usual environment, taking them off to a quiet place, providing isolated practice in particular skills, and then restoring them to the classroom, these therapists work right in the classroom along with the regular staff. They do their best to seize opportunities for meaningful practice that occur as the child is involved in ongoing activities. This procedure means not only that the needed language skill is integrated into the child's ordinary life but also that the staff has the chance to observe and learn how to provide continued practice in those skills when the therapist is not present (Justice, 2004). (Refer to chapter 5 for a more detailed discussion of how this interdisciplinary approach works.)

It is in this regard that the child's teacher can be the most help—not by nagging the child but by encouraging conversation. During such talk an occasional puzzled look of not understanding what the child is saying followed by pleased comprehension if the child repeats the word more clearly will encourage better articulation habits. Of course, all the children will benefit from consistent auditory discrimination activities included in group time, just as they will from the many other means of developing language ability discussed earlier in this chapter.

Children with Delayed Speech

Although articulation disorders are encountered with greater frequency, the teacher is more likely to notice the child who does not talk or who talks very little. Such children are often referred to preschools and children's centers by pediatricians and in certain cases can be helped effectively by that teacher.

Causes of Delayed Speech

Causes of delayed speech are many and range from the child's being hard of hearing to having a neuromuscular disorder such as cerebral palsy. Low intelligence is another common cause of delayed speech; being unfamiliar with Standard American English and negativism or extreme shyness also take their toll (ASHA, 2004b; Horton-Ikard, 2006; Jalongo, 2008). Lack of sufficient environmental stimulation or low parental expectations may also mean a child has not developed to full verbal potential (Moore & Barbarin, 2003).

In such cases the teacher needs to take a deep, continuing look at the child to try to determine what lies behind the lack of speech. Making a home visit can help ascertain whether the child just does not talk at school or whether the nonverbal behavior is consistent in all situations. Using standardized means of language assessment when the child does not speak Standard American English at home will yield inaccurate re-sults. Communication with the family is essential for determining the child's language development (Horton-Ikard, 2006).

It is often difficult or impossible for someone who is not specially trained to spot the cause of lags in speech development. There have been instances in which children with mild or even moderate cognitive delays were denied help and appropriate teaching be-cause the cardinal symptom of delayed speech went unquestioned by an inexperienced teacher because the child "looked normal." The services of a competent psychologist can be enlisted to identify the slow learner. Neuromuscular disorders do not always manifest themselves in obvious ways either; so when such a condition appears to be a likely possibility, a referral to the child's pediatrician is a sound approach to take.

Children who restrict themselves from talking because they are overwhelmed by the newness of school, who speak a different language, or who do not talk because they appear to have been deprived of sufficient speech stimulation or too low expec-tations at home are the ones with the brightest prognosis. In these cases the teacher can gently draw them forth and elicit more speech by responding positively to their venturings. Many of these children will make a heartening gain in fluency during the year or two they spend at school if the methods described in the previous section on developing language skills are applied to them, especially when teachers work with the child's family, too (Horton-Ikard, 2006; Jalongo, 2008; Kirmani, 2007; Moore & Barbarin, 2003).

Children with Disorders of Hearing

Another useful way teachers can help the children in their care is to be on the look-out for those who do not hear well. This is a surprisingly common disorder, yet it often goes by unnoticed.

Studies show that as many as *one out of every three young children has some form of hear-ing loss* and more than 80% of children suffer an ear infection by age 3 (Jalongo, 2008; Schering-Plough Corporation & *Scholastic Early Childhood Today*, n.d.). Ironically, the most common kind of loss, a conductive hearing loss resulting from trouble in the mid-dle ear and often the result of infection, is not usually picked up in screening tests; thus many children who have had their hearing tested slip through the testing screen with this disability not identified. This is particularly unfortunate because middle-ear-type losses account for about 90% of all hearing losses in children and are also most amenable to cure or correction once detected. For these reasons it is important to educate families that they should request a test for conductive hearing loss called a *tympanometric test*, as well as a pure tone audiometer test, when having their children's hearing evaluated.

Children attending centers are particularly likely to get these middle-ear infections (*otitis media*) because they are exposed to more colds and upper respiratory diseases, which often lead to infections and loss of hearing acuity in the middle ear. If left un-treated, these infections can last for months and make a real difference in how well children hear and ultimately in how clearly they speak. Families tend to adjust to this condition without realizing their children's hearing has diminished, so it is particu-larly important for teachers to be alert to the sometimes rather subtle symptoms of hearing loss.

The following behaviors or conditions should alert the teacher to the possibility that a child may be hard of hearing:

- The child who does not talk
- The child who watches you intently but often "just doesn't seem to understand"
- The child who does not respond or turn around when the teacher speaks in a normal tone of voice from behind the child
- The child who consistently pays little attention during story hour or who always wants to sit right in front of the teacher
- The child whose speech is indistinct and difficult to understand, most particularly if high-frequency sounds such as *f* and *s* are missing from the child's speech
- The child who talks more softly or loudly than most of the other children
- The child whose attention you have to catch by a touch on the shoulder
- The child who often asks you to repeat sentences or says "Huh?" a lot
- The child who has a perpetual cold, runny nose, frequent earaches, or usually breathes through the mouth
- The child who consistently ignores you unless you get right down and make direct eye contact as you talk
- Any child who has recently recovered from measles, meningitis, scarlet fever, or a severe head injury

Such children are prime candidates for audiometric testing. Of course, it is also true that children talk indistinctly, want to sit close to the teacher, or fail to pay attention for reasons other than hearing loss. But *particularly if more than one of these symptoms describe the child's usual behavior,* the possibility of a hearing deficit is worth investigating. Referrals may be made to an otolaryngologist (a doctor who treats ear and throat disorders) or to the pediatrician, who will send the child to the best place to receive help.

Hearing losses can result from many causes besides otitis media. Sometimes the loss can be remedied through surgery; but if the loss is permanent, continued professional guidance will be necessary. Although hearing aids do not alleviate all forms of deafness, they can be effective in many cases. Hearing aids combined with speech therapy and auditory training are helpful for many children who have loss of hearing.

Children Who Stutter

Although we do know that an easy, unself-conscious form of repetitive speech is often observed in children under age 5, we do not yet understand why this should be the case. This first stage of repetitive speech differs markedly from the strained, emotion-laden hesitancies and repetitions of the confirmed stutterer and is likely to vanish *if teachers and family do not react to it with concern and tension.*

Teachers can play an effective role in helping families deal with their concern over this potential problem. First, they should encourage families to relax and not to direct attention to the behavior. This includes *not* saying to the child, "Now, just slow down; I'll wait 'til you're ready," or, "Don't talk so fast," or, "Your ideas just get ahead of your tongue; take it easy" (Ainsworth & Fraser, 2002; ASHA, 2004d). They should also reassure the family by explaining that this behavior is common in young children who are undergoing the stress of learning to talk. The goal here is to encourage parents to relax and reduce stressful situations in the home so that children will not become concerned about their speech.

Since stuttering increases when children are undergoing stress, it can be helpful to avoid hurrying them when possible, to allow plenty of time for them to speak, to speak a little slowly when carrying on conversations with them, to provide them your full but relaxed attention when they speak to you, and to avoid putting them on the spot by asking direct questions or by urging them to talk in front of others during group time (Ainsworth & Fraser, 2002; ASHA, 2004d).

It is also wise to inquire of the family whether something is currently making life more difficult for the child at home. Do what you can to relieve that situation. Tension-relieving activities such as dramatic play, water play, and various forms of sublimated aggressive activities can be provided that may reduce some of the child's tensions and attendant stuttering.

As with other speech disorders, it is also necessary to have some rule of thumb for referral when working with a child who stutters. It seems wise to refer the family for further help if they are reacting strongly to the behavior and are unable to control their signs of concern, if they seem unable to reduce the tension-generating situations without outside help, or if the stuttering persists. The Stuttering Foundation of America, listed in Related Organizations and Online Resources, can help to determine if a referral is in order.

SUMMARY

The development of language skills in young children has become of cardinal interest to their teachers as evidence mounts that linguistic competence and mental ability go hand in hand.

Children appear to acquire language partially as a result of an inborn ability to do so and partially in response to environmental stimulation and conditioning. Much remains to be learned in this area, and a complete explanation of how language is acquired remains one of the tantalizing mysteries of human development.

In recent years the science of pragmatics, which stresses the interactional importance of the social and developmental aspects of language acquisition, has come increasingly to the fore. In this area studies relating to the way children learn to use conversation have been of particular interest to early childhood teachers.

Teachers of young children can do many things to facilitate children's language acquisition:

- Listen carefully to what children have to say.
- Provide a meaningful base of experience to talk about.
- Encourage conversation among children.
- Talk to the children themselves.

- Use questions to generate speech and develop language.
- When necessary, seek professional assistance for children who require it.

In this chapter the questions of bilingualism and the use of African American English in school were also discussed, and some suggestions were included about teaching English as a second language.

Finally, four common disorders of speech and hearing were identified: disorders of articulation, delayed speech, deficient hearing, and stuttering. Recommendations were made for classroom treatment and remediation of these disorders, and suggestions for referral were included.

Questions and Activities

1. Identify some factors in the school where you teach that encourage the development of conversation between children and adults. What are some things that discourage conversation between them?
2. List some additional conversation starters you have found useful in getting young children involved in talking with the teacher or with other children.
3. List some ways in which listening skills can be taught to young children.

Diversity Questions

1. Do you believe that teachers have the right to change something as personal as a child's dialect or dominant language? Under what circumstances do you think doing this is warranted or unwarranted?
2. Suppose you had a child in your room who did not speak any English. How could you help the child feel comfortable and gradually learn a second language?
3. The teacher in the room next door says to you, "I certainly admire you for taking that Spanish class so you can talk to Miguel and Angelica, but if I were you I wouldn't bother. After all, this is America, and if they want to be American, they'd better learn to talk English!" What would be your response?

Predicament

1. A mother calls and says her pediatrician has suggested that she place Talia in your center because she has been a little slow in learning to talk. As you become acquainted with Talia, it does appear to you that her speech is slow to develop. She is 3 years old and still communicates mainly by grunting, nodding her head, or pointing when she wants

something. List some possible reasons why her speech might be developing so slowly. How would you go about determining which cause is the most likely one? Propose a course of action that would be most appropriate for each probable cause.

Self-Check Questions for Review
Content-Related Questions

1. Describe three theories that attempt to explain the process by which children learn to talk.
2. List some important principles that teachers should remember for encouraging conversation between themselves and the children.
3. What are the four most common types of speech and language disorders in young children, and what might be the symptoms for each of these that the teacher should look for?

Integrative Questions

1. Which theory—the nativist or the behaviorist—offers more hope to a teacher who has a 3-year-old child in class who isn't talking yet? Explain why you selected that theory.
2. A friend has brought a nanny goat to visit your group of 4-year-olds at school and is milking her. Sarah Lee says, "Bubbles. See the bubbles!" Give an example of what you would reply if Sarah were 2-1/2 years old and how you would change your reply if she were 4 years old.

Reference for Further Reading

Weitzman, E., & Greenberg, J. (2002). *Learning language and loving it: A guide to promoting children's social and language development in early childhood settings* (2nd ed.). Toronto, Canada: Hanen Centre. This is a comprehensive guide to promoting children's social, language, and literacy development in children's centers.

Related Organizations and Online Resources

American Speech-Language-Hearing Association (ASHA). ASHA is the association for more than 115,000 language and hearing professionals. Many excellent resources about children's language development, African American English, bilingualism, intervention, and referrals for evaluation and professional assistance are at http://www.asha.org/public/speech/development/.

Center for Applied Linguistics (CAL). CAL has resources on English language learners, refugee integration, dialects, and foreign languages at http://www.cal.org/.

Stuttering Foundation. Free online resources, services, and support to those who stutter and their families are provided at http://www.stuttersfa.org/.

CHAPTER thirteen

Fostering the Emergence of Literacy

What to say when families suggest you teach the 4-year-olds to read?

What people are talking about when they mention *emergent literacy?*

When children should be able to read and write?

. . . IF YOU HAVE, THE MATERIAL ON THE FOLLOWING PAGES WILL HELP YOU.

Reading opens up marvelous vistas for those who possess sufficient skills . . . reading offers a gateway to ideas and information that have power to improve the self and world. Reading is magical. Reading can transport one to worlds unknown, reveal aspects of the inner self previously undiscovered, and raise possibilities unimagined.

Oscar A. Barbarin (2002, p. 1)

Stories are the first satisfying social context. We have a need in our brain from the beginning for activities that have the connection making that stories do. It reveals the natural scope of the imagination.

Vivian Paley (2004)

Children at every age possess certain literacy skills, although these skills are not fully developed or conventional, as we recognize mature reading and writing to be. Emergent literacy acknowledges as rudimentary writing a child's scribble marks on a page, even if not one letter is discernible. The child who knows the difference between such scribbles and drawings certainly has some sense of the difference between writing and illustration. Similarly, when a child narrates a familiar storybook while looking at the pictures and print and gives the impression of reading, we acknowledge the activity as legitimate literacy behavior.

Lesley M. Morrow (1997, p. 131)

A current concern of many preprimary teachers is the pressure some parents and school districts are putting on them to present a highly structured reading program in the preschool (Paulson et al., 2004; Strickland & Riley-Ayers, 2007). For those who teach kindergarten and in the early primary grades, the pressure is even greater as all children must be proficient at reading and writing in order to take the No Child Left Behind tests in third grade (Strickland & Riley-Ayers, 2007).

Such expectations are inappropriate for preschoolers and often result in overemphasis on testing—rather than understanding and true mastery—in the elementary grades (Bowman, 2002; McVicker, 2007; Neuman, Copple, & Bredekamp, 2000; Strickland & Riley-Ayers, 2007). However, rather than just deploring this pressure, it is wiser to understand what families (and, hence, school districts) want and then to understand how to reassure them while protecting the children from unreasonable expectations.

Families truly want what's best for their children. They see the world as a difficult place to grow up in, they see technology advancing at a frightening pace, and they want their children to be successful, competent grown-ups who can cope with that world. They know that intellectual competence is one key to effective functioning in that world, and they think of the ABCs and reading as being cognitive skills that will provide their children with that competence.

Teachers should conduct a careful educational campaign with the children's families to inform them about what the children are learning at the early childhood center. The teachers should explain that what they are doing *is* appropriate for the children's ages and developmental stages and that it paves the way for learning to read more easily later on. Several organizations offer free resources that can be used to help educate and involve families in your center's early literacy program (see Related Organizations and Online Resources at the end of this chapter).

Part of this information will inevitably involve explaining how children learn from play; all the benefits children derive from being involved in such school activities as blocks, sand, and water; and how they help form the foundation upon which later skills are built (Copple & Bredekamp, 2009; Elkind, 2007; Epstein, 2007; Kalmar, 2008; McVicker, 2007; National Research Council and Institute of Medicine, 2000). But it should also include clear-cut descriptions of the various reasoning and problem-solving skills that are incorporated into the curriculum each day, accompanied by explanations of how these abilities underlie later competence in school. These skills are discussed in detail in chapter 14.

In addition to these explanations, the teacher needs to add information about all the language development activities that are part of a good early childhood curriculum. It is important to emphasize that these activities construct the foundation upon which reading is later built (refer to chapter 12). These range from learning new words to telling a coherent story about what happened on the way to school. They include using language in conversation or using it to make the child's desires known, as well as learning that books can be a source of fascinating pleasure at group time (Bowman, 2002; Epstein, 2007; Jalongo, 2004, 2008; Kalmar, 2008; McVicker, 2007; Neuman et al., 2000; Rosenquest, 2002; Strickland & Riley-Ayers, 2007).

Activities such as these form the foundation for later reading and writing. Families need to understand that learning to read is a lengthy process and that much preparation and maturation must take place before it can be accomplished successfully (Epstein, 2007; Fields, Groth, & Spangler, 2004; Jalongo, 2008; Lawhon & Cobb, 2002; McVicker, 2007; Neuman et al., 2000; Rosenquest, 2002; Strickland & Riley-Ayers, 2007). Once families realize the teachers know what they are doing and that they are "really teaching the children something" that will form a solid foundation for later learning at the elementary school level, they generally stop asking about reading per se and become supportive of what is provided at the school.

Elementary school teachers need also to communicate with families about the literacy curriculum. One of the major goals of the No Child Left Behind Act is to inform families about their child's reading and writing skills. Teachers must assure parents that their children are developing the necessary skills to succeed in school and in the larger culture as they mature into adulthood. The importance of literacy skills cannot be undervalued in children's development because the child's ability to read and write will greatly affect success in school (Bowman, 2002; Jalongo, 2008; Strickland & Riley-Ayers, 2007). Researchers estimate between 20% and 45% of children in the United States have difficulty learning to read (Iaquinta, 2006), and we must work diligently to give each child in our class successful experiences in literacy development.

An excellent way to inform families of the educational value of your program—particularly with regard to literacy development—is by practicing a technique developed in Reggio Emilia called "documentation." According to an American teacher who has adapted the Reggio approach to her kindergarten classroom, Pam Oken-Wright (2001), "Documentation allows us to look at children's thinking through their representation, conversation, and play" (p. 5).

There are many ways to document children's thinking—from taking photographs to displaying the children's own creations such as drawings or sculptures, in addition to writing down verbatim what the children say. When this documentation is then attractively displayed in the classroom, the children can "revisit" their thoughts and perhaps revise them. In addition, the richness of children's learning becomes visible to their families in a very effective and meaningful way. By displaying children's conversations and words, a print-rich environment is created and it is especially powerful because it is the language and thinking that come directly from the children (Edwards, Gandini, & Forman, 1993, 1998; Fu, Stremmel, & Hill, 2002; Gandini, Hill, Cadwell, & Schwall, 2005; Hendrick, 1997, 2004; Tarini, 1993; Wien, 2008).

According to Oken-Wright, tape-recording, transcribing, and displaying children's words and creative work has a strong effect on both children and families:

> Through our documentation of their play, conversation, and representation, children understand that teachers value their work. . . . I have found that through documentation, parents' investment in the program grows. . . . Through documenting, we assure that no child is invisible. . . . The process of documentation feeds the collaborative effort between home and school. (2001, p. 6)

The process of documentation is far more extensive than what could be discussed here. The beginning teacher is encouraged to explore the Reggio texts further, such as the Reggio classic, *The Hundred Languages of Children* by Edwards et al. (1993, 1998) or *First Steps Toward Teaching the Reggio Way* by Hendrick (1997). In the meantime, teachers can begin by simply writing down the children's words—exactly as they say them, while they are playing or engaged in an activity. They can then read them back to the children, revise as necessary, and finally, display them in the classroom for others—including the children's families—to view. It will become apparent how much power is there when children find their voice and also find that their voices are heard.

WHAT IS THE DIFFERENCE BETWEEN FOSTERING EMERGENT LITERACY AND TEACHING CHILDREN TO READ AND WRITE?

From one point of view it is unnecessary to discuss implementing literacy in the early childhood classroom since children have been doing it for years, anyway! For example, every time a child singles out his name tag and puts it on, or finds the book he has been hunting for, or supplies the phrase the gingerbread boy says as he runs from his potential captors, or counts the number of spoonfuls needed pictured on a recipe card, the child is using literacy-related skills. Every time a child substitutes a pretend spoon for a real one, or tells what's happening in a picture, or uses language in any form, then, too, he is engaged in emerging literacy activities because all these activities and hundreds like them are examples of the array of skills that underlie the ultimate skills of reading and writing (Epstein, 2007; McVicker, 2007; Neuman et al., 2000; Paulson et al., 2004; Strickland, 2006; Strickland & Riley-Ayers, 2007).

This understanding of what constitutes true literacy makes it clear that its development entails far more than learning skills such as handwriting, decoding the printed word, and spelling. Paulson et al. (2004) point out:

> Early literacy refers to behaviors seen in very young children, typically 2- to 3-year-olds, as they attempt reading and writing acts without the awareness or understanding of letter-sound relationships. Emerging literacy refers to behaviors observed in 4- to 5-year-old children when an awareness and understanding of letter-sound relationships begin to develop. (p. 169)

Sojin Yi

Early literacy refers to the behaviors seen in very young children as they attempt reading and writing acts without the awareness or understanding of letter-sound relationships.

However, *emergent literacy* does *not* mean we are going to teach the children to read—far from it. Research has shown time and time again that the arts of reading and writing (for the two must go together) rely on the prior acquisition of a great many foundation concepts and strategies—strategies that teachers of young children have been encouraging children to develop for many years. Figure 13.1 lists many activities that are basic to helping children develop literacy. Note that all of them are frequently part of the early childhood curriculum. In sum, we support young children's literacy abilities when we allow them "opportunities to see, share, act, sing, classify, observe, make decisions, develop sequencing skills, recognize and understand relationships, read and tell stories, interact, talk, listen, and play" (Lawhon & Cobb, 2002, p. 113).

By the time children are in kindergarten, they typically understand that written symbols and print convey meaning and long to do so themselves. By the time they are in third grade they can read fluently and write expressively using different forms such as stories, poems, and reports. Figure 13.2 lists curriculum activities that support children's learning to read and write in the primary grades.

myeducationlab

Go to MyEducationLab and select the topic "Emergent Literacy and Language Arts." Under Activities and Applications, read the strategy *Emergent Literacy*. Consider how you can support children's emergent literacy.

---

1. Establish a language-rich atmosphere.

Model the art of good conversation with children, their families, and other adults. Discuss the children's ideas as they arise throughout the day. Ask children interesting questions; respond to them; build on their ideas and language. Engage children in language games, rhymes, riddles, and songs. Encourage dramatic play and the language that goes with it. Use daily classroom activities and routines to talk about words, such as asking what the words of a song or rhyme mean. Encourage all children to express their ideas and feelings with words.

2. Create a print-rich environment.

Provide pleasurable reading experiences throughout the day. Give children free access to many good books that suit their interests; change available books frequently. Write down children's words as they tell a story, make an artistic creation, or engage in dramatic play. Post children's words for families to read and discuss. Post labels and captions throughout the classroom. Print children's names on their cubbies, belongings, and work. Have children help create signs for the classroom and outdoors, such as, "Please close the gate."

3. Provide experiences that inspire children to talk.

Take the children on walks, scavenger hunts, and field trips. Introduce new vocabulary beforehand and discuss the events afterward. Provide plenty of opportunities for symbolic representation experiences, such as dramatic play with props, drawing, painting, clay, music, dance, and so forth.

4. Provide pressure-free opportunities to experiment with writing and reading.

Have plenty of markers, pencils, and types of paper available to the children every day. Support and discuss their drawing, scribbling, first attempts at writing, and invented spelling. Ask children to "read" their own work or books from memory. Provide clues when they read text. Help them match print to spoken words.

5. Involve the children's families in literacy development activities.

Invite family members to come in to read a book to the children or take dictation. Encourage families to model a love of language and reading. Lend books to families and talk about what they are reading to their child at home.

Figure 13.1
Teaching strategies to help children develop literacy

1. Promote listening.

- Provide a listening corner with playback equipment and headphones where children can listen to music, audio books, and their own self-created recordings (classroom sounds, birds outside, a field trip, their family at dinner, etc.).

- Ask children to conduct interviews (with other children, teachers, guest speakers, their family members). Then have them summarize to another child what they learned.

- Play listening games (for example, "Telephone" where one child whispers a phrase to the next child, who whispers it to the next, until the very last child says aloud what he heard—usually *not* the original phrase).

- In small- or large-group time, ask children to explain their theories about an issue of concern or how things work or why things are. When there are differing opinions, encourage each child to explain his viewpoint more clearly.

2. Promote reading.

- Read daily to the children.

- Give children plenty of opportunities for independent reading practice.

- Create a literacy-rich environment with signs and words displayed throughout the classroom.

- Use a variety of reading sources: newspapers, computer programs, shopping lists, surveys of class opinions, books, magazines, dictionaries, a thesaurus, maps, and so forth.

- Communicate with families about reading; send reading materials home with the child to read with a family member.

- Use books and other reading materials as a basis for projects and creative expression. Have children act out favorite scenes or dress up as favorite characters, paint a mural of what the scenery would look like, and so forth.

3. Value writing.

- Provide a wide range of materials for writing and ample opportunity for practice.

- When a real-life situation presents itself, ask the children to use writing to communicate to others. For example, if something is needed in the classroom, ask the children to write a note to the principal or their families or the janitor.

- Have children keep tallies of things in the classroom and write lists.

- Have the children make their own labels and signs for the classroom.

- Create publishing activities such as books, newsletters, and maps to the classrooms. Provide realistic and quality materials for the children's publications.

- Incorporate writing into other activities. If there is an open house for families, have the children write invitations and make tickets for entrance.

Figure 13.2
Activities that support children's learning to read and write in the primary grades

SOME FUNDAMENTAL PRINCIPLES TO KEEP IN MIND

Encourage Families to Read to the Children at Home

When concerned families ask teachers, "When are the children really going to learn something?" what they often have in mind is the alphabet and similar skills. Rather than brushing aside these well-meant requests, it is more productive to think of them as providing a wonderful opportunity not only to explain the foundation reading skills incorporated in the curriculum but also to enlist the parents' cooperation in reading to their children at home. It is equally important that families of elementary school children also read to them at home on a regular basis. Research has shown that the single most important activity for enhancing literacy skills is reading aloud to children (Bowman, 2002; Dickinson & Tabors, 2002; Neuman et al., 2000; Paulson et al., 2004).

Admittedly getting parents to read to their children is not always easy to do. For reasons as varied as exhaustion and illiteracy, some children rarely or never see their parents read anything. A recent study showed that only 58% of children ages 3 to 5 years were read to on a daily basis by a family member (Ohl, 2002). This does not mean, however, that teachers should not do all they can to encourage reading at home; some families are always willing to "give it a try" once they understand how important it is to take an active part in their children's learning to read. Perhaps it is reading the funny papers to their child, or perhaps it is leafing through a picture book lent from school and talking about the pictures, or reading the directions on a lottery ticket. Just about anything that emphasizes the value of the written word is worth encouraging.

If the school provides a lending library of inexpensive, good-quality paperback picture books, the children's enthusiasm makes it likely these will go home to be enjoyed. Talking with families about finding a regular time to read to their children is also worth encouraging. Once this part of the program is going well, some of the families will be interested in learning how to make their book time even more effective by getting the child to comment about the book, too—and, the ultimate of ultimates, tell the story back to the parent. Offering a program on family night with a catchy title such as "Teaching Your Kids to Read—Let's Begin Now!" and demonstrating how to have fun with a book and engage the children in conversation makes it much easier to understand. The importance of encouraging home reading should not be underestimated. In one study, parents attended a series of four 1-hour workshops about reading, and their children's literacy skills improved significantly after 7 months (Sharif, Ozuah, Dinkevich, & Mulvihill, 2003). If your center or a family cannot afford to purchase books, contact the Reading Is Fundamental campaign listed in Related Organizations and Online Resources to see about their free book distribution program.

Teachers Should Make It Plain That They Value the Wonderful World of Books

Teachers can show that they value books if they clearly enjoy the good books they read aloud as much as the children do. There is no substitute for this infectious enthusiasm (Epstein, 2007; Jalongo, 2004; Neuman et al., 2000; Rosenquest, 2002).

Benjamin La Framboise

Every early childhood program must place a high value on books.

Teachers can also give children the opportunity to listen to books on their own by providing a cozy corner with audio books, the print version of the book, and a player with headsets.

Since children's literary and aesthetic tastes are being formed every time they come in contact with a book, it is important to select books with great care. There's really no excuse for offering children "cute" but essentially worthless books when all it takes is a trip to the library to find wonderful, beautifully illustrated ones. The high value the teacher places on good books is also shown in subtler ways by the care that everyone in the room takes of them. Books belong in people's laps or enjoyed in the rocking chair—not left on the floor to be trampled. Old favorites should be promptly mended and torn pages carefully taped with the children's help.

Teachers Should Emphasize How Useful the Written Word Can Be

As an example of how teachers can emphasize the usefulness of the written word, the shared experience of writing a note asking the janitor to leave up their block construction can make this usefulness obvious to the block builders. Empowering children by encouraging them to follow an illustrated recipe on their own provides the satisfaction of accomplishment for independent 4-year-olds. "You didn't even have to tell me nothin'!" chortled one of the youngsters in our center the other day. "I read it all!"—and he had. Labeling containers and activity areas also helps tie together the idea that written words stand for real objects.

Opportunities that encourage children to incorporate various forms of language into their play are yet another effective way to foster emerging literacy skills. For example, Strickland and Schickedanz (2004) suggest that the housekeeping corner could include a telephone book, cookbooks, coupons, marketing list materials, play money, and calendars, just to name a few possibilities. Office play could use envelopes, telephone message pads, magazines, and, of course, paper, pencils, an old typewriter or perhaps a computer, stamps, and a stamp pad.

EVEN VERY YOUNG CHILDREN CAN AND SHOULD BE INVOLVED IN PRODUCING THE WRITTEN WORD

It is helpful to think about children's writing from two aspects. The first aspect focuses on the children's attempts to write for themselves. The second is dictating what they want to say to someone else.

Writing on Their Own

A surprising number of children have little or no practice writing at home—because materials are not available, or parents do not realize beginning scribbles may be early attempts at writing, or they think pencils are dangerous, or they don't want the children to mark up walls, tables, or so forth.

Whatever the reason for the inexperience, the teacher who wants to encourage the link between spoken language and the printed page needs to provide many opportunities for children to "do writing" on their own. Having materials available for them to use, such as felt pens, crayons, soft pencils, interesting paper, and old envelopes, nicely sorted and attractively arranged, is essential.

Many schools set up a communication center where the children have their own mailboxes. Children can leave drawings, little gifts such as found flowers or stones, and their own "written" notes. A message center helps children develop an understanding of back-and-forth communication and the idea that there is a "writer" and a "reader." Through message center communications, valuable preliteracy skills are taught, developed, and practiced in a way children find fun and exciting. By empowering children to express their own feelings and ideas to others, they experience firsthand the social power of their words. That is the type of literacy learning that is so valuable to the child—and so important to convey to the families.

Just as essential as having materials consistently available is showing respect for the children's efforts. These efforts, of course, won't look like much to start with. Over time they will gradually advance through a series of steps progressing from wavy lines, dots, and scribbles all the way through to consistent, reasonably accurate printing in primary school (Epstein, 2007; Neuman et al., 2000; Strickland, 2006; Strickland & Riley-Ayers, 2007). Such comments as, "Look at all that writing you're working on!" and, "It looks to me like you're saying something there" [pause, expectant glance to see whether the child wants to tell you about it] will encourage the children to make further attempts.

Pam Oken-Wright

Respect the child's efforts at writing.

Writing in the Primary Grades

Opportunities for writing should be available to children throughout the day as well as during planned writing activities. Teachers can encourage children to use writing as a tool for thinking, learning, and communicating in a wide range of interesting ways—from writing their own name tags, to making invitations to the family potluck, to creating their own books. In addition to providing these sorts of activities, the elementary school teacher will assist children's learning by using the following strategies:

- Help children identify the sounds of letters and how the letters combine to make words.
- Introduce new words and teach children methods for sounding out and spelling unfamiliar words.
- Encourage children to share their writing with others—peers, school community, and family members.
- Teach children to distinguish and write in different forms: poems, stories, reports, shopping lists, charts, and so forth.
- Teach children how to proofread, revise, and edit their work.
- Use appropriate terms and model them for children, such as, "Now I am going to proofread this newsletter before I give it to your families."

- Begin to emphasize the importance of correct spelling in finished writing projects.
- Point out correct grammar.

Having Someone Write for Them

Another way children can experience turning language into written text is by dictating stories, letters, or ideas for the teacher to write down. Doing this emphasizes the relationship between reading and writing while empowering the child to express ideas more completely and freely.

When pursuing creative stories in early childhood, the teacher should be prepared for considerable literalness in stories by younger children and a greater use of fantasy and imagination by older ones. But since the stories are personal descriptions and reflections of the children's feelings and perceptions, they may also be considered self-expressive and hence creative.

The following two examples of dictated stories are both quite expressive of feelings. The first—illustrated with the artwork shown in Figure 13.3—is by an older child and demonstrates his use of fantasy, whereas the second shows the literalness common in younger preschoolers.

Tony the Robot

Tony the robot had chicken pox. Tony the robot and his friends went to the candy store. Tony the robot ate a red lollipop. When he ate it, a lot of the chicken pox went away. The next morning he woke up and said, "Hip hip hooray! I got no more chicken pox!"

Tony the robot had a baby robot. The baby was magic and he walked on clouds. If the baby robot was in a hurry, he had special bones to walk. He did *not* have wheels.

Figure 13.3
Tony the robot had chicken pox

My House Story

This first page will be about my dog. His name is Toulouse. Sometimes I can't play with him because he goes to dog school. At dog school, somebody makes him fetch sticks and makes him beg. Then he comes home and he shows me what he has learned. I also have a cat. His name is Goya, named after a painter. We always name our animals after painters.

Now about my grandmother and grandfather. My grandmother goes to Weight Watchers. They weigh her there without her shoes on.

Now about my grandfather. He drives a car. It's a red Datsun wagon pickup.

My house is white with a white picket fence. My grandma, grandpa, mommy, and me all live in the house.

My grandfather went to the hospital the day before yesterday. He had his operation yesterday. I don't like to have him in the hospital. He's not here to read me a bedtime story.

I miss him.

These stories mattered a lot to the children who wrote them. At that time the teachers were using little handmade books for recording the stories so that the children were free to illustrate them if they wished. This provided an additional way to work off their feelings and be creative. But it is not necessary to make storytelling that elaborate an occasion. Taking the story down as the child dictates it often provides sufficient encouragement for the young storyteller. Waiting until a child is either sitting quietly or playing alone and then saying, "Tell me a story. What would your story be about?" is a good way to get started. Of course, children sometimes do not want to participate. In this case the teacher just says, "Well, I expect you'll want to do it another time. I'll ask you then." Many teachers find children enjoy telling stories about the pictures they have just painted or drawn, or other creations they have made or are in the process of making, such as objects of play dough or clay.

As with other creative materials, the teacher should scrupulously avoid suggesting what the story should be about or what might happen next. But it does encourage the creator to ask, "Then what happened?" "Then what did he do?" or, "Do you want to tell me anything else?" These questions will help sweep the child along into the narrative.

to MyEducationLab and select the topic "Emergent Literacy and Language Arts." Under Activities and Applications, watch the video *Literacy*. Notice the many ways teachers support children's literacy learning and use strategies that are appropriate for the children's developmental levels.

Having children "revisit" their work from an earlier time can also extend their interest and creativity. Young children may not string a lengthy story together in one sitting. Going back to what the child started a day or two earlier and asking if there is anything to add on or change can inspire further ideas.

Creative stories can also be stimulated by providing hand puppets or flannel board materials, which can be set out for the children to use as they feel the need or used at group time for this purpose. Rubber dolls and toy animals offer another medium for imaginative stories and play. Creative stories can also be stimulated by providing pictures, which may be used as starting points for discussion.

Besides dictating and telling stories, children can learn to value written language by chanting, "I think I can, I think I can, I think I can," as the teacher points to the words while reading the beloved *Little Engine That Could* (Piper, 1980). They can listen as the teacher reads aloud to them the note that is being sent home to their families, and they can mail their letters at the post office before Valentine's Day. If attractive writing materials are assembled in a convenient spot, the children can elaborate on their scribbles and enclose the messages in old envelopes.

Writing the story down as the child dictates is a wonderful way to encourage the young storyteller.

Although these literacy activities and others like them should be spread throughout the curriculum, just as *whole language* is integrated into the curriculum of many elementary schools, there is one particular experience during the day that provides an outstanding opportunity to foster emergent literacy. This is the experience of group time.

SUGGESTIONS FOR PRESENTING A LANGUAGE-RICH GROUP-TIME EXPERIENCE

A well-planned group time can be a high spot of the day for teachers and children, or it can become a dreaded encounter between them as the children thrash about and the teacher struggles to maintain a semblance of order.

Successful group times depend on careful advance planning by the teacher that takes into consideration such things as including enough variety, making certain the material is interesting, providing opportunities for the children to interact with the teacher, and knowing how to pace activities so that they sustain the children's interest. The primary goal, of course, is to provide wonderfully enriching opportunities for the use of language and the development of emergent literacy.

Include a Variety of Activities

Of course, books, particularly nonsexist and multicultural ones, are an essential ingredient of group time, but it is a pity to restrict this potentially rich language experience to only a book and, if luck is with us, a song, when the group can do together so many other interesting language-related activities. Poetry, fingerplays, auditory discrimination skills activities, and chances for discussions that involve problem solving, thinking, and reasoning skills are additional activities that merit inclusion at least once a week, and more often than that, if possible.

Some Specific Suggestions About Materials to Include

Do Include a Book and Poetry

The selection of a fine children's book is usually the best place to begin when planning the time together, and many good lists of books are available (Norton, 2003). Poetry should also be offered on a daily basis. Like the books, this should be good-quality poetry, rather than the nondescript examples generally included in so-called activity books.

Music and Fingerplays Are Important, Too

Singing has its merits because it fosters language, memory, musical development, and pleasure. It takes a good deal of repetition for children to learn a new song; teachers should be prepared to sing one or two verses with them three or four times and then repeat the same song for several group times so that children can learn it well enough to sing it with verve.

Fingerplays are another fine ingredient to include during groups. Again, experience has shown that 2- and 3-year-olds are likely to be able to do just the actions at first and then later will add the words. But you should not be discouraged. If you persevere long enough, keep the pace slow enough, and keep the material brief enough, then they will eventually be able to put words and actions together, which they love to do.

Auditory Training Should Also Be Provided

A well-planned group time includes at least two additional kinds of activities besides those previously listed. The first of these is some activity that provides for auditory training and discrimination. Sometimes this can be included as part of a fingerplay or poem, and sometimes it needs to be a special activity. Children need work on learning to tell sounds apart and to tell when they are the same, and group time provides a fine chance to practice this skill. It is a valuable activity since it may be a helpful introduction to phonics, and it is definitely helpful for teaching children to discriminate among sounds so that they speak more clearly.

Perhaps during a song they could sing as loud as they can and then as soft as they can; or listen to high and low notes on the autoharp, standing up when they hear a high one, and sitting down when they hear a low one; or perhaps half the children can clap their hands when they hear the sound "eee" and the other half listen for "iii."

Some other examples of activities include matching the sounds of shakers, some of which have been filled with sand, some with beans, and some with rice; everyone shutting their eyes and opening them when a particular sound is heard; listening for words left out of familiar nursery rhymes; or having the children signal when they hear sentences that do not make sense, such as "When I went to the market, I bought a camelope"—a game that appeals strongly to 4-year-olds.

Group Time Is an Ideal Time to Provide Practice in Cognitive Skills

The second kind of activity that should be but is only rarely included in group time is one that provides practice in thinking and reasoning (such activities are described in more detail in chapter 14). These include practice in the midlevel mental ability skills, such as matching and temporal ordering, and also practice in the higher level skills of talking problems over and discussing how the group might solve them. Offering these activities during group time ensures that all the children are receiving practice in these vital skills.

One way to encourage the development of cognitive skills in group time is to ask open-ended questions. By asking questions that don't require a specific response, the teacher must *really listen* to the children and thereby learn what they are thinking—not whether they can recite back the "correct" answer (Bardige & Segal, 2004; Jalongo, 2008; Kalmar, 2008; Rinaldi, 2002). In contrast, a sure way to squelch creative thought and expression in young children is to lecture them on a topic and then drill them with questions to which the teacher already knows the answers. "Open-ended questions . . . invite conversation. We ask them because we really want to know the answers" (Bardige & Segal, 2004, p. 17).

In group time it is important to maintain an openness to the children's ideas—as opposed to trying to control and directly "teach" them. Notice what happens in the two different styles of teacher questioning:

Example of Close-Ended Questioning

Child: We got a new puppy yesterday.
Teacher: What's your puppy's name?
Child: Snoopy.
Teacher: Is Snoopy a boy or a girl?
Child: A girl.
Teacher: What color is Snoopy?
Child: Black and white.
Teacher: What kind of dog is it?
Child: I dunno.

Example of Open-Ended Questioning

Child: We got a new puppy yesterday.
Teacher: How did you get the puppy?
Child: Daddy took me to that place where they have pets that get lost.
Teacher: Yeah, the pound. They have lots of pets there. How did you decide which one to get?
Child: . . . Snoopy was the cutest. And she liked me!
Teacher: I bet she liked you. How did you know? What did she do?
Child: She kept wagging her tail and running around her cage. When they let her out, she climbed in my lap and licked my face! (Bardige & Segal, 2004, p. 18)

These two examples illustrate that if the teacher wants to encourage the emerging literacy skills of storyline and vocabulary development, it is necessary to ask open-ended questions. Indeed, research supports this, showing that when teachers use more suggestions, open-ended questions, and elaborative statements with children, the children exhibit higher levels of social, language, and cognitive competence (Wilcox-Herzog & Ward, 2004).

Group Time Should Provide Multiracial, Nonsexist Subject Matter

Two additional ingredients should also be woven into group time. Every group should contain some multiethnic or nonsexist material, or both, and conversely should not contain material that is sexist or racist. This means the teacher will have to appraise carefully the material in songs, books, and poetry before presenting them and either discard those that possess objectionable material or draw it to the children's attention and discuss it.

For example, if the teacher chooses to read a book about going to the hospital, where all the doctors are White males and the nurses White females, a discussion should ensue about whether there are female doctors and male nurses and whether only White people can work at such jobs. Figure 13.4 offers additional suggestions for teachers in selecting multicultural and nonsexist books.

1. Analyze the content.

- Select stories that include a variety of cultures and different family compositions. Look for books that include grandparents, single parents, and extended families.

- Make sure minority characters are represented and that it is in a positive way.

- Avoid books that perpetuate stereotypes.

- Check for accuracy—especially in nonfiction.

- Look beyond who the main characters are. In a study of multicultural children's literature, Mendoza and Reese (2001) found Mexican main characters who lied to get work and who pushed others out of the way to get work.

2. Analyze the illustrations.

- Choose books with illustrations that depict people from different races in positive ways. Look for accurate, respectful depictions of characteristics. Avoid stereotypical caricatures of physical features.

- Screen for stereotypes: oversimplified generalizations (usually negative but not always) about a group, race, or sex.

- Screen for tokenism. If there are ethnically or racially diverse characters, make sure they have other than a supporting role for the White characters and are depicted accurately (i.e., with identifying features, not simply shaded a different color to indicate race).

3. Analyze the characters.

- Look at who is doing what. Who is active and who is passive? Who has power and who is subservient?

- Are characters who are outside of the mainstream culture depicted in a positive way or are they belittled?

- Who is a hero or heroine and what characteristics do they possess?

- Who is successful and what does it take to be successful?

4. Analyze the overall effect.

- Imagine you are the children in your class. How do you think the book would affect their self-image?

- How will the girls relate to the story and characters? How about the boys? How about the African Americans, the Hispanics, the Asians, and others? How will non-White, female children feel when only White boys and men are depicted as virtuous, interesting, and powerful?

- Is there a positively depicted character in the story with whom a minority child can identify?

5. Analyze the author and illustrator s background.

- Look at the biographical material. Are they of the group they are writing about and if not, what qualifies them to do so? Do they exhibit knowledge and sensitivity about the group they are depicting?

6. Screen for equity.

- Watch for insulting words, such as *lazy*, *weak*, *wily*, *backward*, and so forth.

- Watch for exclusionary or sexist language. Find books that use words like *firefighters* instead of *firemen* and books that speak of *parents* or *fathers* rather than only *mothers*.

Figure 13.4
Providing multicultural, nonsexist books

Management Suggestions to Help Group Time Go More Smoothly

It Is Always Wise to Plan More Activities Than You Are Likely to Use

Particularly for inexperienced teachers, it is difficult to know in advance which activities will go well and which will not. It is also difficult to estimate the amount of time a particular activity will absorb. So it is better to be safe and have extra reserves than to be caught short and run out of things to do. You can always use them next time.

Make Certain the Children Talk, Too

Include opportunities for children to respond to the teacher. During group time, children should be encouraged to think, reason, and guess (hypothesize) about what is being discussed: "What would you do if you were Peter and Mr. MacGregor chased you into the potting shed?" "What *is* a potting shed, anyway?" "Do you think Peter was really sick when he got home?" "Was that the best punishment his mother could do, to put him to bed without dinner?" "What does *your* mother do when you're naughty?" and so forth. These opportunities for discussion are an invaluable part of the group experience.

Make Certain the Material Is Interesting

Part of the secret of making sure the material is interesting is to read the material first yourself. If you don't think it's interesting, it's a sure thing the children won't either. It helps a lot to select books the children genuinely enjoy. Unfortunately the world abounds in dull books designed to improve children's minds but not lift their spirits. When books full of charm and humor are selected, the teacher will enjoy them right along with the children, and they will arouse much comment and discussion from everyone. Remember that when a book is dull and the children are not interested, it is not necessary to read grimly through to its end; it is better simply to set it aside and go on to a more attractive choice.

Think, too, about how to present material so that it captures the children's attention. Using visual aids such as flannel boards helps, as does simply telling a story rather than

Leisa Maloney

For an exciting group time, have the children read aloud their own self-made books.

reading it (Trelease, 2001). Children are often absolutely enraptured by this activity, and telling stories lets the teacher look at the children all the time and be more responsive to them as they listen. Using a hand puppet also increases appeal (Neuman et al., 2000).

Another technique sure to provoke the children's interest is to have them read, demonstrate, or tell about their own work—and there can be no doubt about it being developmentally appropriate!

Keep the Tempo of Group Time Upbeat

Pace has a lot to do with sustaining interest. Some teachers are so nervous and afraid of losing control that they rush the children through the experience, ignoring children's comments and wiping out the potential richness of interchange between themselves and the children. A relaxed but definite tempo is a better pace to strive for to hold the children's attention while not making them feel harassed.

At the same time it is important not to drag things out. This is why it is deadly in a group to go all around in the circle and have each child say something. When this happens, attention lags among the other children and restlessness rises like a tide. Far better to include children spontaneously as the opportunity presents itself—a few adding suggestions to the story, others putting figures on the flannel board, and the entire group participating in a fingerplay.

Assess the difficulty of what the children will be learning, and present anything that is new or potentially difficult to understand *early* in the group time, while the children are still feeling rested. A new mental ability activity, for instance, should follow the opening songs, rather than come at the very end of the time together.

Opportunities for the group to move around a bit also provide a needed change of pace. Singing a song during which children get up and down answers the need for large-muscle activity, just as fingerplays about the "eensy weensy spider" harness the energy inherent in wiggly fingers.

Some Advice About Starting and Stopping

Start as soon as the children begin to gather, and quit while you're ahead. It is not necessary to wait until all the children have arrived to begin group activities. The children who have come promptly need something to do other than just sit and wait for stragglers. A good action song or fingerplay is a fine way to begin. It catches the group's attention and involves them immediately, and it is easy for latecomers to join in unobtrusively while this is going on. If such late arrivals are welcomed with a quick smile rather than a reproachful look, they will want to arrive more quickly next time.

Closing a group time well is equally important. Some teachers do this by ending with the same song every time to give the children a sense of finishing or completion. Children love the sense of ceremony this conveys. Others just anticipate its ending by saying something like "Well, we certainly did a lot of interesting things in group today, didn't we?" and then summarizing what was done. Still others just move smoothly into some sort of dismissal routine: "Everyone who is wearing blue jeans can go first today" (or everyone who has spotted socks, or who has freckles, or who ate oatmeal for breakfast). Children enjoy this sort of thing, and it has the advantage of not sending the entire herd off at once in a thundering way.

The most important points about finishing group time are that the children have a clear idea of what they are expected to do next and that group time ends before the youngsters are so exhausted that the experience has degenerated into a struggle to maintain order. *Finishing a group time while the children are still interested and attentive makes it more likely they will want to return because they recall group time as being a satisfying experience they enjoyed.*

What to Do About Undesirable Behavior

It is important for everyone's sanity that the material is geared to the age of the children. The younger the children, the shorter the books, poetry, and songs should be and the more opportunities should be provided for moving around. Whatever the age of the children, teachers must remain sensitive to the group—tuned in—so that they can sense when a shift of material is necessary to hold their attention.

To obtain maximum benefit from such experiences, groups should be kept as small as possible. Larger groups almost always produce problems because of lack of involvement and inattention. What typically happens is that assistant teachers spend their time admonishing some children, patting others on the back, and holding still other unwilling participants on their laps. A far better solution, when a second teacher is available, is to split the group in half so that each staff member works with a smaller number of children. Under these circumstances there can be a better balance between teacher-dominated activities and conversation and discussions, and the children will pay closer attention and develop their language skills more richly.

But these recommendations do not deal with the problem of what to do about the child who is punching a neighbor, rolling over and over on the floor, or continually drifting away from the group to play in the housekeeping area.

The teacher can deal with this situation in several ways. Making certain the material is interesting is the first thing to consider. Sometimes it is effective to have the disruptive youngster sit beside you as you read, turning the pages or doing other helpful things. Sometimes it is enough just to separate two children. Sometimes the behavior can be overlooked. And as a final resort sometimes the child loses the privilege of staying in the group and must be sent away. The problem with this method is that an adult really has to go with the child.

When a child has consistent difficulties enjoying group time, we should take a careful look at possible reasons within the child for this behavior because, if most of the children are enjoying the activity, there may be some special reason why this particular child is not. Possibilities to consider when this is the case include hearing and vision difficulties. These are common but frequently overlooked reasons for inattentiveness. The other common reason is immaturity. Perhaps the material being presented is above the child's level. Any of these conditions require sensitive discussion with the family, as well as special diagnosis by an appropriate professional person.

Try Breaking into Smaller Groups

This is a particularly effective strategy with children in elementary school but can also be used with preschoolers. For example, instead of the often disastrous and seemingly never-ending "show and tell" when each of 20 or so students speaks to the entire group, you can break into smaller groups. A couple days in advance, designate four or five children as sharers for the day. On their day, each sharer goes to a designated place in the room. Assign the rest of the children to a sharer and every so often, have the listeners change to another sharer. This method is described by teacher Kathleen Dailey:

> During the activity, the teacher can walk among the groups to observe children's interactions, or enter a sharing center as a participant and role model. The teacher can encourage language development and dialogue by asking open-ended questions. . . . (Jalongo, 2008, p. 81)

Breaking into smaller groups for guided reading is an effective strategy for elementary teachers. Because children are at different levels in their reading ability, it is a good idea to form groups of children who are at a similar place in their development and have them take turns reading aloud. The teacher moves from child to child and uses prompts and open-ended questions to further the child's learning. Children are also encouraged to ask questions and engage in discussion in their reading groups. In this way, each child's level of reading development is supported and children feel like they are part of a community of readers (Iaquinta, 2006).

Summary

The current approach to preparing children for learning the later skills of reading and writing is termed *emergent literacy*. This term includes the underlying concepts and strategies related to developing all aspects of literacy, whether written or oral. Literacy learning begins in infancy and continues throughout school.

This chapter stresses that teachers should make it plain they value good books and emphasize the usefulness of the written word by providing ways for children to use written literacy materials in their play, by writing down children's dictated stories, by encouraging older children to write themselves, and by including carefully planned group-time experiences. Group time presents a particularly rich opportunity for fostering emergent literacy, and the chapter includes practical suggestions for making that experience satisfying for both children and teachers.

Questions and Activities

1. Role-play a story hour in which the teacher seems to do everything possible to prevent the children from talking.
2. For the sake of variety and to extend your language-building skills with the children, resolve not to use books at all during group time for a month! What will you offer instead that will enhance the language abilities of the children? How will you make sure books are not forgotten in the curriculum?
3. Make up blank paper "books" and invite the children to dictate stories to you on any relevant subject. Many children will relish adding illustrations to these tales if they are encouraged to do so. Have older children create more complex books, including all the usual elements: cover,

acknowledgments, table of contents, and author's biography.

Diversity Question

1. In what ways do children's books support cultural diversity, and in what ways do they support cultural prejudices? Look at the books at your center and examine them for their cultural messages. What do you find?

Predicament

1. The father of a child in your group glows as he tells you his 3-year-old is so smart—he knows all his ABCs, and at home they are drilling him every night with flash cards to help him learn to read. What, if anything, do you think you should do about this?

Self-Check Questions for Review

Content-Related Questions

1. Give three examples of emergent literacy activities a preschooler might participate in with pleasure.
2. What are three fundamental principles for developing literacy that teachers should keep in mind?
3. Name three additional kinds of language activities besides songs and stories that should be regularly included in group time.
4. Discuss some possible ways teachers can reduce disruptive behavior during group time.

Integrative Questions

1. The teacher next door who works with 4-year-olds complains to you that the children keep interrupting during group time. Explain why you would or would not agree that this is undesirable behavior on the children's part.
2. Picture in your mind's eye one book you most enjoy reading to children. Propose three questions based on that book that would promote discussion between you and them.
3. Then, using that book as the central idea or theme, suggest a poem, an auditory discrimination activity, and a nonsexist or multicultural idea you could use along with the book during a group time for 3- or 4-year-olds. Now do the same thing for a group time with elementary school children.

Reference for Further Reading

Neuman, S. B., Copple, C., & Bredekamp, S. (2000). *Learning to read and write: Developmentally appropriate practices for young children*. Washington, DC: National Association for the Education of Young Children. This comprehensive book is essential reading for teachers of young children. It opens with the joint position statement on teaching children reading by the International Reading Association and the National Association for the Education of Young Children. It is packed full of research, theory, and practical teaching ideas related to literacy development.

Related Organizations and Online Resources

American Library Association. This is the oldest and largest library association in the world. Its mission is to promote the highest quality library and information services and public access to information. There is a good list of children's recommended books at http://www.ala.org/.

Children's Book Council (CBC). The CBC is a nonprofit trade organization dedicated to encouraging literacy and the use and enjoyment of children's books, and it is the official sponsor of Young People's Poetry Week and Children's Book Week each year. Information is available at http://www.cbcbooks.org/index.html.

International Reading Association (IRA). This organization was founded in 1956 as a professional organization of those involved in teaching reading to learners of all ages. There is an early literacy and children's special interest group as well as journals and many downloads available at http://www.reading.org.

National Council of Teachers of English (NCTE). The NCTE is devoted to improving the teaching and learning of English and language arts at all levels of education. Resources are available at http://www.ncte.org/.

Reading Is Fundamental (RIF). RIF prepares and motivates children to read by delivering free books and literacy resources to those children and families who need them most. Information can be found at http://www.rif.org/.

CHAPTER fourteen

Supporting the Development of the Cognitive Self

Why studying Piaget is so important?

What specific mental abilities the children could work on that lead to academic success?

How to include practice in these abilities and keep it fun, too?

. . . IF YOU HAVE, THE MATERIAL IN THE FOLLOWING PAGES WILL HELP YOU.

Children are impressive problem solvers. They are learning how to learn and learning the rules of the "reasoning game." Problem posing and problem solving are effective ways for children to express their inventiveness and integrate their learning. They develop mathematics, language, and creativity. And they build connections among these—the essence of learning to think inventively.

Douglas H. Clements and Julie Sarama (2006, p. 26)

Throughout the early years of life, children notice and explore mathematical dimensions of their world. They compare quantities, find patterns, navigate in space, and grapple with real problems such as balancing a tall block building or sharing a bowl of crackers fairly with a playmate. Mathematics helps children make sense of their world outside of school and helps them construct a solid foundation for success in school.

National Association for the Education of Young Children (NAEYC) and National Council of Teachers of Mathematics (NCTM) (2002, p. 1)

Mucking around in the dirt, picking up earthworms, and asking questions—that's how you learn science. Kids need to ask questions, realize some of the flaws, and make mistakes.

Paul Kuerbis (2004, p. 2)

317

The recent research on brain development indicates how important early experiences are on the child's growing mind and mental abilities (O'Hara, Demarest, & Shaklee, 2005; Schiller & Willis, 2008). As Yoon and Onchwari point out, "These studies emphasize developing effective early education programs because 'rich' experiences produce 'rich' brains" (2006, p. 419). Providing enriching and appropriate cognitive experiences for children is the teacher's mandate—both figuratively and literally as the No Child Left Behind Act requires testing of all public school third graders in their cognitive skills.

One of the most satisfying aspects of teaching is witnessing how the children's mental abilities flourish. Yet many teachers overlook this joy as pressures mount to get the children to perform well on tests or otherwise demonstrate (often to insistent families) just what "Little Einsteins" they are. Rather than developing problem-solving skills and creativity in thinking, many children are learning how to memorize, respond quickly to drill questions, and take tests (Copley, 2003; Neuman, 2006; Varol & Farran, 2006; West, 2007; Wien, 2008).

Research has shown that math and science concepts begin developing in infancy and throughout the early childhood years. Research has also shown that memorization, testing, and drills are the least effective ways to bolster children's burgeoning understandings. Deeper learning is fostered by concrete, hands-on experiences that are related to the children's lives and meaningful to them, the opportunity to experiment and form hypotheses, and ample time to try out their ideas through play (Clements & Sarama, 2006; Elkind, 2006; Epstein, 2007; NAEYC & NCTM, 2002; O'Hara et al., 2005; Schickedanz, 2008; West, 2007).

But play alone is not enough. "Significant benefits are more likely when teachers follow up by engaging children in reflecting on and representing the mathematical ideas that have emerged in their play. Teachers enhance children's mathematics learning when they ask questions that provoke clarifications, extensions, and development of new understandings" (NAEYC & NCTM, 2002, p. 11).

The early childhood teacher's task is not an easy one: meet school, state, and federal learning standards, provide appropriate and enriching cognitive experiences for the children, and really make sure they *are* learning—not just learning to ace tests! Fortunately, there is a wealth of theoretical knowledge born from centuries of practice in the classroom that can aid the novice teacher in planning curriculum to support the development of the child's cognitive self.

APPROACHES TO SUPPORTING THE DEVELOPMENT OF THE COGNITIVE SELF

Three very different approaches can be used in combination to ensure that children's mental abilities are enhanced in the early childhood program: the information approach, the conventional approach to midlevel mental abilities, and the emergent curriculum approach.

The information approach is what laypeople generally think of when they conjure up the image of a teacher standing in front of the class imparting knowledge to the "blank slates" that are the students. The information approach is used frequently in elementary schools when children learn from teacher-directed activities and then are tested to see if they have mastered the content. In early childhood education, the information approach is necessary when children learn specific types of knowledge that the adult is responsible for teaching, such as the meaning of a word or how to wash their hands properly after toileting or how to hold a pencil and make the correct lines to form the letter "A." These are not lessons that the child can learn through self-discovery and experimentation. Piaget maintained that some types of learning must be taught by direct social transmission—not only by hands-on experiences in the world. The information approach supports these types of necessary learning. The teacher need not shy away from this approach, although it should be used only when necessary and in conjunction with other approaches.

The conventional approach is important to include because it provides practice in certain midlevel mental abilities that underlie the development of later academic skills. Therefore, we need to understand what these skills are and why they are important. This approach is the focus of this chapter. The experiences for developing midlevel mental abilities are enhanced when embedded in emergent curriculum and this will be discussed at length in chapter 16.

Table 14.1 shows how the role of the teacher and child is quite different for each of the approaches, but this should not imply that one role should be selected and the other ignored. Skillful teachers combine the approaches to present a truly balanced curriculum for the children's cognitive selves.

The main difference between the conventional and the emergent approaches is the degree of responsibility assumed by the teacher. When a teacher is using the conventional approach to work on midlevel reasoning skills, the curriculum is predetermined to a greater extent by the teacher. Although experienced teachers also seize spontaneous opportunities for practicing specific abilities as these arise, the majority of the learning materials are typically generated in advance and presented to the children for their pleasure and practice as *faits accomplis*. For example, to provide practice in common relations the teacher might make up pairs of animals and their feet and ask the children which feet belong to the ducks, which to the robins, ostriches, and so on. The children are expected to apply the concept of common relations by pairing feet and animal bodies together, thereby obtaining practice in common relations and the mathematical concept of one-to-one correspondence (DeVries, Zan, Hildebrandt, Edmiaston, & Sales, 2002; Epstein, 2007; Hohmann & Weikart, 1995).

In contrast, when one is working with the emergent, problem-solving approach, the curriculum must be more fluid because the teacher cannot predict in advance what solutions the children may propose and what direction the investigatory pathway may take. Of course, *planning and direction remain necessary*, but they are done on a more ongoing basis. The result in the emergent approach is that learning becomes less teacher dominated and more of a mutual, collaborative experience as teacher and children share their ideas together (Gandini, Hill, Cadwell, & Schwall, 2005; Helm & Beneke, 2003; Helm, 2008; Helm & Katz, 2001; Hendrick, 1997, 2004; Jones & Nimmo, 1994; Katz & Chard, 2000; Wien, 2008; Wurm, 2005).

Table 14.1
A comparison of learning opportunities using the conventional or the emergent creative approach

	Information Approach	Emergent Constructivist Approach for Teaching Creative Thinking and Problem Solving	Conventional Approach for Teaching Midlevel Abilities
Value of approach	Provides information base needed as foundation for midlevel and problem-solving skills. Widens knowledge of world.	Allows children to develop full range of mental powers. Encourages application of prior knowledge to solving new problems. Empowers children to try out ideas and explain what they know to other children and adults.	Provides diversified practice in applying specific mental ability skills (concepts), which are valuable beginning literacy and beginning mathematical skills.
Examples of kinds of mental ability skills developed by approach	Pay attention. Process information. Retain information. Recall information. Reconstruct information.	Generate ideas on own. Form hypotheses (reasons) why something happens and try them out. Assess and evaluate possibilities. Pursue interests in depth.	Apply specific concepts such as matching, grouping, perceiving common relations, seriated and temporal ordering, cause-and-effect relationships, and conserving.
Teacher's role	Supply information to children and/or help them find information for themselves.	Listen to children; follow their lead to select pathway to investigate. Plan curriculum ahead but alter and adjust plans as pathways develop direction. Encourage generation of ideas by "provoking" children to consider problems and solve them. Develop opportunities with children to try out their ideas.	May use children as source to determine interest around which to build a theme. Plan ahead to think up and present activities and experiences for children that provide opportunities for practice and application of specific concepts.
Child's role	Soak up interesting information and store it in memory. Be able to recall, reconstruct, and repeat information when needed.	Collaborate (toss ball of ideas back and forth) with teacher to pursue interests. Think up ways to express ideas and solve problems. Try ideas out. Express ideas and what is found out through language, graphics, and child-constructed models.	Participate in learning activities provided by teacher, thereby practicing various midlevel mental ability skills. Acquire mental ability concepts and apply them by reasoning. Express what the child knows by manipulating teacher-provided materials.

When using the conventional approach, the teacher prepares activities in advance for the specific learnings she'd like the children to experience, such as charts that show the grouping of different ideas.

This chapter concentrates on developmentally appropriate ways to use the more conventional approach by presenting activities that provide practice in the midlevel reasoning skills. This curriculum approach is based on the work of Jean Piaget.

WHAT IS THE PIAGETIAN-BASED "CONVENTIONAL APPROACH" IN EARLY CHILDHOOD EDUCATION?

Basic Concepts of Piagetian Psychology

Although it is not within the scope of this book to attempt a comprehensive summary of Piaget's work, any discussion of the thought processes of young children must begin with at least a brief review of his work because he devoted a lifetime to studying the mental development and characteristics of young children (Piaget, 1926, 1950, 1962, 1963, 1965, 1983; Piaget & Inhelder, 1967, 1969). He was primarily interested in how people come to know what they know—the origins of knowledge—and his work has important implications for teachers interested in the cognitive development of the children in their care because he provided evidence that children really *do* think differently than adults do.

Many of Piaget's ideas are bound to sound both familiar and comfortable to the contemporary student since a good deal of what he said for 60 years has been practiced in nursery schools and child care centers during the same period and is similar in part to the philosophy of Dewey and Montessori (because of its emphasis on the value of experience). Although his own realm of investigation was primarily in the cognitive

myeducationlab

Go to MyEducationLab and select the topic "Curriculum/Program Models." Under Activities and Applications, watch the video *Supporting Inquiry in Early Childhood: Alec Learns to Use a Dropper.* Note how the teacher uses the conventional approach to plan activites to support the children's cognitive development.

area, Piaget agreed that affective, social, and cognitive components go hand in hand (Piaget, 1981; Wadsworth, 1989). Because these components are interdependent, it is evident that a school in which good mental health policies are practiced and sound social learning is encouraged will also be one in which mental growth is more likely to occur.

Piagetian Categories of Knowledge

Piaget theorized that children acquire three kinds of knowledge as they grow. *Social-conventional knowledge* is the first kind. This is information that society has agreed on and that is often learned through direct social transmission. For example, English-speaking people agree that the word *table* stands for a flat object supported by four legs. Rules that define what acceptable behavior is provide another example of socially transmitted knowledge.

The second kind of knowledge is *physical knowledge*. It is information children gain by acting on objects in the real world. Information about the quality of things and what they do are examples of physical knowledge.

The third kind of knowledge is less tangible because it cannot be directly observed. It is knowledge developed (constructed) in the mind as the child thinks about objects. Piaget called this *logico-mathematical knowledge*. The development of logico-mathematical thought, which we might also think of as being the ability to reason, ultimately enables children to develop ideas of relationships between objects. When they can grasp what it is that items in a group have in common, for instance, they are able to assign a common name to that group, thereby classifying or grouping the things together. For example, the children might divide a set of pictures, sorting them into things you can wear and things you can eat, and name the groups "clothing" and "food." This idea of a common property exists only in the mind. It is not inherent in the pictures themselves; it is an *idea*, not a physical property. It is important to remember that reasoning knowledge is closely tied to physical knowledge since reasoning usually requires a foundation of factual information, but it also differs from factual information.

This gradual development of logico-mathematical ability frees children from being tied to concrete experience because it enables them to think with symbols and to deal with abstractions. However, it takes many years for children to reach that level of maturity. To attain it, Piaget and colleagues identified a series of stages through which children must pass as they develop. These stages are outlined in Table 14.2.

Research conducted over a period of more than 60 years convinced Piaget that the order of the stages through which children progress cannot be changed, although the age at which the stage occurs may vary. He demonstrated this convincingly in his detailed reports of investigations in which he presented problems to children and then asked them questions about their answers.

Piagetian Stages of Development

Of greatest interest to early childhood teachers is the *preoperational stage*, which extends roughly from age 2 to age 7. During this stage children make the profound transition from depending on the way things appear to depending on logic and reasoning when making a decision. They become able to keep two ideas in their minds at once. In other words children acquire the ability to think back to the original starting point and at the same time compare it in their minds with a current situa-

Table 14.2
Summary of the Piagetian model

Basic Stages in Developing the Ability to Think Logically	Behavior Commonly Associated with the Stage
Sensorimotor Stage (0–2 years)* Understanding the present and real	Composed of six substages that move from reflex to intentional activity, involving cause-effect behavior. Involves direct interactions with the environment.
Preoperational Stage (2–7 years) Symbolic representation of the present and real Preparation for understanding concrete operations (this is a tremendous period of transition)	Overt action is transformed into mental action. Child uses signifiers: mental images, imitation, symbolic play, drawing, and language to deal with experience. Understands verbal communication. Uses play to assimilate reality into self. Believes what is seen; is "locked into" the perceptual world. Sees things from own point of view, only one way at a time ("centering"), and is learning to decenter. Thinking is not reversible. Intensely curious about the world. Busy laying foundations for understanding at the later concrete operational stage, which involves grasping concepts of *conservation, transitivity, classification, seriation,* and *reversibility.*
Concrete Operational Stage (7–11 years) Attainment of and organization of concrete operations Learns to apply logical thought to concrete problems	Has probably acquired the following concepts: *conservation, reversibility, transitivity, seriation,* and *classification;* that is, now believes that length, mass, weight, and number remain constant; understands relational terms such as *larger than* and *smaller than;* is able to arrange items in order from greatest amount to least amount; can group things according to more than one principle; can manipulate things in own mind, but these things are real objects. Becomes interested in following rules; games are important.
Formal Operational Stage (11–15 years) Hypothesis-making testing possible Masters logical reasoning	Age of abstract thinking; logical reasoning. Able to consider alternative possibilities and solutions. Can consider "fanciful," hypothetical possibilities as a basis for theoretical problem solving; abstract thinking, can make logical deductions and generalizations; can think about thinking.

*Note that the ages represent the *average* age of acquisition. This means that there is considerable variability in the time different children acquire the ability.

tion. Piaget called this mental operation *reversibility*, and it is a good example of what is meant when we say children are freed from concrete experience, since they perform this logico-mathematical reasoning process in their minds.

But young children in the preoperational stage do not possess this ability. Because they cannot consider two possibilities at once, they are unable to *conserve;* that is, they do not understand that quantity stays the same despite a change in appearance. This is because they cannot keep one idea in their minds while considering a second one. Thus they are likely to believe that a taller jar contains more water than a shorter jar does, even though they have previously been shown that the quantity was the same before pouring. For preoperational children, seeing is believing.

At this stage children may also have difficulty shifting objects into more than one kind of category (e.g., sorting according to size and then shifting to color), taking two attributes into account at the same time (e.g., sorting large pink circles and pink squares, small blue circles and blue squares into separate categories), or arranging a long series of graduated cylinders in regularly ascending order. Adults, however, no longer have difficulty grasping these concepts. This difference in the way children and adults think illustrates an important Piagetian principle: The thinking of children and adults differs in kind from each other. Children reason differently from the way adults do and thus often reach different conclusions.

Additional Basic Concepts of Value

Although Piaget has been criticized on such grounds as inconsistency of theory, obscure terminology, and poor scientific rigor, there is little doubt that he made many significant contributions to our understanding of the growth of children's mental abilities. Among these contributions is the idea that mental development is a dynamic process that results from the interaction of the child with the environment. Children act on their own world, and by means of interaction with it they construct their own knowledge. This is why Piaget favored the saying that "construction is superior to instruction" (Siegler, 2005). This close observer of children maintained that they use language and play to represent reality, and for this reason Piaget (1932) emphasized the extraordinary value of play as a basic avenue through which young children learn. Finally, he stressed the importance of actual involvement of children with materials (as compared with observation and teacher explanation) and the significance of experience as a medium for learning.

Currently it appears that in addition to his general theoretical ideas, Piaget's identification of significant cognitive concepts and the steps and means by which they develop may be the most helpful contribution he has made to our understanding of the cognitive self. Siegler (2005) summed this up well when he concluded that despite recent clarifications and contradictions provided by more recent research, Piaget's theory remains valuable since "it provides us with a good feel for what children's thinking is like at different points in development" (p. 51). This understanding makes it possible for teachers to generate a curriculum for stimulating the growth of certain cognitive abilities, rather than to merely teach children an endless array of facts.

From a Piagetian Perspective, What Can Teachers Do to Help Children Develop Fully at Each Cognitive Stage?

Of course, it is neither desirable nor even possible to accelerate children markedly through the stages of cognitive development. What teachers should do instead is assist children to develop richly and fully at each stage, thereby paving the way for successful attainment of the next stage at the appropriate time. This is especially important for children with developmental delays. The teacher must be sure to provide children who have disabilities in the cognitive realm with experiences appropriate for their developmental level. These cognitive learning activities—as with all good early education—should be challenging (but not too frustrating), stimulating, and fun, and they should be experienced with other children. Refer to chapter 5 for resources on adapting the early childhood curriculum to include children with disabilities.

Piaget maintained that four factors work together to promote cognitive growth: *maturation, experience, socialization,* and *equilibration.* The thoughtful teacher can make a helpful contribution to each of these factors while leading children through the day.

For example, first, physical maturation underlies cognitive maturation, and the good health practices followed by children's centers can make a definite contribution to physical development by providing the sound nutrition, rest, and physical activity so necessary for the child's growing body and particularly the brain to thrive.

Second, the provision of real experience with the physical world so stressed by Piaget is an essential cornerstone of early childhood education. These experiences should include many opportunities for children to arrange things in order, to return substances to their prior state, and to group them according to their common properties *as well as the chance to talk about why they have put them in particular configurations.* Opportunities for exploring other relationships such as cause and effect, as well as the basic skill of telling same from different, should also be included. (The remainder of this chapter presents many examples of ways such experiences may be integrated into the daily life of the school.)

Third, socialization, too, is something most early childhood teachers know a good deal about. However, here a special point requires emphasis when discussing cognition from a Piagetian point of view. Whereas early childhood teachers often think of socialization as lying in the realm of teaching children how to get along together or

Benjamin La Framboise

Children need plenty of real experiences with the physical world to explore the properties of things (such as sand) and relationships (such as cause and effect).

teaching them language (a profoundly useful social skill), Piaget thought of socialization as having another important facet. He maintained that interaction between children, particularly discussion, which he termed *argument*, is of extraordinary importance. Through such exchanges of ideas children test and modify what they think. And these modifications of what they think lead to the fourth factor that influences cognitive growth—equilibration.

Equilibration is the mechanism that brings maturation, experience, and social interaction into balance. It is the mechanism by which children regulate their ideas and "put things all together."

So if teachers wish to strengthen cognitive growth, in addition to providing optimum opportunities for physical maturation and real experience, they should also encourage dialogue *among* the children (as well as carrying out discussions between themselves and the children). The result will be that children figure out more things for themselves. This enables them to coordinate their existing knowledge with their newly acquired knowledge by exercising the faculty of equilibration.

Thus, when the children complain it's no fun to swing because their feet drag on the ground, instead of obligingly shortening the swing, the teacher might ask the children to propose what might be done to change that situation. Could they make their legs shorter? Could someone push them so that they could hold their legs out straight? Or . . . ? Children can think up and debate many possibilities once provided the chance to do so. Such discussions and proposed solutions enable children to construct knowledge for themselves, construction that is so much more valuable than instruction.

How Is Piagetian Theory Linked with Such Midlevel Skills as Matching and Grouping?

In addition to more encompassing ideas such as equilibration, Piaget (1983) was also interested in how children develop their ability to perform more specific mental operations including classification, seriation, cause and effect, and conserving quantity (understanding that the amount remains the same despite changes in appearance).

The beginning levels of these skills are what teachers term *matching, grouping, common relations, graduated ordering, cause-and-effect relationships,* and *initial understanding of the principles of conservation of quantity*. These skills are valuable not only because they are the precursors of later, more sophisticated Piagetian mental operations but also because, as Table 14.3 illustrates, they are vital foundation stones for building academic skills related to reading and mathematical understanding.

For example, *matching* (being able to tell whether things are the same or different) is an important prerequisite for being able to read. If one cannot tell the difference between *d* and *b,* how can one tell the difference between *dog* and *bog*? *Grouping* (identifying the common property of several nonidentical items) underlies the concept of class inclusion, which is necessary for understanding set theory. Grouping is also an essential element of such sciences as botany, in which classification is very important. *Seriation* (arranging things in regular, graduated order) gives real meaning to enumeration. Finally, *common relations* (the ability to identify pairs of items associated together) helps children learn to draw analogies. This fascinating ability to move from one known relationship to a second by perceiving parallels in the two sets involves transferring ideas and making such linkages. It is surely an indispensable element in creative thought.

Table 14.3
Links between basic mental abilities and later school-related skills

Ability	Value
Matching: Can identify which things are the same and which things are different *Basic question:* Can you find the pair that is exactly the same?	The ability to discriminate is crucial to development of other mental abilities. An important aspect of gaining literacy: discriminate between letters (such as *m* and *w*). Promotes understanding of equality. Encourages skill in figure/ground perception (separating a significant figure from the background).
Grouping: Can identify the common property that forms a group or class *Basic question:* Can you show me the things that belong to the same family?	Fosters mathematical understanding: set theory and equivalency. Children must discriminate, reason, analyze, and select in order to formulate groups. Regrouping encourages flexibility of thought. Depending on manner of presentation, may foster divergent thinking—more than one way to group items. Requires use of accommodation and assimilation. Classification is a basic aspect of life sciences: allows people to organize knowledge.
Common relations: Can identify common property or relationship between a *nonidentical pair* *Basic question:* Which thing goes most closely with what other thing?	Fosters mathematical understanding: one-to-one correspondence. Fosters diversity of understanding concepts: many kinds of pairs (opposites, cause-effect, congruent). Can teach use of analogies and riddles.
Cause and effect: Can determine what makes something else happen: a special case of common relations *Basic question:* What makes something else happen?	Basis for scientific investigations. Conveys sense of order of world. Conveys sense of individual's ability to be effective: act on the world and produce results, make things happen. Encourages use of prediction and generation of hypotheses. Introduces child to elementary understanding of the scientific method.
Seriation: Can identify what comes next in a graduated series *Basic question:* What comes next?	Fosters mathematical understanding. Relationship between quantities: counting (enumeration) with understanding, one-to-one correspondence, equivalency, estimation. If teacher presents series going from left to right, fosters basic reading skill.
Temporal ordering: Can identify logical order of events occurring in time *Basic question:* What comes next?	Fosters mathematical understanding. Conveys a sense of order and a sense of time and its effect. Relationship between things: cause-and-effect and other relationships. Prediction. Requires memory: what happened first, then what happened?
Conservation: Can understand that a substance can return to its prior state and that quantity is not affected by mere changes in appearance *Basic question:* Are they still the same quantity?	Idea of constancy (reversibility) is fundamental as a foundation for logical reasoning, basic for scientific understanding; it is also the basis for mathematical calculations involving length, volume, area, and so forth.

327

Each of these concepts develops over time by building on lower level concepts. Practice in these abilities entails the use of and practice in some additional mental skills that must be so generally employed that they apply to all the abilities. These are listed here rather than being repeated in Table 14.3. They include the ability to pay attention, observe carefully, make comparisons, and use symbols (representations) in place of actual objects. The symbols might consist of models, pictures, language, or simply imaginary items as is done in play.

HOW TO PROVIDE OPPORTUNITIES FOR PRACTICING CONCEPT FORMATION SKILLS

Develop Needed Materials

There are two ways to obtain materials to use for teaching these midlevel skills. The easiest, most expensive, and most obvious way is to rely on commercially developed tabletop activities. Many such materials are available, particularly in the areas of matching and seriation. The trouble with them is that they often are not related closely to curriculum topics, and they generally use only pictures as the medium of instruction. (Montessori materials are a welcome exception to this trend.) The most significant danger to guard against is offering only commercially developed activities for concept development. This results in a presentation that is too narrow, sensorily limited, and dull to be fully effective.

The second way to introduce opportunities for this kind of concept development is to embed them directly in the curriculum. This is likely to be more work for the teacher, who will have to develop materials for the children's use, but it is also more satisfying since it gives the teacher a chance to be creative and to use a much wider variety of materials and activities. Best of all, teacher-developed experiences mean the activities can be directly related to and coordinated with the topics that have interested the children. It is not difficult to generate such ideas and there are a wealth of activities books available in educational libraries for such purposes.

Provide Consistent Opportunities for Practice

It is necessary to provide repeated opportunities for experience and practice. One or two repetitions to practice grouping, matching, or ordering are not sufficient. To build strong connections between neurons and to understand these concepts fully and richly, children need to practice them consistently, using many materials and moving from simpler to more difficult activities as their skills increase (American Association for the Advancement of Science [AAAS], 1998; Koralek, 2003; Koralek & Colker, 2003; NCTM, 2000; Worth & Grollman, 2003).

Above All, Make Certain the Activities Are Fun

Teachers are able to devise and construct a great many activities to stimulate mental development. Indeed, teachers seem to have a much better basic grasp of how to devise appealing materials than most manufacturers do. The teacher-made activities are so much more colorful, and they reflect a real familiarity with what young children really care about.

Pleasure is also increased for the children when the activities are at the right developmental level. As Vygotsky maintained, the satisfaction of meeting the challenge of an activity that is just a little bit but not too much harder than what the child has already mastered is obviously gratifying. Suggestions are included with the discussions of specific abilities showing how the levels of difficulty can be increased. The strategies summarized here might be used with any of the abilities to increase the challenge. These include adding more choices, asking whether there is another way to do it, asking the children to put what they are doing into words, using a different sensory mode in place of vision (e.g., using only touch or only hearing), using memory, asking the children to tell you something in reverse order, or using items that are less familiar. A word of caution: We have had children in our center, usually 5-year-olds, who enjoyed being challenged in all these ways; however, the key word here is *enjoyed*. The purpose is not to make things so difficult that children sweat and struggle over them.

Another caution is the *undesirability* of resorting to competition and comparison to generate "fun." Setting up activities with the aim of seeing who can do something quickest or "best" takes a lot of fun out of it for everyone else. It is fairly easy to substitute something like suspense in place of competition to sustain interest. Suspense strategies can be as simple as having children pull things out of a mystery bag and then decide where they should go, or asking them to choose something from one hand or the other held behind the teacher's back.

Develop and offer materials to children that promote cognitive midlevel abilities such as matching. This matching game becomes much more fun when the children create the design for other children to copy, then project it for all to see on an overhead projector.

Leisa Maloney

Some Practical Suggestions About Presenting Midlevel Thinking and Reasoning Skills in the Curriculum

Before embarking on a detailed discussion of specific reasoning abilities, it is important to stress once again that the purpose of including the following material is not to foster precocity in young children. It is hoped that regular exposure to these kinds of activities will furnish all children with beginning skills that will stand them in good stead as they move on to the next stage of intellectual development.

Note that the following descriptions of activities include suggestions for children who are less advanced, as well as suggestions for those who are more mature. They also stress that a diversity of experiences should be offered, *including large-muscle activities*. All too often this kind of curriculum is limited to small-muscle, tabletop experiences, which is most unfortunate.

Matching

Matching is the ability to perceive that two items are *identical,* and it depends on the child's grasping the concept of sameness and differentness. At our center we have found this to be one of the easier concepts for young children to acquire. Even 2- and 3-year-olds will work at this occupation with interest and diligence if the materials are attractive and not too detailed.

Many commercial materials are available that may be used to provide practice in matching. These range from simple, obvious pictures with few details to quite elaborate discrimination tasks that contain a great deal of detail and subtle differences. Lotto and bingo games are probably the most prevalent examples of such materials. But matching should not be limited to these kinds of activities. Younger children can grasp this concept by matching buttons (a perennial favorite), matching animal stamps or stickers, or playing simple picture dominoes. Fabric swatches and wallpaper samples are also fun to use for this purpose and can be surprisingly difficult. Incidentally, putting blocks back so that all of one kind go in the same place is a matching— *not* grouping—exercise, since the blocks are identical.

Matching experiences need not be limited to the sense of vision, of course. Children will also enjoy matching by touch (for texture and thickness), by hearing (duplicating simple sounds, rhythms, or melodies), and by taste and smell (it is interesting to cut up a variety of white fruits and vegetables, for instance, and ask the children to taste bits of them and find the ones that are the same). Imitation can also be thought of as an attempt to match actions; shadow or mirror dancing, Follow the Leader, and Simon Says may be employed for this purpose. Large-muscle activities may be further incorporated by setting out two or three pictures and choosing a child to walk over to match one of them with the picture in his hand. (He then has the privilege of picking the next child to do this.) Children who are proficient at pumping may be asked whether they can match the arc of their swings with that of the child beside them.

When asking children to complete a match, the teacher should use sentences such as, "Show me the one that matches," or, "Find me one that's just the same," rather than, "Show me two that are just alike," because an occasional child is misled by the term *alike* and will blithely select something to show the teacher, saying, "Here, I like this one best!"

As the child becomes more skilled, matching tasks may be increased in difficulty by making the matches more complex and difficult to analyze. This is usually accomplished by increasing the number of details that must be inspected in each picture and by increasing the number of items to be compared. Ultimately the material shifts from depending on pictorially meaningful content to more symbolic form. This leads, finally, to using the symbols of the alphabet and numbers (Koralek, 2003).

Grouping

The word *grouping* is used here in place of *classification* to emphasize that we are discussing an elementary form of the more sophisticated skill described by Piaget (1965) wherein older children can form hierarchical classes or classify items according to more than one property at the same time. Preschool children perform at a simpler level than classification, but 4- and 5-year-olds in particular are able to sort objects or pictures into categories meaningful to them. Elementary school children are at a more advanced level and delight in true classification games.

Other examples of meaningful categorizing are placing dollhouse furniture into rooms according to their function (e.g., kitchen equipment in the kitchen) and sorting shells according to whether they are clams or mussels or pectins, rough or smooth, large or small. Teachers encourage categorizing every time they ask children, "Are airplanes birds? Why not?" or say, "Show me all the buttons that belong together." In these instances the child is being asked to determine what it is that various items have in common—to determine the common property that defines the class—and then the child is usually expected to decide whether an additional item also possesses this property and can be included.

In essence such material may be presented in three ways. First, children can be confronted with an assembled group and be asked to choose things to add to it (perhaps it is pictures of clothing such as a sweater, dress, and shirt, and the additional pictures might be a doll, a pair of pants, and an ice cream cone). Second, they can be presented with an assembled group and be asked to remove items that do not belong (e.g., "Everyone who isn't wearing a plaid top, sit down."). Finally, children can be given a melange of articles or pictures and be asked to sort them according to whatever criteria they establish.

It is wise to encourage children to determine the categories for themselves whenever possible. If the teacher hands a child a box of little animals and says, "Pick out all the red ones" or "Pick out all the ones we saw at the zoo," the teacher has done most of the thinking for the child. But if the teacher says, "Show me which ones you think belong together," and follows this with, "How come you put those together?" the child must do more of the thinking. This is quite different from and more valuable than expecting the child to "discover" the category the teacher has thought up.

Of course, it is not necessary to limit "grouping" activities to small-muscle experiences. Every time children are asked to show how many different ways they can run or to choose what equipment they need to play house with in the sandbox, they are essentially thinking of things that fit a particular category or class just as they are determining categories when the teacher asks them, "Do you think the wheelbarrow should be kept with the wagons and scooters or with the garden equipment?" Additional practice is also provided by asking older 4- to 6-year-olds to select three or four children from the group who are wearing something similar—boots, perhaps, or striped clothing— and then have the rest of the children guess what it is they have in common.

Occasionally teachers become confused and attempt to teach grouping by using identical items for this purpose. Although being able to pick out things that are exactly the same and to tell them apart from those that are different is a useful literacy skill, it is not grouping; it is simple matching. *To teach grouping, it is necessary to use materials that possess common properties but are not identical.*

The easiest form of grouping is sorting that requires simple responses to a prominent sensory quality such as color. The task may be made more difficult by asking the children to think of a way the materials can be regrouped: by using more complex materials, by increasing the emphasis on verbalization, or by asking them to group materials according to several properties at the same time (AAAS, 1998; Koralek, 2003; Koralek & Colker, 2003). Once in elementary school, children become adept at true classification skills where they can attend to a number of properties at the same time and categorize them by subgroups (NAEYC & NCTM, 2002).

Perceiving Common Relations

The basic skill required in developing the concept of common relations is the ability to identify and *pair* items that are usually associated together but that are *not* identical. The activity of perceiving common relations is similar to grouping because it depends on the identification of a common property or bond. It differs from grouping because it involves *pairing* such items, rather than working with larger numbers of them. It is useful to cultivate because it probably forms the basis for the later understanding and formulation of analogies (e.g., ring is to finger as belt is to . . . waist, buckle, or sash?). Because these combinations are usually culturally based (salt and pepper, shoes and socks, hat and head), it is important to know the home backgrounds of the children to be able to develop pairs likely to be familiar to them.

Opposites can also be included in this activity since there is also a true relationship between them. Thus hot can be contrasted with cold, up with down, and thick with thin.

Young children relish pairing up an assortment of items that are either presented all together in a box or in more gamelike form in which several items are set out and their related members are drawn out of a bag one by one. Some commercial materials on the market are useful for this purpose, such as two-piece puzzles linking animals with their homes, or occupations with appropriate tools. (We call these *congruent relationships*.) It is also helpful to acquire many pairs of real objects or models of them that belong together and to keep a reserve of these handy to be brought out from time to time for the fun of it.

When the teacher is working with these combinations, it is usually effective to ask the child to pick out the thing that *goes most closely* with a selected item or that *belongs best* with it. This is language that the children understand and that is clear enough for them to be able to follow the directions.

Perceiving common relations may be made more difficult for more mature children by including less familiar combinations, by increasing the number of choices, or by setting up true analogies in which the child has to ascertain the quality common to both pairs of items.

Understanding the Relationship Between Simple Cause and Effect

Although it takes children a long time to develop clear ideas of physical causality (Piaget, 1963), they can begin to acquire this concept while attending the early learning center. Indeed, much of the social learning that goes on in the children's center already supports the development of causality, such as when children experience the logical consequences of their behavior. Thus the child who pulls all the blocks off the shelf is expected to help restack them, and the youngster who dumps milk on the table must get the sponge and wipe it up.

In addition to understanding cause and effect in terms of social consequences, children age 4 and older can often handle cause-related questions that are phrased as "What would happen if . . . ?" or "What do you think made (something) happen?" These questions are sound to use since they do not require children to apply or explain scientific principles that lie beyond their understanding but depend instead on what they can see happen with their own eyes or on what they can deduce from their own experience (AAAS, 1998; Koralek, 2003; Koralek & Colker, 2003; NCTM, 2000; Worth & Grollman, 2003).

Following are some examples of successful questions:

- What will happen if we add some sugar to the dough?
- What will happen to your shoes if you go out in the rain without your boots on?
- How come Matthew dropped the hot pan so fast?
- What made the kittens mew when mama cat got up?
- What made the egg get hard?

Finding the answers to these questions can be accomplished by setting up simple experiments to identify the most probable causes. These experiments enable the children to try out suggested causes, compare results, and then draw conclusions about the most likely reason for something happening, thereby introducing them to the scientific method (AAAS, 1998; Koralek & Colker, 2003; Worth & Grollman, 2003).

Lori Pickert

Provide fascinating materials that inspire curiosity. This home-made table has lights and mirrors under a clear Plexiglas top. The children are given an assortment of colorful objects to make interesting arrangements.

Young children are continually forming theories and hypotheses about why things are, and they enjoy experiments to test their ideas. Remember it is much more valuable for children to propose possibilities, make predictions, try them out, and gather and analyze data, than for teachers to guide them to thinking of possibilities the teachers have thought up already. This is the basis of the scientific method that forms the core of science education in elementary school and beyond.

Ordering

Ordering means arranging objects or events in logical order. The two kinds of ordering that appear to be most useful are (a) arranging a variety of items according to a graduated, seriated scale (spatial ordering, the beginning of Piagetian seriation) and (b) arranging events as they occur in time (temporal ordering). The basic question the child must be able to answer when dealing with either of these concepts is, What comes next? Many interesting activities require a child to answer this question and to infer the logical order of either a spatial or temporal series.

Spatial Seriated Ordering

Almost any kind of item that comes in graduated sizes may be used for the purpose of teaching spatial, or seriated, ordering: various sizes of bolts and nuts, sets of measuring cups or spoons, nested mixing bowls, and empty tin cans of assorted sizes. Montessori cylinders are excellent for this purpose, and an examination of equipment catalogs will reveal many additional possibilities as varied as nesting blocks and flannel board materials. Hardwood blocks, of course, present classic opportunities for becoming acquainted with the relationship between varying lengths, as well as for studying the regular relationships of equivalency that occur in block construction, because blocks may vary in length but generally are of the same width and depth.

Variations on seriation can be used to teach gradations in quality. Grades of sandpaper can be provided so that children have opportunities to arrange them in order from rough to smooth; flavors can be provided that range from sweet to sour; tone bells can be arranged from high pitch to low pitch. Large-muscle experiences that will draw the children's attention to graduated sizes might include having the children arrange themselves from shortest to tallest. (This can be fun to do if everyone lies down side by side and their heights are marked on a big roll of paper and then the same paper is used again later in the year to measure their growth.)

The easiest kinds of seriation problems are ones in which the child is asked to choose which items should be added to a chain of two or three to continue an upward or downward trend. Very young children often grasp this principle best if it is presented in terms of "This is the Papa Bear, and this is the Mama Bear; now show me what comes next." The activity may be made more difficult by increasing the number of objects to be arranged, and even more difficult by asking the child to arrange a series and then adding one or two items that must be inserted somewhere in the middle to make the series more complete. Finally, the challenge can be increased even more by asking the child to arrange two sets of objects in corresponding order or, more difficult yet, in contrasting order—for example, going from low to high for one set and high to low on a parallel set. This is *very* difficult! Nuts and bolts make particularly nice items to use for this purpose, as do padlocks and various sizes of keys and paper dolls with appropriately sized clothing.

Temporal Ordering

Recalling or anticipating the order of events as they occur in time is called *temporal ordering*. Children can be asked to recount the order in which they got ready that morning: "First you got up, and then you went to the bathroom, and then. . . ." Flannel board stories are another fine way to help children visualize the order in which things happen, and some social occasions also make excellent topics for discussion and pictures. Birthday parties, for example, often run quite true to form: First the guests arrive, then the birthday child opens the presents, and so forth. Recipes, too, can be set out with the ingredients arranged in the order in which they will be needed. Many of these orderly events can be played through as well as discussed; recapitulation through play is a most valuable way to rehearse the order in which events take place.

Although even 2-year-olds are keenly aware of the order in which daily events occur and are sticklers for maintaining that order, as many families will attest, older preschoolers also need continuing practice with this concept. The level of difficulty for these more sophisticated children can be increased by adding more episodes to each event, asking the child to arrange a series of pictures and then to interpolate additional ones after the series has been formulated, asking the child to arrange the events in reverse, or asking the child to consider what might happen if something occurred out of order ("What if you got in the bathtub and then took your clothes off?" To which one child replied, "Nothing, as long as I don't turn the water on!"). Asking children to plan an activity step by step in advance also provides practice in temporal ordering.

Conserving

Perhaps no mental ability has come under more investigation than the ability to conserve quantity (Siegler, 2005). When children possess this ability, they are able to recognize that the amount of the substance remains the same despite changes in its appearance. Before that time, when they are too young to be able to conserve (typically in our culture before age 6 or 7), the child is deceived by appearances into reasoning that the quantity has increased or decreased because a change in shape has made the material look like more or less. For instance, two glasses of water that have been judged equivalent will then be judged unequal when one is poured into a squat, low dish and another into a tall, thin cylinder and the two are compared again, or two balls of clay previously demonstrated to be the same amount will be judged different in quantity when one has been mashed flat or divided into many little balls.

Early childhood teachers should see to it that the children in their groups have many occasions to try out and experiment with the results of pouring liquids back and forth into containers of various shapes to learn that shape does not alter quantity. Blocks present outstanding opportunities to demonstrate conservation of mass since it is relatively simple to see that a tower of four contains the same number of units as does a two-by-two stack. Clay and dough also lend themselves well to providing opportunities for youngsters to acquire this concept. In short, any material, whether liquid or solid, that can be divided and put together again may be used to investigate the principle of conservation.

It is also worthwhile to provide opportunities for measuring to demonstrate equality or inequality. Scales are useful in this regard, and yardsticks and measuring tapes are also valuable. Or children can create their own units of measure, using cutouts of feet or paper clips or Popsicle sticks. However, the teacher must realize that despite

myeducationlab

Go to MyEducationLab and select the topic "Curriculum/Program Models." Under Activities and Applications, watch the video *Supporting Different Learning Styles: A First Grade Mathematics Lesson.* Which midlevel mental abilities does this activity address?

these aids, children who are too immature to grasp the principle of conservation will continue to insist that what their eyes tell them to be true is true.

The teacher's role in this area lies in providing many opportunities for the children to manipulate materials and experiment with changing their forms and with returning them to their prior state (reversing the reaction). In addition to supplying experiences, they should make a point of talking with the children and drawing their attention to the unchanging nature of quantity as they manipulate the materials. This is also an excellent time to build related vocabulary, such as *more than, less than,* and *equal to*. Finally, besides talking with the children themselves, teachers should foster discussion and "argument" among the children about the nature of conservation, since research supports Piaget's contention (1926) that such interaction among children will help them reach correct conclusions.

USE QUESTIONS THAT "PROVOKE" THE CHILDREN INTO THINKING FOR THEMSELVES AS THEIR IDEAS AND MENTAL ABILITIES EMERGE

Sort Out the Different Kinds of Teacher-Generated Questions: Understand the Difference Between Using Fact and Thought Questions

All questions are not alike because some elicit convergent and others divergent replies. This is easiest to understand if one thinks of questions related to mental development as being of three kinds: (a) *convergent fact questions,* which request the child to reply with one right answer; (b) *figuring-out questions,* which require the child to apply a concept such as grouping or common relations to arrive at one or more right answers; and (c) *open-ended questions,* which elicit an original idea (hypothesis) or solution from the youngster.

Fact questions are the simplest and, regrettably, most frequently used kind of question. They can usually be spotted because they request information ("Do you make cookies in the oven or in the broiler?" "You're right! It *is* a rabbit. What else do you know about rabbits?"), request labeling or naming ("Let's see, I have some things in this bag, and I wonder if you can tell me what they are"), or request the child to recall something from memory ("How about telling us what happened when you went to the pet store? Did you buy rabbit food?"). All these questions are "closed" or convergent questions because they anticipate simple, correct-answer replies.

Figuring-out questions are a big step up from fact questions, but in the final analysis they are still going to produce right (convergent) answers. They are more advanced than fact questions because, to answer the question, the child must be able to apply a concept to a situation and reason out the reply. For example, to select the pictures that are the same (e.g., playing Bingo), a child must understand the concept of sameness and then be able to apply it by matching the pictures that are identical. Or if asked how birds are not the same as butterflies, the child must analyze what is the same about them and what is different. Even though there would be several differences to identify, and even though more analysis and insight is involved than is required just to say, "It's called a butterfly," the final result is the production of closed-end, correct answers. These midlevel intellectual skills are useful because they form part of the foundation for verbal and mathematical literacy later on, but they do not provide children opportunities to express the full range of what they know and to produce unique solutions.

Open-ended questions, in contrast, foster the production of original, divergent ideas and solutions. They are termed *open-ended* because the questioner does not know what the answer will turn out to be. Open-ended questions encourage the development of mathematical and scientific thinking, and the more experience young children have with them in early childhood programs, the more proficient they become at math and science in later years (Epstein, 2007; NAEYC & NCTM, 2002; O'Hara, et al., 2005; Schickedanz, 2008).

Fortunately, producing open-ended questions is really easy if you think of them as coming in three types: *opinions, reasons for the opinions, and possible ways to try out the opinions to see whether they are sound.*

For example, with the first type, *asking-for-opinion questions*, the teacher might ask, "In your opinion, what could we do to help the ducks feel happy?" or, "Oh, oh! We've got the tub over in the shade, but how in the world can we get enough water over there to fill it," or, "What do you think we should feed them?"

Examples of the second type, *asking-for-reasons-for-opinion questions*, are, "Why'd you choose the bucket, Ben?" or, "How come you think they'd like the lettuce best?" or, "Why do you think the hose is better to use than the bucket?"

The third type, *asking-how-can-we-find-out questions*, typically encourages the children to think up ways to try out their type 1 opinions. "Now let's think about this. Shanti thinks we should feed them hot dogs, Will is voting for lettuce, and Mya thinks peanuts would be just right. How are we going to find out which the ducks like best?"

Wait for Answers and Ask Only a Few Questions at a Time

One of the most important things about asking questions is learning to *wait* for an answer. This is surprisingly hard to do. Many teachers ask excellent questions but then plunge right ahead and answer them themselves. But children, like adults, need time to collect their thoughts and formulate their replies. Pausing allows them to do this.

Something else to beware of is asking too many questions. In our zeal to help children think, we must remember that most young children are not highly verbal and that they do not enjoy long, drawn-out intellectual dialogues. To prevent questions from becoming burdensome, it is best to weave them into general discussions while the actual experience is going on, as well as to provide all possible opportunities for children to put their suggestions into practice promptly.

Resist the Impulse to Always Answer the Children's Questions Yourself

Asking opinion-type questions and waiting for the children to answer them is only half of what teachers need to know about the inquiry approach. The other half is knowing how to respond when children ask *them* questions.

Of course, many times teachers can help children make satisfying progress by supplying information they couldn't figure out for themselves, but *just as often* the children can figure things out on their own if teachers do not rush in and furnish the fact immediately. When other children can be drawn into the discussion and encouraged to add their suggestions, comments, and evaluations, even more learning will take place.

Encourage the Child or the Group to Produce More Than One Answer

Since more than one correct answer is possible in divergent thinking, teachers need to learn how to encourage children to propose more than one possible solution to a problem.

The kinds of questions that often lead children to generate more ideas related to creative problem solving are sometimes called "what-else?" and "what-if?" questions. Questions such as "What else could you do?" or "Is there another way?" will stimulate many suggestions from the children. This kind of elementary brainstorming can be done quite successfully with young children in a playful way. It encourages them to see that questions can have several right answers and to develop the habit of looking for more than one solution to a problem.

What-if? questions encourage even freer and more creative answers than what-else? questions do. A problem can be postulated, such as, "What if we didn't have any blankets at nap; how could we keep warm?" Then all kinds of possibilities can be suggested. (One of our little boys replied, "Grow fur.")

The use of open-ended questions by the early childhood teachers encourages a sense of open-minded wonder about the world, as well as a delight in experimentation and hypothesis testing. This is one of the best ways we can support the development of cognitive growth in young children: by giving them the gift of scientific inquiry.

SUMMARY

Piaget made many significant contributions to our understanding of cognition. Among these are his identification of various categories of knowledge and stages of intellectual development. He maintained that mental development is a dynamic process that results from the child's actions on the environment, that play is an important avenue of learning, and that children construct their own knowledge base.

The chapter provides detailed discussions of some basic thinking and reasoning skills that form the foundation for later, more sophisticated cognitive abilities and academic learning. These include matching, grouping, perceiving common relations, temporal and seriated ordering, conservation, and understanding elementary cause-and-effect relationships.

The chapter concludes with a discussion of open-ended questioning methods and how they support scientific inquiry.

Questions and Activities

1. Pick up on a current interest of the children in your group and propose some midlevel thinking activities that could be based on that interest.

2. Concoct activities that fit the various mental abilities, such as ordering and grouping, and try them out with the children. Then add variations to the activities that make them easier or more difficult in order to suit the needs of individual children in the group. Set aside some shelves in your school where these materials can be accumulated.

3. Review the activities related to mental ability in the school where you teach and identify the ones that foster literacy skills that lead to reading. If you teach in elementary school, which standards are in place that address specific mental abilities?

Diversity Question

1. How should midlevel cognitive activities be adapted for children with developmental delays? Do you think the teacher should try to "speed up" a child's development in order to keep up with the other children? Explain the reasons for your answer.

Self-Check Questions for Review

Content-Related Questions

1. Piaget identified three kinds of knowledge involved in children's thought. What are they?
2. List at least four important ideas Piaget contributed to cognitive education.
3. From a Piagetian point of view, explain what teachers can do to assist the cognitive development of young children.
4. What is the main difference between the teaching style needed to teach the midlevel mental abilities and the teaching style needed for the problem-solving approach?

Integrative Questions

1. Explain why *matching* and *perceiving common relations* are examples of logico-mathematical knowledge.
2. Which of the following mental abilities is most likely to foster mathematical understanding: (a) matching, (b) seriation, or (c) cause-and-effect? Explain why you selected the answer you did.
3. How are *common relations* and *grouping* the same? How do they differ?
4. How do *matching* and *grouping* differ?

Reference for Further Reading

DeVries, R., Zan, B., Hildebrandt, C., Edmiaston, R., & Sales, C. (2002). *Developing constructivist early childhood curriculum: Practical principles and activities*. New York: Teachers College Press. Rheta DeVries, one of the founders of constructivist early education, and her colleagues illustrate how Piagetian, constructivist theory can be generalized from cognitive development per se to actual classroom practice.

Related Organizations and Online Resources

High/Scope Educational Research Foundation. This independent nonprofit organization develops curricula and assessment instruments, trains teachers, conducts research, and publishes educational books and materials. High/Scope's educational approach emphasizes Piagetian "active participatory learning." Many curriculum activities that support children's cognitive development are at http://www.highscope.org.

Jean Piaget Society. This membership organization for scholars, teachers, and researchers was established in 1970. This is a serious scholarly group, but students can find some good information and resources at http://piaget.org/aboutPiaget.html.

Basic information about Piaget can be found in *Time* magazine's year 2000 issue on "The 100 Most Important People of the Century" available at http://www.time.com/time/time100/scientist/profile/piaget.html.

National Council of Teachers of Mathematics. (NCTM). NCTM is a public voice of mathematics education, providing leadership and professional development to support teachers in ensuring equitable mathematics learning of the highest quality for all students. Information is available at http://www.nctm.org.

Developmental standards for preschoolers through grade 8 can be found at http://www.nctm.org/focalpoints/.

The joint position statement of the National Association for the Education of Young Children and NCTM can be accessed at http://www.naeyc.org/about/positions/psmath.asp.

National Science Teachers Association (NSTA). Founded in 1944 and with more than 55,000 members, NSTA is the largest organization in the world committed to promoting excellence and innovation in science teaching and learning for all. Information is available at http://www.nsta.org/default.aspx.

The site is primarily for teachers in elementary grades and up but there is a discussion group for early childhood educators with activity ideas and project descriptions at http://blogs.nsta.org/EarlyYearsBlog/default.aspx.

CHAPTER fifteen

Nurturing the Development of the Creative Self

How the creative energy young children possess can be sustained?

How to explain to families why your school doesn't send home paper plates with little faces glued on them?

What other arts activities can be offered in addition to the usual markers, dough, and paint easels?

. . . IF YOU HAVE, THE MATERIAL IN THE FOLLOWING PAGES WILL HELP YOU.

Creativity focuses on the process of forming original ideas through exploration and discovery. In children, creativity develops from their experiences with the process, rather than concern for the finished product. Creativity is not to be confused with talent, skill, or intelligence. Creativity is not about doing something better than others, it is about thinking, exploring, discovering, and imagining.

Mary Ann Kohl (2007, p. 1)

An education in the arts benefits society because students of the arts gain powerful tools for understanding human experiences, both past and present. They learn to respect the often very different ways others have of thinking, working, and expressing themselves. They learn to make decisions in situations where there are no standard answers. By studying the arts, students stimulate their natural creativity and learn to develop it to meet the needs of a complex and competitive society.

Consortium of National Arts Education Associations (1994, Summary, p. 1)

A belief in the child's right to creative thought and expression transforms the classroom. . . . our most enlightened visions of education will be connected by the common thread of imagination, creative thought, and enhanced opportunities for creative expression. As we look ahead, it will no doubt be possible to trace society's greatest innovations and achievements back to an abiding respect for creative thought processes during childhood.

Mary Renck Jalongo (2003, p. 226)

The ability to be creative and make artistic imagery has been a part of the human experience since prehistoric cave dwellers represented their world in drawings of bison and horses. One need only witness today's preschoolers—intensely absorbed in representing their own world of mommies and daddies and beloved pets—to appreciate the same natural desire to express the creative human spirit. The experience of being involved in creative activity satisfies people in ways that nothing else can, and appears not only to reflect but also to foster emotional health. The act of creation enhances the child's feelings of self-esteem and self-worth. Something about creating a unique product or idea leaves people feeling good about themselves.

While providing that emotional sustenance, such activities also foster cognitive growth by providing endless opportunities for trying out ideas and putting them into practice, for ensuring many alternative ways to solve problems, and for encouraging use of symbols in place of "real" objects to represent ideas and feelings.

What Is Creativity?

Many people (including both teachers and parents) think only of the arts when considering the topic of creativity. However, creativity has more to do with a way of thinking and processing the world rather than the production of art projects. Creativity is the life force of play, indeed, of early childhood. Creativity plays a significant role in the cognitive realm, such as mathematical and scientific thinking (Ashbury

Leisa Maloney

The experience of creative activity satisfies people in ways that nothing else can.

& Rich, 2008; Geist & Geist, 2008; Loomis, Lewis, & Blumenthal, 2007; Shore & Strasser, 2006; Viadero, 2008). Creative thinking involves imagination, thinking up new ideas and testing them out (i.e., hypothesis testing), communication, physical manipulations, problem posing, problem solving, making interpretations, and using symbols (Deasy & Stevenson, 2002; Gardner, 2007).

E. Paul Torrance was known for his pioneering research in creativity and developed an inventory of four abilities that are essential components of the creative process (Khatena & Khatena, 1999; Torrance, 1966/1984):

1. Fluency—the ability to produce a number of different ideas
2. Flexibility—the ability to approach situations and develop solutions from a number of different perspectives
3. Originality—the ability to have a new or novel idea
4. Elaboration—the ability to extend ideas

The Torrance Tests of Creative Thinking (TTCT) are the most widely used tests to measure children's creativity and have been in use since the 1960s. By familiarizing ourselves with these characteristics of creative thinking, we are better able to plan curriculum for young children that helps their fluency, flexibility, originality, and elaboration in thinking to flourish. Precisely how the teacher does this is discussed further in this chapter, and in chapter 16.

THE IMPORTANCE OF CREATIVITY

Creativity Supports Emotional Development

Creative experiences provide unparalleled opportunities for expressing emotions and, by gaining relief and understanding through such expression, for coming to terms with them (Ashbury & Rich, 2008; Consortium of National Arts Education Associations, 1994; Eisner, 2002; Loomis, Lewis, & Blumenthal, 2007). Because they have this strong affective component, they provide a balance for the emphasis on intellectual development that may overwhelm the rest of the program unless it is carefully managed.

Creativity plays an important function in the theory of multiple intelligences that was developed by Howard Gardner in 1983. (Gardner's theory of multiple intelligences is discussed in more detail in chapter 16.) In this theory, the traditional concept of intelligence that has formed the basis for American schools is viewed as far too limited. People possess different sensibilities and potentials beyond those that can be measured by IQ tests—or that have typically been taught in academically focused schools. For example, some people seem to have an advanced sense of "intrapersonal" or "emotional intelligence." According to Gardner (1986), the creative arts are a valuable way of supporting intrapersonal intelligence: "An artistic medium provides the means for coming to grips with ideas and emotions of great significance, one that cannot be articulated and mastered through ordinary conversational language" (p. 90).

Teachers can enhance children's emotional learning through creative arts activities by encouraging children to express their feelings: "I hear that you are angry right now. Why don't you paint a picture of what that feels like?" In discussing children's (or any artist's) work, get in the habit of asking, "How does this painting make you feel?" or "What were you feeling when you made this?" Play different types of music that evoke varying moods and discuss it with the children. Mood music can accompany other activities throughout the day, such as Mozart while painting or African drumming while pounding dough.

Creativity Supports Social Development

For children, creativity is often a social act. Singing, painting, dancing, playing make-believe, and so forth are all much more fun when done with friends. Through many of the creative arts, such as play-acting, puppetry, theater, video, call-and-response singing, and dance, the child learns to pay attention to others as well as the rules of social give-and-take. When the child shares creative expression with the rest of the class or with the family, the child gains a connection to other people through the use of art.

Teachers can enhance children's social learning through creative activities by encouraging children to pair up or work in small groups, and to discuss their creative expression and ideas with others. Displaying children's creative work throughout the classroom also engenders social connection, as does encouraging children to question and critique others' work in a constructive way. Employing the arts to foster social development is one of the cornerstones of the Reggio approach. Loris Malaguzzi, originator of the Reggio philosophy, emphasized the relationship between social growth and creativity when he stated, "The most favorable situation for creativity seems to be interpersonal exchange, with negotiation of conflicts and comparison of ideas and actions being the decisive elements" (1993, p.76).

Pam Oken-Wright

For children, creativity is often a social act.

Creativity Supports Physical Development

Creative experiences such as drawing, cutting with scissors, tearing, working with wire and clay, and painting help develop fine-motor skills and eye-hand coordination. Other types of creative arts such as woodworking, large construction projects, mural painting, dance, and theater help develop the child's gross-motor skills.

Teachers can enhance children's fine-motor development by allowing frequent free-choice opportunities to practice skills with tools and instruments. An arts or communication center should be available throughout the day where the child has a wide array of age-appropriate papers, markers, crayons, pencils, scissors, glue, yarn, ribbon, beads, and so on (see Appendix E for suggestions for some appropriate and inexpensive materials to have in the classroom).

Teachers can enhance children's gross-motor development through creative expression by offering plenty of movement and dance activities in the curriculum. Challenge the children (without resorting to competition) to use their bodies in novel ways, "How can you get over to that tree without walking?" "Can you think of another way to get the paint on this butcher paper without using your hands?" Large construction projects with use of wheelbarrows and hauling of materials should also be encouraged, and are especially interesting to elementary school children.

These types of creative experiences support "bodily-kinesthetic intelligence," which is proposed in Gardner's theory of multiple intelligences. Bodily-kinesthetic intelligence involves handling objects and tools skillfully and exhibiting coordination and control of one's body movements. A person who uses the hands or body in a problem-solving way is employing this form of intelligence. Dancers, athletes, surgeons, and craftspeople are adept at this form of intelligence, and teachers should plan curriculum to enhance its development in early childhood.

Creativity Supports Language and Literacy Development

Creative experiences seem naturally connected to language. Often young children engage in private speech as they describe what they're doing while creating art. Observe a group of preschool children working on an art project and you are likely to hear at least one child who voices a running commentary: "Now I need the roof for my house. Red—just like my house. There we go. Red roof. Perfect!"

Most children like to talk about their creations with others and to tell the underlying story. It is a good idea to couple verbal storytelling with the artistic creation. Taking dictation while a child paints, draws, or creates out of clay and then displaying the child's words along with the creation is quite satisfying. This is the idea behind the documentation that is used in the Reggio schools where beautiful displays of the children's work and words are seen throughout the hallways and classrooms. Not only is the documentation aesthetically pleasing, but it also creates a strong sense of community. Parents, grandparents, children, and teachers are drawn to the fascinating and beautiful documentation displays and gather around informally to discuss them (Gandini, Hill, Cadwell, & Schwall, 2005; Hendrick, 2004).

Language happens naturally when children work on projects side by side or in small groups. In group projects, children must communicate with each other and the teachers to describe their intent to others, acquire the proper materials and tools, plan the project, and evaluate it as it progresses.

Teachers can enhance language learning through creative expression, first, by incorporating listening activities into the program. As discussed in chapter 12, listening is typically the first aspect of language learning. Playing different types of music that convey different moods and discussing it with the children will help them appreciate the expressive qualities of music. Offer children a range of musical instruments to experiment with and listen to. Ask them to talk about their favorite instruments and the sounds that they make. Using creative music experiences helps develop one of the eight multiple intelligences described by Gardner, that of musical intelligence.

Language can also be supported through creative activities by asking open-ended questions about the child's work. It is also good practice to encourage the children to explain their work, their intent, and the processes used to other children. Refer the child who asks, "How do you make green?" to another child who has recently done so, and encourage their joint exploration of color mixing. In this way, verbal exchange is sure to ensue.

The ability to write develops from the preliteracy activities of drawing and scribbling. Any creative arts activity that requires fine-motor coordination helps the child develop the ability to write letters and numbers.

Creativity Supports Cognitive Development

Creative experiences are a pathway to cognitive growth. The creative arts help children develop attention skills and memory strategies that apply to other academic skills and cognitive learning. Creativity makes full use of the imagination and encourages the child to come up with ideas that are new and unusual. The creative process requires a sense of open exploration because there is no set, predetermined way to achieve a goal. Divergent thinking is thus encouraged, as the child must try out a variety of different ideas to bring a concept to fruition. Creativity involves exploration and problem solving, which leads to the development of deeper critical thinking skills (Ashbury & Rich, 2008; Deasy & Stevenson, 2002; Gardner, 1982, 2004, 2007).

Creative arts activities enhance premath and math learnings (Ashbury & Rich, 2008; Geist & Geist, 2008; Shore & Strasser, 2006). Concepts such as less and more are explored through the use of paint, dough, clay, and color. One-to-one correspondence is used when children try to match colors or shapes in their creations. Even a young preschool child begins to explore number concepts when the child paints each family member and gives each of them two legs. Grouping and classification come into play as the child creates more complex drawings of people and objects in the world. Elementary school children learn math by measuring and using rulers in their woodworking and sewing projects. Mixing clay, paint, or glue also requires measuring, and the ability to see transformations. Studies have shown that music training and math learning are related as the child attends to patterns and progressions (Ashbury & Rich, 2008; Geist & Geist, 2008; Shore & Strasser, 2006).

Science learning is also developed through creativity. Creative thinking itself supports the scientific method of hypothesis forming and testing, gathering data,

Benjamin La Framboise

Creative art experiences help children to see things in new ways and to realize that sometimes there is no "right" or "wrong" way of doing something. Why not paint with string?

analyzing it, and drawing conclusions. This is the process employed by a young child who manipulates clay and has the idea to make a dog from the material. How will he get it to stand up? The child experiments with different methods and perhaps finally settles on rolling out sturdy legs for support or propping it up with sticks if it topples over. All this learning stems from the child's creative imagination, the physical manipulations of materials, and the mental conclusions he makes after several trial-and-error experiments.

Children learn about physics through creative experiences. They discover the physical properties of objects and materials through hands-on manipulations during the creative process. They learn that wet paint eventually dries and feels quite different, that glaze changes color after firing, and that covering a clay project with wet cloth will keep it soft for the next day.

Teachers can enhance childrens' cognitive learning through the use of creative experiences by respecting the childrens' ideas and valuing their divergent thinking. Encourage the children to make theories and hypotheses about the world and then test them out. When we encourage children to explore and experiment—and make mistakes (sometimes very messy mistakes)—without judgment or reprimand, their creative thinking and spirit of wonder is unleashed. They feel free to imagine, invent, create, and try out new ways to do things.

Elliot Eisner is a professor of art and education, and past president of the John Dewey Society, who has written extensively about the need for creative education. In Figure 15.1, Eisner details some of the most important benefits students reap from engaging in the creative arts.

PEARSON **myeducationlab**)

Go to MyEducationLab and select the topic "Teaching Strategies." Under Activities and Applications, watch the video *Samantha Makes an Octopus Puppet*. Consider which learning domains are supported through this creative arts activity.

The arts teach children to make good judgments about qualitative relationships. Unlike much of the curriculum in which correct answers and rules prevail, in the arts, it is judgment rather than rules that prevail.

The arts teach children that problems can have more than one solution and that questions can have more than one answer.

The arts celebrate multiple perspectives. One of their large lessons is that there are many ways to see and interpret the world.

The arts teach children that in complex forms of problem solving purposes are seldom fixed, but change with circumstance and opportunity. Learning in the arts requires the ability and a willingness to surrender to the unanticipated possibilities of the work as it unfolds.

The arts make vivid the fact that neither words in their literal form nor numbers exhaust what we can know. The limits of our language do not define the limits of our cognition.

The arts teach students that small differences can have large effects. The arts traffic in subtleties.

The arts teach students to think through and within a material. All art forms employ some means through which images become real.

The arts help children learn to say what cannot be said. When children are invited to disclose what a work of art helps them feel, they must reach into their poetic capacities to find the words that will do the job.

The arts enable us to have experience we can have from no other source and through such experience to discover the range and variety of what we are capable of feeling.

The arts' position in the school curriculum symbolizes to the young what adults believe is important.

Figure 15.1
Ten lessons the arts teach

Source: Eisner, E. W. (2002). The arts and the creation of the mind. *New Haven, CT: Yale University Press. Reprinted with permission of the National Art Education Association.*

THE STAGES OF DEVELOPMENT IN CHILDREN'S CREATIVITY

As is true in other areas, children pass through general stages of development in their creative growth, for example, in their use of creative materials (Althouse, Johnson, & Mitchell, 2003; Jalongo & Stamp, 1997). First, *they explore the material itself* and investigate its properties. For instance, 2- and 3-year-olds spend many satisfactory hours in what appears to be mainly manipulation and exploration of paints and brushes or in relishing the mixing of play dough, and they employ all their senses to do this. Who has not seen such a child meticulously painting his hands up to the elbow, or beheld another squeezing the sponge in the paint bucket, or a third looking thoughtfully into the distance while licking the back of the play dough spoon?

Once the qualities of the material have been explored and some skill has been gained in its manipulation, the child is likely to move on to what is called the *nonrepresentational stage*. Paintings at this stage, for example, seem to have more design and intention behind them, but the content is not readily recognizable by anyone but the painter. Because painting at this stage is not always done with the intention of depicting something in particular, the teacher must beware of asking, "What is it?" lest such a question unintentionally put the child on a spot.

Ultimately children reach the pictorial or *representational stage*, in which they quite deliberately set out to reproduce or create something. The child may paint a self-portrait, or the sun in the sky, or a fascinating event such as a toilet overflowing or children going trick-or-treating.

One peak period for creative self-expression in our culture occurs between the ages of 4 and 6 years (Schirrmacher, 1998). This stage correlates well with Erikson's developmental stage for this age, which he identified as the stage of *initiative versus guilt*. Erikson's (1963) stage is characterized by reaching out, exploring, and experimenting and reflects an increase in creative behavior that is partially characterized by this same kind of activity.

IMPLICATIONS FOR TEACHERS IN NURTURING CHILDREN'S CREATIVITY

One implication to be drawn from the fact that children pass through sequential stages of development is that teachers should permit children countless opportunities

Leslie Gleim

Children pass through developmental stages in their creative growth and in their use of materials and tools.

Pam Oken-Wright

Notice how this older child uses materials and tools to create a pictorial representation.

to experience and explore expressive materials. *This learning is fundamental to the creative experience.* The full knowledge gained through such exploration extends the ways children may use the material, thereby enriching their creative opportunities; and the freedom to explore is also likely to keep alive their interest and openness to the medium (Althouse et al., 2003; Amabile, 1996; Cadwell, 2002; Loomis, Lewis, & Blumenthal, 2007; Pelo, 2007).

The second developmental implication is that young children, when using expressive materials, should not be expected to produce a finished product. Some 4-year-olds will do this, of course, but because many will not, the expectation of some sort of recognizable result is not a reasonable creative goal to set for children in their early years (Althouse et al., 2003; Copple & Bredekamp, 2009).

Use *Lots* of Self-Expressive Materials to Foster the Creative Self

Expressive materials include such diverse media as painting, collage, dough and clay, woodworking, sewing, and dance—and those are just the tip of the iceberg. Although the materials themselves are different, some basic principles apply to all of them (see Figure 15.2).

PEARSON
myeducationlab

Go to MyEducationLab and select the topic "Creative Arts." Under Activities and Applications, watch the video *Creative Arts*. How can early childhood programs support the development of children's creativity?

- **Interfere as Little as Possible**

Let children explore the materials as their impulses and feelings require, intervening only when needed. Many teachers unthinkingly limit and control the use of expressive materials more than is necessary. Thus they may refuse to permit a child to use the indoor blocks on the table "because we always use them on the floor," or they may insist the child use only one paintbrush at a time despite the fact that using two at once makes such interesting lines and patterns. These ideas are essentially harmless ones and should be encouraged because of their originality.

- **Never Provide a Model for the Children to Copy**

A copy is not an original. The teacher who really wishes to foster originality and the child's self-expression will avoid models and make-alike activities. Merely set out the materials and let the children go to it themselves. However it is good practice to provide real-life models such as leaves, flowers, or whatever objects the children are interested in for them to observe and use in their own work.

- **Understand That the Process, Not the Product, Matters Most to the Young Child**

We live in such a work-oriented, product-centered culture that sometimes we lose sight of the simple pleasure of doing something for its own sake. For young children, however, getting there is more than half the fun. They savor the process and live for the moment. Therefore, it is important not to hurry them toward finishing something or to overstress the final result. They will love to take their creations home, of course, and all such items should be carefully labeled, at least occasionally dated, and put in the children's cubbies so that this is possible, but the primary emphasis should remain on doing.

- **Allow Plenty of Time and Opportunity for the Children to Use Materials So That Their Experiences Are Truly Satisfying**

Children need the chance to work themselves into the experience and to develop their feelings and ideas as they go along. For this reason it is important to schedule time periods that allow for many children to move in and out of the expressive experience as their needs dictate. For real satisfaction this opportunity needs to be available for 60 to 90 minutes at a time.

- **Provide Enough of Whatever the Children Are Using**

Nothing is sadder than children making do with skimpy little fistfuls of dough when they need large, satisfying mounds to punch and squeeze. The same thing holds true for collage materials, woodworking, and painting. Children need plenty of material to work with, as well as the chance to make as many things as they wish.

Providing enough material for the children means that teachers must develop their scrounging and pack rat instincts to the ultimate degree. They not only must ferret out sources of free materials but also must find time and energy to pick them up regularly and produce a place to store them until they are needed. Families can be helpful in collecting materials if the teacher takes the time to show them examples of what is needed. Any community has many sources of such materials. (Appendix E is included to inspire the beginner.)

- **Variety in Materials Is Crucial**

Creative activity should not be limited to easel painting and paper collage. Other creative experiences should be offered frequently, including movement activities and dance, music making, woodworking, weaving, puppetry, shadow play, theatrical performances, singing, clay, wire, mural making, sewing, and so on. In Reggio, the original author of this text— once witnessed a small group of children doing welding—and using real equipment (with protective gear and close supervision). You will find examples of variations suggested in a number of resources, but it is important to rememer that there is a difference between the use of self-expressive materials and many craft-type projects advocated for preschool children, even when these materials do not require making something just like the model.

Figure 15.2
Practical ways to encourage the creative aspect of self-expressive materials

Remember to Make Self-Expressive Opportunities Available for Children with Disabilities

One has only to peruse the majority of textbooks about early childhood special education to realize the subject of self-expressive materials is rarely touched upon, and yet children with disabilities enjoy and need them just as much as other children do. Indeed, offering them the chance to participate in these kinds of activities is of particular value to such children because it provides them the sometimes rare opportunity to take control and make independent choices about what they are doing—and experience success on their own terms.

Although space does not permit an extensive list of suggestions, here are a few possibilities worth considering. For children who are poorly coordinated or movement restricted it is relatively easy to include movement education activities scaled to their abilities. This might mean modifications in the height of equipment, provision of additional handholds, or inclusion of safety mats. Children who are vision impaired will do best with art materials if the table is well lit and the materials are clearly contrasting in tone and texture. Light tables are particularly nice to use with them. Clay and other sensorily appealing modeling materials are worthwhile to offer. Children who are hearing impaired can be stimulated to try out all sorts of self-expressive materials if they are encouraged to come and see what is available for their delight. Children who are cognitively delayed will enjoy the same materials set out for the children who are more intellectually developed but will use the materials at a more exploratory level. They will benefit from clear, simple instructions about whatever limits are necessary in relation to the activity.

Foster an Appreciation of Beauty

In these days of grotesque cartoons, garish advertising, and urban squalor to which so many children are exposed, it is more important than ever to make certain that the *children's* center—their special place—does not reflect that ugliness (Cadwell, 2002; Edwards, Gandini, & Forman, 1993, 1998; Epstein, 2007; Gandini et al., 2005; Isenberg & Jalongo, 2006; Jalongo & Stamp, 1997).

Sometimes teachers are so caught up in the functional aspects of room arrangement and curriculum development they forget that the school has an important influence on developing the children's concepts of what is beautiful. When the room—which is really the children's home away from home—is accented with pretty curtains, colorful pillows, well-proportioned furniture, and tastefully arranged activity centers, it has a significant influence on forming the children's taste—their aesthetic appreciation.

Children's creations should be included, too, because they add so much verve, joy, and loveliness to the surroundings. By choosing to display the children's own work rather than adult-made, mass-produced "art," the value we place on the children's ideas and creations is conveyed to them and their families. And when we take care to display children's work in a really attractive way—not just taped sloppily to the wall— doesn't it look better, anyway?

Lori Pickert

The children's center should be a place where beauty is appreciated and expressed. A few things to mention about this attractive classroom: it's full of beautiful, living plants and the children's work is displayed just about everywhere—at child eye level, adult eye level, even from the ceiling and strewn with colorful lights to add more appeal.

SUMMARY

Early childhood teachers have always valued the creative part of the child's self and have sought to enhance its development by fostering the use of self-expressive materials. Today we also seek to foster creativity in additional ways, which include generating creative play and encouraging originality of thought.

It is important for the teacher to support creativity in many ways throughout the curriculum because it teaches to the child's multiple intelligences. As well, creative experiences help develop other domains of learning, including emotional development, social development, physical development, language and literacy development, and cognitive development.

The teacher should provide opportunities for creative expression every day. When presenting self-expressive materials for the children's use, teachers should avoid making models for them to copy, emphasize the process rather than the product, and allow plenty of time and opportunity for the children to use the material. But the most important thing is to make the materials freely available and let the children explore them as their impulses and interests dictate.

Questions and Activities

1. The next time you have to solve some sort of problem, take a few minutes and just for fun list all the ways, both silly and practical, that the problem might be solved. Try not to evaluate the merit of the ideas as you produce them, but just play around with many possibilities. Then evaluate them. Is a fresh one included that might be a good, new, though perhaps unconventional, way to solve the problem?

2. Might it be possible that preprimary teachers are depriving children of the right to learn the things that would help them succeed best in elementary school when we stress play, creativity, and mental health, rather than emphasizing such skills as learning the alphabet and counting? What might be the case for placing greater emphasis on academic learning at the preschool level? Do you think creative experiences can be used to support academic learning? Why or why not?

3. Isn't it a waste of time to let children try things out that obviously won't work? Might it not be better just to lead a discussion with them about the proposed solutions, rather than go to the trouble of actually trying out something only to experience failure? Why?

Diversity Question

1. Explain why it is valuable for children who have disabilities to participate in using self-expressive materials. Provide examples of ways materials might be adapted to make that participation more feasible.

Predicaments

1. You have in your room a boy about 4 years old who asks for a lot of assistance. For example, he will ask, "How can I make purple?" or "Why won't my dog [of clay] stand up?" As his teacher, how would you respond to his requests?

2. A parent in your preschool complains that rather than just "playing and dancing to music all day," you should be teaching the children to read and write. How would you respond?

3. Krysta is painting at the easel and gradually begins to spread paint off the paper onto the easel itself, then to paint her hands and arms up to the elbows, and then to flick drops of paint onto a neighboring child and her painting. What should the teacher do?

Self-Check Questions for Review

Content-Related Questions

1. Describe some things teachers can do to include creative experiences in the early childhood curriculum.

2. What are the four components of creativity as described by Torrance? Give an example of how you could support each component in your classroom.

3. What is Gardner's theory of multiple intelligences? How does providing creative experiences for children support this theory?

4. Identify several values the experience of creativity offers to the growing child.

Integrative Questions

1. On a snowy day the children are fascinated with the snow itself because it's the first snow of winter. What are some activities you could do with them that would provide some learning while the children are having fun? Would you incorporate any expressive arts activities? Be sure to identify what the children would be learning and why you think they will enjoy the experiences.

2. The preschool teacher in the next room has had the 3-year-olds make caterpillars out of Styrofoam egg cartons and pipe cleaners. Each child was allowed to decide whether to use purple or red pipe cleaners for the legs and yellow or pink ones for the antennae. The next project is showing the children how to glue artificial flowers onto pipe cleaner stems and stick them into balls of clay for Mother's Day. Evaluate these projects in terms of their potential creative benefit for the children. Be sure to explain why you think these projects would or would not enhance the children's creative selves.

Reference for Further Reading

Althouse, R., Johnson, M. H., & Mitchell, S. T. (2003). *The colors of learning: Integrating the visual arts into the early childhood curriculum.* New York: Teachers College Press.

Related Organizations and Online Resources

National Art Education Association. This nonprofit, educational organization represents over 22,000 art educators from every level of instruction, and anyone and everyone concerned about quality art education in our schools. An excellent list of publications on the effects of arts education on children's learning is available at http://www.naea-reston.org/.

National Standards for Arts Education. This document outlines basic arts learning outcomes integral to the comprehensive K–12 education of every American student. Developed by the Consortium of National Arts Education Associations, the standards can be accessed at http://artsedge.kennedy-center.org/teach/standards/ overview.cfm.

Project Zero. This research group at the Harvard Graduate School of Education has investigated the development of learning processes in children, adults, and organizations since 1967. Project Zero's mission is to understand and enhance learning, thinking, and creativity in the arts, as well as humanistic and scientific disciplines, at the individual and institutional levels. Information about Gardner's theory of multiple intelligences can also be found at http://www.pz.harvard.edu/index.cfm.

CHAPTER sixteen

Developing the Whole Child: Integrating the Five Selves Throughout the Curriculum

How to plan curriculum so that the children's development in all areas is supported?

Just what "child-centered" or "emergent curriculum" really means?

How education can reflect a belief in the value of play, happiness, and joy?

. . . IF YOU HAVE, THE MATERIAL IN THE FOLLOWING PAGES WILL HELP YOU.

The word joy will probably not show up in a curriculum guide. And I don't hear many politicians using that word when they talk about schools and money and accountability. But those of us working hard to ensure a childhood for so many children know that if we did not hear laughter, giggling, hoopla, shouting, and cheering in our centers we couldn't go on. It is the joy of each child that keeps us doing what we do.

Bev Bos (2006, p.1)

Experience shapes the brain.

Daniel Siegel (1999)

Education is not preparation for life; education is life itself.

John Dewey (1916)

SELECTING VALUES AND PRIORITIES IN THE CURRICULUM

Biological and psychological research, as well as our own observations and common sense, confirms how much the work of families and teachers matters in the early years. We must think carefully about what we are providing in the way of experiences and how we are providing them as we plan the curriculum for the whole child. Which learnings are more important, and which less so?

For example, is it more important that children experience joy and verve when learning or that they learn to sit quietly and not interrupt the teacher? Is it more significant that they speak fluently and spontaneously or that they speak Standard American English? Is it more valuable that they be able to think about problems and feel confident about their ability to solve them or that they be able to pick out all the things in the room that are shaped like squares?

It is not that any of these values are reprehensible or should not receive attention: It *is* a question of deciding which goals should receive *primary* emphasis. The teacher who elects to foster joy and verve is likely to employ a different teaching style from one who believes that quietly paying attention is vital to classroom success.

When we began our journey of learning to teach for the whole child in chapter 1, certain elements were suggested as effective, best practices in early childhood programs and schools. These include good human relationships, family inclusion, and a curriculum

Benjamin La Framboise

In considering the child, which learnings are most important? Is it more valuable that she feels confident in her ability to solve problems or that she can say what day of the week it is?

that is developmentally, individually, and culturally appropriate. In this text we have seen how high-quality early education uses reasonable and authentic methods of assessment, incorporates a balance of self-selection and teacher direction, and educates all the child's five selves. High-quality education for young children is based on the principles that learning should be the result of actual experience, that play is a significant mode of learning, and above all that the center should be a place of joy for both children and staff.

It is an unfortunate truth that many teachers today feel overwhelming pressure to conform to mandated standards and to focus class time on preparing for and administering tests. We are stressed about how the children will fare on assessments, whether our school will pass muster, and whether the families feel we are doing a good job with their children. As a result, we often lose sight of the real reasons we were drawn to teaching in the first place, and the many delights we—and the children—can enjoy every day in the early childhood classroom.

In this concluding chapter we will look at various ways of going about this: how to develop curriculum that will support the five selves of the children, how to expand their curiosity about the world, and how to encourage their joy in learning and engagement in school. Keep in mind that the art of teaching involves being open-minded and flexible. The suggestions here are not meant to serve as a blueprint for how you will teach every child, every day for the rest of your teaching career. Your willingness to experiment and learn, and your own sense of wonder and creativity in teaching will help you develop your personal teaching style and methods that inspire joy and laughter. The following priorities are those the authors have recommended in *The Whole Child*, and discussion of them has been woven throughout the text. They are presented to you in this chapter as an organized set for your consideration as you begin your own journey into the teaching profession.

Benjamin La Framboise

In considering curriculum approaches, it is important to develop your own teaching style and methods that inspire joy and laughter in the classroom.

PRIORITY 1: PRACTICE INTENTIONAL TEACHING

Intentional teachers are mindful of their teaching goals and strategies—ever on the lookout for teachable moments and assessing the effects they have on the children, families, and educational community. Rather than discounting standards and assessment, intentional teachers use them for the betterment of the children and for appropriate planning for the individual learners in their care. Intentional teachers have a sense of purpose and devote careful thought to the curriculum, the educational environment they help to create, and most importantly, the relationships they nurture within the classroom. Through caring and intentional teaching, the curricular goals that have been suggested throughout this text can be addressed: inclusion of children with disabilities, family involvement, enhancing the development of the five selves, learning standards and assessment, and meeting academic goals.

In the book *The Intentional Teacher: Choosing the Best Strategies for Young Children's Learning*, Epstein (2007) states:

> The mission of the intentional teacher is to ensure that young children acquire the knowledge and skills they need to succeed in school and in life. To fulfill this mission, intentional teachers conscientiously address every area of early learning—intellectual, social-emotional, physical and creative—with sufficient range and depth. . . . Moreover, intentional teachers attend to their own personal development. They regard themselves as lifelong learners—studying the children in their care, updating their knowledge of the latest child development theory and research, and examining implications for their practice. They are also collaborators, teaming with coworkers and families to apply their expertise and resources toward children's optimal development. (p. 21)

PRIORITY 2: INCORPORATE DEVELOPMENTALLY APPROPRIATE PRACTICE (DAP)

By now it should be clear that each child's development is unique. It is important to know where each child fits in the developmental continuum so as to teach at the appropriate level and inspire the child to go just a bit further. In addition to being knowledgeable about typical development, the teacher must use a variety of assessment techniques throughout the year. We need to know which are areas of strength and which are areas where you can help the youngster gain competence. By incorporating DAP in our teaching, we ensure that each child's needs are considered and met. Whether children are physically disabled, developmentally delayed, or intellectually gifted, whether they are overweight or hyperactive, we are able to provide an educational experience that is suited to each child's interests and abilities and encourages optimal growth.

In working to revise the National Association for the Education of Young Children (NAEYC) position statement of developmentally appropriate practice, Copple and Bredekamp (2008) found widespread agreement in the field that the following aspects are fundamental to DAP:

- Curriculum and experiences that actively engage children
- Rich, teacher-supported play

- Integrated curriculum
- Scope for children's initiative and choice
- Intentional decisions in the organization and timing of learning experiences
- Adapting curriculum and teaching strategies to help individual children make optimal progress (p. 54)

Supporting the child's active engagement is a primary concept of DAP and the underpinning of emergent curriculum which will be discussed in further detail. By developing a curriculum that focuses on children as active participants rather than as passive recipients of information from the adult, we enhance their view of themselves as capable and encourage a positive attitude toward school, which is so important for future academic success.

PRIORITY 3: DEVELOP AN INTEGRATED CURRICULUM THAT SUPPORTS THE FIVE SELVES OF THE WHOLE CHILD AND TEACHES TO MULTIPLE INTELLIGENCES

One of the first American educators to propose an integrated curriculum was John Dewey (1916), founder of the progressive education movement. Integrated curriculum is based on the premise that natural human learning does not occur in isolated segments; it spans different learning domains at the same time. Rather than studying discrete subject matters one at a time, they are combined and intentionally linked. Language, literacy, social studies, music, art, math, science, physical movement, and other subjects can all take place together in curriculum investigations and activities.

Early childhood educators frequently use integrated curriculum. For example, when we read a book that includes counting, in addition to literacy skills, we teach the social skill of listening and answering, basic counting skills, and one-to-one correspondence. In *The Whole Child*, we have proposed that there are five selves of the child that all warrant special attention from the teacher: the physical self, emotional self, social self, cognitive self, and creative self. Using an integrated approach that combines subject matters—at group time, in learning centers, or in projects—is one of the best ways to ensure that all areas of development are addressed.

Integrated curriculum also supports Gardner's theory of multiple intelligences, which was introduced in chapter 15. In this theory there are different types of learning that individuals possess, and teachers should attempt to teach to all of them throughout the curriculum. There are seven types of intelligences proposed in multiple intelligences theory (Gardner, 1983, 1999, 2004):

1. Linguistic intelligence involves the ability to communicate with spoken and written language.
2. Musical intelligence involves the ability to appreciate, perform, and compose music. Musical intelligence includes paying attention to patterns, pitches, tones, and rhythms.

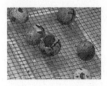

Go to MyEducationLab and select the topic "Math and Science." Under Activities and Applications, watch the video *Exploring Eggs in a Study of Birds.* How are different intelligences supported through this type of integrated curriculum? Which intelligences do you see addressed in the video and how?

3. Logical-mathematical intelligence involves the ability to use logic, analyze problems, perform mathematical operations, experiment, and investigate issues scientifically.

4. Spatial intelligence involves perceiving the visual world accurately, performing transformations on the initial perception, and then mentally "seeing" or figuring out the effects.

5. Bodily-kinesthetic intelligence involves using the body in a highly differentiated and skilled way for expressive and goal-directed purposes. Use of tools and mechanical abilities are also involved in bodily-kinesthetic intelligence.

6. Interpersonal intelligence involves the ability to attend to and understand other people.

7. Intrapersonal intelligence involves the ability to be self-aware and understand one's own emotions, fears, and motivations. It is our sense of self that informs our behavior and relation to the world.

PRIORITY 4: FIND WAYS TO ENCOURAGE CHILD-CENTERED ACTIVE LEARNING; USE AN EMERGENT CURRICULUM APPROACH

Sometimes novice teachers assume the term *emergent* means that every idea must emerge from the children and that the curriculum must be entirely unplanned and spontaneous to fulfill the criteria of emerging. However, in this book *emergent* means that the direction a topic takes develops as the children and teachers investigate it together—each contributing his or her own ideas and possibilities as they evolve, in somewhat the same way the children and teachers in Reggio Emilia do. The teachers do make plans in advance and have ideas for possible topics, just as the children do, but as Rinaldi (1994) put it so well, "these plans are viewed as a compass, not a train schedule."

This image of a curriculum plan serving as a compass indicating direction and intention rather than being a predetermined schedule is particularly helpful to keep in mind when using the emergent approach. After all, if the curriculum is seen as gradually emerging, it cannot be completely scheduled in advance, but it certainly does require a sense of direction and purpose.

If we carry the image of a compass a little further, it also clarifies why we, like Loris Malaguzzi (1992), the founder and architect of the Reggio Emilia preprimary schools, prefer to use the word *pathway*, rather than *project*, to describe the development of a topic. *Pathway* conveys the sense of a continuing journey, rather than a unit that has a preplanned end or goal in mind from the start. As teachers and children venture down the pathway together, learning stems from the social interaction and collaboration that takes place along the way (Edwards, Gandini, & Forman, 1993, 1998; Gandini, Hill, Cadwell, & Schwall, 2005; Hendrick, 1997, 2004; Oken-Wright 2001; Rinaldi, 2002; Wien, 2008; Wurm, 2005).

As this idea of a collaborative, learning-together approach has gained impetus, interest has also grown (in Reggio Emilia as well as in the United States) in the works of a Russian psychologist named Lev Vygotsky because of his emphasis on the value of the child and a more knowledgeable person working in collaboration. Therefore, it makes sense to take a moment to consider some of his most basic ideas.

Some Basic Concepts of Vygotskian Psychology

During his brief life (he died at age 37 from tuberculosis), Vygotsky contributed some insightful ideas about cognitive development and how it takes place. He maintained that language and cognitive ability do not appear automatically as the child passes through landmark stages, but rather that they develop in part because of interaction with other people—other peers, adults, and even imaginary companions as the child grows. As the title of his book *Mind in Society* (1978) emphasizes, the mind develops as the result of society's action on it. Since mental development cannot be separated from the social context in which it takes place, this theory about children's mental development is often spoken of as a sociocultural or sociohistorical theory. All this means is that society (and its past development—hence historical) and the culture it generates have great influence on what children learn and the means by which they learn it.

Perhaps the most familiar Vygotskian concept is the idea of the *zone of proximal development (ZPD)*. Vygotsky (1978) defined this as "the distance between the actual development level [of the child] as determined by independent problem solving and the level of potential development as determined through problem solving under adult guidance in collaboration with more capable peers" (p. 86). Vygotsky

Pam Oken-Wright

Cognitive abilities develop out of interactions with other people.

pointed out that with the assistance of a more knowledgeable person, the child can advance closer to the farther edge of potential ability. In other words there's a difference between the current or actual level of development and the child's potential level of development. The possibility of maximum advancement depends on the assistance lent to the learner by a more knowledgeable person—either an adult or another child.

This concept of the *ZPD*, as it is affectionately called, has encouraged teachers striving to put the emergent curriculum into practice to see their role as first beginning at the children's level of ability and then collaborating with them—by offering questions and cues, as well as more tangible assistance, that may enable children to extend their mental abilities a bit beyond what they were previously able to do.

The other aspect of Vygotsky's theory of particular importance to early childhood teachers is his emphasis on the significance of spoken language as the mediator between the world, the children's minds, and their ability to express, understand, and explain to other people what they know. Vygotsky theorized that by using the tool of language, children are able to master themselves and gain independence and self-control of behavior and thought. It is certainly true that many of us who work with 2-year-olds have heard examples of their attempts to use language to regulate behavior that support this contention. Who has not witnessed a child of that age say, "No! No! Baby!" while reaching simultaneously for the scissors?—or dealt with a 4-year-old reporting prissily on another's misdeeds in the sandbox?

A warning must be noted concerning the use of language with young children: While acknowledging its indispensable value, teachers must also remember not to substitute it for real experiences. For language to have meaning it must be tied to the concrete world, and for the world to acquire meaning, the child must have language.

PEARSON
myeducationlab

Go to MyEducationLab and select the topic "Curriculum/Program Models." Under Activities and Applications, watch the video *Guiding Learning in a Study of Birds*. How does this integrated curriculum approach support Vygotsky's theory of the importance of tying language to real-world experiences?

The Reggio Approach

The Reggio approach, which was introduced in chapter 1, is an emergent curriculum approach that has been in use in the preprimary schools of Reggio Emilia, Italy, since the 1960s. Americans have been studying the Reggio approach since it first landed at the NAEYC national conference in the early 1990s (with one conference presentation!). Since that time, *Newsweek* magazine has cited the Reggio schools as "the best in the world," thousands of teachers have taken study tours there, and there is now an entire Reggio track at the annual NAEYC conference with well over 20 presentations each year.

There has been discussion of the Reggio approach throughout *The Whole Child*, but this has only given you a small taste of a deeply thought-out and philosophical method of teaching. Once teachers witness the full beauty and passion of that city's educational system for young children, most feel inspired to provide the best learning experiences for our children in U.S. cities as well. It is hoped that you will feel inspired by this text to explore the Reggio approach further as you develop your own set of best practices in teaching. Figure 16.1 highlights some of the basic principles that underlie the Reggio Emilia approach.

1. **Image of the child**
   Children are viewed as strong, capable, powerful, curious, full of ideas and theories, and active in constructing their own knowledge through interactions with others.

2. **Education based on relationships**
   Everyone involved in the school—children, teachers, and parents—are constantly learning through their interactions with others. All learners must feel connected to others, loved, and cared for in order for growth and development to blossom.

3. **The role of the teacher**
   The teacher is there to nuture close relationships with the children and families. The teacher works in collaboration with the children, other educators, families, and community to sustain stimulating experiences throughout the school day, to provoke, inspire, and help organize deep learning investigations. Teachers facilitate children's ability to represent what they know and imagine.

4. **Environment as third teacher**
   Through conscious use of space, color, natural light, displays of children's work, and attention to nature and detail, the environment almost serves as an additional teacher. It conveys to children, families, and teachers how the space is to be used and that their presence is valued and respected. The environment serves as an invitation to enter and to participate.

5. **The hundred languages of children**
   Children use many different formats for communicating their ideas and feelings. In addition to talking they are expressive with paint, drawing, clay, woodwork, theater, puppets, collage, and so on. There are a hundred (or more) ways in which children speak to us and others. Schools support fluency in a range of languages by providing materials, an art studio (atelier), and a school artist (atelierista) for advice, training, and collaboration.

6. **Documentation**
   Documentation in Reggio goes beyond simply recording children's words and putting them up on the bulletin board. The purpose of documentation is "to make learning visible," to record the children's theories which are expressed in a variety of media, to diplay their work, and to use it as a basis for discussion and as a basis for where the curriculum will go next. Artists work with the classroom teachers to help explore various creative means of expression with the children, and to display the pathway their learning went in an aesthetically pleasing way.

7. **The role of the families**
   The educational process is seen as involving three equally important participants: children, teachers, and parents. Parents have the right—and are encouraged—to be active contributors in their children's activities and development. Parents collaborate with teachers in curriculum decisions as well as administrative decisions.

8. **The importance of time**
   Projects and themes follow the children's interest and development of concepts. Projects and activities are not "one-shot deals," rather they build upon one another over time, as the children "revisit" their original work and ideas, refining them further through new experiences, activities, and forms of expression. Time is also important in building sustaining, collaborative relationships.

9. **Children with special rights**
   Children with disabilities are welcomed and included in the Reggio classrooms. They are referred to as "children with special rights" because it is not they who need to do anything, it is up to the school to provide and care for them as they do for all children (this reflects the first principle of the image of the child).

10. **Community involvement**
    The Reggio Emilia infant centers and preprimary schools are open to all children in the town, which uses its tax dollars to fund the preprimary schools. The schools grew out of town meetings after World War II has destroyed much of the city, and the people of Reggio wanted to ensure that fascism and war would never happen in their country again. They believed that building and funding the best education possible for the youngest citizens would bring about that goal. The Reggio community at large and city political body are greatly involved in supporting the schools.

Figure 16.1
Basic principles of the Reggio approach

Benjamin La Framboise

A basic principle of the Reggio approach: Education is based on relationships.

SOME BASIC PRINCIPLES TO REMEMBER WHEN USING THE EMERGENT APPROACH

Many teachers, particularly early childhood teachers, are very attracted to this idea of the curriculum unfolding and developing as the children's interest grows. Yet when actually thinking about putting the approach into practice, they feel baffled and unsure about where to begin.

It is really not so difficult once the approach is analyzed into its various aspects and some fundamental concepts are grasped. One of the most important of these is that it is valuable for children to be able to generate their own ideas, figure out answers for themselves, and try out a variety of solutions until they find one that works—in other words, to make connections for themselves.

Foster the Children's Ability to Generate Their Own Creative Ideas

Armstrong's (1997) definition of creativity as the "ability to see things in new ways and make unconventional connections" (p. 32) applies as well to cognitive activity as to play and the use of expressive materials because the ability to put past experiences together to connect in new ways is crucial to developing creative thinking. Of course, sometimes building on past knowledge produces unexpected and delightful results. For example, two young friends were eating lunch together when the following dialogue took place.

> **Henry:** "Well, you know, Andrew, I'm Black. I'm Black all over—from my head right down to inside my shoes. But that's OK! 'Cuz my mother says, 'Black is beautiful!'"

Andrew: "Well," looking thoughtfully at Henry, "I guess being Black's all right—but you know, Henry, if you wuz green, you could hide in the trees!"

Using prior information as Andrew did to produce new possibilities is just one kind of creative thinking. Children are also thinking creatively when they produce more than one answer to a question, or conceive of new uses for familiar materials, or generate uniquely descriptive language and self-expressive stories. To do these things, they need a wealth of experience to draw upon, and they need the help and expertise of the teacher to encourage them.

One person who has helped us understand the difference between the kind of thinking processes in which only one answer is correct and the thinking processes in which many answers might be correct is Paul Guilford (1981). He named the uncreative one-correct-answer sort of thinking *convergent* and the creative many-possible-answers kind of thinking *divergent*.

Convergent thinking is elicited by such questions as, "What color is this?" "Can you tell me the name of this shape?" and, "What must we always do before we cross the street?" Nothing is wrong with this kind of mental activity; children need a variety of commonly known facts at their fingertips. But teaching that stops at the fact-asking information level fails to draw out the child's own ideas. Children who are trained like robots to produce facts when the right button is pushed are unlikely to grow up to produce the new ideas desperately needed in science, medicine, and human relationships (Ashbury & Rich, 2008; Hirsh-Pasek & Golinkoff, 2003; Jalongo, 2003).

Unfortunately most teaching is still geared to convergent, one-answer learning. But just because this has been true of teaching in the past does not mean it must continue. The following examples of ways to encourage children to generate emerging ideas of their own may encourage teachers to produce more divergent thinking in the children in their groups. Doing this is fun, it is interesting, and it can be exciting for both children and teachers when presented in the right manner. All it takes is practice.

Base the Curriculum on the Interests of the Children as Their Ideas Develop

When thinking about the value of basing topics on the children's interests, the question of a former student always comes to mind. She asked most desperately and sincerely, "But what if the children don't have any ideas? What do I do then?"

The answer to this is that the ideas are always there if the teacher asks the right questions, waits for answers, and *listens closely enough*. Even when beginning with a potential topic generated by the teachers, note in the following example how the Reggio staff listened to the children and changed direction according to the interests of the 3-year-olds.

In this particular project described by Gambetti (1993), the teachers initiated the investigation because they thought it would be interesting to find out how the 3-year-olds viewed seasonal events, with late autumn as a particular focus. They began the study by talking with the children and asking them questions such as, "According to you, what is a season?"

As they listened closely to what the children said, it became clear to the teachers that the children were more interested in clouds and what they do than they were in seasons. So they dropped the idea of seasons and decided to follow that lead. Over a considerable period of time a variety of experiences with clouds ensued—some suggested by the teachers and others by the children. These included looking at clouds at different times, observing frost in the morning and how the children's breath made clouds, projecting images of ice and clouds on a shadow screen, and drawing clouds—filled with whatever the children thought should be inside them. Finally the children decided they wanted to make "real" clouds of their own based on what they had learned about them. They journeyed around the school looking for materials from which to form the clouds and materials with which to fill them. These ingredients, which were intended to represent raindrops and snowflakes, were as varied as wedged paper, lace, Styrofoam, bits of mirrors, and actual water. During the investigation the children were challenged (or *provoked*, as they say in Reggio) to produce various hypotheses about clouds and how they work and also to solve some problems. For example, they hypothesized about what's inside clouds, and they solved the problem of how to represent that content and the mechanics of how to hang the clouds up in the classroom "near the sky."

Careful recordings and pictures were made of what the children said as they worked on this project over many days. Their conclusions and explanations of what they did and why they did it were encouraged and written down, and all this information was transcribed onto documentation boards for the children, teachers, and families to review as the pathway developed.

Base the curriculum on children's real interests. These girls wanted to communicate with their bird, which inspired them to draw its portrait and write a friendly message: "PEEP."

Remember to Keep the Pathway Focused: Don't Let It Branch Off in Too Many Directions

Although it is all very well and good to pay attention to the children's interests, the teacher must provide continuing direction to the pathway lest the group lose its way. Only the teacher has the vision to keep the entire forest in view while not losing sight of the individual trees.

Take the example of ducklings, for instance (see Table 16.1 on pp. 371–372). Without consistent direction, interests might spread to barnyard animals in general, baby animals, raising a kitten, how animals swim, how people swim, what comes out of eggs, going duck hunting (remember that many children live in families in which family members hunt as a pastime), what's alive and what's dead, Easter customs from other lands, and so forth.

Such a far-ranging mixture of subjects will most likely provide the children with what Katz (1991) termed "smatterings" of information—mostly factual learning only loosely related to the children's core of interest. How much stronger it would be to focus clearly on a particular aspect of ducklings and to pursue the learning possibilities of that subject in more depth.

The Number of Children's Ideas Will Be Increased If the Teacher Recognizes Their Value and Responds to Them in a Positive Way

An open-minded teacher who keeps on the lookout for spontaneous ideas and suggestions can frequently go along with variations in approach and changes in procedure when they are suggested by the children. The teacher who is willing to let the children put their ideas into practice offers strong positive reinforcement for this behavior, which will nourish problem-solving talent in the children.

Sometimes these ideas can be very simple. For example, one time we offered a cooking project that involved slicing bananas. The inexperienced student in charge thought she could watch only two children working with paring knives at once and therefore sensibly limited the activity to two children at a time. A third little boy hung around and watched, badly wanting to have a chance with the bananas; but the student truthfully explained she was so new that she just couldn't supervise more than two knives at once. Then he said to her, "I tell you what—I could use one of the scissors for the bananas. I know how to do that. I *never* cut myself with scissors." She immediately saw the value of his suggestion and let him snip up as many pieces as he liked.

Another independently minded 2-1/2-year-old was going through a streak of wanting to get into the swing by herself. Since she was short and the swing was high, she struggled and wriggled, doggedly refusing assistance. Finally she rushed away and returned with a large hollow block, which she put under the swing and used successfully as a mounting block.

Use Language Consistently Along with More Tangible Ways of Trying Out Ideas

Although there are perils in overintellectualizing discussions, it is important to remember that language is of genuine value in the development of ideas. Just remember that conversation must not be allowed to take the place of actual involvement with real things.

The staff in Reggio Emilia makes a particular point of valuing language in such interesting ways that these warrant special discussion here. They use tape recordings as well as videotapes and photographs to capture children's comments about topics.

These recordings are then transcribed so that staff can review and talk them over together—searching for clues about what the children know and what turn a pathway might take next (Edwards et al., 1993, 1998; Oken-Wright, 2001; Tarini, 1997).

Transcriptions, though time-consuming to do, have so many uses that they are well worth the extra work. Besides being used for the teachers to study, some of them are used to review events and ideas with the children—allowing the children to revisit (recognize) what they have been doing and thinking about.

In addition, transcriptions often become part of documentation boards assembled as the investigations continue. These boards, which combine written and pictorial documentation, are used for the children's direct benefit and to keep the families informed about what is going on. Ultimately the documentation boards and transcriptions, together with other records, provide concrete evidence of accomplishment that can be very useful for assessment purposes (Cadwell, 2002; Helm & Beneke, 2003; Wien, 2008; Wurm, 2005).

Enable the Children to Translate Their Ideas into Concrete, Tangible Experiences

The real joy and satisfaction of using the emergent approach must not be thought of as stopping at the idea stage. The real satisfaction comes from putting the proposals for solving problems into practice: trying out possible containers for water, determining what works and what lets the water soak through, seeing whether the ducks can manage the steps or really need a ramp to get in and out, and so forth.

This aspect of learning can stretch out over weeks as the children think of what could be done and put their ideas to the test of practicality. It is important to relax and allow plenty of time and an unhurried pace if the children are to obtain maximum value from the experience.

Also Allow Children to Experience Failure

Of course, creative ideas and experiments do not always work. But if the situation is reasonably safe, the children should be allowed to try out their ideas even if the adult knows they will not work. Children are entitled to the right to fail, as well as the right to succeed. The sensitive teacher will be matter-of-fact and low-key about such ineffective trials by saying, "I'm sorry that didn't work out just right, but it was worth a try," or, "Well, what do you want to try next?"

Children can learn as much from experiencing failures as they can from successes. Sometimes they are able to modify the idea and turn it into a later triumph, sometimes not. More important than being successful is learning to accept the experience of failure as part of life while going on to try out other possible solutions.

Make Certain the Children Use Some Form of Expressive Medium to Explain to Other People What They Have Found Out

The most obvious way children can communicate what they've learned is to explain it as the teacher writes it down for them, but there are many additional avenues for such explanations. The various ways in which children can express their feelings and ideas—the hundred languages of children—are boundless and make up some of the most exciting aspects of the child development program. But rather than relying on a textbook for creative teaching ideas, the successful—and happy—teacher will adopt an attitude of experimentation and discovery when it comes to developing a creative curriculum. Why stick to the same old craft-type "recipes" when it just takes a little imagination to come up with some really inspiring experiences for children? There are many resources available to teachers for activities, and hopefully these will be used as a springboard for further creative ideas. Refer to Appendix E for suggestions about creating your own classroom activities using homemade and recycled materials.

An Example of How Midlevel Mental Ability Skills Can Be Included—and Learning Standards Can Be Met—as Part of an Emergent Approach

As we saw earlier in chapter 14, it is not necessary or even desirable to rely exclusively on only one of the two approaches to fostering cognitive development in young children, because both the emergent and conventional approaches have merit. The most desirable strategy is to use the emergent approach as the fundamental foundation for fostering thinking ability and then to enrich it with specific practice in midlevel skills as well. Table 16.1 illustrates how a teacher could use this combination approach to provide maximum benefits for the children.

Table 16.1

Example of how a pathway might emerge based on the children's interests using the emergent and midlevel approaches to cognitive development

Children's Original Concerns and Interests	Adults' Visions of Possible Pathways to Explore	Children's Choices	Adult "Provocations"
[Children actually hatched eggs . . . have cared for ducklings and realized they've outgrown current cage]	Provide some way for ducks to go swimming	Make a pond for the ducks to enjoy	What could we use or make for pond? How can we keep the water in?
During a discussion, they say they want the ducks to feel happy—			How could the ducks get into or out of the water?
1. Find their mother			How can we fill the pond with water?
2. Take them swimming			Could we make a shower for them?
3. Make them a shower			
4. Let them play outside			
5. Fix them a bigger house	Build an outdoor shelter and pen	Maybe later—let's do the pond first . . . that will make them *most* happy	
6. Feed them stuff ducks really like to eat	Investigate relationship of form to function; web feet vs. claws vs. fingers, etc.	Children not interested when topic is brought up	

(*Continued*)

Children's Proposed Solutions	Examples of Higher Order Thinking Skills Tapped Using This Emergent Approach	Companion Midlevel Mental Abilities That Could Be Added by Teacher
Dish pan Galvanized tub Children's pool Dig hole, fill with water	Use imagination to solve problems (What kind of things hold water?) Anticipate outcomes of proposed solutions and/or try them out.	*Matching* Get out spring lotto game made of "Easter" stickers of ducks, chickens, etc. *Grouping* Provide plastic animals for children to sort according to categories—include ducks, fish, farm animals, birds, etc.
Make them a ramp Build stairs from blocks Lift them ourselves (but we have to catch them first!)	Think of alternatives (what to do when hole is dug and water seeps away) Estimate future size of ducks (Find out how to find how big ducks grow) Apply concept of measurement (How long does the hose need to be to reach the pond?)	*Common Relations* Pair different pictures of feet with animals they belong to (ducks and others) *Temporal Ordering* Take photos of ducklings as they grow and arrange them in order of developmental stages
Add pipes onto end of hose Use bucket Squirt hose very hard Move pool	Gain understanding of some principles of physics related to force and pressure (How can you make water run uphill?)	*Graduated (seriated) Ordering* Measure height of ducklings as they grow Make graph comparing growth rate with growth rate of gerbils
Hold watering can up and sprinkle ducks Tie hose to top of slide Use pipes, screw on flexible dish-rinsing hose from kitchen on pipe's end Squirt hose	Value other people's ideas when something doesn't work (What if the cook needs to use the dish-rinsing hose?)	*Cause and Effect* Were the ducks happier when they had the new pond? What made the water come out of the house faster or slower?

PRIORITY 5: FOCUS ON TEACHING HAPPINESS AND JOY IN LEARNING AS MUCH AS ACADEMIC SKILLS

Take a moment to reflect on what you have learned about young children's development and learning, and your role as their teacher. By embarking on a teaching career you have joined the ranks of many educators in history from John Dewey to Jean Piaget, from Maria Montessori to Loris Malaguzzi to your favorite teacher in elementary school (hopefully there was at least one!). The work of early childhood educators is valuable and long-lasting; if we do our job well, we will be appreciated and remembered by the children, families, coworkers, and community members with whom our teaching lives intersect.

With an overemphasis on academic achievement and testing comes the temptation to rush children in their development—just as teachers often rush from topic to topic, filling the day with requirements until there is no room for recess. It is helpful to take a pause, breathe deeply, and reflect on the meaning of teaching. What are our basic goals for education? What goals do you have as a teacher? As Noddings (2006) points out, a wider goal beyond academics is the foundation of American education:

> Some people argue that schools are best organized to accomplish academic goals and that we should charge other institutions with the task of pursuing the physical, moral, social, emotional, spiritual, and aesthetic aims that we associate with the whole child. . . .
>
> Those who make this argument have not considered the history of education. Public schools in the United States—as well as schools across different societies and historical eras—were established as much for moral and social reasons as for academic instruction. (p. 2)

Noddings goes on to suggest that happiness be included as one of our basic educational aims, "We incorporate this aim into education not only by helping our students understand the components of happiness but also by making classrooms genuinely happy places" (p. 3).

It is rare today to hear much talk about happiness in the public discourse about education. With a focus on funding and academic performance, the idea of teaching to improve the quality of a human life and creating well-adjusted, happy members of society has gotten lost. It is hoped that *The Whole Child* will prove valuable to you in your teaching career and that you will find enjoyment and happiness along the way.

PEARSON myeducationlab

Go to MyEducationLab and select the topic "Curriculum/Program Models." Under Activities and Applications, watch the video *Discovery in a Study of Birds*. How can teachers incorporate wonder and joy into the curriculum and how does doing so affect children's learning?

SUMMARY

Biological research about the development of the brain confirms the crucial influence parents and teachers have during the early years of childhood. To determine the most desirable ways to foster learning, the priorities of practicing intentional teaching, incorporating developmentally appropriate practice, teaching to the child's five selves, encouraging child-centered, active learning through emergent curriculum, and including happiness as a goal for school are important to consider.

Vygotsky's concepts of the zone of proximal development and the vital role other people play in the development of the child's mental ability, coupled with his emphasis on the importance of language as the mediator of social experience, have gained prominence during the past few years as exemplars of how teachers can extend children's learning.

Vygotsky's ideas fit comfortably with the philosophy of the emergent curriculum exemplified by the approaches of Reggio Emilia and the project approach. These approaches encourage the use of divergent, creative thinking by the children. To foster such thinking, teachers should learn to use open-ended questions in ways that provoke children into thinking for themselves. They should ask only a few questions at a time, wait for answers, respond to the children's ideas in a positive way, and encourage production of more than one answer.

Finally, probably the most crucial element to consider in developing teaching methods is to include joy and happiness as a curriculum goal.

Questions and Activities

1. The next time you have to solve some sort of problem, take a few minutes and just for fun list all the ways, both silly and practical, that the problem might be solved. Try not to evaluate the merit of the ideas as you produce them, but just play around with many possibilities. Then evaluate them. Is a fresh one included that might be a good, new, though perhaps unconventional, way to solve the problem?
2. Might it be possible that preprimary teachers are depriving children of the right to learn the things that would help them succeed best in elementary school when we stress play, creativity, and mental health, rather than emphasizing such skills as learning the alphabet and counting? What might be the case for placing greater emphasis on academic learning at the preschool level?
3. Isn't it a waste of time to let children try things out that obviously won't work? Might it not be better just to lead a discussion with them about the proposed solutions, rather than go to the trouble of actually trying out something only to experience failure? Why?
4. Make a list of the priorities you think are important to incorporate in your teaching. Keep this list and update or revise it every year.

Diversity Question

1. In Reggio Emilia, teachers use the term "children with special rights." How does this reflect the image of the child who has a disability? Which term do you prefer, "special rights" or "special needs" and why?

Predicaments

1. You have in your room a little girl about 3 years old who asks a lot of questions. For example, she might ask, "Why are we going in now?" When dutifully provided with the reasons, she then asks, "But why do we have to do that?" When answered, she asks, "But why?" If you were her teacher, would you think this type of inquiry should be encouraged? How would you handle it?
2. The teacher next door is starting the year by focusing on bears. She plans to have the children bring teddy bears from home, reward them with little bear stickers when they're good, and tell the story of Goldilocks at group time. Explain why this approach is *not* emergent and suggest some things you and the children might do concerning bears that would reflect the emergent approach more adequately.

Self-Check Questions for Review

Content-Related Questions

1. Describe some things teachers can do that will help cognitive learning be a source of genuine pleasure to the children.
2. Does work on cognitive learning mean the teacher should ignore what is going on emotionally and socially among the children?
3. Name at least two basic concepts of Vygotskian psychological theory.
4. Explain the difference between *divergent* and *convergent* thinking and why each is an important aspect of thought.
5. Does *emergent* mean the teacher should avoid planning the cognitive curriculum in advance? Be sure to explain your answer fully.

Integrative Questions

1. A baby bird has fallen from its nest and is found on the playground. What are some activities you could do with them that would provide some learning? Be sure to identify what the children would be learning and why you think they will enjoy the experiences. What different experiences would you offer that support the 7 multiple intelligences?
2. Select a learning experience based on a natural science subject (e.g., ants) and make up a list of questions on this subject that will require convergent, fact-based answers. Now modify the questions so that they will be more likely to require children to do some creative thinking using opinions, reasons, and (possibly) trying out opinions to answer them.

Reference for Further Reading

Epstein, A. S. (2007). *The intentional teacher: Choosing the best strategies for young children's learning.* Washington, DC: National Association for the Education of Young Children.

Related Organizations and Online Resources

Early Childhood Research and Practice. This is an online journal that usually includes an article highlighting an emergent curriculum project. The spring 2000 issue devoted a special section to the project approach. It is available at http://www.ecrp.uiuc.edu/.

Multiple Intelligences Theory. Information as well as research and programs related to multiple intelligences can be found at the Howard Gardner site at http://www.howardgardner.com and Project Zero at http://www.pz.harvard.edu.

Project Approach Home Page. This Web site, developed by Sylvia Chard, contains a wealth of information about the theory and planning of projects, as well as many fascinating documented projects in various early childhood programs. You can also join the Project Approach discussion group by following the link at http://www.projectapproach.org.

Reggio Emilia Approach. Information about the preprimary schools in Italy, the Hundred Languages of Children exhibit, Reggio-inspired programs in the United States, and the North American Reggio Emilia Alliance can be found at http://www.reggioalliance.org.

Chart of Typical Development

Infancy to 8 Years of Age

MOTOR SKILLS

	0–12 Months	1–2 Years	2–3 Years	3–4 Years	4–5 Years	5–6 Years	6–7 Years	7–8 Years
Gross-motor skills	Sits without support	Walks alone	Runs forward well	Runs around obstacles	Walks backward toe-heel	Runs lightly on toes	Easily cuts soft foods	Strings beads
	Crawls	Walks backward	Jumps in place, two feet together	Walks on a line	Jumps forward 10 times, without falling	Walks on balance beam	Jumps rope with control	Plays instruments
	Pulls self to standing and stands unaided	Picks up toys from floor without falling	Stands on one foot, with aid	Balances on one foot for 5 to 10 seconds	Walks up and down stairs alone, alternating feet	Can cover 2 m (6'6") hopping	Plays hopscotch	Fastens jewelry
	Walks with aid	Pulls toy, pushes toy	Walks on tiptoe	Hops on one foot	Turns somersault	Skips on alternate feet	Plays with hula hoop	Rides a bicycle
	Rolls a ball in imitation of adult	Seats self in child's chair	Kicks ball forward	Pushes, pulls, steers wheeled toys		Jumps rope	Climbs	Swims well
		Walks up and down stairs (hand-held)		Rides (that is, steers and pedals) tricycle		Skates	Throws and catches a ball with ease	Plays sports requiring coordination
		Moves to music		Uses slide without assistance			Moves in time with music	
				Jumps over 15 cm (6") high object, landing on both feet together			Skips	
				Throws ball overhand				
				Catches ball bounced to him or her				
Fine-motor skills	Reaches, grasps, puts object in mouth	Builds tower of three small blocks	Strings four large beads	Builds tower of nine small blocks	Cuts on line continuously	Cuts out simple shapes	Prints name	Prints numerous words
	Picks things up with thumb and one finger (pincer grasp)	Puts four rings on stick	Turns pages singly	Drives nails and pegs	Copies cross	Copies triangle	Copies most shapes and designs	Draws in detail
	Transfers object from one hand to other hand	Places five pegs in pegboard	Snips with scissors	Copies circle	Copies square	Traces diamond	Copies most letters and numbers	Writes in cursive
	Drops and picks up toy	Turns pages two or three at a time	Holds crayon with thumb and fingers, not fist	Imitates cross	Prints a few capital letters	Copies first name	Draws in moderate detail	Reads and writes decimals
		Scribbles	Uses one hand consistently in most activities	Manipulates clay materials (for example, rolls balls, snakes, cookies)		Prints numerals 1 to 5	Prints in upper- and lowercase letters	
		Turns knobs				Colors within lines		
		Throws small ball				Has adult grasp of pencil		

Paints with whole arm movement, shifts hands, makes strokes	Imitates circular, vertical, horizontal strokes Paints with some wrist action; makes dots, lines, circular strokes Rolls, pounds, squeezes, and pulls clay	Has handedness well established (that is, child is left- or right-handed) Pastes and glues appropriately

COMMUNICATION SKILLS
Understanding language

Responds to speech by looking at speaker Responds differently to aspects of speaker's voice (for example, friendly or unfriendly, male or female) Turns to source of sound Responds with gesture to *hi, bye-bye,* and *up* when these words are accompanied by appropriate gesture Stops ongoing action when told *no* (when negative is accompanied by appropriate gesture and tone)	Responds correctly when asked *where* (when question is accompanied by gesture) Understands prepositions *on, in,* and *under* Follows request to bring familiar object from another room Understands simple phrases with key words (for example: *Open the door. Get the ball.*) Follows a series of two simple but related directions	Points to pictures of common objects when they are named Can identify objects when told their use Understands question forms *what* and *where* Understands negatives *no, not, can't,* and *don't* Enjoys listening to simple storybooks and requests them again	Begins to understand sentences involving time concepts (for example, *We are going to the zoo tomorrow*) Understands size comparatives such as *big* and *bigger* Understands relationships expressed by *if-then* or *because* sentences Carries out a series of two to four related directions Understands when told *Let's pretend*	Follows three unrelated commands in proper order Understands comparatives like pretty, prettier, and prettiest Listens to long stories but often misinterprets the facts Incorporates verbal directions into play activities Understands sequencing of events when told them (for example, *First we have to go to the store, then we can make the cake, and tomorrow we will eat it.*)	Demonstrates preacademic skills	Distinguishes between letters, words, sentences, and paragraphs Writes from left to right and top to bottom on paper Comprehends opposites and analogies Can read simple texts Beginning to understand grammar, punctuation, and capitalization Can paraphrase Knows what nouns and verbs are and can identify them in a sentence

0–12 Months	1–2 Years	2–3 Years	3–4 Years	4–5 Years	5–6 Years	6–7 Years	7–8 Years
Spoken language							
Makes crying and noncrying sounds	Says first meaningful word	Joins vocabulary words together in two-word phrases	Talks in sentences of three or more words, which take the form agent-action-object (*I see the ball*) or agent-action-location (*Daddy sit on chair*)	Asks *when*, *how*, and *why* questions	There are few obvious differences between child's grammar and adult's grammar	Completely comprehensible speech	Uses proper punctuation when storytelling
Repeats some vowel and consonant sounds (babbles) when alone or spoken to	Uses single words plus a gesture to ask for objects	Gives first and last name	Tells about past experiences	Uses models like *can, will, shall, should,* and *might*	Still needs to learn such things as subject-verb agreement, and some irregular past tense verbs	Can tell stories with connected relationships between people, objects, and events	
Interacts with others by vocalizing after adult	Says successive single words to describe an event	Asks *what* and *where* questions	Uses *s* on nouns to indicate plurals	Joins sentences together (for example, *I like chocolate chip cookies and milk.*)	Can take appropriate turns in a conversation		
Communicates meaning through intonation	Refers to self by name	Makes negative statements (for example, *Can't open it*)	Uses *ed* on verbs to indicate past tense	Talks about causality by using *because* and *so*	Gives and receives information		
Attempts to imitate sounds	Uses *my* or *mine* to indicate possession	Shows frustration at not being understood	Refers to self using pronouns *I* or *me*	Tells the content of a story but may confuse facts	Communicates well with family, friends, or strangers		
	Has vocabulary of about 50 words for important people, common objects, and the existence, nonexistence, and recurrence of objects and events (for example, *more* and *all gone*)		Repeats at least one nursery rhyme and can sing a song				
			Speech is understandable to strangers, but there are still some sound errors.				

COGNITIVE SKILLS

Follows moving object with eyes	Imitates actions and words of adults	Responds to simple directions (for example, *Give me the ball and the block. Get your shoes and socks.*)	Recognizes and matches six colors	Plays with words (creates own rhyming words; says or makes up words having similar sounds)	Retells story from picture book with reasonable accuracy	Writes original stories of a few sentences	Writes original stories a few paragraphs in length, centered around one distinct subject
Recognizes differences among people; responds to strangers by crying or staring	Responds to words or commands with appropriate action (for example, *Stop that, Get down.*)	Selects and looks at picture books, names pictured objects, and identifies several objects within one picture	Intentionally stacks blocks or rings in order of size	Points to and names four to six colors	Names some letters and numerals	Finds familiar words in objects (e.g., street signs, books.)	Counts to 100
Responds to and imitates facial expressions of others	Looks at storybook pictures with an adult, naming or pointing to familiar objects on request (for example, *What is that? Point to the baby.*)	Matches and uses associated objects meaningfully (for example, given cup, saucer, and bead, puts cup and saucer together)	Draws somewhat recognizable picture that is meaningful to child, if not to adult; names and briefly explains picture	Matches pictures of familiar objects (for example, shoe, sock, foot; apple, orange, banana)	Rote counts to 10	Identifies and writes word patterns and rhymes	Begins to understand how long different activities take to do
Responds to very simple directions (for example, raises arms when someone says *Come* and turns head when asked *Where is Daddy?*)	Recognizes difference between *you* and *me*	Stacks rings on peg in order of size	Asks questions for information (*why* and *how* questions requiring simple answers)	Draws a person with two to six recognizable parts, such as head, arms, legs; can name or match drawn parts to own body	Sorts objects by single characteristics (for example, by color, shape, or size if the difference is obvious)		Understands basic concept of weather
Imitates gestures and actions (for example, shakes head no, plays peek-a-boo, waves bye-bye)	Has very limited attention span	Recognizes self in mirror, saying *baby* or own name	Knows own age	Draws, names, and describes recognizable picture	Is beginning to use accurately time concepts of *tomorrow* and *yesterday*		Can add and subtract up to double-digits
Puts small objects in and out of container with intention	Accomplishes primary learning through own exploration	Can talk briefly about what he or she is doing	Knows own last name	Rote counts to 5, imitating adults	Uses classroom tools (such as scissors and paints) meaningfully and purposefully		
		Imitates adult actions (for example, housekeeping play)	Has short attention span	Knows own street and town	Begins to relate clock time to daily schedule		
			Learns through observing and imitating adults, and by adult instruction and explanation; is very easily distracted		Attention span increases noticeably; learns through adult instruction; when interested, can ignore distractions		
			Has increased understanding of concepts of the functions and groupings of objects (for example, can put dollhouse furniture in correct rooms), and part-whole (for example, can identify pictures of hand and foot as parts of body)				
			Begins to be aware of past and present (for example, *Yesterday we went to the park. Today we go to the library.*)				

0–12 Months	1–2 Years	2–3 Years	3–4 Years	4–5 Years	5–6 Years	6–7 Years	7–8 Years
COGNITIVE SKILLS *(Continued)*							
		Has limited attention span; learning is through exploration and adult direction (as in reading of picture stories) Is beginning to understand functional concepts of familiar objects (for example, that a spoon is used for eating) and part-whole concepts (for example, parts of the body)		Has more extended attention span; learns through observation and listening to adults as well as through exploration; is easily distracted Has increased understanding of concepts of function, time, part-whole relationships; function or use of objects may be stated in addition to names of objects Time concepts are expanding. Can talk about yesterday or last week (a long time ago), about today, and about what will happen tomorrow	Concepts of function increase as well as understanding of why things happen. Time concepts are expanding into an understanding of the future in terms of major events (for example, *Christmas will come after two weekends*).		

SELF-HELP SKILLS

Feeds self cracker	Uses spoon, spilling little	Uses spoon, little spilling	Pours well from small pitcher	Cuts easy foods with a knife (for example, hamburger patty, tomato slice)	Dresses self completely	Capable of buttoning, lacing, and zipping clothes	Can read a clock
Holds cup with two hands; drinks with assistance	Drinks from cup, one hand, unassisted	Gets drink from fountain or faucet unassisted	Spreads soft butter with knife	Laces shoes	Ties bow	Ties knots and bows	Sets goals
Chews food	Removes shoes, socks, pants, sweater	Opens door by turning handle	Buttons and unbuttons large buttons		Brushes teeth unassisted	Can make bed, dust, and sweep	Understands that actions have consequences
Holds out arms and legs while being dressed	Unzips large zipper	Takes off coat	Washes hands unassisted		Crosses street safely	Has a basic understanding of money and time concepts	Begins to take responsibility for basic needs
	Indicates toilet needs	Puts on coat with assistance	Blows nose when reminded				
		Washes and dries hands with assistance					

SOCIAL SKILLS

Smiles spontaneously	Recognizes self in mirror or picture	Plays near other children	Joins in play with other children; begins to interact	Plays and interacts with other children	Chooses own friend(s)	Growing ability to wait turn in group games	Expresses individual opinions
Responds differently to strangers than to familiar people	Refers to self by name	Watches other children, joins briefly in their play	Shares toys; takes turns with assistance	Dramatic play is closer to reality, with attention paid to detail, time, and space	Plays simple table games	Can plan ahead	Beginning to learn how to be a good friend
Pays attention to own name	Plays by self; initiates own play	Defends own possessions	Begins dramatic play, acting out whole scenes (for example, traveling, playing house, pretending to be animals)	Plays dress-up	Plays competitive games	Identifies and distinguishes emotions in others and responds fittingly	Knows how to be a team player
Responds to *no*	Imitates adult behaviors in play	Begins to play house		Shows interest in exploring sex differences	Engages with other children in cooperative play involving group decisions, role assignments, fair play	Understands and follows rules	
Copies simple actions of others	Helps put things away	Symbolically uses objects, self in play					
		Participates in simple group activity (for example, sings, claps, dances)					
		Knows gender identity					

Source: From Mainstreaming Preschoolers: Children with Health Impairments by A. Healy, P. McAreavey, C. S. Von-Hippel, and S. H. Jones, 1978, Washington, DC: U.S. Department of Health, Education and Welfare, Office of Human Development Services, Administration for Children, Youth and Families, Head Start Bureau.

Tips for Success in the First Few Weeks of Teaching

Granted, the first weeks of teaching are not easy, but they need not be impossible either. However, it is wise for you to make allowances for possible stress and not to be disappointed if you feel more tired than usual, or occasionally disheartened or bewildered. These feelings will become less frequent as time passes and the children, staff, and routine become more familiar. They will also diminish as you gain more skill and confidence.

Some Thoughts About Getting Started

Think of yourself as providing a life-affirming environment and use that as a yardstick when working with children

Life-affirming teachers see children and themselves as being involved in a positive series of encounters intended to facilitate growth and happiness. They have faith that children want to do the right thing—that they can grow and change for the better—and they have confidence that teachers and parents can assist them in that task.

Such teachers accept their own humanness and that of other people. They realize that sometimes a child can seem lost in a morass of angry feelings and strike out at others, but they also have confidence that the child knows deep inside that this behavior is not working well. They know it is possible for a life-affirming teacher to lead that child onto the firmer ground of being socially acceptable if the teacher is patient, positive, and consistent.

Observe professional discretion

Family affairs and children's behavior should not be discussed with people outside the school who have no need to know about them. Even amusing events should never be told unless the names of the children either are not mentioned or are changed. Most communities are smaller worlds than a beginning teacher may realize, and news can travel with astonishing rapidity.

In general, student teachers should be wary of being drawn into discussions with parents about their own or other families' children. This kind of discussion is the teacher's prerogative, and it is a wise student who passes off questions about youngsters by making some pleasant remark and referring the parent to the teacher. Nobody is ever antagonized by a student who does this in a tactful way, but disasters can result from well-meant comments by ill-informed or tactless beginners.

In addition, students should not discuss situations they disapprove of at the school where they work or say anything critical about another teacher to outsiders. These remarks have an unpleasant way of returning to the source, and the results can be awkward, to say the least. The principle "If you don't say it, they can't repeat it" is a sound one here. It is better instead to talk the problem over in confidence with the college supervisor.

Observe the chain of command

Just about every organization has a chain of command. It is always wise to avoid going over anyone else's head when making a comment or request. Understandably, teachers hate being put in a bad light by a student's talking a problem over with the school director or principal before talking it over with the teacher first.

A related aspect of this authority structure is being sure to get permission *before* planning a special event such as a field trip or getting out the hoses after a videotape on water play. Answers to such requests are generally yes, but it is always best to check before embarking on a major venture.

Some Recommendations for Starting Out

Although not always possible, it helps to find out some things before beginning the first student-teaching day. For example, it is helpful to talk with the teacher and determine the expected arrival time and recommended style of clothing. Most school guidelines are reasonable and will recommend sensible but professional-looking clothes.

Some schools have written guidelines they can give the student to read. Time schedules and lists of rules are also very helpful to review. If the school does not have these items written down, ask the teacher how basic routines such as eating and taking children to the toilet are handled, and ask about crucial safety rules and for a brief review of the schedule. If the student can come for a visit when the children are not there, the teacher will have a better opportunity to chat. During this visit make a special point of finding out where the children's cubbies are, where sponges and cleanup materials are kept, and where various supplies are stored. Don't hesitate to ask questions; just do your best to remember the answers!

Practical Things to Do to Increase Competence

Gain confidence in your ability to control the group

Almost invariably the first thing students want to discuss is discipline. Because this is the point everyone seems most concerned about, it is recommended that you begin preparation for work by reading chapter 11 on fostering self-discipline and conflict resolution skills in order to build strength in this area. Even though those reviews will help, observation, practice, and seeing situations all the way through are the best ways to gain competence in creating a peaceful, positive classroom environment.

Get to know the children as soon as possible

One way to become familiar with each of the children is to make a list of their names from the sign-in sheet and then jot down a few adjectives or facts to remember about each one. Calling the children by name at every opportunity will help, too. It will not take more than a day or two to become well acquainted, and it will help you belong to the group more quickly.

Develop the proverbial "eyes in the back of the head"

One of the most common failings of inexperienced teachers is their tendency to focus on only one child at a time. It is pleasant and much "safer" to sit down and read a favorite book with one or two charming children and ignore the chaos going on in the block corner, but good teachers form the habit of total awareness. They develop a sense of what is happening in the entire area. This is true outdoors as well as indoors.

Take action in unsafe situations immediately

Since student teachers are sometimes afraid of appearing too restrictive in a liberal atmosphere, they may allow dangerous incidents to happen because they do not know the rule or school policy about it. The general rule of thumb is that when one is unsure whether an activity is dangerous, it is better to stop it and then check to see what the teacher thinks. Stopping a few activities that are safe is better than letting two children wrestle each other off the top of the slide while the student debates indecisively below. Children's behaviors generally look less dangerous to students as they gain experience and feel less anxious, *but it is always better to be safe than sorry.*

Encourage the growth of independence and competence; avoid overteaching, overhelping, and overtalking

As a general principle, we encourage children at the preprimary level to do everything they can for themselves and for other children, too. This is different from the behavior of the teacher who sees the role of the teacher as doing *to* and doing *for* children. It takes self-control to wait while Katy fumbles for the zipper, insight to see how to assist her without taking over, and self-discipline not to talk too much while she is learning. But building competencies in the children by encouraging them to do things for themselves and for others increases their self-esteem so much that practicing restraint is worth the effort.

Encourage originality of self-expression

One of the most frowned-on things students can do is to make models of something for the children to copy when they are working with creative materials. It is easy to be trapped into making one child a clay snake or drawing a man for another youngster, but early childhood teachers dislike providing such models since they limit children's expression of their own feelings and ideas. It is better to relish the materials with the children and help them use the materials for their own purposes.

Keep contacts with the children as quiet and meaningful as possible

Except in a real emergency, walk over to the child to talk, rather than call across the room. Use a low voice and bend down so that the child can see your face and be less overwhelmed by your size. (An excellent way to find out how big an adult is from a child's point of view is to ask a friend to stand up and teach you something while you remain seated on the floor. It's enlightening.)

Expect to do menial tasks

No other profession requires the full range of abilities and effort that preschool teaching does. These extend from inspiring children and counseling parents to doing the most menial types of cleanup. Sometimes students do not realize this, so they feel imposed upon when they are asked to change a child's pair of pants or to mop the floor or clean the guinea pig cage. This kind of work is expected of almost all early childhood teachers as just being part of school life. Not only is cleaning up to be expected, but continual straightening up is also necessary as the day progresses. Blocks

should be arranged on shelves and dress-up clothes rehung several times to keep the room looking attractive. (Unfortunately there is no good fairy who will come along and do this.)

Learn from the start to be ingenious about creating equipment and scrounging materials

Early childhood programs almost always operate on lean budgets, and every school develops some ingenious ways to stretch money and invent equipment. Students can learn from each place they work by picking up these economical ideas from the staff, and they can contribute much by sharing their own ideas about the creative use of materials and new sources of free supplies. Be on the lookout for so-called waste materials that other businesses throw away. The carpet company's colorful scraps can make handsome additions to the collage box, for example, and rubber tires can be used in fascinating ways to make sturdy play equipment.

Organize yourself before beginning to teach

It is very helpful to arrive early on each teaching day so that there is time to get everything together in advance for the morning or afternoon. Nothing beats the feeling of security this preparation breeds. Life is also easier if before going home the student asks what will be happening during the next teaching session. Asking in advance makes reading up on activities ahead of time possible—a real security enhancer!

It increases confidence when you know the schedule well enough to tell what is going to happen next, as well as what time it is likely to happen. This allows time for cleanup and helps avoid the disappointment of moving into a new activity just as the group is expected to wash up for lunch. For these reasons, it is advisable always to wear a watch.

When you need help, ask for it

Mentors usually are not critical when beginners admit they do not know something and have the courage to ask, but they are inclined to resent students who protect themselves by appearing to know everything already or who defend themselves by making constant excuses. When one is unsure of a policy at the school, it never does any harm to say to the child, "I don't know if it's all right to climb on the fence. Let's ask Ms. Green, and then we'll both know."

The chance to chat with your mentor while cleaning up at the end of the morning or at some other convenient time of day is an invaluable time to raise problems and ask questions. During the day itself students often have to muddle through—learning by observation and using their own common sense. Nothing disastrous is likely to take place, and teachers are usually too busy to be corralled for more than a sentence or two of explanation while school is in progress.

Recognize stress and deal with it as effectively as possible

It is inevitable to feel stress when dealing with a new situation such as beginning to teach, and it is valuable to recognize this fact so that you can deal with it effectively, rather than just feel overwhelmed because sometimes you are exhausted at the end of the day. So much about the experience is new. There are so many personalities to deal with and so much to learn, so much uncertainty and excitement, and such a great desire to please without knowing exactly what is expected. This situation is clearly a lot to handle. These stresses do not mean that teaching is bad or unpleasant. Many novel situations such as getting married or receiving a promotion are delightful; but nonetheless they are stressful since they represent change, and change requires learning and adaptation.

Wise teachers acknowledge the possibility of stress and make practical plans for coping so that they can avoid coming down with various ailments or experiencing the excessive fatigue that prevents them from functioning effectively.

Deliberately creating opportunities for relaxation is an effective way of handling stress. Finding a quiet place and letting go from the toes all the way to the forehead and ears can be quieting and refreshing. Such strategies need not take long, but it is necessary to make a point of remembering to use them from time to time.

The Way to Your Mentor's Heart

Be prepared to make the small, extra contribution of time and energy *beyond* what is expected. The student who stays the extra 10 minutes on potluck night to dry the coffee pot is well on the way to becoming a popular member of the staff.

Offer help *before* being asked to lend a hand. Some students are so afraid of being pushy or of making mistakes that they never volunteer. But always having to request help gets tiresome for the mentor teacher, even if the student is willing when asked. It is better to develop an eye for all the little things that must be done and then to do them quietly. Such students are treasured by their mentor teachers.

Besides volunteering to help, teachers also appreciate the student who contributes ideas for projects and activities. After all, it is not the mentor teacher's responsibility to provide all the ideas for your teaching days. Come prepared with a variety of suggestions so that if one or two turn out to be impractical, you can be flexible and propose alternative possibilities.

Finally, let your enthusiasm show through. The vast majority of teachers follow their profession since they love it; the rigors of the job and the relatively low pay weed the others out very quickly. The teachers are therefore enthusiastic themselves. They are often "born" teachers, and they love teaching students as well as young children. Expressing thanks by being enthusiastic yourself will encourage them to keep on making the extra effort entailed in guiding student teachers.

Journals and Newsletters Associated with Early Childhood

Child Care Exchange
(800)221-2864
http://www.childcareexchange.com/

Childhood Education
A publication of the Association for Childhood Education International (ACEI)
(800)423-3563
http://www.acei.org/

Early Childhood Education Journal
(800)777-4643
http://www.springeronline.com

Early Childhood Research Quarterly
A publication of the National Association
for the Education of Young Children
(877)839-7126
http://www.naeyc.org/

Journal of Early Intervention
A publication of the Council for Exceptional
Children (CEC) Division for Early Childhood
(800)818-7243, Extension 0
http://www.dec-sped.org

Journal of Research in Childhood Education
A publication of the Association for Childhood Education International (ACEI)
(800)423-3563
http://www.acei.org/

Scholastic Early Childhood Today
(800)SCHOLASTIC
http://www.earlychildhoodtoday.com/

Young Children
A publication of the National Association
for the Education of Young Children
(800)424-2460
http://www.naeyc.org

Young Exceptional Children
A publication of the CEC Division for Early
Childhood
(800)818-7243, Extension 0
http://www.dec-sped.org

Zero to Three
(202)638-1144
http://www.zerotothree.org/

Recommended Childhood Immunization Schedule, United States, 2006

Vaccines are listed under routinely recommended ages. Bars indicate range of recommended ages for immunization. Any dose not given at the recommended age should be given as a "catch-up" immunization at any subsequent visit when indicated and feasible. Ovals indicate vaccines to be given if previously recommended doses were missed or given earlier than the recommended minimum age.

Age ▶ / Vaccine ▼	Birth	1 mo	2 mos	4 mos	6 mos	12 mos	15 mos	18 mos	24 mos	4–6 yrs	11–12 yrs	13–18 yrs
Hepatitis B	Hep B	Hep B			Hep B						Hep B	
Diphtheria, Tetanus Pertussis			DTaP	DTaP	DTaP		DTaP			DTaP	Td	
H. influenzae type b			Hib	Hib	Hib	Hib						
Inactivated Poliovirus			IPV	IPV	IPV					IPV		
Measles, Mumps, Rubella						MMR # 1				MMR # 2	MMR	
Varicella						Var				Var		
Pneumococcal			PCV	PCV	PCV	PCV			PCV	PPV		
Influenza					Influenza (Yearly)				Influenza (Yearly)			
Hepatitis A										Hepatitis A Series		

------- Vaccines below dashed line are for selected populations ---

Source: Department of Health and Human Services, Centers for Disease Control and Prevention (CDC).

Note: Approved by the Advisory Committee on Immunization Practices (ACIP), the American Academy of Pediatrics (AAP), and the American Academy of Family Physicians (AAFP).

A Beginning List of Homemade, Free, and Recyclable Materials

Material	How Acquired	Suggested Uses
Cornstarch finger paint	Dissolve 1/2 cup cornstarch in 1 cup of cold water and pour mixture into 3 cups boiling water, stir constantly until shiny and translucent. Allow to cool.	Use as a finger paint base, or ladle into jars and stir in tempera or food coloring. If a thicker mixture is desired, be sure to add glycerin to reduce stickiness. Adding a little glycerin or talcum powder makes painting particularly slick. Scents such as oil of cloves may be used to add fragrance. Starch bases can be refrigerated and then offered as a contrast to warmed starch— perhaps one kind for each hand.
Basic play dough	You will need 3 cups flour, 1/4 cup salt, 6 tablespoons oil, enough dry tempera to color it, and about 3/4 to 1 cup water. Encourage children to measure amounts of salt and flour and mix them together with the dry tempera. Add tempera before adding water. If using food coloring, mix a 3-ounce bottle with the water before combining it with the salt and flour. Combine oil with 3/4 cup water and add to dry ingredients. Mix with fingers, adding as much water as necessary to make a workable but not sticky dough.	Allow the dough or clay objects made by the children to harden. Then paint and shellac the objects or dip painted clay objects into melted paraffin to give a "finish." *Occasionally* use dough and clay with accessories such as dull knives for smoothing or cookie cutters and rolling pins to alter form. Offer chilled dough as a contrast to the room temperature variety. Cookie and bread recipes are also dough experiences. Vary the dough experience by changing the recipe.
Basic play dough II	Combine 3 cups self-rising flour, 1 cup salt, 5 tablespoons alum (can be purchased at drug stores), and 1 tablespoon dry tempera. Boil 1 3/4 cups water, add 1/3 cup oil to it, and pour over flour mixture, stirring rapidly.	This dough is lighter and more plastic than the first one; it feels lovely. It thickens as boiling water is poured in and cools rapidly, so children can finish mixing. It keeps exceptionally well in the refrigerator; oil does not settle out, and it does not become sticky— a paragon among doughs!

Material	How Acquired	Suggested Uses
Cardboard rolls	Gift-wrapping section of department stores for empty ribbon rolls; paper towel and toilet paper rolls	Tape two together beside each other, add string, and use as binoculars. Put beans, rice, and so forth, inside, tape closed, and use as shakers. Use as a base for puppets by adding decorative scraps of material. Tape several together lengthwise and use as tunnels for small vehicles. Punch holes 2 in. apart, secure wax paper over one end with a rubber band, and you have a flute.
Wood shavings and scraps	Building scrap piles, carpentry shops	
Material remnants	Interior design stores, upholsterers, clothing manufacturers	
Suede and leather scraps	Leather goods stores	
Pieces of Styrofoam	Throwaways from drug stores, variety stores, radio and TV stores	Buy a supply of plastic colored golf tees, to be hammered easily into Styrofoam chunks—a perfect activity for beginning carpenters. Poke sticks, straws, and so forth, into Styrofoam chunks to make a 3-D collage.
Computer paper used on one side	Almost anywhere computers are used	
Used envelopes	Offices, schools, junk mail	Use large envelopes for safe storage of special projects. Cut the bottom corners off old envelopes and decorate each as a different finger puppet.
Small boxes	Variety stores, hearing-aid stores, department and stationery stores	Stuff with newspaper and tape shut to make building blocks. Cut ⅔ of one side of a flat box (e.g., pudding box), decorate, and fill with scrap paper cut to fit, to make an ideal notepaper holder.
Large boxes	Appliance stores, supermarkets, department stores	Decorate boxes for use as "treasure boxes" to store artistic creations. Tie boxes together to make a train; large boxes also can turn into houses, cars, boats, and so forth. Use a series of large boxes for making an obstacle course or continuous tunnel.

Material	How Acquired	Suggested Uses
Plastic lids and containers	Home throwaways	Cut shapes in the lids to use as shape sorters (make shapes from other household "junk"). Use different-sized containers for stacking and nesting toys. Add a wooden spoon to a large empty container, with lid, to make a perfect drum. Cut interesting shapes in lids and use as stencils for painting or coloring.
Meat trays and aluminum pie plates	Home throwaways	Use as a base for paintings and collages, Christmas ornaments, or table decorations. Put them in the bathtub or swimming pool to use as boats in water play. Equip older children with a dull needle and yarn to sew color patterns on meat trays.
Milk cartons	Home throwaways	Cut an opening in one side, hang it up, and use as a bird feeder. Cut the top off, add a handle, and decorate with ribbon for a springtime basket.
Egg cartons	Home throwaways	Sort small objects into each egg pocket by size, texture, color, and so on. Fill each egg pocket with earth, plant seeds (e.g., beans), and watch them grow. Decorate individual egg pockets and hang upside down for simple but effective bells. In the springtime, use separate egg pockets to house chicks made out of cotton balls painted yellow. Cut lengthwise and add paint and pipe cleaner legs for a cute caterpillar.
Wide-mouth jars	Home throwaways, recycling centers	Make a mini-terrarium by layering charcoal, potting soil, and humus, dampening the soil, and adding small plants; put the lid in place, but open weekly if too much moisture builds up. Glue a 3-D scene to the lid, fill jar with water and sparkles, put lid on, and turn upside down.
Pebbles, leaves, cones, feathers, seed pods, and so forth.	These natural materials abound; bird refuge for unusual feathers	Make collages. Decorate other items.
Wallpaper sample books	Wallpaper stores	Decorate play areas or dollhouses.

Material	How Acquired	Suggested Uses
Rug scraps	Carpet and department stores	Decorate dollhouses.
Burlap	Horse-boarding barns	Various art projects
Ticker tape and newsprint rolls and ends	Local newspaper office	
5-gallon ice cream containers	Drive-ins and ice cream stores	
Art papers of various sizes and colors	Print shops	
1- or 2-day animal loans	Local pet shops, families	

Source: Some materials and sources suggested by the Principles and Practices class, 1972, of Santa Barbara City College, CA; other materials and suggested uses from the resource sheet "Recycling for Fun: Creating Toys and Activities for Children from 'Beautiful Junk '" by the Canadian Child Day Care Federation and the Canadian Association of Toy Libraries and Parent Resource Centres, and from the authors' experience.

REFERENCES

Adams, C. (2008, January/February). What are your expectations? The challenge of teaching across race. *Instructor*, 26–30.

Adams, H. (1907). *The education of Henry Adams*. New York: Oxford University Press.

Ainsworth, M., Blehar, M. C., Waters, E., & Wall, S. (1978). *Patterns of attachment*. Mahwah, NJ: Erlbaum.

Ainsworth, S., & Fraser, J. (2002). *If your child stutters: A guide for parents* (6th ed.). Memphis, TN: Stuttering Foundation of America.

Alat, K. (2002). Traumatic events and children: How early childhood educators can help. *Childhood Education*, 79(1), 2–8.

Allen, E. K., & Schwartz, I. S. (2001). *The exceptional child: Inclusion in early childhood education*. Albany, NY: Delmar.

Althouse, R., Johnson, M. H., & Mitchell, S. T. (2003). *The colors of learning: Integrating the visual arts into the early childhood curriculum*. New York: Teachers College Press.

Amabile, T. M. (1996). *Creativity in context: Update to The Social Psychology of Creativity*. Boulder, CO: Westview/HarperCollins.

American Academy of Ophthalmology. (1993). *Amblyopia*. San Francisco: Author.

American Academy of Pediatrics (AAP). (2002). *Caring for our children*. Elk Grove Village, IL: Author.

American Academy of Pediatrics (AAP). (2005). *Television: How it affects children*. Elk Grove Village, IL: Author.

American Academy of Pediatrics (AAP) (2008). *Car safety seats: A guide for families—2008*. Elk Grove Village, IL: Author.

American Association for the Advancement of Science (AAAS). (1998). *Dialogue on early childhood science, mathematics, and technology education*. Washington, DC: Author.

American Dietetic Association (ADA). (1999). Dietary guidance for healthy children aged 2 to 11 years. *Journal of the American Dietetic Association*, 99, 93–101.

American Heart Association. (2005). *Heart disease and stroke statistics*. Dallas, TX: Author.

American Speech-Language-Hearing Association (ASHA). (2004a). *Children and bilingualism*. Rockville, MD: Author. Retrieved December 14, 2004, from http://asha.org/public/speech/development/Bilingual-Children.htm

American Speech-Language-Hearing Association (ASHA). (2004b). *Frequently asked questions: Helping children with communication disorders in the schools—speaking, listening, reading, & writing*. Rockville, MD: Author. Retrieved December 14, 2004, from http://asha.org/public/speech/development/schools_faq.htm

American Speech-Language-Hearing Association (ASHA). (2004c). *Pragmatics, socially speaking*. Rockville, MD: Author. Retrieved December 14, 2004, from http://asha.org/public/speech/development/pragmatics.htm

American Speech-Language-Hearing Association (ASHA). (2004d). *Stuttering*. Rockville, MD: Author. Retrieved December 14, 2004, from http://asha.org/public/speech/disorders/stuttering.htm

Anti-Defamation League. (2005). *Bias-free foundations: Early childhood guidebook and activities for educators*. New York: Author.

Armstrong, T. (1997). Seeing things in new ways. *Scholastic Early Childhood Today*, 11(5), 32–35.

Aronson, S. (1997). Food allergies can be fatal. *Child Care Information Exchange*, 118, 88–91.

Ashbury, C., & Rich, B. (Eds.). (2008). *Learning, arts, and the brain*. New York/Washington, DC: Dana Press.

Association for Childhood Education International (ACEI). (2004). *Obesity and children*. Olney, MD: Author.

Autism facts. (2003). Washington, DC: Autism Society of America.

Axline, V. (1969). *Play therapy* (Rev. ed.). New York: Ballantine Books.

Bailey, B. (1997). *There's gotta be a better way: Discipline that works.* Oviedo, FL: Loving Guidance.

Baker, A. C., & Manfredi/Petitt, L. A. (2004). *Relationships, the heart of quality care.* Washington, DC: National Association for the Education of Young Children.

Bandura, A. (1977). *Social learning theory.* Upper Saddle River, NJ: Merrill/Prentice Hall.

Bandura, A. (1997). *Self-efficacy: The exercise of control.* New York: Freeman.

Bank Street. (1998). *Bank Street: A private college at work in the public schools.* New York: Author.

Barbarin, O. A. (2002). The Black-White achievement gap in early reading skills: Familial and social-cultural context. In B. Bowman (Ed.), *Love to read: Essays in developing and enhancing early literacy skills of African American children.* Washington, DC: National Black Child Development Institute, 1–15.

Bardige, B., & Segal, M. (2004). Conversations in child care. *Zero to Three, 25*(1), 16–22.

Bardige, B. S., & Segal, M. M. (2005). *Building literacy with love: A guide for teachers and caregivers of children birth through age 5.* Washington, DC: Zero to Three.

Barnes, S. B., & Whinnery, K. W. (2002). Effects of functional mobility skills training for young students with physical disabilities. *Exceptional Children, 68*(3), 313–324.

Barnett, W. S., Jung, K., Wong, V., Cook, T., & Lamy, C. (2007). *Effects of five state prekindergarten programs on early learning.* New Brunswick, NJ: National Institute for Early Education Research.

Barnett, W. S., Hustedt, J. T., Friedman, A. H., Boyd, J. S., & Ainsworth, P. (2007). *The state of preschool 2007.* New Brunswick, NJ: National Institute for Early Childhood Research.

Barrera, I. (2003). From rocks to diamonds: Mining the riches of diversity for our children. *Zero to Three, 23*(5), 8–15.

Barrera, I., Corso, R. M., & Macpherson, D. (2003). *Skilled dialogue: Strategies for responding to cultural diversity in early childhood.* Baltimore: Brookes.

Barrera, R. M. (2001). Bringing home to school. *Early Childhood Today, 16*(3), 44–56.

Barrera, R. M. (2004). In Profiles in culture. *Early Childhood Today, 19*(3), 46–48.

Bazron, B., Osher, D., & Fleischman, S. (2005). Creating culturally responsive schools. *Educational Leadership, 63*(1), 83–84.

Beatty, B. (1995). *Preschool education in America: The culture of young children from the colonial era to the present.* New Haven, CT: Yale University Press.

Bergen, D. (2004). *ACEI speaks: Play's role in brain development.* Retrieved November 2, 2004, from http://www.acei.org/brainspeaks.pdf

Berk, L. E. (2006). Looking at kindergarten children. In D. F. Gullo (Ed.), *K today: Teaching and learning in the kindergarten year* (pp. 11–25). Washington, DC: National Association for the Education of Young Children.

Berkowitz, M. W. & Bier, M. C. (2005). Character education: Parents as partners. *Educational Leadership, 63*(1): 64–69.

Biber, B. (1984). *Early education and psychological development.* New Haven, CT: Yale University Press.

Black, D. L. (2000, November 29). Progressive education means business. *Education Week, XX*(13), reprint.

Black, S. M. (1999). HIV/AIDS in early childhood centers: The ethical dilemma of confidentiality versus disclosure. *Young Children, 54*(2), 39–45.

Blair, C. (2003). *Self-regulation and school readiness.* Champaign, IL: Clearinghouse on Early Education and Parenting.

Bloom, L. (1998). Language acquisition in its developmental context. In D. Kuhn & R. S. Siegler (Eds.), *Handbook of child psychology: Cognition, perception, and language* (5th ed., Vol. 2). New York: Wiley.

Bodrova, E. D., & Leong, D. (2008). *Introduction to the state standards database.* Retrieved May 24, 2008, from http://nieer.org/standards/

Bodrova, E. D., Leong, D., Henson, R., & Henninger, M. (2000). Imaginative, child-directed play: Leading the way in development and learning. *Dimensions of Early Childhood, 28*(4), 25–30.

Bodrova, E. D., Leong, D., & Shore, R. (2004). *Child outcome standards in pre-kindergarten programs: What can we do to make them work? Preschool Policy Matters #5.* New Brunswick, NJ: National Institute for Early Education Research.

Bos, B. (2006). Child development. *ExchangeEveryDay.* Retrieved May 26, 2008, from exchangeeveryday@ccie.com

Bowlby, J. (1973). *Attachment and loss: Separation* (Vol. 1). New York: Basic Books.

Bowlby, J. (1980). *Loss: Sadness and depression*. New York: Basic Books.

Bowman, B. (Ed.). (2002). *Love to read: Essays in developing and enhancing early literacy skills of African American children*. Washington, DC: National Black Child Development Institute.

Bowman, B. (2006a). Resilience: Preparing children for school. In B. Bowman & E. K. Moore (Eds.), *School readiness and social-emotional development: Perspectives on cultural diversity* (pp. 49–57). Washington, DC: National Black Child Development Institute.

Bowman, B. T. (2006b). Standards at the heart of educational equity. *Young Children, 61*(5) 42–48.

Bowman, B. T., Donovan, M. S., & Burns, M. S. (Eds.). (2000). *Eager to learn: Educating our preschoolers*. Washington, DC: National Research Council.

Bradburn, E. (1989). *Margaret McMillan: Portrait of a pioneer*. London: Routledge.

Bradley, J., & Kibera, P. (2006). Closing the gap: Culture and promotion of inclusion in child care. *Young Children, 61*(1), 34–40.

Bredekamp, S. & Copple, C. (1997).

Brittain, W. L. (1979). *Creativity, art, and the young child*. New York: Macmillan.

Bronfenbrenner, U. (1969). Preface. In H. Chauncey (Ed.), *Soviet preschool education: Teacher's commentary* (Vol. 2). New York: Holt, Rinehart & Winston.

Bronfenbrenner, U. (1979). *The ecology of human development*. Cambridge, MA: Harvard University Press.

Bronson, M. B. (2004). Choosing play materials for primary school age children (ages 6–8). In

D. Koralek, (Ed.), *Spotlight on young children and play*. Washington, DC: National Association for the Education of Young Children.

Bronson, M. B. (2006). Developing social and emotional competence. In D. F. Gullo (Ed.), *K today: Teaching and learning in the kindergarten year*. Washington, DC: National Association for the Education of Young Children.

Brown, S. E. (2004). *Bubbles, rainbows, and worms: Science experiments for preschool children* (Rev. ed.). Beltsville, MD: Gryphon House.

Bruner, J. S. (1978). Learning the mother tongue. *Human Nature, 1*(9), 42–49.

Bruner, J. S. (1983). *Child's talk: Learning to use language*. Oxford, UK: Oxford University Press.

Buell, M. J., & Sutton, T. M. (2008). Weaving a web with children at the center: A new approach to emergent curriculum planning for young preschoolers. *Young Children, 63*(4), 100–105.

Butterfield, P. M., Martin, C. A. & Prairie, A. P. (2004). *Emotional connections: How relationships guide early learning*. Washington, DC: Zero to Three.

Cadwell, L. B. (2002). *Bringing learning to life: The Reggio approach to early childhood education*. New York: Teachers College Press.

Carpenter, E. M., & Nangle, D. W. (2001). The Compass program: Addressing aggression in the classroom. *Head Start Bulletin, 73*, 27–28.

Carroll, D. W. (1999). *Psychology of language* (3rd ed.). Pacific Grove, CA: Brooks/Cole.

Caulfield, R. (2002). Babytalk: Developmental precursors to

speech. *Early Childhood Education Journal, 30*(1), 59–62.

Cavanaugh, S. (2008). Playing games in classroom helping pupils grasp math. *Education Week, 27*(35), 10.

Cavner, D. (2008). Teaching empathy. *Exchange, 179*, 92–95.

Center for the Child Care Workforce. (2002). *Current data on child care salaries and benefits in the United States*. Washington, DC: Author.

Center on Hunger, Poverty, and Nutrition Policy. (1999). *Childhood hunger, childhood obesity: An examination of the paradox*. Medford, MA: Center on Hunger, Poverty, and Nutrition Policy & Tufts University.

Center on the Social and Emotional Foundations for Early Learning. (2004). *What works briefs*. Champaign, IL: Author. Retrieved November 27, 2004, from http://www.csefel.uiuc.edu/whatworks.html

Centers for Disease Control and Prevention (CDC). (1996). Asthma mortality and hospitalization among children and young adults. *Morbidity and Mortality Weekly Report, 45*, 350–353.

Centers for Disease Control and Prevention (CDC). (2000). *National health and nutrition examination survey*. Atlanta, GA: Author.

Centers for Disease Control and Prevention (CDC). (2004). *Flu deaths in children*. Atlanta, GA: Author.

Check playgrounds for safety. (1996). *Oklahoma Child Care, 3*, 18–19.

Chen, D. W. (2003). Preventing violence by promoting the development of competent conflict resolution skills: Exploring roles and responsibilities. *Early*

Childhood Education Journal, 30(4), 203–208.

Chick, K. A., Heilman-Houser, R., & Hunter, M. W. (2002). The impact of child care on gender role development and gender stereotypes. *Early Childhood Education Journal, 29*(3), 149–154.

Child abuse. (1999, April). *Education Week,* p. 6.

Children and Adults with Attention-Deficit/Hyperactivity Disorder (CHADD). (2005). *The disorder named AD/HD.* Landover, MD: Author.

Children's Defense Fund (CDF). (2001). *Child care basics.* Retrieved October 21, 2004, from http://childrensdefense.org

Children's Defense Fund (CDF). (2004). *Key facts about American children.* Retrieved October 21, 2004, from http://www.childrensdefense.org

Children's Defense Fund (CDF). (2005). *Protect children not guns.* Washington, DC: Author.

Children's Defense Fund (2005). *State of America's children.* Washington, DC: Author.

Choi, D. H., & Kim, J. (2003). Practicing social skills training for young children with low peer acceptance: A cognitive-social learning model. *Early Childhood Education Journal, 31*(1), 41–46.

Chomsky, N. (1968). *Language and mind.* New York: Harcourt Brace.

Churchill, S. L. (2003). Goodness-of-fit in early childhood settings. *Early Childhood Research Journal, 31*(2), 113–118.

Cleaver, S. (2007a, November/December). How green classrooms are reconnecting kids with nature. *Instructor,* 20–25.

Cleaver, S. (2007b, September/October). Too much of a good thing? *Instructor,* 31–35.

Clements, D. H., & Sarama, J. (2006). All around the math room! *Scholastic Early Childhood Today, 21*(2), 25–30.

Close, N. (2002). *Listening to children: Talking with children about difficult issues.* Boston: Allyn & Bacon.

Cohany, S. R. & Sok, E. (2007). Married mothers in the labor force. *Monthly Labor Review* (February): 9–16.

Cohen, S. (1998). *Targeting autism: What we know, don't know, and can do to help young children with autism and related disorders.* Berkeley: University of California Press.

Coie, J. D., & Dodge, K. A. (1998). Aggression and antisocial behavior. In W. Damon (Series Ed.) & N. Eisenberg (Vol. Ed.), *Handbook of child psychology: Social, emotional, and personality development* (5th ed., Vol. 3). New York: Wiley.

Cole, C. L., & Arndt, K. (1998). Autism. In L. A. Phelps (Ed.), *Health-related disorders in children and adolescents.* Washington, DC: American Psychological Association.

Connor, C. M., & Craig, H. K. (2006). African American preschoolers' language, emergent literacy skills, and use of African American English: A complex relation. *Journal of Speech, Language, and Hearing Research, 49,* 771–792.

Consortium of National Arts Education Associations. (1994). *National standards for arts education: Dance, music, theater, and visual arts: What every young American should know and be able to do in the arts.* Reston, VA: Music Educators National Conference.

Consumer Product Safety Commission. (1997). *A handbook for public playground safety.* Washington, DC: Author.

Cook, R. E., Tessier, A., & Klein, M. D. (2003). *Adapting early childhood curricula for children with special needs* (6th ed.). Upper Saddle River, NJ: Merrill/Prentice Hall.

Copley, J. V. (2003). Assessing mathematical learning: Observing and listening to children. *Child Care Information Exchange, 151,* 47–50.

Copple, C., & Bredekamp, S. (2008). Getting clear about developmentally appropriate practice. *Young Children, 63*(1), 54–55.

Copple, C., & Bredekamp, S. (Eds.). (2009). *Developmentally appropriate practice in early childhood programs serving children birth through age 8. (3rd ed.).* Washington, DC: National Association for the Education of Young Children.

Cox, M. (1997). *Drawings of people by the under-5's.* London: Falmer Press.

Crawford, L. (2004). *Lively learning: Using the arts to teach the K-8 curriculum.* Greenfield, MA: Northeast Foundation for Children.

Cuellar, D. (2007). *Preparing teachers to work with young Hispanic children in the United States.* Paper presented at the National Task Force for Early Childhood Education for Hispanics. Retrieved May, 12, 2008, from http://www.ecehispanic.org

Curtis, P., & Carter, M. (2003). *Designs for living and learning: Transforming early childhood environments.* St. Paul, MN: Redleaf Press.

Curwood, J. S. (2007, August). What happened to kindergarten: Are academic pressures stealing childhood? *Instructor,* 28–32.

De Mesquita, P. B., & Fiorella, C. A. (1998). Asthma (childhood). In L. A. Phelps (Ed.), *Health-related disorders in children and adolescents.* Washington, DC: American Psychological Association.

Deasy, R., & Stevenson, L. (2002). *The arts: Critical links to student success.* Washington, DC: The Arts Education Partnership.

Derman-Sparks, L. (1994). Empowering children to create a caring culture in a world of differences. *Childhood Education, 70*(2), 66–71.

Derman-Sparks, L., & ABC Task Force. (1989). *Anti-bias curriculum: Tools for empowering young children.* Washington, DC: National Association for the Education of Young Children.

Derman-Sparks, L., Higa, C. T., & Sparks, B. (1980). Children, race, and racism: How race awareness develops. *Interracial Books for Children Bulletin, 11*(3/4), 3–9.

Derman-Sparks, L., & Phillips, C. B. (1997). *Teaching/learning anti-racism: A developmental approach.* New York: Teachers College Press.

Derman-Sparks, L., & Ramsey, P. G. (2006). *What if all the kids are white? Anti-bias multicultural education with young children and families.* New York: Teachers College Press.

Desouza, J. M. S., & Czerniak, C. M. (2002). Social behaviors and gender differences among preschoolers: Implications for science activities. *Journal of Research in Childhood Education, 16*(2), 175–188.

Desrochers, J. (1999). Vision problems: How teachers can help. *Young Children, 54*(2), 36–38.

Dettore, E. (2002). Children's emotional growth: Adults' role as emotional archaeologists. *Childhood Education, 78*(5), 278–281.

DeVries, R., Hildebrandt, C., & Zan, B. (2000). Constructivist early education for moral development. *Early Education and Development, 11*(1), 9–35.

DeVries, R., & Kohlberg, L. (1990). *Constructivist early education: Overview and comparison with other programs.* Washington, DC: National Association for the Education of Young Children.

DeVries, R., & Zan, B. (1996). A constructivist perspective on the role of the sociomoral atmosphere in promoting children's development. In C. T. Fosnot (Ed.), *Constructivism: Theory, perspectives, and practice.* New York: Teachers College Press.

DeVries, R., Zan, B., Hildebrandt, C., Edmiaston, R., & Sales, C. (2002). *Developing constructivist early childhood curriculum: Practical principles and activities.* New York: Teachers College Press.

Dewey, J. (1916). *Democracy and education.* New York: Macmillan.

Dickinson, D. K., & Tabors, P. O. (2002). Fostering language and literacy in classrooms and homes. *Young Children, 57*(2), 10–18.

Dillon, S. (2006, March 26). In response to law, schools cut back subjects to push reading and math. *The New York Times,* pp. A1, A16.

Division for Early Childhood and the National Association for the Education of Young Children (2000). *Including all children: Children with disabilities in early childhood programs.* Washington, DC: National Association for the Education of Young Children.

Doctoroff, S. (2001). Adapting the physical environment to meet the needs of all children for play. *Early Childhood Education Journal, 29*(2), 105–109.

Dougy Center for Grieving Children. (1999, April 18). *Norman, Oklahoma, transcript.*

Drew, W. F., Christie, J., Johnson, J. E., Meckley, A. M., & Nell, M. L. (2008). Constructive play: A value-added strategy for meeting early learning standards. *Young Children, 63*(4), 38–44.

East, K., & Thomas, R. L. (2007). *Across cultures: A guide to multicultural literature for children.* Westport, CT: Libraries Unlimited.

Eastman, P. D. (1960). *Are you my mother?* New York: Random House.

Edelman, M. W. (2001). Circle of hope: Children's natural resilience can inspire us to feel hopeful about their futures. In *Special: Keeping kids safe.* New York: Scholastic Early Childhood Today and Parent & Child.

Edwards, C., Gandini, L., & Forman, G. (Eds.). (1993). *The hundred languages of children: The Reggio Emilia approach to early childhood education.* Norwood, NJ: Ablex.

Edwards, C., Gandini, L., & Forman, G. (Eds.). (1998). *The hundred languages of children: The Reggio Emilia approach— Advanced reflections.* Norwood, NJ: Ablex.

Edwards, C., & Raikes, H. H. (2002). Extending the dance: Relationship-based approaches to infant/toddler care and education. *Young Children, 57*(4), 10–17.

Eisner, E. W. (2002). *The arts and the creation of the mind*. New Haven, CT: Yale University Press.

Elias, C. L., & Berk, L. E. (2002). Self-regulation in young children: Is there a role for sociodramatic play? *Early Childhood Research Quarterly, 17*(2), 216–238.

Elias, M. (2008, May 2). New antipsychotic drugs carry risks for children. *USA Today,* pp. A1, A4.

Elkind, D. (1987). *Miseducation: Preschoolers at risk*. New York: Knopf.

Elkind, D. (2001). Instructive discipline is built on understanding. *Child Care Information Exchange, 141,* 7–8.

Elkind, D. (2004a). Thanks for the memory: The lasting value of true play. In D. Koralek (Ed.), *Spotlight on young children and play* (pp. 36–41). Washington, DC: National Association for the Education of Young Children.

Elkind, D. (2004b). The ethical young child: Pipe dream or possibility? *Exchange, 160,* 46–47.

Elkind, D. (2006). The values of outdoor play. *Exchange, 171,* 6–8.

Elkind, D. (2007). *The power of play: Learning what comes naturally*. Philadelphia: DeCapo Press.

Ellis, R. (1994). *The study of second language acquisition*. New York: Oxford University Press.

Epilepsy Foundation of America. (n.d.). *Epilepsy*. Landover, MD: Author.

Epstein, A. (2003, Spring). All about High/Scope. *High/Scope Resource,* 5–7.

Epstein, A. S. (2007). *The intentional teacher: Choosing the best strategies for young children's learning*. Washington, DC: National Association for the Education of Young Children.

Epstein, A. S., Schweinhart, L. J., DeBruin-Parecki, A., & Robin, K. B. (2006). *Preschool assessment: A guide to developing a balanced approach*. New Brunswick: National Institute for Early Education Research.

Erikson, E. (1963). *Childhood and society* (2nd ed.). New York: Norton.

Erikson, E. H. (1959). Identity and the life cycle. *Psychological Issues, 1*(1), Monograph 1.

Erikson, E. H. (1982). *The life cycle completed: A review*. New York: Norton.

Falconer, R. C., & Byrnes, D. A. (2003). When good intentions are not enough: A response to increasing diversity in an early childhood setting. *Journal of Research in Childhood Education, 17*(2), 188–200.

Fenichel, E. (Ed.). (2003). The impact of adult relationships on early development. *Zero to Three, 23*(3), entire issue.

Fields, M. V., Groth, L., & Spangler, K. (2004). *Let's begin reading right* (5th ed.). Upper Saddle River, NJ: Merrill/Prentice Hall.

Finn, E., & Wolpin, S. (2005). Dental disease in infants and toddlers: A transdisciplinary health concern and approach. *Zero to Three, 25*(3), 28–34.

First five L.A.'s 2002–2003 annual report. (2004, October). Los Angeles: L.A. Public School District.

Forman, G. E., & Hill, F. (1980). *Constructive play: Applying Piaget in the preschool*. Monterey, CA: Brooks/Cole.

Fox, L., & Lentini, R. H. (2006). "You Got It!" Teaching social and emotional skills. *Young Children, 61*(6), 36–42.

Freud, S. (1959). Two encyclopaedia articles: (A) Psycho-analysis and (B) The libido theory. In J. Strachey (Ed. & Trans.), *Collected papers of Sigmund Freud* (Vol. 5, pp. 107–130). London: Hogarth Press. (Original work published 1922)

Froebel, F. (1889). *Autobiography of Friedrich Froebel* (E. Michaelis & K. Moore, Trans.). Syracuse, NY: Bardeen.

Froschl, M., & Sprung, B. (2008). Let's work it out: Helping young children address teasing and bullying. *Exchange, 179,* 12–14.

Frost, J. (2008, May 29). History of play. *ExchangeEveryDay,* p.1.

Frost, J. L., Wortham, S. C., & Reifel, S. (2005). *Play and child development* (2nd ed.). Upper Saddle River, NJ: Merrill/Prentice Hall.

Fu, V., Stremmel, A., & Hill, L. (Eds.). (2002). *Teaching and learning: Collaborative exploration of the Reggio Emilia approach*. Upper Saddle River, NJ: Merrill/Prentice Hall.

Fuhr, J. E., & Barclay, K. H. (1998). The importance of appropriate nutrition and nutrition education. *Young Children, 53*(1), 74–80.

Galdone, P. (1981). *Three billy goats gruff*. New York: Ticknor & Fields.

Galdone, P. (1985). *The three bears*. New York: Ticknor & Fields.

Galinsky, E., Howes, C., Kontos, S., & Shinn, M. (1994). *The study of children in family child care and relative care:*

Highlights of findings. New York: Families and Work Institute.

Gallahue, D. L., & Ozmun, J. C. (2001). *Understanding motor development: Infants, children, adolescents and adults* (5th ed.). New York: McGraw-Hill.

Gambetti, A. (1993). *The cloud project*. Conference at Wayne State University, Traverse City, MI.

Gandini, L. (2008). Introduction to the schools of Reggio Emilia. In L. Gandini, S. Etheredge, & L. Hill (Eds.), *Insights and inspirations from Reggio Emilia: Stories of teachers and children from North America* (pp. 24–27). Worcester, MA: Davis Publications.

Gandini, L., Hill, L., Cadwell, L., & Schwall, C. (Eds.). (2005). *In the spirit of the studio: Learning from the atelier of Reggio Emilia*. New York: Teachers College Press.

Garbarino, J. (2001). Power struggles: Early experiences matter. *Child Care Information Exchange, 137,* Beginnings Workshop Insert. Retrieved October 21, 2002, from *ExchangeEveryDay* @ccie.com newsletter.

Gardner, H. (1983). *Art, mind, and brain: A cognitive approach to creativity*. New York: Basic Books.

Gardner, H. (1999). *Intelligence reframed: Multiple intelligences for the 21st century*. New York: Basic Books.

Gardner, H. (2004). *Frames of mind: The theory of multiple intelligences* (20th-anniversary edition). New York: Basic Books.

Gardner, H. (2007). *Project Zero at Harvard Graduate School of Education: Update on current work*. Cambridge, MA: Project Zero.

Gartrell, D. (2004). *The power of guidance: Teaching social-emotional skills in early childhood classrooms*. Clifton Park, NY: Delmar/Thomson and National Association for the Education of Young Children.

Gartrell, D. (2006). Guidance matters: Boys and men teachers. *Beyond the Journal, Young Children on the Web,* May.

Gartrell, D. (2008). Comprehensive guidance. *Young Children, 63*(1), 44–45.

Geist, K., & Geist, E. A. (2008). Do re mi, 1-2-3 that's how easy math can be: Using music to support emergent mathematics. *Young Children, 63*(2), 20–25.

Gerber Products Company. (2003). *Feeding infants and toddlers study*. Parsippany, NJ: Author.

Gesell, A., Halverson, H. M., Thompson, H., & Ilg, F. (1940). *The first five years of life: A guide to the study of the preschool child*. New York: Harper & Row.

Ginsburg, K. R. (2007). The importance of play in promoting healthy child development and maintaining strong parent-child bonds. *Pediatrics, 119* (1), 182–191.

Girls, Inc. (2006). *The supergirl dilemma: Girls grapple with the mounting pressure of expectations*. New York: Author.

Gleim, L. (2007). *A moment of learning*. Retrieved June 30, 2008, from http://www.midpac. edu/elementary/PG/2007/10/ an_ordinary_moment_of_ learning.php

Goleman, D. (1995). *Emotional intelligence*. New York: Bantam Books.

Gonzalez-Mena, J. (2000). *Multicultural issues in child care* (3rd ed.). New York: McGraw-Hill.

Gonzalez-Mena, J. (2007). *Diversity in early care and education: Honoring differences* (5th ed.). New York: McGraw-Hill.

Gonzalez-Mena, J., & Eyer, D. W. (2006). *Infants, toddlers and caregivers: A curriculum of respectful, responsive care* (7th ed.). New York: McGraw-Hill.

Greenberg, M. T., Domitrovich, C. E., Graczyk, P. A., & Zins, J. E. (2005). The study of implementation in school-based preventive interventions: Theory, research, and practice. *Promotion of Mental Health and Prevention of Mental and Behavioral Disorders, 2005 Series, 3.*

Greenman, J. (1998). *Places for childhoods: Making quality happen in the real world*. Redmond, WA: Child Care Information Exchange.

Greenman, J. (2003). Making outdoor learning possible. *Child Care Information Exchange, 151,* 75–80.

Greenman, J. (2005). *Caring spaces, learning places: Children's environments that work*. Redmond, WA: Exchange Press.

Greenspan, S. (1998). Recognizing and responding to language delays. *Scholastic Early Childhood Today, 13*(1), 67–69.

Greenspan, S. I. (2004). Working with the child who shows attention problems. *Early Childhood Today, 19*(1), 24–25.

Greenspan, S. I. (2006). Working with the child who may have ADD. *Early Childhood Today, 21*(1), 21–22.

Greenspan, S. I., & Wieder, S. (1998). *The child with special needs: Encouraging intellectual and emotional growth*. Reading, MA: Addison-Wesley.

Grisham-Brown, J., Hallam, R., & Brookshire, R. (2006). Using authentic assessment to evidence children's progress toward early learning standards. *Early Childhood Education Journal, 34*(1), 45–51.

Grusec, J. E., & Arnason, L. (1982). Consideration for others: Approaches to enhancing altruism. In S. G. Moore & C. R. Cooper (Eds.), *The young child: Reviews of research* (Vol. 3). Washington, DC: National Association for the Education of Young Children.

Guilford, J. P. (1981). Developmental characteristics: Factors that aid and hinder creativity. In J. C. Gowan, J. Khatena, & E. P. Torrance (Eds.), *Creativity: Its educational implications* (2nd ed.). Dubuque, IA: Kendall/Hunt.

Guralnick, M. J. (1999). The nature and meaning of social integration for young children with mild developmental delays in inclusive settings. *Journal of Early Intervention, 22*(1), 70–86.

Guralnick, M. J. (Ed.). (2001). *Early childhood inclusion: Focus on change.* Baltimore: Brookes.

Guralnick, M., Neville, B., Hammond, M., & Connor, R. T. (2007). The friendships of young children with developmental delays: A longitudinal analysis. *Journal of Applied Developmental Psychology, 28*(1), 64–79.

Gurian, M., & Stevens, K. (2004). With boys and girls in mind. *Educational Leadership, 62*(3), 21–26.

Gurian, M., & Stevens, K. (2005). *The minds of boys: Saving our sons from falling behind in school and life.* San Francisco: Jossey-Bass.

Hainstock, E. G. (1997). *The essential Montessori: An introduction to the woman, the writings, the method, and the movement.* New York: Plume.

Hakuta, K. (1998). Improving education for all children: Meeting the needs of language minority children. In D. Clark (Moderator), *Education and the development of American youth.* Washington, DC: Aspen Institute.

Hall, K. W. (2008). The importance of including culturally authentic literature. *Young Children, 63*(1), 80–84.

Hallam, R. A., Buell, M. J., & Ridgley, R. (2003). Serving children and families living in poverty. *Journal of Research in Childhood Education, 16*(2), 115–124.

Harper, L. V., & McCluskey, K. S. (2002). Caregiver and peer responses to children with language and motor disabilities in inclusive preschool programs. *Early Childhood Research Quarterly, 17*(2), 148–166.

Harris, T. T., & Fuqua, J. D. (2000). What goes around comes around: Building a community of learners through circle times. *Young Children, 55*(1), 44–47.

Haugland, S. W., Bailey, M. D., & Ruiz, E. A. (2002). The outstanding developmental software and web sites for 2001. *Early Childhood Education Journal, 29*(3), 191–200.

Head Start Bureau. (2001). Head Start child outcomes framework. *Head Start Bulletin, 70.* Washington, DC: Author.

Head Start Bureau. (2004). *Head Start facts.* Washington, DC: Author.

Heft, T. M., & Swaminathan, S. (2002). The effects of computers on the social behavior of preschoolers. *Journal of Research in Early Childhood Education, 16*(2), 162–188.

Helm, J. H. (2004). Projects that power young minds. *Educational Leadership, 62*(1), 58–62.

Helm, J. H. (2008). Got standards? Don't give up on engaged learning! *Young Children, 63*(4), 14–20.

Helm, J. H., & Beneke, S. (Eds.). (2003). *The power of projects: Meeting contemporary challenges in early childhood classrooms—strategies and solutions.* New York: Teachers College Press.

Helm, J. H., & Katz, L. G. (2001). *Young investigators: The project approach in the early years.* New York: Teachers College Press.

Helping young children in frightening times. (2001). *Young Children, 36*(6), 6–7.

Hemmeter, M. L., Ostrosky, M. M., Artman, K. M., & Kinder, K. A. (2008). Moving right along: Planning transitions to prevent challenging behavior. *Young Children, 63*(3), 18–25.

Hendrick, J. (1973). *The cognitive development of the economically disadvantaged Mexican American and Anglo American four-year-old: Teaching the concepts of grouping, ordering, perceiving common connections, and matching by means of semantic and figural materials.* Doctoral dissertation, University of California, Santa Barbara.

Hendrick, J. (1975). *The whole child: New trends in early education.* St. Louis, MO: C. V. Mosby.

Hendrick, J. (Ed.). (1997). *First steps toward teaching the Reggio way.* Upper Saddle River, NJ: Merrill/Prentice Hall.

Hendrick, J. (Ed.). (2004). *Next steps toward teaching the Reggio way: Accepting the challenge to change.* Upper Saddle River, NJ: Merrill/Prentice Hall.

Hendrick, J., & Stange, T. (1991). Do actions speak louder than words? An effect of the functional use of language on dominant sex role behavior in boys and girls. *Early Childhood Research Quarterly, 6*(4), 656–676.

Hickman-Davis, P. (2002). Cuando no hablan ingles: Helping young children learn English as a second language. *Dimensions of Early Childhood, 30*(2), 3–10.

Hill, P. S. (1992). *Kindergarten*. Olney, MD: Association for Childhood Education International. (Original work published 1942).

Hirsch, E. S. (Ed.). (1996). *The block book* (3rd ed.). Washington, DC: National Association for the Education of Young Children.

Hirsh-Pasek, K., & Golinkoff, R. M. (2003). *Einstein never used flashcards: How our children really learn—and why they need to play more and memorize less.* New York: Rodale Press.

Hodges, W. (1987). Teachers-children: Developing relationships. *Dimensions, 15*(4), 12–14.

Hogan, N., & Graham, M. (2001). Helping children cope with disaster. *ACEI Focus on Pre-K & K, 14*(2), 1–6.

Hohmann, M., & Weikart, D. (1995). *Educating young children: Active learning practices for preschool and child care.* Ypsilanti, MI: High/Scope.

Holloway, J. H. (2003). What promotes racial and ethnic tolerance? *Educational Leadership, 60*(6), 85–86.

Honig, A. S. (2002). *Secure relationships: Nurturing infant/toddler attachment in early care settings.* Washington, DC: National Association for the Education of Young Children.

Honig, A. S., & Hirallal, A. (1998). Which counts more for excellence in childcare staff—years in service, education level, or ECE coursework? *Early Childhood Development and Care, 145,* 31–46.

Hoot, J. L., Szecsi, T., & Moosa, S. (2003). What teachers of young children should know about Islam. *Early Childhood Education Journal, 31*(2), 85–90.

Hopkins, E. (2008, January/February). Bias proof your classroom: Interview with G. Thompson. *Instructor, 32.*

Horton-Ikard, R. (2006). The influence of culture, class, and linguistic diversity on early language development. *Zero to Three, 27*(1), 6–12.

Housman, A. E. (1922). *Last poems, XII.* New York: Holt.

Howard, V. F., Williams, B. F., & Lepper, C. E. (2005). *Very young children with special needs: A formative approach for today's children* (3rd ed.). Upper Saddle River, NJ: Merrill/Prentice Hall.

Howes, C., & Ritchie, S. (2002). *A matter of trust: Connecting teachers and learners in the early childhood classroom.* New York: Teachers College Press.

Hoyt, C. (2005, December/January). Wiping out prejudices before they start. *Child Magazine.* Retrieved May 12, 2008, from http://www.parents.com/family-life/better-parenting/teaching-tolerance/wiping-out-kid-prejudices-before-they-start/?page1

Huffman, L. C., Mehlinger, S. L., & Kerivan, A. S. (2000). Risk factors for academic and behavioral problems at the beginning of school. In *Off to a good start: Research on the risk factors for early school problems and selected federal policies affecting children's social and emotional development and their readiness for school.* Chapel Hill: University of North Carolina, FPG Child Development Center.

Hulit, L. M. (1996). *Straight talk on stuttering: Information, encouragement, and counsel for stutterers, caregivers, and speech-language clinicians.* Springfield, IL: Charles C Thomas.

Hurless, B., & Gittings, S. (2008). Weaving the tapestry: A first grade teacher integrates teaching and learning. *Young Children, 63*(2), 40–46.

Hyson, M. (Ed.). (2003). *Preparing early childhood professionals: NAEYC's standards for programs.* Washington, DC: National Association for the Education of Young Children.

Hyson, M. (2008). *Enthusiastic and engaged learners.* Washington, DC: National Association for the Education of Young Children.

Iaquinta, A. (2006). Guided reading: A research-based response to the challenges of early reading instruction. *Early Childhood Research Journal, 33*(6), 413–418.

Imhoff, G. (Ed.). (1990). *Learning two languages: From conflict to consensus in the reorganization of the schools.* New Brunswick, NJ: Transaction Publishing.

Isaacs, J. B. (2008). *Impacts of early childhood programs.* Washington, DC: First Focus and the Brookings Institute.

Isenberg, J. P., & Jalongo, M. R. (2006). *Creative thinking and arts-based learning: Preschool through fourth grade* (4th ed.). Upper Saddle River, NJ: Merrill/Prentice Hall.

Isenberg, J. P., & Quisenberry, N. (2002). *Play: Essential for all children—A position paper of the Association for Childhood Education International.* Olney, MD: Association for Childhood Education International.

Jablon, J. R., & Wilkinson, M. (2006). Using engagement strategies to facilitate children's learning and success. *Young Children, 61*(2), 12–16.

Jacklin, C. N., & Baker, L. A. (1993). Early gender development. In S. Oskamp & M. Costanzo (Eds.), *Gender issues in contemporary society.* Newbury Park, CA: Sage.

Jalongo, M. R. (2003). A position paper of the Association for Childhood Education International: The child's right to creative thought and expression. *Childhood Education, 79*(4), 218–228.

Jalongo, M. R. (2004). *Young children and picture books: Literature from infancy to six* (2nd ed.). Washington, DC: National Association for the Education of Young Children.

Jalongo, M. R. (2008). *Learning to listen, listening to learn.* Washington, DC: National Association for the Education of Young Children.

Jalongo, M. R., & Stamp, L. N. (1997). *The arts in children's lives: Aesthetic education in early childhood.* Boston: Allyn & Bacon.

Jensen, E. (2006). *Enriching the brain: How to maximize every learner's potential.* San Francisco: Jossey-Bass.

Johnson, L. G., Rogers, C. K., Johnson, P., & McMillan, R. P. (1993). *Overcoming barriers associated with the integration of early childhood settings.* Presented at the conference of the National Association for the Education of Young Children, Anaheim, CA.

Johnson, R. T. (2000). *Hands off! The disappearance of touch in the care of children.* New York: Peter Lang.

Johnson, S. P. (2008). The status of male teachers in public education today. *Education Policy Brief, 6*(4), 1–11.

Jones, E., & Cooper, R. M. (2006). *Playing to get smart.* New York: Teachers College Press.

Jones, E., & Nimmo, J. (1994). *Emergent curriculum.* Washington, DC: National Association for the Education of Young Children.

Justice, L. M. (2004). Creating language-rich preschool classroom environments. *Teaching Exceptional Children, 37*(2), 36–44.

Kagan, S. L., & Lowenstein, A. E. (2004). School readiness and children's play: Contemporary oxymoron or compatible option? In E. F. Zigler, D. G. Singer, & S. J. Bishop-Josef (Eds.), *Children's play: The roots of reading* (pp. 59–76). Washington, DC: Zero to Three Press.

Kaiser, B., & Rasminsky, J. S. (2003). *Challenging behavior in young children: Understanding, preventing, and responding effectively.* Boston: Allyn & Bacon.

Kaiser Family Foundation. (2006). *The media family: Electronic media in the lives of infants, toddlers, preschoolers, and their parents.* Washington, DC: Author.

Kalmar, K. (2008). Let's give children something to talk about! Oral language and preschool literacy. *Young Children, 63*(1), 88–92.

Kamii, C. (1975). One intelligence indivisible. *Young Children, 30*(4), 228–238.

Kamii, C. (1982). *Number in preschool and kindergarten: Educational implications of Piaget's theory.* Washington, DC: National Association for the Education of Young Children.

Kamii, C. (1985). *Young children reinvent arithmetic: Implications of Piaget's theory.* New York: Teachers College Press.

Kamii, C., Miyakawa, Y., & Kato, Y. (2004). The development of logico-mathematical knowledge in block building activity at ages 1–4. *Journal of Research in Childhood Education, 19*(1), 44–57.

Katz, L. (1991). Keynote address at the Reggio Conference, Oklahoma City, OK.

Katz, L., & Chard, S. C. (2000). *Engaging children's minds: The project approach* (2nd ed.). Norwood, NJ: Ablex.

Katz, L., & McClellan, D. E. (1997). *Fostering children's social competence: The teacher's role.* Washington, DC: National Association for the Education of Young Children.

Kauffman Early Education Exchange. (2002). *Set for success: Building a strong foundation for school readiness based on the social-emotional development of children.* Kansas City, MO: Ewing Marion Kauffman Foundation.

Kemple, K. M. (2004). *Let's be friends: Peer competence and social inclusion in early childhood programs.* New York: Teachers College Press.

Kendrick, A. S., Kaufmann, R., & Messenger, K. P. (Eds.). (2002). *Healthy young children: A manual for programs* (Rev. ed.). Washington, DC: National Association for the Education of Young Children.

Kersey, K. C., & Malley, C. R. (2005). Helping children develop resiliency: Providing supportive relationships. *Young Children, 60*(1), 53–58.

Khatena, J., & Khatena, N. (1999). *Developing creative talent in art: A guide for parents and teachers.* Stamford, CT: Ablex.

Kindlon, D., & Thompson, M. (1999). *Raising Cain: Protecting the emotional lives of boys.* New York: Ballantine.

King, J. R. (1998). *Uncommon caring: Learning from men who teach young children.* New York: Teachers College Press.

Kirk, S. A., Gallagher, J. J., & Anastasiow, N. J. (2003). *Educating exceptional children* (10th ed.). Boston: Houghton Mifflin.

Kirmani, M. H. (2007). Empowering culturally and linguistically diverse children and families. *Young Children, 62*(11), 94–98.

Klein, T. P., Worth, D., & Linas, K. (2003). Play: Children's context for development. *Young Children, 58*(3), 38–45.

Knudsen, E. I., Heckman, J. J., Cameron, J. L., & Shonkoff, J. P. (2006). Economic, neurobiological, and behavioral perspectives on building America's future workforce. *Proceedings of the National Academy of Sciences, 103*(27), 10155–10162.

Koch, P. K., & McDonough, M. (1999). Improving parent-teacher conferences through collaborative conversations. *Young Children, 54*(2), 11–15.

Kohl, M. A. (2007). Fostering creativity. *Early Childhood News.* http://www.earlychildhoodnews.com/

Kohn, A. (1999). *Punished by rewards: The trouble with gold stars, incentive plans, A's, praise, and other bribes* (Rev. ed.). Boston: Houghton Mifflin.

Kohn, A. (2001). Five reasons to stop saying "Good job!" *Young Children, 56*(5), 24–28. http://www.eric.ed.gov:80/ERICDocs/data/ericdocs2sql/content_storage_01/0000019b/80

Kolb, K., & Weede, S. (2001). *Teaching prosocial skills to young children to increase emotionally intelligent behavior.* Champaign, IL: Clearinghouse on Early Education and Parenting.

Kontos, S., & Wilcox-Herzog, A. (1997). Teachers' interactions with children: Why are they so important? *Young Children, 52*(2), 4–12.

Koplow, L. (1996). *Unsmiling faces: How preschools can heal.* New York: Teachers College Press.

Koralek, D. (Ed.). (2003). *Spotlight on young children and math.* Washington, DC: National Association for the Education of Young Children.

Koralek, D. (Ed.). (2004). *Spotlight on young children and play.* Washington, DC: National Association for the Education of Young Children.

Koralek, D., & Colker, L. (Eds.). (2003). *Spotlight on young children and science.* Washington, DC: National Association for the Education of Young Children.

Kostelnik, M. (2004). Modeling ethical behavior in the classroom. *Child Care Information Exchange, 16,* 34–37.

Kranowitz, C. S. (1994). Kids gotta move: Adapting movement experiences for children with differing abilities. *Child Care Information Exchange, 5*(94), 37.

Kremenitzer, J. P., & Miller, R. (2008). Are you a highly qualified, emotionally intelligent early childhood educator? *Young Children, 63*(4), 106–112.

Kristal, J. (2005). *The temperament perspective: Working with children's behavioral styles.* Baltimore: Brookes.

Kritchevsky, S., & Prescott, E. (1977). *Planning environments for young children: Physical space.* Washington, DC: National Association for the Education of Young Children.

Kuerbis, P. (2004, December 24). Tests take toll on science education. *The Denver Post,* pp. B1–B2.

Labov, W. (1970). The logic of nonstandard English. In F. Williams (Ed.), *Language and poverty.* Chicago: Markham.

Lally, R. J., Griffin, A., Fenichel, E., Segal, M., Szanton, E., & Weissbourd, B. (2003). *Caring for infants and toddlers in groups: Developmentally appropriate practice* (Rev. ed.). Arlington, VA: Zero to Three/National Center.

Landy, S. (2002). *Pathways to competence: Promoting healthy social and emotional development in young children.* Baltimore: Brookes.

Larkin, M. (2001). Providing support for student independence through scaffolded instruction. *Teaching Exceptional Children, 34*(1), 30–32.

Lavatelli, C. S. (1970a). *Early childhood curriculum: A Piaget program.* Boston: American Science and Engineering.

Lavatelli, C. S. (1970b). *Piaget's theory applied to an early childhood curriculum.* Boston: American Science and Engineering.

Lawhon, T., & Cobb, J. B. (2002). Routines that build emergent literacy skills in infants, toddlers, and preschoolers. *Early Childhood Education Journal, 30*(2), 113–118.

Levin, D. E. (1998). *Remote control childhood? Combating the hazards of media culture.* Washington, DC: National Association for the Education of Young Children.

Levin, D. E. (2003). *Teaching young children in violent times: Building a peaceable classroom* (2nd ed.). Washington, DC: National Association for the Education of Young Children and Educators for Social Responsibility.

Lewin-Benham, A. (2006). One teacher, 20 preschoolers, and a goldfish: Environmental awareness, emergent curriculum, and documentation. *Young Children, 61*(2), 28–34.

Lillie, T., & Vakil, S. (2002). Transitions in early childhood for students with disabilities: Law and best practice. *Early Childhood Education Journal, 30*(1), 53–58.

Loeffler, M. H. (Ed.). (1992). *Montessori in contemporary American culture*. Portsmouth, NH: Heinemann.

Loomis, K., Lewis, C., & Blumenthal, R. (2007). Children learn to think and create through art. *Young Children, 62*(5), 79–83.

Louv, R. (2005). *Last child in the woods: Saving our children from nature-deficit disorder*. Chapel Hill, NC: Algonquin Books of Chapel Hill.

Louv, R. (2005). *Last child in the woods: Saving our children from nature-deficit disorder*. Chapel Hill, NC: Algonquin Books.

Louv, R. (2008). *Last child in the woods: Saving our children from nature-deficit disorder*. (Rev. ed.) Chapel Hill, NC: Algonquin Books of Chapel Hill.

Maccoby, E. E. (1980). *Social development: Psychological growth and the parent-child relationship*. New York: Harcourt Brace Jovanovich.

Maccoby, E. E., & Jacklin, C. N. (1980). Sex differences in aggression: A rejoinder and reprise. *Child Development, 512,* 964–980.

MacDonald, S. (2001). *Block play: The complete guide to learning and playing with blocks*. Beltsville, MD: Gryphon House.

MacDonald, A. (2007). *Brain development in childhood*. Washington, DC: The Dana Foundation. Accessed April 5, 2008. http://www.dana.org/news/brainhealth/detail.aspx?id=10054

Malaguzzi, L. (1992). *A message from Loris Malaguzzi: An interview by Lella Gandini, April, 1992, La Villetta School, Reggio Emilia*. Amherst, MA: Performanetics.

Malaguzzi, L. (1993). A bill of three rights. *Innovations in Early Education: The International Reggio Exchange, 2*(1), 9.

Malaguzzi, L. (1998). History, ideas, and basic philosophy: An interview with Lella Gandini. In C. Edwards, L. Gandini, & G. Forman (Eds.), *The hundred languages of children: The Reggio Emilia approach—Advanced reflections*. Norwood, NJ: Ablex.

Mallory, B. L., & New, R. S. (Eds.). (1993). *Diversity & developmentally appropriate practices: Challenges for early childhood education*. New York: Teachers College Press.

Mann, T., Steward, M., Eggbeer, L., & Norton, D. (2007). Zero to Three's task force on culture and development: Learning to walk the talk. *Zero to Three, 27*(5), 7–16.

Marano, H. E. (2008). *A nation of wimps*. New York: Broadway Books.

Maratsos, M. (1998). The acquisition of grammar. In D. Kuhn & R. S. Siegler (Eds.), *Handbook of child psychology: Cognition, perception, and language* (5th ed., Vol. 2). New York: Wiley.

Marion, M. (1998). *Guidance of young children* (5th ed.). Upper Saddle River, NJ: Merrill/Prentice Hall.

Marshall, N. L., Robeson, W. W., & Keefe, N. (1999). Gender equity in early childhood education. *Young Children, 54*(4), 9–13.

Martini, M. (2002). How mothers in four American cultural groups shape infant learning during mealtimes. *Zero to Three, 22*(4), 14–20.

Mash, E. J., & Barkley, R. Q. (Eds.). (1998). *Treatment of childhood disorders* (2nd ed.). New York: Guilford.

Masters, W. H., Johnson, V. E., & Kilodny, R. C. (1994). *Heterosexuality*. New York: HarperCollins.

McAfee, O., Leong, D. J., & Bodrova, E. (2004). *Basics of assessment: A primer for early childhood educators*. Washington, DC: National Association for the Education of Young Children.

McClelland, M. M., & Morrison, F. J. (2003). The emergence of learning-related social skills in preschool children. *Early Childhood Research Quarterly, 18*(2), 206–224.

McDaniel, G. L., M. Y. Isaac, H. M. Brooks, & A. Hatch. (2005). Confronting K-3 teaching challenges in an era of accountability. *Young Children, 60*(2), 20–26.

McIntosh, K., Herman, K., Sanford, A., McGraw, K., & Florence, K. (2004). Teaching transitions: Techniques for promoting success between lessons. *Teaching Exceptional Children, 37*(1), 32–38.

McLean, M., Wolery, M., & Bailey, D. B. (2004). *Assessing infants and preschoolers with special needs* (3rd ed.). Upper Saddle River, NJ: Merrill/Prentice Hall.

McMillan, M. (1929). *What the open-air nursery school is*. London: Labour Party.

McNair, S., Kirova-Petrova, A., & Bhargava, A. (2001). Computers and young children in the classroom: Strategies for minimizing computer bias. *Early Childhood Education Journal, 29*(1), 51–55.

McVicker, C. J. (2007). Young readers respond: The importance of child participation in emerging literacy. *Young Children, 62*(3), 18–22.

Meisels, S. J., & Atkins-Burnett, S. (2005). *Developmental screening in early childhood* (5th ed.). Washington, DC: National

Association for the Education of Young Children.

Mendoza, J., Katz, L. G., Robertson, A. S., & Rothenberg, D. (2003). *Connecting with parents in the early years.* Champaign, IL: Clearinghouse on Early Education and Parenting.

Mendoza, J., & Reese, D. (2001). Examining multicultural picture books for the early childhood classroom: Possibilities and pitfalls. *Early Childhood Research and Practice, 3*(2).

Menteach. (2006). *Data about men teachers.* Retrieved May 14, 2008, from http://menteach.org/resources/data_about_men_teachers

Mercurio, C. M. (2003). Guiding boys in the early years to lead healthy emotional lives. *Early Childhood Education Journal, 30*(4), 255–258.

Michigan Department of Education. (2002). *Fact sheet: What research says about parents' involvement in children's education.* Lansing, MI: Author.

Miller, K. (2003). *The crisis manual for early childhood teachers, updated: How to handle the really difficult problems.* Beltsville, MD: Gryphon House.

Miller, N. B., & Sammons, C. C. (1999). *Everybody's different: Understanding and changing our reactions to disabilities.* Baltimore: Brookes.

Mistry, K. B., Minkovitz, C. S., Strobino, D. M., & Borzekowski. D. L. G. (2007). Children's television exposure and behavioral and social outcomes at 5.5 years: Does timing of exposure matter? *Pediatrics, 120*(4), 762–769.

Moffitt, M., & Omwake, E. (n.d.). *The intellectual content of play.* New York: New York State Association for the Education of Young Children.

Montessori, M. (1912). *The Montessori method: Scientific pedagogy as applied to child education in "The Children's House" with additions and revisions by the author* (A. E. George, Trans.). New York: Frederick A. Stokes.

Montie, J. E., Xiang, Z., & Schweinhart, L. J. (2006). Preschool experience in 10 countries: Cognitive and language performance at age 7. *Early Childhood Research Quarterly, 21,* 313–331.

Montie, J. E., Xiang, Z., & Schweinhart, L. J. (Eds.). (2007). *Role of preschool experience in children's development in 10 countries.* Ypsilanti, MI: High/Scope Press.

Moomaw, S. (1997). *More than singing: Discovering music in preschool and kindergarten.* St. Paul, MN: Redleaf.

Moomaw, S., & Hieronymus, B. (1995). *More than counting: Whole math activities for preschool and kindergarten.* St. Paul, MN: Redleaf.

Mooney, C. M. (2000). *Theories of childhood: An introduction to Dewey, Montessori, Erikson, Piaget & Vygotsky.* St. Paul, MN: Redleaf.

Moore, E. K., & Barbarin, O. A. (2003). Respecting the voices of parents: How the Spirit of Excellence Parent Empowerment Project connects with African American parents. In J. Mendoza, L. G. Katz, A. S. Robertson, & D. Rothenberg (Eds.), *Connecting with parents in the early years.* Champaign, IL: Clearinghouse on Early Education and Parenting.

Morrison, G. (2004). *Early childhood education today* (9th ed.). Upper Saddle River, NJ: Merrill/Prentice Hall.

Morrow, L. M. (1997). *Literacy development in the early years: Helping children read and write* (3rd ed.). Boston: Allyn & Bacon.

Morse, L. W., & Shine, A. E. (1998). Sickle cell anemia. In L. A. Phelps (Ed.), *Health-related disorders in children and adolescents.* Washington, DC: American Psychological Association.

Moyer, J. (Ed.). (1995). *Selecting educational equipment and materials for school and home* (Rev. ed.). Wheaton, MD: Association for Childhood Education International.

Murkoff, H. (2003). *The what to expect babysitter's handbook.* New York: Workman Publishing.

Murphy, D. M. (1997). Parent and teacher plan for the child. *Young Children. 52*(4), 32–36.

Mussen, P. H., Conger, J. J., & Kagan, J. (1969). *Child development and personality.* New York: Harper & Row.

National Association for Sport and Physical Education (NASPE). (2002). *Early childhood physical activity guidelines.* Reston, VA: Author.

National Association for the Education of Young Children (NAEYC). (1995). *National Association for the Education of Young Children position statement: Responding to linguistic and cultural diversity: Recommendations for effective early childhood education.* Washington, DC: Author.

National Association for the Education of Young Children (NAEYC). (1996). *National Association for the Education of Young Children position statement: Technology and young children—ages 3 through 8.* Washington, DC: Author.

National Association for the Education of Young Children (NAEYC). (1997). National Association for the Education of Young Children position statement on the prevention of child abuse in early childhood programs and the responsibilities of early childhood professionals to prevent child abuse. *Young Children, 52*(3), 42–46.

National Association for the Education of Young Children (NAEYC). (1998a). NAEYC: Change agent for a changing world: NAEYC annual report. *Young Children, 53*(6), 43–54.

National Association for the Education of Young Children (NAEYC). (1998b). What would you do? Real-life ethical problems early childhood professionals face. *Young Children, 53*(4), 52–54.

National Association for the Education of Young Children (NAEYC). (2001). *Helping children cope with disaster.* Retrieved November 16, 2004, from http://www.naeyc.org/coping_with_disaster.htm

National Association for the Education of Young Children (NAEYC). (2005). *Code of ethical conduct and statement of commitment: Guidelines for responsible behavior in early childhood education.* Washington, DC: Author.

National Association for the Education of Young Children (NAEYC). (2006). *Where we stand on standards for programs to prepare early childhood professionals.* Washington, DC: Author.

National Association for the Education of Young Children (NAEYC). (2007). *September 1, 2006–August 31, 2007 annual report.* Washington, DC: Author.

National Association for the Education of Young Children

(NAEYC) & National Association of Early Childhood Specialists in State Departments of Education (NAECS/SDE). (1991). Guidelines for appropriate curriculum and assessment in programs serving children ages 3 through 8. *Young Children, 46*(3), 21–38.

National Association for the Education of Young Children (NAEYC) & National Association of Early Childhood Specialists in State Departments of Education (NAECS/SDE). (2001). *Joint position statement: STILL unacceptable trends in kindergarten entry and placement.* Washington, DC: NAEYC.

National Association for the Education of Young Children (NAEYC) & National Association of Early Childhood Specialists in State Departments of Education (NAECS/SDE). (2002). *Joint position statement: Early learning standards: Creating the conditions for success.* Washington, DC: NAEYC.

National Association for the Education of Young Children (NAEYC) & National Association of Early Childhood Specialists in State Departments of Education (NAECS/SDE). (2003). *Joint position statement: Early childhood curriculum, assessment, and program evaluation: Building an effective, accountable system in programs for children birth through age 8.* Washington, DC: NAEYC.

National Association for the Education of Young Children (NAEYC) & National Association of Early Childhood Specialists in State Departments of Education (NAECS/SDE). (2004). *Where we stand on early learning standards.* Washington, DC: NAEYC.

National Association for the Education of Young Children

(NAEYC) & National Council of Teachers of Mathematics (NCTM). (2002). *Joint position statement: Early childhood mathematics: Promoting good beginnings.* Washington, DC: NAEYC.

National Center on Birth Defects and Developmental Disabilities. (2007). *Autism spectrum disorders overview.* Washington, DC: Centers for Disease Control and Prevention.

National Center for Children in Poverty. (2004). *Promoting the emotional well-being of children and families–Policy paper #1: Building services and systems to support the healthy emotional development of young children—An action guide for policymakers.* Washington, DC: Author.

National Council of Teachers of Mathematics (NCTM). (2000). *Principles and standards for school mathematics.* Reston, VA: Author.

National Council of Teachers of Mathematics (NCTM). (2006). *Curriculum focal points for prekindergarten through grade 8 mathematics: A quest for coherence.* Reston, VA: Author.

National Dissemination Center for Children with Disabilities (NICHCY). (2003). *Who are the children in special education?* Research Brief (RB2). Washington, DC: Author.

National Dissemination Center for Children with Disabilities (NICHCY). (2008). *IDEA.* Retrieved May 16, 2008, from http://www.nichcy.org/idea.htm

National Early Childhood Accountability Task Force, 2007. *Taking stock: Assessing and improving early childhood learning and program quality.* Washington, DC: Pew Charitable Trusts, the Foundation for Child Development, and the Joyce Foundation.

National Education Goals Panel. (1999). *The national education goals report: Building a nation of learners, 1999.* Washington, DC: U.S. Government Printing Office.

National Institute of Child Health and Human Development (NICHD) Early Child Care Research Network. (2000). The relation of child care to cognitive and language development. *Child Development, 71,* 958–978.

National Pediatric & Family HIV Resource Center. (1999, April 18). *Children living in a world with AIDS: Guidelines for children's participation in HIV/AIDS programs.* Available at www://pedhivaids.org

National Research Council and Institute of Medicine. (2000). *From neurons to neighborhoods: The science of early childhood development.* Washington, DC: National Academy Press.

Natural Learning Initiative. (n.d.). Retrieved October 27, 2004, from Counteracting Sendentary Lifes. http://www.naturalearning.org/

Needlman, R., & Needlman, G. (1997). Dispelling the myths about epilepsy. *Scholastic Early Childhood Today, 11*(4), 12–13.

Neuman, S. B. (2006). N is for nonsensical. *Educational Leadership, 64*(2), 28–31.

Neuman, S. B., Copple, C., & Bredekamp, S. (2000). *Learning to read and write: Developmentally appropriate practices for young children.* Washington, DC: National Association for the Education of Young Children.

Noddings, N. (2003). *Happiness and education.* Cambridge, UK: Cambridge University Press.

Noddings, N. (2006). What does it mean to educate the whole child? *Educational Leadership, 63,* 2–6.

Norton, D. (2003). *Through the eyes of a child: An introduction to children's literature* (6th ed.). Upper Saddle River, NJ: Merrill/Prentice Hall.

Nourot, P. M. (1998). Sociodramatic play: Pretending together. In D. P. Fromberg & D. Bergen (Eds.), *Play from birth to twelve and beyond: Contexts, perspectives, and meaning.* New York: Garland.

Novick, R. (2002). Learning to read the heart: Nurturing emotional literacy. *Young Children, 57*(3), 84–89.

O'Connor, K. J. (2000). *The play therapy primer.* New York: Wiley.

Odom, S. L. (Ed.). (2002). *Widening the circle: Including children with disabilities in preschool programs.* New York: Teachers College Press.

O'Hara, P., Demarest, D., & Shaklee, H. (2005). *Research abstract: Emergent mathematics.* Boise, ID: University of Idaho.

Ohl, J. (2002). Linking child care and early literacy: Building the foundation for success. *Child Care Bulletin, 27,* 1–6.

Oken-Wright, P. (2001). Documentation: Both mirror and light. *Innovations in Early Education: The International Reggio Exchange, 8*(4), 5–15.

Pacific Oaks College Faculty. (1985). *The anti-bias curriculum.* Paper presented at the National Association for the Education of Young Children Conference, New Orleans.

Paley, V. (2004, September). *Speech at Appalachian State University.* Boone, NC: Appalachian State University.

Park, B., Neuharth-Pritchett, S. & Reguero de Atiles, J. (2003). Using integrated curriculum to connect standards and developmentally appropriate practice. *Dimensions of Early Childhood, 31*(3), 13–17.

Parke, R. D., & Buriel, R. (1998). Socialization in the family: Ethnic and ecological perspectives. In W. Damon (Series Ed.) & N. Eisenberg (Vol. Ed.), *Handbook of child psychology: Social, emotional, and personality development* (5th ed., Vol. 3). New York: Wiley.

Parten, M. B. (1932). Social participation among preschool children. *Journal of Abnormal and Social Psychology, 27,* 243–269.

Parten, M. B. (1933). Social play among preschool children. *Journal of Abnormal and Social Psychology, 28,* 136–147.

Patrick, S. (1993). Facilitating communication and language development. In T. W. Linder (Ed.), *Transdisciplinary play-based intervention: Guidelines for developing a meaningful curriculum for young children.* Baltimore: Brookes.

Paulson, L. H., Kelly, K. L., Jepson, S., van den Pol, R., Ashmore, R., Farrier, M., & Guilfoyle, S. (2004). The effects of an early reading curriculum on language and literacy development of Head Start children. *Journal of Research in Childhood Education, 18*(3), 169–178.

Pawl, J. (2002). Protecting our children. *Zero to Three, 22*(3), 21–22.

Payne, F. G., & Rink, J. E. (1997). Physical education in the developmentally appropriate integrated curriculum. In C. H. Hart, D. C. Burts, & R. Charlesworth (Eds.), *Integrated* curriculum and developmentally appropriate practice: Birth to age eight. Albany: State University of New York Press.

Peisner-Feinberg, E. S., Burchinal, M. R., Clifford, R. M., Culkin, M. I., Howes, C., Kagan, S. I., et al. (1999). *The children of the cost, quality, and outcomes study go to school: Technical report.* Chapel Hill, NC: Frank Porter Graham Child Development Center, University of North Carolina at Chapel Hill.

Peisner-Feinberg, E. S., Burchinal, M. R., Clifford, R. M., Culkin, M. L., Howes, C., Kagan, S. L., et al. (2001). The relation of preschool child-care quality to children's cognitive and social developmental trajectories through second grade. *Child Development, 72* (5), 1534–1553.

Pelo, A. (2007). *The language of art: Inquiry-based studio practices in early childhood settings.* St. Paul, MN: Red Leaf Press.

Perry, B. D. (2001). Responding to children's stress. *Special: Keeping Kids Safe.* New York: Scholastic Early Childhood Today and Parent & Child.

Perry, J. P. (2004). Making sense of outdoor pretend play. In D. Koralek (Ed.), *Spotlight on young children and play* (pp. 17–21). Washington, DC: National Association for the Education of Young Children.

Pflaum, S. W. (1990). *The development of language and literacy in young children* (3rd ed.). Upper Saddle River, NJ: Merrill/Prentice Hall.

Piaget, J. (1926). *The language and thought of the child.* New York: Harcourt Brace & World.

Piaget, J. (1932). *The moral judgment of the child.* London: Routledge & Kegan Paul.

Piaget, J. (1948). *The moral judgment of the child.* Glencoe, IL: Free Press.

Piaget, J. (1950). *The psychology of intelligence.* London: Routledge & Kegan Paul.

Piaget, J. (1959). *The construction of reality in the child.* New York: Basic Books.

Piaget, J. (1962). *Play, dreams, and imitation in childhood.* New York: Norton.

Piaget, J. (1963). *The origins of intelligence in children.* New York: Norton.

Piaget, J. (1965). *The child's conception of number.* New York: Norton.

Piaget, J. (1981). *Intelligence and affectivity: Their relationship during child development.* Palo Alto, CA: Annual Reviews.

Piaget, J. (1983). Piaget's theory. In P. H. Mussen (Series Ed.) & W. Kessen (Vol. Ed.), *Handbook of child psychology: History, theory, and methods* (4th ed., Vol. 1). New York: Wiley.

Piaget, J., & Inhelder, B. (1967). *The child's conception of space.* New York: Norton.

Piaget, J., & Inhelder, B. (1969). *The psychology of the child* (H. Weaver, Trans.). New York: Basic Books.

Pianta, R. C., & Stuhlman, M. (2004). Teacher-child relationships and children's success in the first years of school. *School Psychology Review, 33,* 444–458.

Pica, R. (1998). *Moving and learning across the curriculum: 315 activities and games to make learning fun.* Albany, NY: Delmar.

Pica, R. (2003). *Your active child: How to boost physical, emotional, and cognitive development through age-appropriate activity.* New York: McGraw-Hill.

Piirto, J. (1999). *Talented children and adults: Their development and education* (2nd ed.). Upper Saddle River, NJ: Merrill/Prentice Hall.

Piper, W. (1980). *The little engine that could.* New York: G. P. Putnam.

Powell, D. R. (1998). Research in review: Reweaving parents into the fabric of early childhood programs. *Young Children, 53*(5), 60–67.

Prince, D. L., & Howard, E. M. (2002). Children and their basic needs. *Early Childhood Education Journal, 30*(1), 27–31.

Profiles in culture. (2004). *Early Childhood Today, 19*(3), 46–48.

Pruitt, D. B. (Ed.). (2000). *Your child: Emotional, behavioral, and cognitive development from birth through preadolescence.* New York: HarperCollins.

Rafanello, D. (2000, Summer). Facilitating language development. *Healthy Child Care America.* Oak Grove Village, IL: American Academy of Pediatrics.

Raines, S. C., & Canady, R. J. (1989). *Story s-t-r-e-t-c-h-e-r-s: Activities to expand children's favorite books.* Beltsville, MD: Gryphon House.

Raines, S. C., Miller, K., & Curry-Rood, L. (2002). *Story s-t-r-e-t-c-h-e-r-s for infants, toddlers, and twos: Experiences, activities, and games for popular children's books.* Beltsville, MD: Gryphon House.

Ramani, G. B., & Siegler, R. S. (2007). *Promoting broad and stable improvements in low-income children's numerical knowledge through playing number board games.* Unpublished manuscript, Pittsburgh, PA: Carnegie Mellon University.

Raver, C. C. (2003). *Young children's emotional development and school readiness*. Champaign, IL: Clearinghouse on Early Education and Parenting.

Raver, S. A. (1999). *Intervention strategies for infants and toddlers with special needs: A team approach* (2nd ed.). Upper Saddle River, NJ: Merrill/Prentice Hall.

Ray, A., Bowman, B., & Brownell, J. O. (2006). In B. Bowman & E. K. Moore (Eds.), *School readiness and social-emotional development: Perspectives on cultural diversity* (pp. 7–22). Teacher-child relationships, social-emotional development, and school achievement. Washington, DC: National Black Child Development Institute.

Reynolds, G., & Jones, E. (1997). *Master players: Learning from children at play*. New York: Teachers College Press.

Rimm-Kaufman, S. E., Pianta, R. B., & Cox, M. J. (2000). Teachers' judgments of problems in transition to kindergarten. *Early Childhood Research Quarterly, 15*, 147–166.

Rinaldi, C. (1993). *Opening remarks: The Reggio Emilia approach in the United States*. Traverse City, MI: Wayne State University, Merrill-Palmer Institute.

Rinaldi, C. (1994). *The philosophy of Reggio Emilia*. Reggio Emilia, Italy: Reggio Emilia Seminar.

Rinaldi, C. (2001). The pedagogy of listening: The listening perspective from Reggio Emilia. *Innovations in Early Education: The International Reggio Exchange, 8*(4), 1–4.

Rinaldi, C. (2002). Research and learning. *Child Care Information Exchange, 145*, 16–20.

Riojas-Cortez, M. (2001). Preschoolers' funds of knowledge displayed through sociodramatic play episodes in a bilingual classroom. *Early Childhood Education Journal, 29*(1), 35–40.

Rogers, C. (1961). *On becoming a person: A therapist's view of psychotherapy*. London: Constable.

Rogers, C. R., & Dymond, R. F. (1954). *Psychotherapy and personality change*. Chicago: University of Chicago Press.

Roseberry-McKibben, C., & Brice, A. (2004). *Acquiring English as a second language: What's normal, what's not*. Rockville, MD: American Speech-Language-Hearing Association. Retrieved December 14, 2004, from http://asha.org/public/speech/development/easl.htm

Rosenquest, B. B. (2002). Literacy-based planning and pedagogy that supports toddler language development. *Early Childhood Education Journal, 29*(4), 241–249.

Rothenberger, A., & Banaschewski, T. (2005). Informing the ADHA debate. *Scientific American Mind, 1*(1), 50–55.

Rotigel, J. V. (2003). Understanding the young gifted child: Guidelines for parents, families, and educators. *Early Childhood Research Journal, 30*(4), 209–214.

Ruble, D. N., & Martin, C. L. (1998). Gender development. In W. Damon (Series Ed.) & N. Eisenberg (Vol. Ed.), *Handbook of child psychology: Social, emotional, and personality development* (5th ed., Vol. 3). New York: Wiley.

Rushton, S., & Larkin, E. (2001). Shaping the learning environment: Connecting developmentally appropriate practices to brain research. *Early Childhood Education Journal, 29*(1), 25–33.

Rutledge, D. (2000). Neurons and nurture in the early years. *Education Canada, 39*(4), 16–19.

Sandall, S. R. (2004). Play modifications for children with disabilities. In D. Koralek (Ed.), *Spotlight on young children and play* (pp. 44–45). Washington, DC: National Association for the Education of Young Children.

Sandall, S. R., Hemmeter, M. L., Smith, B. J., & McLean, M. E. (2005). *DEC recommended practices: A comprehensive guide*. Longmont, CO: Sopris West.

Sandall, S. R., Schwartz, I. S., Joseph, G. E., Chou, H. Y., Horn, E. M., & Wolery, R. (2002). *Building blocks for teaching preschoolers with special needs*. Baltimore: Brookes.

Sanders, K. (2002). Men don't care? *Young Children, 57*(6), 44–48.

Sanders, S. W. (2002). *Active for life: Developmentally appropriate movement programs for young children*. Washington, DC: National Association for the Education of Young Children.

Saracho, O. N., & Spodek, B. (Eds.). (2003). *Contemporary perspectives on play in early childhood education*. Greenwich, CT: Information Age Press.

Sargent, P. (2002). Under the glass: Conversations with men in early childhood education. *Young Children, 57*(6), 22–30.

Schering-Plough Corporation & *Scholastic Early Childhood Today*. (n.d.). *Healthy ears, healthy learning* (Scholastic supplement). New York: Author.

Schickedanz, J. A. (2008). *Increasing the power of instruction: Integration of language, literacy, and math across the preschool day*. Washington, DC: National Association for the Education of Young Children.

Schiller, P (2001). Brain research and its implications for early childhood programs: Applying research to our work. *Child Care Information Exchange, 140*: 14–18.

Schiller, P., & Willis, C. A. (2008). Using brain-based teaching strategies to create supportive early childhood environments that address learning standards. *Young Children, 63*(4), 52–55.

Schirrmacher, R. (1998). *Art and creative development for young children* (3rd ed.). Albany, NY: Delmar.

Schlank, C. H., & Metzger, B. (1997). *Together and equal: Fostering cooperative play and promoting gender equity in early childhood programs*. Boston: Allyn & Bacon.

Schultz, T., & Kagan, S. L. (2005). *Taking stock: Assessing and improving early childhood learning and program quality*. Report of the National Early Childhood Accountability Task Force, Philadelphia: Pew Charitable Trusts.

Schweinhart, L. J. (2008, March 18). Creating the best prekindergartens: Five ingredients for long-term effect and returns on investment. *Education Week*. Retrieved April 4, 2008 from http://www.edweek.org/login .html?source=http://www.edweek .org/ew/articles/2008/03/19/ 28schweinhart.h27.html &destination=http://www.edweek .org/ew/articles/2008/03/19/28 schweinhart.h27.html&levelId= 2100

Schweinhart, L. J., Montie, J., Yiang, Z., Barnett, W. S., & Belfield, C. R. (2005). *Lifetime effects: The High/Scope Perry Preschool project through age 40*. Ypsilanti, MI: High/Scope.

Schweinhart, L. J., & Weikart, D. P. (1997). *Lasting differences: The High/Scope Preschool Curriculum Comparison Study through age 23*. Ypsilanti, MI: High/Scope.

Scott-Little, C., Kagan, S. L., & Frelow, V. S. (2006). State standards for children's learning: What do they mean for child care providers? *Exchange, 168,* 27–34.

Scott-Little, C., Lesko, J., Martella, J., & Milburn, P. (2007). Early learning standards: Results from a national survey to document trends in state-level policies and practices. *Early Childhood Research and Practice, 9*(7).

Sharif, I., Ozuah, P. O., Dinkevich, E. I., & Mulvihill, M. (2003). Impact of a brief literacy intervention on urban preschoolers. *Early Childhood Education Journal, 30*(3), 177–180.

Shelov, S. P., & Hannemann, R. E. (Eds.). (2004). *The American Academy of Pediatrics complete and authoritative guide: Caring for your baby and young child, birth to age 5* (4th ed.). New York: Bantam.

Shillady, A. L. (2004, January). Choosing an appropriate assessment system. *Beyond the Journal, Young Children on the Web*. Retrieved February 13, 2008 from http://www.journal .naeyc.org/btj/ 200401

Shipley, C. C. (1993). *Empowering children: Play-based curriculum for lifelong learning*. Scarborough, Ontario: Nelson.

Shirah, S., & Brennan, L. (1990). *Sickle cell anemia*. Paper presented at the National Association for the Education of Young Children, Washington, DC.

Shonkoff, J. P., & Meisels, S. J. (Eds.). (2000). *Handbook of early intervention* (2nd ed.). New York: Cambridge University Press.

Shore, R. (1997). *Rethinking the brain: New insights into early development*. New York: Families and Work Institute.

Shore, R., & Strasser, J. (2006). Music for their minds. *Young Children, 61*(2), 62–67.

Siegel, D. J. (1999). *The developing mind: Toward a neurobiology of interpersonal experience*. New York: Guilford.

Siegler, R. W. (2005). *Children's thinking* (4th ed.). Upper Saddle River, NJ: Merrill/Prentice Hall.

Sigel, I. (1987). Does hothousing rob children of their childhood? *Early Childhood Research Quarterly, 2*(3), 211–225.

Smilansky, S. (1990). *Sociodramatic play: Its relevance to behavior and achievement in school, in children's play and learning*. New York: Teachers College Press.

Smilansky, S., & Shefatya, L. (1990). *Facilitating play: A medium for promoting cognitive, socio-emotional, and academic development in young children*. Gaithersburg, MD: Psychosocial & Educational Publications.

Smith, P. K., Morita, Y., Junger-Tas, J., Olweus, D., Catalano, R., & Slee, P. (Eds.). (1999). *The nature of school bullying: A cross national perspective*. London: Routledge.

Snow, C. E., Burns, S. M., & Griffin, P. (Eds.). (1998). *Preventing reading difficulties in young children*. Washington, DC: National Academy Press.

Snow, C. E., Burns, S. M., & Griffin, P. (1999). Language and literacy environments in preschools. *CEEP DIGESTS, EDO-PS-99-1*. Champaign, IL: Clearinghouse on Early Education and Parenting.

Soderman, A. K., Gregory, K. M., & O'Neill, L. T. (1999). *Scaffolding emergent literacy: A child-centered approach for preschool through grade 5*. Boston: Allyn & Bacon.

Sorte, J. M., & Daeschel, I. (2006). Health in action: A program approach to fighting obesity in young children. *Young Children,* *61*(3), 40–48.

Soundy, C. S., & Stout, N. L. (2002). Pillow talk: Fostering the emotional and language needs of young learners. *Young Children, 57*(2), 20–24.

Spaggiari, S. (1998). The community-teacher partnership in the governance of the schools: An interview with Lella Gandini. In C. Edwards, L. Gandini, & G. Forman (Eds.), *The hundred languages of children: The Reggio Emilia approach—Advanced reflections.* Norwood, NJ: Ablex.

Spolsky, B. (1999). Second-language learning. In J. A. Fishman (Ed.), *Handbook of language & ethnic identity.* New York: Oxford University Press.

Stanford, B. H., & Yamamoto, K. (Eds.). (2001). *Children and stress: Understanding and helping.* Olney, MD: Association for Childhood Education International.

Steele, M. M. (2004). Making the case for early identification and intervention for young children at risk for learning disabilities. *Early Childhood Education Journal, 32*(2), 75–79.

Steglin, D. A. (1997). Early childhood professionals and HIV/AIDS-impacted children and families: Strategies for professional preparation. *Journal of Early Childhood Teacher Education, 18*(3), 26–34.

Stephens, K. (2006a). Family referrals: A tool for supporting children and families. *Exchange, 172,* 28–31.

Stephens, K. (2006b). Primed for learning: The young child's mind. In B. Neugebauer (Ed.), *Curriculum: Brain research, math, science* (pp. 7–11). Redmond, WA: Exchange Press.

Stone, J. G. (2001). *Building classroom community: The early childhood teacher's role.* Washington, DC: National Association for the Education of Young Children.

Strickland, D. S. (2006). Language and literacy in kindergarten. In D. F. Gullo (Ed.), *K today: Teaching and learning in the kindergarten year.* Washington, DC: National Association for the Education of Young Children.

Strickland, D. S., & Riley-Ayers, S. (2007). *Literacy leadership in early education: The essential guide.* New York: Teachers College Press.

Strickland, D. S., & Schickedanz, J. A. (2004). *Learning about print in preschool: Working with letters, words, and beginning links with phonemic awareness.* Newark, DE: International Reading Association.

Sussna Klein, A. G. (2002). Infant and toddler care that recognizes their competence: Practices at the Pikler Institute. *Dimensions of Early Childhood, 30*(2), 11–18.

Sutcliffe, J. (1997). *The complete book of relaxation techniques.* Allentown, PA: People's Medical Society.

Sutton, R. E. (1991). Equity and computers in the schools: A decade of research. *Review of Educational Research, 61,* 475–503.

Swick, K. J. (2006). Families and educators together: Raising caring and peaceable children. *Early Childhood Education Journal, 33*(4), 279–287.

Swick, K. J., & Freeman, N. K. (2004). Nurturing peaceful children to create a caring world: The role of families and community. *Childhood Education, 81*(1), 2–8.

Swinney, B. (1999). *Healthy food for healthy kids.* New York: Meadowbrook Press.

Sykes, M. (2001). On building ties with families. *Early Childhood Today, 16*(3), 57–58.

Tabors, P. O. (1997). *One child, two languages: A guide for preschool educators of children learning English as a second language.* Baltimore: Brookes.

Tarini, E. (1993). What is documentation? *Innovations in Early Education: The International Reggio Exchange, 1*(4).

Tarini, E. (1997). Introducing message boxes. In J. Hendrick (Ed.), *First steps toward teaching the Reggio way.* Upper Saddle River, NJ: Merrill/Prentice Hall.

Taylor, A. S., Peterson, C. A., McMurray-Schwarz, P., & Guillou, T. S. (2002). Social skills interventions: Not just for children with special needs. *Young Exceptional Children, 5*(4), 19–26.

Teele, D. W., Klein, J. O., & Rosner, B. A. (1989). Epidemiology of otitis media during the first seven years of life in children in greater Boston: A prospective cohort study. *Journal of Infectious Diseases, 160,* 83–94.

Tekene, L. (2008). Questions as a technique for scaffolding children's learning. *Exchange, 179,* 51–53.

Thigpen, B. (2007). Outdoor play: Combatting sedentary lifestyles. *Zero to Three, 28*(1), 19–23.

Thomas, E. M. (2004). *Aggressive behaviour outcomes for young children: Change in parenting environment predicts change in behaviour.* Ontario, Canada: Statistics Canada.

Thomas, P. (2003). *Using Tai Chi and visualization to reduce chil-*

dren's stress. St. Paul, MN: Redleaf Press.

Thomas, R. M. (1999). *Comparing theories of child development* (5th ed.). Monterey, CA: Brooks/Cole.

Thompson, M. (2006). Let's be friends! *Scholastic Parent & Child, 14*(3), 52–53.

Tokarz, B. (2008). Block play: It's not just for boys anymore. *Exchange, 181,* 68–71.

Torrance, E. P. (1966/1984). *The Torrance tests of creative thinking.* Bensenville, IL: Scholastic Testing Service.

Trelease, J. (2001). *The new read-aloud handbook* (5th ed.). New York: Penguin.

Turnbull, R., & Cilley, M. (1999). *Explanation and implications of the 1997 amendments to IDEA.* Upper Saddle River, NJ: Merrill/Prentice Hall.

Tutwiler, S. W. (1998). Diversity among families. In M. L. Fuller & G. Olsen (Eds.), *Home-school relations: Working successfully with parents and families.* Boston: Allyn & Bacon.

United Nations. (2006). *Convention on the rights of persons with disabilities.* New York: Author.

U.S. Census Bureau. (1999, Spring). *Who's minding the kids? Child care arrangements.* Washington, DC: Author.

U.S. Census Bureau. (2005). *Foreign-born population tops 34 million.* Washington, DC: Author.

U.S. Census Bureau. (2005). *Who's minding the kids? Child care arrangements: Spring, 2005.* Washington, DC: Author.

U.S. Department of Education. (2001). *Twenty-fourth annual report to Congress on the implementation of the Individuals with Disabilities Education Act (IDEA).* Washington, DC: Author.

U.S. Department of Education. (2004). *26th annual report to Congress on the implementation of the Individuals With Disabilities Education Act, 2004: Volumes I & II.* Washington, DC: Author.

U.S. Department of Education, National Center for Education Statistics. (2003). *Computer and Internet use by children and adolescents in 2001* (NCES 2004–014). Washington, DC: Author.

U.S. Department of Education, National Center for Education Statistics. (2006a). *Digest of education statistics, 2005* (NCES 2006-030, chap. 2). Washington, DC: Author.

U.S. Department of Education, National Center for Education Statistics. (2006b). *Digest of education statistics, 2005* (NCES 2006–030), Table 42 Washington, DC: Author.

U.S. Department of Education, Office of Special Education and Rehabilitative Services. (2006b). *OSERS Homepage.* Retrieved May 15, 2008, from http://www.ed.gov/about/offices/list/osers/osep/index.html

U.S. Department of Health and Human Services. (2000). *Report of the Surgeon General's conference on children's mental health: A national action agenda.* Washington, DC: U.S. Government Printing Office.

U.S. Department of Health and Human Services. (2004). *Child maltreatment 2002.* Washington, DC: U.S. Government Printing Office.

U.S. Department of Health and Human Services (2008). *Insure kids now!* Washington, DC: Author.

UNICEF. (2003).*The state of the world's children, table 3: Health.* New York: UNICEF House, Division of Communication.

Vacca, J. J. (2006). EVALUATE children with disabilities: Recommendations for early childhood educators. *Dimensions of Early Childhood, 34*(2), 11–18.

Vakil, S., Freeman, R., & Swim, T. J. (2003). The Reggio Emilia approach and inclusive early childhood programs. *Early Childhood Education Journal, 30*(3), 187–192.

Vance, E., & Weaver, P. J. (2002). *Class meetings: Young children solving problems.* Washington, DC: National Association for the Education of Young Children.

Varol, F., & Farran, D. C. (2006). Early mathematical growth: How to support young children's mathematical development. *Early Childhood Education Journal, 33*(6), 381–387.

Viadero, D. (2007). Teachers say NCLB has changed classroom practice. *Education Week, 26*(42), 6, 22.

Viadero, D. (2008). Insights gained into arts and smarts. *Education Week, 27*(27), 1, 10–11.

Vygotsky, L. (1962). *Thought and language.* Cambridge: MIT Press.

Vygotsky, L. (1978). *Mind in society: The development of higher psychological processes* (M. Cole, V. John-Steiner, S. Scribner, & E. Souberman, Eds.). Cambridge, MA: Harvard University Press.

Wadsworth, B. J. (1989). *Piaget's theory of cognitive and affective development* (4th ed.). White Plains, NY: Longman.

Walsh, B. A., & Blewitt, P. (2006). The effect of questioning style during storybook reading on novel vocabulary acquisition of preschoolers. *Early Childhood Education Journal, 33*(4), 273–278.

Warner, L., & Lynch, S. (2003). Classroom problems that won't go away. *Childhood Education, 79,* 97–100.

Washington, V. (2002). Why early childhood matters now more than ever. *Early Childhood Today, 17*(3), 5.

Watson, M. W., & Peng, Y. (1992). The relation between toy gun play and children's aggressive behavior. *Early Education and Development, 3*(4), 370–389.

Weikart, D. P. (1990). *Quality preschool programs: A long-term social investment.* New York: Ford Foundation.

Wellhousen, K. (2001). *Outdoor play everyday: Innovative play concepts for early childhood.* Albany, NY: Delmar.

Wender, P. H. (2000). *ADHD: Attention-deficit hyperactivity disorder in children and adults.* New York: Oxford University Press.

West, M. M. (2007). Problem solving: A sensible approach to children's science and social studies learning—and beyond. *Young Children, 62*(5), 34–41.

White, H. (2008). *Connecting today's kids with nature: A policy action plan.* Reston, VA: National Wildlife Federation.

Whitebook, M., Sakai, L., Gerber, E., & Howes, C. (2001). *Then and now: Changes in child care staffing, 1994–2000 (technical report).* Washington, DC: Center for the Child Care Workforce.

Wien, C. A. (2004). *Negotiating standards in the primary classroom: The teacher's dilemma.* New York: Teachers College Press.

Wien, C. A. (2008). *Emergent curriculum in the primary classroom: Interpreting the Reggio Emilia approach in schools.* New York: Teachers College Press.

Wilcox-Herzog, A., & Ward, S. L. (2004). Measuring teachers' perceived interactions with children: A tool for assessing beliefs and intentions. *Early Childhood Research and Practice, 6*(2). Retrieved January 1, 2005 from http://ecrp.uiuc.edu/v6n2/herzog.html.

Willis, C. A. (2002). The grieving process in children: Strategies for understanding, educating, and reconciling children's perceptions of death. *Early Childhood Education Journal, 29*(4), 221–226.

Wiltz, N. W., & Klein, E. L. (2001). "What do you do in child care?" Children's perceptions of high and low quality child care. *Early Childhood Research Quarterly, 16*(2), 209–236.

Wolkoff, S. (2002). The babies push us to be strong and stay loving. *Zero to Three, 22*(3), 14–15.

Wong, L. (2004). In Profiles in culture. *Early Childhood Today, 19*(3), 46–48.

Wood, C. (2007). *Yardsticks: Children in the classroom ages 4–14.* Turners Falls, MA: Northeast Foundation for Children.

Worth, K., & Grollman, S. (2003). *Worms, shadows, and whirlpools.* Portsmouth, NH: Heinemann.

Wurm, J. P. (2005). *Working in the Reggio way: A beginner's guide for American teachers.* St. Paul: Redleaf Press.

Yell, M. L., & Dragsow, E. (2005). *No child left behind: A guide for professionals.* Upper Saddle River, NJ: Merrill/Prentice Hall.

Yoon, J., & Onchwari, J. A. (2006). Teaching young children science: Three key points. *Early Childhood Education Journal, 33*(6), 419–423.

York, S. (2003). *Roots and wings: Affirming culture in early childhood programs* (Rev. ed.). St. Paul, MN: Redleaf.

Zeece, P. D. (2004). Promoting empathy and developing caring readers. *Early Childhood Education Journal, 31*(3), 193–199.

Zigler, E. F., Singer, D. G., & Bishop-Josef, S. (Eds.). (2004). *Children's play: The roots of reading.* Washington, DC: Zero to Three Press.

INDEX